Reluctant Europeans

Reluctant Europeans

Britain and European Integration,
1945–1998

DAVID GOWLAND

and

ARTHUR TURNER

 LONGMAN

An imprint of **PEARSON EDUCATION**

Harlow, England · London · New York · Reading, Massachusetts · San Francisco · Toronto · Don Mills, Ontario · Sydney
Tokyo · Singapore · Hong Kong · Seoul · Taipei · Cape Town · Madrid · Mexico City · Amsterdam · Munich · Paris · Milan

Pearson Education Limited
Edinburgh Gate,
Harlow, Essex CM20 2JE, United Kingdom
and Associated Companies throughout the world.

Visit us on the world wide web at
http://www.pearsoned-ema.com

© Pearson Education Limited 2000

First published 2000

ISBN 0–582–36957–6 CSD
ISBN 0–582–36956–8 PPR

British Library Cataloguing in Publication Data

A catalogue entry for this title is available from the British Library

Library of Congress Cataloging-in-Publication Data

Gowland, D. A.
Reluctant Europeans: Britain and European integration, 1945–1998
/ David Gowland and Arthur Turner.
p. cm.
Includes bibliographical references and index.
ISBN 0–582–36957–6. — ISBN 0–582–36956–8 (pbk.)
1. European Economic Community—Great Britain. 2. European Union—
Great Britain. 3. Great Britain—Politics and government—1945–
I. Turner, Arthur (Arthur S.) II. Title.
HC241.25.G7G675 1999
337.4041—dc21 99–20912
CIP

Set by 35 in 10/12pt Baskerville
Produced by Addison Wesley Longman Singapore (Pte) Ltd.,
Printed in Singapore

For Helen and Susan

Frontispiece

I remember being much amused last year, when landing at Calais, at the answer made by an old traveller to a novice who was making his first voyage. 'What a dreadful smell!' said the uninitiated stranger, enveloping his nose in his pocket handkerchief. 'It is the smell of the continent, sir,' replied the man of experience. And so it was.

Mrs Frances Trollope (1835)

England still stands outside Europe. Europe's voiceless tremors do not reach her. Europe is apart and England is not of her flesh and blood.

John Maynard Keynes (1919)

The Sun will not flinch from opposing the euro. We are against it economically, politically and constitutionally. *We will fight, fight, fight.* And even if we lose, we hope people will use the words of one of the greatest of our statesmen, Winston Churchill, and say ... *This was their finest hour.*

The Sun, 24 June 1998

Contents

Abbreviations Used in the Text   ix

Introduction   1

1. Britain, Europe and the Audit of War   9

2. Western Union and the Reconstruction of
    Western Europe   25

3. 'We are not ready': Britain and the Schuman Plan   40

4. The Case for Association   55

5. The 'Special Relationship' and European Unity   69

6. The Commonwealth Dimension   83

7. From Messina to Rome   96

8. On the Defensive   110

9. From Application to Veto   125

10. Ancient Rivalries   141

11. Labour's Retreat into Europe   152

12. Mission Accomplished   168

13. Renegotiating 'Tory Terms'   184

14. 'Full-hearted Consent': the 1975 Referendum   198

15. Semi-detached: the Callaghan Government
    and Europe   214

16. More U-turns: Labour and the EC in the 1980s   230

17. 'Megaphone Diplomacy': Thatcher and the EC,
    1979–1984   244

18. Fatal Attraction: Thatcher and the Single
    European Act   259

19. 'At the Heart of Europe'?   275

20. Opting out: the Maastricht Treaty Review   284

21. Eurosceptics versus Europhiles   293

22. 'War at Last': the Beef Crisis of 1996   310

23. Under New Management: the General Election
    of 1997   322

24. After Amsterdam: Enlargement, Employment
    and the Euro   341

25. New Labour, Old Problems: The British Presidency
    of 1998   354

    Suggestions for Further Reading   365

    Chronological Table   374

    Map: The Enlargement of the European Community   381

    Index   382

Abbreviations Used in the Text

ACP	African, Caribbean and Pacific States
APEX	Association of Professional, Executive, Clerical and Computer Staff
ASTMS	Association of Scientific, Technical and Managerial Staffs
BSE	Bovine Spongiform Encephalopathy
BTO	Brussels Treaty Organisation
CAP	Common Agricultural Policy
CBI	Confederation of British Industry
CFP	Common Fisheries Policy
CJD	Creutzfeldt-Jakob disease
CLPD	Campaign for Labour Party Democracy
DEA	Department of Economic Affairs
EAEC	European Atomic Energy Community
EC	European Community/ies
ECA	Economic Cooperation Administration
ECB	European Central Bank
ECJ	European Court of Justice
ECOFIN	EU Council of Finance Ministers
ECSC	European Coal and Steel Community
ECU	European Currency Unit
EDC	European Defence Community
EEC	European Economic Community
EFTA	European Free Trade Association
EMS	European Monetary System
EMU	Economic and Monetary Union
EP	European Parliament
EPC	European Political Cooperation
EPU	European Payments Union
ERDF	European Regional Development Fund
ERM	Exchange Rate Mechanism
ERP	European Recovery Programme
ETUC	European Trade Union Confederation

EU	European Union
FDP	Free Democratic Party (Federal Republic of Germany)
FTA	Free Trade Area
GATT	General Agreement on Tariffs and Trade
GDP	Gross Domestic Product
GNP	Gross National Product
IGC	Intergovernmental Conference
IMF	International Monetary Fund
MEP	Member of the European Parliament
MRP	Mouvement Républicain Populaire
NATO	North Atlantic Treaty Organisation
NEC	National Executive Committee
NFU	National Farmers' Union
NOP	National Opinion Polls
NRC	National Referendum Campaign
NUR	National Union of Railwaymen
OECD	Organisation for Economic Cooperation and Development
OEEC	Organisation for European Economic Cooperation
OPEC	Organisation of Petroleum Exporting Countries
PLP	Parliamentary Labour Party
PSBR	Public Sector Borrowing Requirement
QMV	Qualified Majority Voting
SDP	Social Democratic Party
SEA	Single European Act
SPD	Social Democratic Party of Germany (Federal Republic of Germany)
TGWU	Transport and General Workers' Union
TUC	Trades Union Congress
UPW	Union of Post Office Workers
USDAW	Union of Shop, Distributive and Allied Workers
VAT	Value Added Tax
WEU	Western European Union

Introduction

In May 1948 the British Labour government and party boycotted The Hague Congress of Europe. They did so partly on the grounds that this large gathering of European public figures, which played a formative role in the creation of the Council of Europe a year later, was too closely associated with the idea of a federal Europe. Shortly afterwards Ernest Bevin, the British Foreign Secretary, reluctantly acquiesced in British membership of the Council of Europe. In doing so, he not only ruled out any federalist designs, but also rejected a Franco-Italian proposal to invest the new organisation with the title of the European Union.[1] This outcome preserved British leadership of Europe, at least in the minds of British policy-makers. At the time of the Congress, however, the British ambassador to The Netherlands reported that the Dutch, who were usually more sympathetic to British views about Europe than other continental countries, harboured considerable doubts about Britain's willingness or ability 'to make common cause with Western Europe which their spokesmen professed themselves anxious to make'.[2]

Fifty years later, as Britain's six-month presidency of the European Union (EU) drew to a close in June 1998, it appeared that another British Labour government shared at least some common ground with that of 1948 in conveying the image of self-styled European leadership while maintaining a highly qualified British approach to European unity. In early May 1998 Britain stood on the sidelines as eleven of the fifteen member states of the EU agreed to advance towards the third and final stage of economic and monetary union symbolised by the introduction of a single currency – the euro – on 1 January 1999. A few weeks later the European

---

1. Bevin was advised by one Foreign Office [hereafter FO] official that the phrase 'European Union' should be avoided on the grounds that it suggested to the English ear 'such things as "the Union of South Africa" or even the "Soviet Union"': Public Record Office [hereafter PRO], FO 371/79262, Jebb to Bevin, 31 January 1949.
2. PRO, FO 371/73095, Nichols to FO, 19 May 1948.

1

Parliament expressed its disenchantment with Britain's presidency of the EU when it defeated the customary motion congratulating the outgoing presidency. At the end of the presidency, moreover, the British Prime Minister, Tony Blair, registered strong opposition to the idea of a federal European superstate. He further maintained that the EU was moving in line with British thinking as Chancellor Kohl of Germany and President Chirac of France jointly declared that the idea of a European superstate was dead. What remained unclear, however, was whether Blair, the product of a highly centralised system of government, attached the same meaning to the concept of a federal Europe as either Kohl, the representative of a federal system of government, or Chirac, the head of a relatively decentralised system of government.

In the intervening period, the process of European integration often resulted in a marked contrast between British and continental perceptions of the UK's role in and views about Europe. Furthermore, during this period few subjects in British politics attracted as much continuing attention and controversy as British involvement in European integration. This highly contested issue frequently divided governments, political parties, interest groups and the wider public to such an extent that any attempt to manufacture a national consensus in favour of closer union with continental Europe was fraught with difficulties. Public debate about specific European policies, in fact, invariably exposed major differences of opinion over more general questions touching on national identity, independence and sovereignty. Such divisions, in turn, strengthened the view in continental circles that the British were reluctant Europeans: their insular tradition and global outlook rendered them incapable of overcoming a deep-seated detachment from continental Europe and of playing more than a peripheral role in furthering European integration. The sense of being separate from continental Europe on the British side reinforced these perceptions and remained in being long into the period covered by this book. In 1960, for example, Foreign Office officials made the then novel suggestion that a keynote speech by the Foreign Secretary should be entitled 'British policy in Europe' rather than 'British policy towards Europe'.[3] To this day 'Britain and Europe' is a common expression in British quarters.

This book offers an historical account of the relationship between Britain and European integration in the period from the end of

3. PRO, FO 371/154503, Wilford to Peck.

the Second World War to the conclusion of the British presidency of the EU in June 1998. It examines and analyses the distinctive features of British policy and attitudes towards the process of integration associated with the European Community (EC) in the period 1950–91 and with the EU since the Maastricht Treaty on European Union (1992). The book considers the wide variety of factors that have shaped and continue to shape British policy in this sphere. The impact of Britain's changing role and power in the world, the strategic concerns of policymakers, the influence of national politics, the activities of interest groups and the significance of economic, financial and commercial trends, all receive detailed attention.

We have adopted a broadly chronological approach to the subject matter. This dimension is also evident in the more theme-based chapters that explore particularly important aspects. The first half of the book deals with the period 1945–72 when British governments first remained aloof from the origins and early development of the European Community (EC) in the 1950s, then unsuccessfully attempted to obtain membership in the 1960s before finally joining the Community on 1 January 1973. The second half of the book focuses especially on the problems of adjusting to membership in the first instance and on subsequent difficulties as the drive towards greater integration gathered momentum with the Single European Act (1986) and the Maastricht Treaty. This section provides substantive treatment of post-Maastricht developments, including Britain's current exercise (1998) of its right to 'opt-out' of the third and final stage of economic and monetary union.

A major feature of this historical analysis is the emphasis on national government and party politics in determining the nature and extent of British involvement in European integration. Within this state-centred framework, much attention is given to the role, influence and interplay of internal and external conditions in accounting for the stance of successive governments towards European integration. In particular, we consider the interrelationship between domestic and foreign policy and the changing mixture of constraints and opportunities that faced policymakers. We examine the British contribution to the course of European integration and also deal with the impact of EC/EU membership on British politics and economic performance, including the 'Europeanisation' of policymaking on matters previously under exclusively national control and jurisdiction.

The book also studies Britain's relationship with the EC/EU in the context of the former's bilateral and multilateral relations with other European and non-European states. British policymakers' perceptions of the changing configuration of the international system since 1945 are particularly important in illuminating the contrasting phases in the evolution of British policy towards Europe during the second half of the twentieth century. A key element of the study in this respect is the relationship between Britain's descent from global power status in this period and its emergence as a primarily regional European power still heavily influenced by long-standing images of itself as playing a major role in world affairs and by the continuing appeal of extra-European ties.

We should emphasise two points concerning our characterisation of the British as reluctant Europeans. First, this description is primarily based on the conduct of British governments in managing this transformation. It is not derived from any comparative judgement involving other European states. In fact some of these states, like Denmark and Greece, have long shared British doubts about major plans for the EC/EU. Furthermore, Britain has not played a uniformly laggardly role in the EC/EU. For example, it has an above-average record for implementing EC/EU legislation. It has also figured prominently in promoting major changes such as the reform of the Common Agricultural Policy (CAP) and the speedy implementation of single market legislation.

Secondly, it is not part of our argument that the continental European states principally distinguished themselves from Britain by a more idealistic and less state-centred approach towards the process of European integration. Contrasting British and continental views of the nature and extent of European integration since 1945 have been rooted in diverse historical experiences rather than diametrically opposing views of the role and functions of the state in the international system. European integration for many continental states has long been harnessed to a number of strategic national purposes. In Germany, it has offered an opportunity to reinvent and locate the state in a stable European framework. In France, it has provided a mechanism for advancing a programme of national economic modernisation and enhanced international status. In Britain, too, the idea of European integration has been perceived in terms of serving the 'national interest'. Unlike that of the continental states, however, British policy has been far less governed by the idea of European integration as the centrepiece of a long-term strategy for national renewal. Much greater emphasis has been placed in the British case on the risks of exclusion from the EC/EU and on reconciling European commitments with global interests. In addition, British policymakers have frequently demonstrated a greater concern about the level of public support for integration than their continental counterparts. As the Macmillan government edged towards making the first application for membership, for example, a Cabinet committee chaired by Macmillan reviewed the arguments in favour of this decision and concluded: 'But perhaps the strongest argument for joining the Six [the EC] was based on the potential dangers of staying outside; as the Six consolidated, we would inevitably enter into a period of relative decline . . . This, however, was a difficult argument to present publicly.'[4] Why involvement in European integration has had less resonance in Britain, why it has often been viewed as a disagreeable necessity rather than a positive benefit, and why policymaking has frequently consisted of a set of tactical adjustments to suit the needs of the moment and to preserve a 'wait and see' position towards plans for further integration, are among the questions addressed in this study.

The institutional character, aims and identity of the EU require some introductory comment. First and as a matter of nomenclature, we should explain the use of the title 'European Community' (EC) in large parts of this book. The legally correct title is the 'European Communities', comprising the European Coal and Steel Community (ECSC), based on the Treaty of Paris (1951), and the European Economic Community (EEC) and the European Atomic Energy Community (EAEC), founded on the Treaties of Rome of 1957. The institutions of these three Communities were merged in 1967, though the separate treaties remained in existence. Unless indicated otherwise, EC in the text normally refers to the most significant of these Communities – the EEC or Common Market, as it was popularly called in Britain until the later 1970s. For the post-1992 period, we have used the EU title derived from the Maastricht Treaty. This treaty established a three-pillar structure for the EU. The first pillar, known as the European Community, replaces the EEC and incorporates the economic dimension and policies of the EU including the Single Market and Economic and Monetary Union. The second and third pillars involve a Common Foreign and Security Policy (CFSP) and co-operation on Justice and Home Affairs respectively.

4. PRO, CAB 134/1821, E.Q.(61) 4th Meeting, 17 May 1961.

Further, it should be noted that the origins and development of the EC/EU have attracted much debate about the dynamics of European integration. A dictionary definition of integration as the action or process of combining separate parts or elements does not carry the reader very far into this debate. European integration as a process or as a means has been surrounded by a wide variety of explanations and aspirations concerning its course and direction.[5] The collective existence, experience and aims of the EC/EU states have often been portrayed in terms of interchangeable words like 'unity', 'unification' and 'union'. The underlying purpose of the EC/EU, as specified in the preamble to the EEC Treaty and endorsed by the Maastricht Treaty, is 'to create "an ever closer union" among the peoples of Europe'.[6] This declaration has proved sufficiently imprecise to accommodate some polarised visions of the EC/EU's potential in terms of federal and confederal systems of government or supranational and intergovernmental forms of decision-making.

Two main schools of thought, federalism and functionalism, emerged shortly after the Second World War and offered very different models of European integration. Federalism is associated with the idea of constitution-making. It subscribes to the view that historical change is effected by a deliberate political act which in this case transfers some of the powers and responsibilities of the European states to federal institutions responsible for dealing with matters of common concern. The early exponents of functionalism, however, envisaged European integration as an incremental process. They advocated the introduction of supranational controls over particular sectors of governmental activity and, according to some accounts, such a course of action promised a 'spill-over' effect leading to the integration of other sectors. This form of integration suggests a much less dramatic and longer-term transformation of relations between states than the federalist model.

Neither of these models satisfactorily accounts for the often untidy mix of elements and chequered history of the EC/EU. It is rather the case that the EC/EU is a unique political system that defies classification either as a conventional international organisation or as a sovereign state. In many ways the hybrid character of

5. For an introductory guide to the subject see S. Henig, *The Uniting of Europe: From Discord to Concord* (1997). For more detailed studies of European integration see D.W. Urwin, *The Community of Europe: A History of European Integration since 1945* (1995); A.M. El-Agraa (ed.), *The European Union: History, Institutions, Economics and Policies* (1998); P. Gowan and P. Anderson (eds), *The Question of Europe* (1997).

6. C.H. Church and D. Phinnemore, *European Union and European Community: A Handbook and Commentary on the Post-Maastricht Treaties* (1994), p. 53.

the Maastricht Treaty reflected rather than resolved this problem of categorisation. The treaty's first pillar (European Community) exemplifies what is commonly called the Community method and most clearly approximates to the principle of supranational integration. Decision-making under this system involves three of the four main institutions of the EC/EU. The Commission as the executive body is independent of national governments and possesses the exclusive right to initiate proposals. The Council of Ministers represents the governments of the member states and as the decision-taking body makes widespread use of qualified majority voting (QMV). The European Parliament (EP), a directly elected body, is extensively involved in consultation concerning proposals and also has some specific powers concerning the passage of the annual budget, the dismissal of the Commission and, in certain circumstances, the right to reject proposed legislation. The fourth main institution, the European Court of Justice (ECJ), is responsible for ensuring the uniform interpretation of European Community law. The second and third pillars of the Maastricht Treaty, however, represent an intergovernmental method of operation. Under this arrangement, the Commission's right of initiative is shared with the member states, while the Council of Ministers acts on the principle of unanimity. The EP plays only a consultative role, and the ECJ is of marginal significance.

The history of the EC/EU has displayed a fluctuating balance between supranationalism and intergovernmentalism. This pattern, in turn, has had a bearing on the changing position of the EC/EU on the spectrum between confederal and federal forms of government. The supranational principle and the idea of sector integration found expression in the ECSC Treaty of Paris, which established a supranational High Authority and is the only EC/EU treaty to employ the term supranational. The EEC Treaty of Rome committed its founder member states to creating a common market allowing for the free movement of goods, capital, labour and services. The member states were in this case less inclined to make explicit reference to the supranational principle than they had been on the formation of the ECSC. Nevertheless, this form of general economic integration still held out the possibility of extending the process to other more political spheres of activity involving the member states. The evolution of the EEC in the 1960s and 1970s, however, confounded the expectations of the proponents of federalist and functionalist theory. Some of the governments of the member states, notably France under de Gaulle's leadership, challenged the notion of a European superstate and espoused the idea of a European confederation of states. By the 1970s, the EEC at times resembled a traditional international organisation with a strong emphasis on intergovernmental cooperation and a form of decision-making based on the lowest common denominator.

During the past twenty years the relationship between the EU and its constituent states has shifted yet again. The adoption of QMV as a result of the Single European Act of 1986 has greatly undermined the exercise of a national veto by a single member state within the Council of Ministers. The Maastricht Treaty shifted the balance even further towards the federal end of the spectrum, most evidently so in that the institutional infrastructure of economic and monetary union includes a European Central Bank (ECB) empowered to operate independently of the governments of the member states. Against all that, however, the EU still remains delicately poised between a confederation of states and a federal state. The populations of its member states are EU citizens, yet the EU still falls short of possessing the competences of a state whether organised on federal or unitary lines. It has no independent powers to tax its citizens, and it has neither the right nor the resources to exercise the legitimate use of force within and beyond its borders. In recent years, the concept of a 'multi-speed' Europe with some member states more willing and able than others to advance towards common objectives has further clouded the identity and future development of the EU as a single undifferentiated entity.

Opposition to the idea of a federal Europe has been one of the enduring characteristics of British political rhetoric over the past fifty years, no less pronounced in the 1990s, when federalism became the horrifying 'F' word in British politics, than in the 1940s when a federal Europe was regarded as the far-fetched notion of defeated continental Europeans. It was in response to British objections that the phrase 'federal goal' was struck from the proposed opening article of the Treaty of Maastricht. None of the other EU states expressed similar anxieties. Furthermore, none was surprised by this episode in view of the tortuous saga of Britain's problematical adjustment to the process of European integration since 1945. As will be seen in this study, the singular features of this British experience can be traced back in the first instance to the impact of the Second World War on Britain and to the main aims and assumptions of British policymakers in dealing with the problems of peacetime Europe.

CHAPTER ONE

Britain, Europe and the Audit of War

At the end of the Second World War in Europe in May 1945, Britain occupied a distinctive position in the world that reflected both long-standing interests as a global maritime power and the immediate mixed legacy of war. As one of the 'Big Three' along with the US and the USSR in the victorious alliance against the Axis powers, Britain confirmed its status as a great power. It also stood in marked contrast to the continental European states, with their wartime experience of occupation, division and defeat. At the same time, the price of victory was proportionately higher for Britain than for the other two major wartime allies, which had more power to shape the postwar world. In their response to these conditions, British policymakers subscribed to a particular set of priorities and views that governed their attitudes to early postwar interest in the idea of European unity and cooperation.

A key recurring feature of British policy towards European developments centred on the belief that Europe could not be separated from the global dimensions of British foreign policy. Nor could the European continent be viewed as the major, exclusive area of British strategic interest. Any European policy, and especially one involving a British contribution to the collective efforts of European states, had to be formulated in the light of British interests, connections and relations beyond Europe. This British presence in the wider world shaped the widespread perception of Britain as a great power. In 1954 Lord Franks, a leading British official throughout this period, succinctly summarised the deeply ingrained view of the British political establishment: 'Britain is going to continue to be what she has been, a Great Power.'[1]

1. *The Times*, 8 November 1954.

Some of the most obvious manifestations of British status during the course of the war were evident in the diplomatic, military and imperial fields. As one of the triumvirate of wartime allies, Britain had been at war with Germany longer than the other two. British leaders participated at the highest levels in the planning and prosecution of the war and in negotiations concerning a postwar settlement. They attended the wartime and postwar conferences of the 'Big Three' at Tehran (November–December 1943), Yalta (January–February 1945) and Potsdam (July–August 1945), and were closely involved in the conduct of inter-allied diplomacy. They also supervised British armed forces comprising some 5.1 million personnel stationed across Europe, the Middle East, Africa and the Far East at the end of the war. Such widespread military commitments were in themselves indicative of the vast, sprawling complex of worldwide commitments, interests and influence associated with the British Empire and Commonwealth. This principal expression of British great power status, which stretched across approximately one-quarter of the world's land mass, was held together by a wide variety of strategic, political, economic and cultural ties. It consisted of diverse elements, ranging from the white self-governing dominions like Australia, Canada, New Zealand and South Africa to colonies in Africa, Asia, the Caribbean and the Mediterranean which were still under direct control.

This global presence and influence served to maintain the view of Britain as a great power whose policymakers had every intention of safeguarding such a position. It was thus almost a foregone conclusion that any new symbol of great power status and independence in the postwar world should also be possessed by Britain. This was particularly the case when, following the successful explosion and use of the atomic bomb by the US in July/August 1945, the Labour government took the decision in January 1947 to manufacture a British atomic bomb. Ernest Bevin, Foreign Secretary and one of the few members of the government privy to this decision, pressed the case for such a British device in characteristically colourful language: 'We've got to have the bloody Union Jack flying on top of it.'[2]

Some later accounts of the conduct of Britain's international role at this time have emphasised the extent to which the country emerged from the war not only as an overcommitted and over-extended state in the international system, but also as one given to

2. A. Bullock, *Ernest Bevin: Foreign Secretary 1945–1951* (1983), p. 352.

illusions of grandeur in peacetime and to a persistent failure to achieve a balance between resources and commitments.[3] This inability or unwillingness to set aside the symbols of, and nostalgia for, past greatness and to fashion a strategy based on current reduced capabilities was occasionally questioned in the highest quarters. In 1944, for example, John Maynard Keynes, economic adviser to the Chancellor of the Exchequer, responded to arguments about the likelihood of a leading role for sterling in the postwar world by commenting: 'All our reflex actions are those of a rich man.'[4] Two years later the Prime Minister, Clement Attlee, unsuccessfully challenged Whitehall orthodoxy when he put the case for considering Britain as 'an easterly extension of a strategic area the centre of which is the American continent rather than as a power looking eastwards through the Mediterranean to India and the East'.[5] Certainly policymakers at the time were aware, if incompletely so, of the extent to which Britain had become a disabled great power, not least because of the cost of the war (see below) and the superior resources of the other two major allies. Few were more conscious of these grim realities than Winston Churchill who, as leader of the wartime coalition government, had seen at first hand British dependence on the US for wartime supplies and the extent of Soviet military power in Europe. At the Tehran conference in 1943 Churchill pictured himself as the poor little English donkey seated between the great Russian bear and the great American buffalo. The disparity in international weight conveyed by this simple image became even more pronounced as the war drew to a close, by which time Sir Alexander Cadogan, the Permanent Under-Secretary at the Foreign Office, judged that it was now more appropriate to speak of the 'Big 3 (or $2\frac{1}{2}$)'.[6]

It is nevertheless true to say that most British policymakers tended to view this relative decline in power as transient. As war gave way to peace, their central preoccupation was to restore Britain's credentials as a world power on an equal footing with, and independent of, the US and the USSR. There was strong opposition to the

3. For contrasting assessments see, for example, E. Barker, *The British between the Superpowers, 1945–50* (1983); C. Barnett, *The Lost Victory: British Dreams, British Realities* (1995).

4. Barnett, *The Lost Victory: British Dreams, British Realities*, p. 111.

5. Cited in A. Gorst, ' "We must cut our coat according to our cloth": the making of British defence policy, 1945–8', in R.J. Aldrich (ed.), *British Intelligence Strategy and the Cold War, 1945–51* (1992), p. 148.

6. Cited in A. Adamthwaite, 'Britain and the world 1945–9: the view from the Foreign Office', *International Affairs*, vol. 61 (1985).

view that the heavy strain on British resources should be relieved by an immediate, massive withdrawal from onerous overseas obligations. A policy of 'splendid isolation' was ruled out, partly on the grounds that it was not a viable option for an economy so dependent on international trade, and partly because it amounted to a grave loss of political prestige and influence in the highly interdependent network of the country's overseas commitments and interests. 'The abandonment of any one obligation', the Foreign Office warned in 1950, 'may start a crumbling process which may destroy the whole fabric.'[7] In their approach to the task of enhancing Britain's strength as a world power, British policymakers demonstrated the global rather than European concerns that affected their definition of British interests in Europe. This global dimension was particularly apparent in several major spheres of British involvement in the international environment.

First, the evolution of British foreign policy was greatly influenced by relations between the three wartime allies. The idea of peacetime cooperation between these three was a central feature of British plans for developing a stable postwar international order. It was recognised that the wartime alliance was a marriage of convenience that would be severely tested as the allies competed for power and influence in the postwar world. As President Franklin D. Roosevelt told Congress in a message of 6 January 1945: 'The nearer we come to vanquishing our enemies the more we inevitably become conscious of the differences among the victors.'[8] There was also in British governing circles a clear appreciation of the extent to which the other two allies presented different types of threats to British interests. Furthermore, there was much concern about the possibility of US/USSR cooperation at Britain's expense or of American abandonment of the 'special' Anglo-American wartime relationship for a mediatorial role in postwar Anglo-Soviet disputes. In these circumstances, British policymakers supported the principle of great power cooperation in order to reinforce Britain's world power status, to reduce the risk of independent action against Britain by the other two major powers, and to provide a collective means for preventing threats to world peace. Whitehall viewed the developing institutional apparatus for giving expression to this principle – wartime gatherings of the 'Big Three', the formation of the Council of

---

7. *Documents on British Policy Overseas* [hereafter *DBPO*], series II, vol. II, no. 43.
8. Cited in R.M. Hathaway, *Ambiguous Partnership: Britain and America, 1944–1947* (1981), p. 104.

Foreign Ministers and the creation of the United Nations Organisation – as instruments for promoting great power cooperation
in peacetime. The vital importance of this framework meant that
British policy towards continental Europe was governed by British
involvement in inter-allied relations. This emphasis was to be seen,
for example, in an important Foreign Office paper of July 1945
entitled 'Stocktaking after VE-day'. Its author, Orme Sargent, whose
view was endorsed by Foreign Secretary Eden, advocated a British-
led attempt to organise the west European states in order to counter American and Soviet impressions of Britain as a 'secondary Power'
and to establish equality of status for Britain among the 'Big Three'.[9]

Secondly, the Empire and Commonwealth also had an important impact on British policy towards postwar schemes for European
unity and cooperation. This multi-faceted enterprise, with its mixture of tradition, sentiment and interest, symbolised British power
and independence in the world. During the war it had served as a
major source of economic and military assistance, including a global
network of bases. Wartime and immediate postwar developments,
however, raised doubts about the long-term future of this British-
led formation. In the Far East Japanese expansion and the fall of
Singapore in 1942 had dramatically exposed British weaknesses.
On the Indian sub-continent the granting of independence to India
and Pakistan in 1947 and to Burma and Ceylon in 1948 signified a
notable change, foreshadowing a process of decolonisation that was
to result in independence from British rule for some 49 countries
over the next 30 years. In addition, the absence of a central political authority and the presence of centrifugal tendencies among
the self-governing dominions greatly restricted the Commonwealth's
potential as a single power in peacetime. Nevertheless the Empire
and Commonwealth had survived the war. The subsequent transition
from 'British Empire and Commonwealth' into 'The Commonwealth', which was facilitated by the arrangements of the Commonwealth prime ministers' conference of 1949 to keep a republican
India within the fold, served to mask Britain's declining power in
the world. During the early postwar years at least Whitehall regarded
the Commonwealth as a highly prized asset, not only in terms of
strategic value and prestige, but also as an economic, commercial
and financial enterprise. It provided access to scarce resources and,
as the world's largest trading bloc via the operation of the imperial
preference system, offered an assured market for British goods.

9. PRO, FO 371/50912, Sargent, 'Stocktaking after VE-day', 11 July 1945.

Furthermore, Britain acted as the central banker of the associated sterling area, which comprised the Empire and Commonwealth (except Canada) and also extended to a number of third countries including Burma, Iceland, Ireland, Iraq (from 1952), Egypt (until 1947), Jordan, Libya and the Persian Gulf Territories.[10] The currencies in the sterling area were tied to the pound. By this means London played a prominent role in the world's financial system at a time when some 50 per cent of all international payments were in sterling.

At the end of the war, the protection of these interests was considered more important by British policymakers than involvement in postwar European affairs. This order of priorities was particularly evident in efforts to counter what were perceived as the two main threats to British power beyond mainland Europe. One of these threats, clearly identified by the Cabinet's Post-Hostilities Planning Committee in 1944, concerned Soviet military and political pressure against British positions in the eastern Mediterranean and the Middle East.[11] This region was of such vital strategic importance to Britain, especially in terms of sea routes to the Empire via the Suez Canal – the Empire's 'jugular' – and as a source of oil supplies, that it produced some of the earliest intimations of tension in postwar UK–USSR relations: over Turkey and the Straits, Iran and Tripolitania. It also attracted more attention than Europe because of the greater scale of British assets there. British defence policy in the early postwar years was formulated on the basis of these priorities, with its emphasis on three pillars – the defence of the UK, the sea lanes and the Middle East. The other major threat came from the US. American foreign economic policy was driven by a determination to move away from the highly protectionist, restrictive international economy of the inter-war period towards a more open, multilateral free-trading system. Here the chief concern of British policymakers was the accompanying American insistence on dismantling the discriminatory economic, financial and commercial controls of the imperial preference system and the sterling area. On the termination of Lend-Lease in August 1945, Washington informed the Attlee government that it expected all such controls to be eliminated in accordance with the terms of the Mutual Aid Agreement of 1942.

---

10. C.R. Schenk, *Britain and the Sterling Area: From Devaluation to Convertibility in the 1950s* (1994), p. 8.
11. Barker, *The British between the Superpowers*, p. 7.

Thirdly, British plans for the reconstruction of the postwar international economy focused on the global rather than the European economy. The principal British effort in devising a new world economic system concentrated on the making of the Bretton Woods agreements of 1944. These agreements were mainly shaped by US–UK negotiations, although the US was in the driving seat. They aimed to create a stable, growth-oriented trading and monetary regime. Arrangements were made to assist states in balance of payments difficulties (through the International Monetary Fund), to finance long-term economic arrangements (through the World Bank), to reduce tariff barriers (the 1947 General Agreement on Tariffs and Trade), and to maintain a fixed exchange rate system in which the value of the dollar would be pegged to gold and all other national currencies tied to the value of the dollar. British involvement in the making and development of this system greatly influenced the UK's response to the idea of participation in any exclusively European forms of economic cooperation. It was always the case that any British involvement in a European initiative covering trade and payments had to mesh with, and not mark a departure from, this wider global system – later known as the 'one world' approach to international trade. Expansion of multilateral world trade was given far greater priority by Britain than by the original member states of the European Community (EC), which were principally concerned to foster intra-European trade. Herein lay a difference of material interest and perspective that was to exercise a long-standing influence on commercial relations between Britain and the EC in the postwar period.

Fourthly, the nature and extent of British interest in, and commitment to, continental Europe in the early postwar period was greatly influenced by UK–US relations. In wartime the 'special relationship' between the two countries had taken a variety of forms. Most notably there was the close personal relationship between Churchill and Roosevelt that was cemented by regular consultations – occasionally in unusual circumstances: 'The Prime Minister of Great Britain has nothing to conceal from the President of the United States', declared Churchill, as he emerged from a White House bath to face a startled Roosevelt.[12] Joint institutions like the Combined Chiefs of Staff reflected the collective purpose of the two countries in the prosecution of the war, as did the provision of

12. Cited in D. Reynolds, 'A "special relationship"? America, Britain and the international order since the Second World War', *International Affairs*, vol. 62 (1986).

US supplies to Britain under the Lend-Lease programme. The gross imbalance of power in this relationship became increasingly obvious, however, as American views, whether on military strategy or on plans for the postwar international economy, took precedence over British. On the British side, as exemplified in Churchill's thinking about the postwar order, there was a growing recognition of the need to maintain the special wartime relationship in peacetime. One of the basic calculations in this respect was that only the US possessed the resources both to provide short-term economic relief to Britain and to take on an enhanced role in the international system that would considerably ease its burden. By this means it was hoped to maintain Britain's standing as a great power – the second major power in the western hemisphere – and to ensure that the US took its interests into account.

The importance of enlisting US support in the immediate aftermath of war first became apparent on the economic front as Attlee's Labour government, elected in July 1945, counted the cost of war. The government's domestic programme, fuelled by popular aspirations and supported by the first overall parliamentary majority (146) for a Labour government, included major commitments to policies ensuring full employment, universal social security and nationalisation. The economic conditions for establishing this 'New Jerusalem', however, were decidedly problematical. By the time fighting ceased Britain had accumulated massive external debts and had incurred such losses that the country faced what Keynes described as 'a financial Dunkirk' and virtual bankruptcy.[13] Wartime debts amounted to £4.7 billion, a substantial proportion of them (£3.5 billion) based on the arrangement whereby Britain obtained materials from sterling area countries, notably India, Pakistan and Egypt, for which payment was deferred – a system of IOUs known as the sterling balances. The other important source of wartime finance was US credits via the Lend-Lease system. This assistance effectively meant that essential imports for wartime production could be obtained even while exports shrank to some 30 per cent of their pre-war level: in sum Lend-Lease accounted for approximately two-thirds of the funds needed to finance the total external deficit in wartime. The heavy cost of financing the war was also evident in other ways, not least in the sale of some £1.1 billion of overseas assets which had long yielded invisible income compensating for any visible trade deficit.

13. *DBPO*, series I, vol. III, no. 6.

The disastrous impact of war on Britain's overseas balance sheet was detailed by Keynes in a paper entitled 'Our Overseas Financial Prospects', which was sent to the Cabinet in August 1945. Keynes calculated that for the year 1945 total overseas income would amount to £800 million, made up of £350 million from exports, £350 million in receipts from allies for military equipment and services, and £100 million net invisible income and sundry repayments. Total overseas expenditure would amount to £2.9 billion: £1.25 billion on imports excluding munitions, £850 million on munitions and £800 million on other government expenditure overseas. The resulting shortfall of £2.1 billion would be met, so it was hoped, through Lend-Lease (£1.1 billion), Canadian Mutual Aid (£250 million), and sterling area credits (£750 million). But this temporary assistance, soon to be terminated in the case of Lend-Lease at the end of the war in the Far East, did not address the problem of a continuing deficit. According to Keynes's guesstimates this would amount to £1.7 billion for the period 1946–8. 'Where, on earth, is all this money to come from?' enquired Keynes.[14] His answer was that only the US was in a position to offer sufficient funds. Consequently, the first major decision of the Labour government was to dispatch Keynes to Washington in September 1945 to seek a loan. Early British hopes of a free gift, or at least an interest-free loan, were soon dashed. By the terms of the resulting Anglo-American Financial Agreement of December 1945, Britain obtained a loan of $3.75 billion (plus $650 million to write off Lend-Lease debts) at 2 per cent interest. The most onerous and contentious condition of the loan was the US insistence on making sterling freely convertible within twelve months of the agreement taking effect. The Americans also extracted a British commitment to forming an International Trade Organisation: in the event, the General Agreement on Tariffs and Trade (GATT) was to be a less ambitious substitute. The proposed aims of this body were to foster free trade and non-discriminatory commercial policies. A major threat was thus posed to the entire edifice of the imperial preference system, though the British negotiators in Washington ensured that dollar aid was not made immediately conditional on scrapping preferences, but was linked to a general scheme for reducing tariffs. In the course of the loan negotiations, moreover, other issues surfaced that indicated the essentially patron–client character of Anglo-American relations, most notably US interest in acquiring military bases in nine

14. *Ibid.*

British-administered islands in the Pacific and in seeking the abandonment of British claims to sovereignty over 25 disputed islands in the Pacific.

The loan negotiations, like the wartime Lend-Lease system, highlighted British dependence on the US for the preservation of its great power standing. It was clearly difficult to maintain the notion of such a status in these circumstances, and it is significant that many of the bitterly contested issues that were later to mark Britain's relations with Europe – including national independence and economic sovereignty – were first raised in the parliamentary debate on the terms of the US loan. Robert Boothby, a Conservative MP, described acceptance of the loan as 'a monetary Munich', while the *Manchester Guardian* expressed a widespread mood of resentment at American attempts to dictate the conduct of Britain's economic relations with the rest of the world.[15] Two hundred MPs voted against the loan and a further 167 abstained. Their indignation at the terms of the loan was expressed by *The Economist*, 'It is aggravating to find that our reward for losing a quarter of our national wealth is to pay tribute for half a century to those who have been enriched by the war.'[16] No less significant, and also indicative of the great power mentality of the British policymakers, was the rejection of alternatives to a loan. The possibility of writing off the sterling balances, for example, was dismissed as an unlikely way of safeguarding Britain's imperial ties and financial interests. There were also strong strategic reasons for fulfilling obligations towards creditor countries in the Middle East and the Indian subcontinent, which were considered key regions in the developing Cold War struggle with the Soviets in the early postwar years. Nor could massive cuts in public spending be contemplated in view of the government's domestic programme and the importance of defence spending in protecting the country's overseas interests. To be sure, there were many illusions about what the country could afford to do, and these were soon to be put to the test in the European context, whether in meeting the cost of maintaining an occupation zone in Germany or in continuing to supply aid to Greece and Turkey. There were few illusions, however, about what would happen in the absence of a dollar loan. Keynes presented the grim alternative as 'Starvation Corner', while Hugh Dalton, the Chancellor of the Exchequer,

---

15. *Parliamentary Debates (Hansard) House of Commons Official Report* [hereafter *H.C. Deb.*], vol. 425, col. 1616.

16. Cited in Bullock, *Ernest Bevin: Foreign Secretary 1945–1951*, p. 203.

held out the bleak prospect of 'less than an Irish peasant's standard of living for the British people'.[17]

The priority accorded by British policymakers to these four major spheres of interest in the wider world – 'Big Three' relations, the Empire–Commonwealth, the global economy and the 'special' US–UK relationship – was a powerful determinant of British policy on the postwar reconstruction of continental Europe. The main features of Britain's wartime planning for postwar Europe reflected a combination of traditional considerations and immediate wartime conditions and experiences. Policymakers shared a mental map of the European environment that emphasised both the dangers of continental entanglements and the need to maintain a balance of power in Europe so as to avoid domination of the continent by a single state. Such strategic concerns did not conduce to widespread support for the idea of British involvement in schemes for European unity. This much had been evident in the inter-war period, notably in Britain's response to the Briand Memorandum of 1930 proposing the creation of a United States of Europe. The Foreign Office described the French Foreign Minister's proposal as 'a surprising and disappointing work . . . permeated by a vague and puzzling idealism'. The same proposal prompted Churchill to make the well-known observation: 'We are with Europe, but not of it. We are linked but not compromised. We are interested and associated but not absorbed'[18] – a fair summary of a Janus-faced British attitude towards Europe that held sway long thereafter. Certainly Churchill himself was to be involved as wartime leader in promoting an exceptionally radical scheme for the union of two states – the Franco-British Union (16 June 1940). On the French side the initiative was essentially the product of the fertile imagination of Jean Monnet, one of the prime movers in the origins of the EC. But this hastily conceived plan, seen in British government circles mainly as a device to keep France in the war against Germany, failed to win the support of a French government that was suspicious of British motives and saw no alternative to seeking an armistice with Germany.

There were divided and often shifting opinions about the organisation of postwar Europe in the upper reaches of the wartime coalition government. Some of the earliest indications of Churchill's views on the subject were expressed in a private paper written in

17. H. Dalton, *High Tide and After: Memoirs 1945–1960* (1962), p. 85.

18. Cited in A. Shlaim, *Britain and the Origins of European Unity 1940–51* (1978), p. 17. See also R. Boyce, 'British capitalism and the idea of European unity between the wars', in P.M.R. Stirk (ed.), *European Unity in Context: The Interwar Period* (1989).

January 1943 ('Morning Thoughts') and in a radio broadcast of March 1943 which envisaged the formation of a Council of Europe as the European component of a world peace-keeping organisation.[19] Such thinking was principally influenced by the need to devise a European framework that could adequately contain postwar Germany. Churchill's growing fears about the rising tide of Soviet power in Europe, however, increasingly modified his assessment of the value of British involvement in a European organisation.[20] He had grave misgivings about the likelihood of weak continental states clamouring for postwar aid from a hard-pressed Britain. His anxieties increased as serious shortages of food, fuel and other raw materials accompanied the end of the war in Europe. Another cause of alarm was the prospect of maintaining a large peacetime British army on the continent to compensate for the failings of French and other military forces there. By the end of the war, he had come to the conclusion that a British-led European bloc or security system was simply insufficient to contain Soviet power and that only a close Anglo-American peacetime relationship would be capable of dealing with this threat.

The Foreign Office, under Anthony Eden, was initially sceptical of Churchill's proposal for a regional European body including Britain. It took the view that such a scheme scarcely buttressed the idea of great power cooperation within the framework of a global security system. Indeed, a British-organised European bloc was thought likely to undermine great power cooperation, in that it would be treated by Moscow as an anti-Soviet measure and by Washington as evidence of a bloc-building or sphere of influence mentality that conflicted with its globalist plans for the postwar world. Unlike Churchill, Eden and his Foreign Office advisers were slow to acknowledge that Soviet power, rather than a revived Germany, would represent the most serious threat to Europe's security after the war. They maintained that the construction of a durable European system to control postwar Germany required the maintenance of an alliance with the Soviets.

During the last twelve months of the war, however, the Foreign Office was far more receptive to the idea of what was described as a Western Group or a regional association of Western Europe based

19. For the text of 'Morning Thoughts' see M. Howard, *Grand Strategy vol. IV August 1942–September 1943* (1972), pp. 637–9.
20. On the eve of the Tehran conference in November 1943, Churchill expressed his fears to Harold Macmillan, 'The real problem now is Russia', and he added, 'I *can't* get the Americans to see it': cited in K. Robbins, *Churchill* (1992), p. 138.

on an Anglo-French treaty. This idea first surfaced during Foreign Office preparations for the Dumbarton Oaks conference (August–October 1944) where the 'Big Three' and China settled arrangements for what was to become the United Nations Organisation, including provision for regional associations. In the wake of this conference, Eden, with the backing of the Chiefs of Staff, sought to persuade Churchill of the general value of a Western Group as a bulwark against 'another Hitler, whencesoever he may come'.[21] In Eden's view, such an arrangement offered particular advantages in helping to control postwar Germany, to reinforce Britain's 'Big Three' status, to reassure west European states that might otherwise fall prey to Soviet influence, and to give defence in depth to the UK. The Foreign Office also acknowledged the benefits of close economic association between members of the proposed Western Group. It was recognised, however, that any successful scheme involving the formation of a customs union would present formidable difficulties for Britain in view of Commonwealth interests and likely American opposition.[22] While Eden hereby indicated his greater concern with the Soviet threat in the postwar world, he was still convinced that British involvement in any west European grouping must not jeopardise relations with the other two allies and must be clearly subordinated to the 'Big Three' alliance.

Churchill remained largely unimpressed by the notion of a Western Group, though he agreed that an Anglo-French treaty was required in the first instance. There was little likelihood, however, of concluding a treaty with General Charles de Gaulle, the head of the French provisional government. Prior to the Franco-Soviet treaty of December 1944, de Gaulle spurned a British suggestion for an Anglo–French–Soviet pact, and his prickly relations with London were worsened by Anglo-French differences over Middle Eastern affairs and the treatment of postwar Germany. In the event, Churchill's wartime coalition government took no decision about the proposal for a Western Group, and none of the related plans for this organisation came to fruition before the end of the war, apart from the largely British-inspired effort at the Yalta conference to include France as an Occupying Power. Such plans nevertheless revealed the likely nature and extent of British interest in the postwar organisation of Europe, especially in their emphasis on defence and

21. *DBPO*, series I, vol. I, no. 119, Eden to Churchill, 29 November 1944.
22. For the views of Whitehall officials on Britain's economic relations with Western Europe at the end of the war see, for example, PRO, T 236/779, Minutes of a meeting held at the Foreign Office on 25 July, 1945.

security and their underlying assumption that Britain would be the leading spokesman for non-communist Europe. The widespread view in Whitehall was that Britain's European leadership credentials were further enhanced by the unfavourable image of the Americans and Soviets in Western Europe. In his 'Stocktaking after VE-day' paper, for example, Sargent commented that 'Unlike our two great partners we are not regarded in Western Europe as gangsters or go-getters.'[23]

Britain's record in the war and its harbouring of many wartime European governments-in-exile established its reputation as the leader of the European states. This exceptional wartime status, as compared with the altogether different experiences of the continental European states, permeated the attitudes of British policymakers towards the postwar idea of European unity and removed them from direct experience of many of the influences contributing to this idea. This detachment was not simply a case of traditionally insular British attitudes towards the continent expressed in the so-called 'Channel complex' – 'Fog in the English Channel, continent cut off'. It was also indicative of the contrasting impact of the war on British and continental societies. A substantial, albeit incalculable, difference in this respect was that the British nation-state had not only survived the war intact, but had actually been strengthened in the process. The cessation of hostilities in 1945 did not mark some kind of 'Year Zero' or abrupt break with the past in the case of Britain. Indeed, the wartime record was long to remain a matter of celebration, affirming rather than calling in question Britain's status as one of the great powers and further reinforcing the concept of national sovereignty. The absence of any fundamental reassessment of the country's political institutions or its role in the wider world was later to be remarked on by Jean Monnet: 'I never understood why the British did not join the European Community, which was so much in their interest. I came to the conclusion that it must have been because it was the price of victory – the illusion that you could maintain what you had without change.'[24] A not untypical expression of this frame of mind was provided by Hugh Dalton at the Labour Party conference of 1950: 'We intend to hold what we have gained here in this island.'[25] In some respects,

23. PRO, FO 371/50912, Sargent, 11 July 1945.

24. Cited in M. Charlton, *The Price of Victory* (1983), p. 307.

25. Cited in S. Dejak, 'Labour and Europe during the Attlee Governments: the image in the mirror of R.W.C. Mackay's "Europe Group", 1945–50', in B. Brivati and H. Jones (eds), *Reconstruction to Integration: Britain and Europe since 1945* (1993), p. 56.

Dalton was merely voicing a commonplace Labour Party view of the marked contrast between the achievements of the Attlee government and turbulent political conditions on the continent, where there was an ebbing tide of support for the socialist parties, especially in France, Germany and Italy. But he was also subscribing to a deeply rooted and enduring consensus of opinion in British political circles which held that the relationship between European integration and the nation-state exhibited all the features of a zero-sum game between opposing rather than complementary concepts.

The wartime experience of occupation, division and defeat suffered by so many continental European states made for a different climate of opinion, one that was often based on a desire to expunge recent history or to reverse wartime verdicts – whether that of 1940 in the case of France or 1945 in the case of Germany. In these circumstances, there was an understandable preoccupation with the idea of a new beginning, a marked commitment to the process of renewal and modernisation, and a critical assessment of the role and functions of the new or reconstructed state. A heightened sense of the value of European unity was stimulated by a variety of influences that had little or no resonance in Britain. Many of these influences reflected the adverse impact of occupation on national unity and the attractions of European unity for defeated states seeking international rehabilitation. British political culture, moreover, was largely cut off from bodies of continental opinion that were closely associated with advancing the cause of European unity, most notably the resistance movement in wartime and the new political force of Christian Democracy in the early postwar years. The absence of any British counterpart to the continental Christian Democratic parties resulted in a distancing from a common ideology and a burgeoning network of ties, especially between Christian Democratic elements in France, Italy and West Germany, that greatly contributed to the subsequent course of European integration.

The gulf between Britain and continental Europe arose, too, out of widely diverging views concerning the importance of European ties as against interests in the wider world. Britain's global connections meant that Europe was treated as but one part of a larger whole. Many of the continental states, by contrast, viewed Europe as their sole or primary sphere of interest in the outside world. This was most apparent in the case of the defeated powers, as Germany had lost its colonies in the aftermath of the First World War, while Italy was formally dispossessed of its north African empire in 1946. Other European states remained colonial powers – notably France,

Belgium and The Netherlands. Yet their overseas possessions scarcely matched the size and influence of the British Empire in the workings of the global economy. Nor did they attract so much attention as to undermine the importance of a European-focused strategy.

A further distinction between Britain and the continental European states that accounted for marked differences of attitude towards the idea of European unity and cooperation lay in the relatively stronger economic position of Britain during the period of postwar reconstruction. Certainly contemporary British perceptions of this difference often overestimated the disastrous effects of war on the European economies and underestimated its adverse impact on British economic fortunes. Even so, it was still the case that Britain occupied a dominant position over its European neighbours in the economic and commercial fields. In 1951, for example, Britain still accounted for one-third of the total industrial production of non-communist Europe (roughly equivalent to the combined industrial production of France and Germany) and enjoyed a pronounced lead over other European manufacturers in sectors like merchant shipbuilding, cars and aircraft. In addition, the volume of British exports was equal to that of French and German exports put together. Extra-European trading links were far more important to Britain's postwar economic recovery than European markets: in the period 1952–4 only 13 per cent of total British exports went to the states which later constituted the EC, whereas 47 per cent went to the Commonwealth.[26] This trading pattern meant that, at best, there was heavily qualified support among British policymakers for the idea of forging close economic ties with the continental states.

At the end of the war, there was no blueprint in British government circles concerning relations with the European states and the idea of a collective European entity including Britain. While Churchill was increasingly inclined to view the prospect of a British-led Europe as a weak reed, Foreign Office support for such a venture could make little headway and was, in any case, tempered by the workings and constraints of the wartime alliance. It was in the aftermath of war that Britain's European policy had perforce to be more clearly defined. This process can be seen most clearly in connection with the origins and outcome of a British-inspired plan for Western Union that was formally launched in January 1948.

---

26. PRO, T 234/195, Relative values of UK trade with the Commonwealth, Sterling Area and Western Europe: 1952–4 (annual average).

CHAPTER TWO

Western Union and the Reconstruction of Western Europe

The period 1945–9 represented a crucial phase in the evolution of British policy towards the idea of European cooperation. This was true both in terms of identifying the limits of the Labour government's interest in becoming embroiled in organisations facilitating the reconstruction of Western Europe and also in fashioning the background against which this same government declined full involvement in the Schuman Plan of 1950. Major developments in the international context during this period greatly influenced British policy, notably the failure of the wartime allies to cooperate in peacetime, the emergence of an adversarial relationship – or Cold War – between the Western powers and the USSR, and the accompanying division of Europe into two blocs and of occupied Germany into two states. One of the most significant features of this pattern of events on the Western side was the American commitment to the economic recovery and security of Western Europe, culminating in the North Atlantic Treaty of 1949. This unprecedented undertaking by a peacetime US administration first found expression in the 'Truman doctrine' of March 1947 by which President Truman promised US assistance in containing communism and identified Europe as the top priority area in the world for this exercise. Shortly afterwards, in June 1947, the hitherto globalist character of US policy was further modified to allow for regional cooperation when George Marshall, the Secretary of State, offered American economic aid to Europe. The Soviet rejection of this offer sealed the economic division of Europe. The sixteen west European states that took it up created the Organisation for European Economic Cooperation (OEEC). This, the first major postwar west European organisation in the field of economic cooperation, came into existence in April 1948, at the same time as the first instalment of US aid became available through the four-year European Recovery Programme (ERP) – commonly known as the Marshall Plan. A few months later, in July 1948, the US and five west European states embarked on discussions that eventually resulted in the North Atlantic Treaty.

These events had a pronounced impact on the character and scope of British interest in the area of European cooperation. The evolution of the views of Foreign Secretary Bevin during this period clearly demonstrated some of the effects of these general developments. In a meeting with senior Foreign Office officials on 13 August 1945, soon after taking up office, Bevin emphasised the long-term importance of cultivating close political, economic and commercial relations between Britain and the countries on the Mediterranean and Atlantic fringes of Europe. Here, as elsewhere in the handling of his foreign policy brief, Bevin reflected a consensus between the wartime coalition government and the incoming Labour administration. In this particular case, as we noted earlier, the Foreign Office was already receptive to the idea of forming a west European bloc. On the wider international stage, Bevin was to emerge as a pugnacious defender of Britain's great power status, possessing a 'bulldog patriotism' in the Churchillian mould. From the outset he had an intuitive grasp both of the likelihood of worsening UK–USSR relations and of the importance of close ties with the US. On the development of links between Britain and the west European states, Bevin insisted that this process should begin with the establishment of better relations with France, and he raised the possibility of a Franco-British alliance or the formation of a Western Group. Five years later, however, in April 1950, Bevin was arguing that it was necessary 'to get away from talk about Europe', to recognise that Europe did not constitute a separate and self-contained unit, and to acknowledge the importance of the Atlantic Pact.[1] By this time, in fact, the conventional wisdom in British foreign policymaking circles was that European policy had to be shaped in accordance with the model of Britain as the centre of three great interlocking or concentric circles – Europe, the Atlantic and the Commonwealth – with Europe as the decidedly subordinate circle. This model further reinforced the British view of European integration as a zero-sum game in that the idea of closer involvement in

1. *DBPO*, series II, vol. II, no. 52. At a Cabinet meeting on 8 May 1950 Bevin commented that 'for the original conception of Western Union we must now begin to substitute the wider conception of the Atlantic Community': PRO, CAB 128/17, CM(50) 29th Conclusions, 8 May 1950.

Europe was invariably dismissed on the grounds that it would automatically entail losses for British interests in the other two circles. In the intervening period it was the origin, substance and outcome of one of Bevin's major initiatives that registered this change of emphasis in British thinking and also indicated the limits beyond which the Labour government was not prepared to venture in the field of European cooperation.

This initiative was formally launched by Bevin in a House of Commons speech on 22 January 1948. Bevin called for a Western Union to resist what was perceived as a growing Soviet threat at a time of considerable uncertainty and rising tension in international affairs – 'a critical moment', in Bevin's words, in the organisation of the postwar world.[2] The general thrust of his argument was that the time had arrived to emphasise the spiritual unity of the West, to mobilise its resources and, in particular, to create some form of union in Western Europe – whether of a formal or informal character – which would be backed by the North American continent and the Commonwealth. This grand design was immediately accompanied by some specific recommendations, including a proposed treaty with the Benelux states (Belgium, The Netherlands and Luxembourg), talks on Germany between the Western occupying powers and cooperation between the west European colonial powers.[3] Beyond that, however, there was limited detail of what exactly this most positive British endorsement of the principle of west European union might amount to in practice. Some Foreign Office officials, who were not involved in the planning stage of this initiative, were completely mystified, the immediate response of one of their number being: 'What do we mean by a spiritual union? A United States of Europe? A Customs Union? A regional defence arrangement?'[4]

2. *H.C.Deb.*, vol. 446, no. 45, col. 385. See also, for example, PRO, FO 371/73069, Record of a conversation between Bevin and the US ambassador to Britain, 26 February 1948: Bevin commented that 'we were now in the critical 6 to 8 weeks' which would 'decide the future of Europe'. For the background to the Western Union initiative see PRO, CAB 129/23, CP(48)6; PRO, CAB 128/12, CM 48(2), 8 January 1948; PRO, FO 800/444, Record of conversation between Bevin and the Canadian High Commissioner, 17 December 1947; PRO, FO 371/73045, memorandum by Bevin, 12 January 1948.

3. For a detailed discussion of Bevin's views on collaboration between the European colonial powers see J. Kent, *British Imperial Strategy and the Origins of the Cold War 1944–49* (1993). There was little support in Whitehall for Anglo-French cooperation in the utilisation of colonial resources. See, for example, PRO, FO 371/67673, Interdepartmental meeting of officials, 8 October 1947.

4. PRO, FO 371/73045, Makins to Sargent, 21 January 1948.

The significance of this initiative has been a matter of dispute among commentators ever since. Some have viewed it as an integral part of Bevin's effort to lure the US into giving military backing to Western Europe in the face of the Soviet threat. According to this explanation, the Western Union initiative was 'a sprat to catch a mackerel'[5]: it was primarily designed to demonstrate that the west European powers were prepared to make collective defence arrangements but clearly required US backing to make these effective. Bevin's underlying purpose was thus fulfilled in the Atlantic Pact of 1949 – the 'crowning achievement' of his foreign secretaryship, according to this account. Other commentators, however, have argued that Western Union was not initially conceived as a first step in this direction. Rather, it was part of a general, long-term design to reassert British power and influence via a British-led Western Europe extending to and utilising Western Europe's overseas links and colonies. In effect, Bevin aimed to organise the 'middle of the planet' and thus create a 'Third Force' in the international system that was on a par with, and independent of, the US and the USSR. Still other commentators have maintained that this idea of Britain organising the 'middle of the planet' was a fanciful notion reflecting illusions of grandeur and offering an insubstantial basis for dealing with the pressing problems of Western Europe's economic weakness and defencelessness.[6] These explanations are not mutually exclusive. It might be argued, indeed, that they epitomise the way in which Bevin himself took up or set aside different options in response to a rapidly changing set of international conditions. This was especially the case in the first half of 1948, as the Cold War intensified with the Communist coup in Czechoslovakia in February and the beginnings of the Berlin blockade in June, as the US Congress finally approved Marshall Aid appropriations in April, and as the Vandenberg resolution in the American Senate in June opened the way to US defence cooperation with Western European states. The course and outcome of Bevin's Western Union initiative is illustrative of this process.

In the wake of the Western Union initiative, the nature and extent of British interest in some form of union in Western Europe

5. Cited in J.W. Young, *Britain and European Unity 1945–1992* (1993), p. 17.

6. For a review of some of the different assessments of Bevin's concept of Western Union see J. Melissen and B. Zeeman, 'Britain and Western Europe, 1945–51: opportunities lost?', *International Affairs*, vol. 63 (1987). See also S. Croft, *The End of Superpower: British Foreign Office Conceptions of a Changing World, 1945–51* (1994); Kent, *British Imperial Strategy and the Origins of the Cold War*.

was to be tested in the military, economic and political fields. The most immediate consequence of the initiative was the signing of the Brussels Treaty in March 1948 by Britain, France and the Benelux states. By this mutual assistance pact, the five powers undertook to provide military and other aid in the event of an attack on a member state. They also agreed to collaborate in economic, social and cultural matters and to establish the institutional apparatus for such purposes – the Brussels Treaty Organisation (BTO), which was to operate under the supervision of an intergovernmental body of ministers. This development suggested the outlines of a west European bloc under British leadership and consistent with British views concerning the organisation of Western Europe. In fact, however, the BTO soon emerged as a forum within which Britain and France were the leading representatives of contrasting views on west European cooperation. Both states were also increasingly engaged in a contest for the leadership of Western Europe.

A major difference of opinion in the first instance centred on the military aspects of the Brussels Treaty. The British attached most importance to the symbolic value of the treaty, recognising that its paper guarantees – in the absence of military capability – did not begin to meet the Soviet threat: a British Chiefs of Staff plan, dated March 1948, concluded that on the basis of one month's preparation the Soviets could amass a force of 75 divisions, 5,000 tactical aircraft and 800 heavy bombers while the Western powers could assemble only ten divisions and 950 tanks. It was envisaged that British occupation forces in Germany would form the British contribution to BTO, but these amounted to only two divisions and were, in any case, primarily given over to civilian duties. The main concern of the French, however, was to obtain the commitment of British military forces to continental Europe (i.e. other than for occupation purposes), and to develop the closest form of military cooperation between London and Paris. The British were determined to avoid such an undertaking: 'We do not want any more Dunkirks', declared Bevin.[7] This was also the view of the Chiefs of Staff, who opposed a major commitment of British ground forces to Europe at a time when the 'three pillars' of British defence policy – defence of the UK mainland, control of the lines of sea communication and defence commitments in the Middle East

---

7. PRO, FO 371/73045, memorandum by Bevin, 12 January 1948.

– took priority.[8] Furthermore, the idea of close cooperation with the French on sensitive issues of military strategy was resisted by British military planners. They regarded France as a security risk, not least because of Communist representation (until May 1947) in the postwar French government.[9] There was also the fear that substantive cooperation was bound to reveal British and American plans to evacuate their occupation forces from Germany in the event of a Soviet invasion. The Chiefs of Staff, for example, did not wish to arouse French suspicions that 'we intend to desert them in the event of Russian aggression'.[10] By contrast, there was a greater willingness in London to participate in highly secret talks with the Americans than with the BTO allies. This US–UK dialogue was most evident in exchanges before and after the beginning of formal discussions resulting in the Atlantic Pact of 1949: the exploratory Pentagon talks of 22 March–1 April 1948 on the possibility of US involvement in a Western defence system were restricted to American, British and Canadian delegates. The French were excluded on security grounds – ironically so in view of the fact that one of the British delegates, Donald Maclean, was later to be exposed as a Soviet spy.

British resistance to French pressure for a stronger UK commitment to continental defence and for closer military cooperation between the two countries was symptomatic of the often very ambivalent attitudes of British policymakers towards France in these early postwar years. On the one hand, Bevin was convinced that any form of west European cooperation had to be based on an Anglo-French axis and that every effort had to be made to strengthen France in order to enhance west European stability and security. His commitment to such a policy found expression in the signing of the Anglo-French Dunkirk Treaty (March 1947), in the joint British and French response to the Marshall Aid offer and the formation of the OEEC, and in the making of the Brussels Treaty. On the other hand, British policymakers frequently voiced both anxiety and disdain about France's military deficiencies, low morale,

---

8. This view was reinforced by uncertainty about American policy towards the defence of Western Europe. In March 1948, for example, Alexander (Minister of Defence) warned Bevin that there could be no British commitment to military action on the Continent 'until we are clear on the scope and scale of American cooperation': PRO, FO 371/73052, Alexander to Bevin, 10 March 1948.

9. Bevin was advised to impress on the French government the importance of taking remedial action to prevent Communist penetration of its Service Departments: PRO, FO 371/73052, Alexander to Bevin, 10 March 1948.

10. Cited in P. Cornish, *British Military Planning for the Defence of Germany 1945–50* (1995), p. 139. See also PRO, FO/371/73052, Alexander to Bevin, 10 March 1948.

political instability and economic problems. A Foreign Office paper of October 1948, for example, took the view that the French political system was so discredited, the economy was so rapidly deteriorating and national defence was so wholly neglected that France was 'the weakest link in the western chain'.[11] In April 1950, an equally gloomy Foreign Office review concluded that in building on France 'we shall perhaps be building on sand'. To this Bevin added as a post-script: 'almost too optimistic, but even then a sad story'.[12]

The second and eventually more significant gauge of British interest in west European union was in the field of economic coop-eration. The particular litmus test of British policy in this respect was the question of whether or not to participate in the formation of a west European customs union. This issue had come to promin-ence following the Marshall Aid offer, when there was mounting American support for a single market in Western Europe, and when the principle of a customs union attracted interest in French circles and resulted in efforts to develop a customs union between France, Italy and the Benelux states. The prospective recipients of Marshall Aid formed an intergovernmental study group in November 1947 to consider the subject. This development has special significance in view of later history, for ten years were to elapse before the Treaty of Rome established the EEC with a customs union as its centre-piece, i.e. a tariff-free trading bloc with a common external tariff.

Prior to and at the time of the Western Union initiative, there were significant differences of opinion in Whitehall about the pos-sibility of British membership of a west European customs union. Bevin and the Foreign Office recognised the political advantages of British involvement in such a scheme, especially in giving substance to the concept of Western Union. Bevin himself had a long-standing

11. PRO, FO 371/73105, Kirkpatrick, 8 October 1948. See also, for example, PRO, FO 371/79076, Harvey to Bevin, 28 October 1949. In his annual review of French politics in 1949, Harvey (British ambassador in Paris) warned that 'until American weapons arrive, this country is virtually disarmed': PRO, FO 371/89166, Harvey to FO. For Anglo-French relations in the early postwar period see J.W. Young, *Britain, France and the Unity of Europe 1945–1951* (1985); R. Woodhouse, *British Policy towards France, 1945–51* (1995); S. Greenwood,'Return to Dunkirk: The origins of the Anglo-French treaty of March 1947', *The Journal of Strategic Studies*, vol. 6 (Decem-ber 1983).

12. PRO, FO 371/89173–89174, FO paper on France, 22 April 1950. In August 1950 a British embassy report, seen by Bevin and forwarded to Attlee, reported that 'With very few exceptions, no member of the Embassy staff or of the Consulates knows personally of any individual Frenchman who means to fight in the event of war in the near future': PRO, FO 371/89176, Hayter to FO, 16 August 1950. See also, for example, PRO, FO 371/89246, Harvey to FO [report on the French army], 21 March 1950.

interest in this idea that stretched back to the inter-war period when he had been greatly impressed by the advantages of a large common market enjoyed by American industry: at the 1927 TUC conference, for example, he had called for a European customs union to encourage the free movement of trade and labour. After the war he soon emerged as a vigorous exponent of this idea, as early as October 1946 producing a paper on the subject that led the Cabinet to appoint a committee of experts to consider the matter. In the event, the committee's report of August 1947 opposed British membership of a customs union, for reasons discussed below.[13] Bevin's immediate reaction came in his TUC speech in the following month when he advocated a customs union encompassing Britain, the Commonwealth and Western Europe. He then obtained Cabinet support for the appointment of an interdepartmental committee to examine the whole question. It was against this background that one of the earliest attempts to flesh out the idea of Western Union in the economic field was a Foreign Office paper of February 1948 that predictably and forcefully argued the case for a west European customs union including Britain. It did so primarily on the grounds that no other solution would yield comparable benefits, whether in terms of the political and economic strengthening of Western Europe or in relation to the long-term competitive efficiency of the British economy: 'For better or for worse', the paper concluded, 'our fate is in large part bound up with that of Western Europe.'[14]

This view, however, had already fallen foul of weighty objections elsewhere in Whitehall – particularly at the Treasury and the Board of Trade – and was soon to fall by the wayside altogether.[15] There were several strands to this opposition. First, it was feared that Britain's

13. Shortly afterwards Duff Cooper (British ambassador in Paris) commented in a dispatch to Bevin, 'The mere words "customs union" produce a shudder in the Treasury and nausea in the Board of Trade': PRO, FO 371/67674, Cooper to Bevin, 16 October 1947.

14. PRO, FO 371/71766, FO paper on a west European customs union, 27 February 1948.

15. For Treasury and Board of Trade views immediately prior to the Western Union initiative see, for example, PRO, CAB 134/215, EPC 47 6th meeting, 7 November 1947. By late March 1948 the Cabinet had decided, as one senior FO official put it, 'to put their money on economic integration in Western Europe' through the European Recovery Programme and the OEEC rather than the alternative policy of joining a customs union: PRO, FO 371/71776, Makins, 23 March 1948. In the following month Bevin suggested to his French counterpart, Bidault, that a Western Union bank facilitating trade expansion between the west European states might be a better solution than a customs union: PRO, FO 371/73057, Record of a conversation between Bevin and Bidault, 17 April 1948.

far more important trading and financial interests beyond Europe would be placed at risk. The overriding priority, it was felt, was to ensure that sterling's role as an international trading currency was unimpaired and that the imperial preference system remained intact. The general view was that British membership of a European customs union was unacceptable on a number of counts. In particular, it was reckoned that British membership of such a customs union would result in a loss of British trade in Commonwealth countries that could not be offset by comparable gains in the more competitive European markets. Much emphasis was also placed on the view that membership of a European customs union was incompatible with maintenance of the Commonwealth preferential trade system.[16] Moreover, any attempt to merge the Commonwealth system with a European customs union would entail a net loss for British exporters and for British management of the sterling area. All in all, the Empire–Commonwealth was considered to hold far greater attractions than Europe in helping to improve Britain's external trade and payments position. This was hardly surprising in view of the fact that the whole of Europe accounted for only 20 per cent of British trade, while the Commonwealth accounted for almost 50 per cent.

Secondly, the dramatic downturn in Britain's economic fortunes in 1947 lent further weight to the argument against membership of a European customs union. The ballooning trade and payments deficit with the dollar area, the short-lived and disastrous attempt in July–August to make sterling convertible and the rapid exhaustion of the US loan of 1945 all combined to confront the Labour government with the gravest crisis in its period of office. These conditions put a premium on measures that contributed to the goal of economic viability. Under the forceful leadership of Stafford Cripps, Chancellor of the Exchequer since November 1947, the Treasury was intent on pressing ahead with a programme mainly designed to increase dollar-earning exports and to reduce dollar-costing imports. Given these priorities, a European customs union was viewed by the Treasury as at best irrelevant and at worst an obstacle to reducing

16. A British government paper produced for the Commonwealth Prime Ministers' Conference of October 1948 insisted that 'a settlement of the preference problem on lines satisfactory to all countries concerned is a *sine qua non* of our even considering entering a customs union'. It was noted that other prospective members of a customs union might be unable or unwilling to offer adequate compensation to other Commonwealth countries for any loss of preference in their export trade to Britain: PRO, CAB 133/88.

the dollar deficit. Indeed, officials in the department persistently drew a distinction between what was required to achieve economic viability and plans to use Marshall Aid as a vehicle for promoting European economic unity. In making this distinction, the Treasury believed that others – notably the Americans and the French – were hopelessly confusing these two aims, to the detriment of economic viability as the major target. According to the Treasury argument, a customs union would simply encourage British production for the dollar-starved European market rather than for the dollar area or for other markets in the Commonwealth where payment was to be had in dollars. It was on these grounds, for example, that Bevin's support for close Anglo-French economic relations to serve strategic and political purposes buckled under the weight of the Treasury's view of the limited economic value of such relations. Treasury opposition to any Anglo-French-inspired customs union for Western Europe dwelt much on the view that exporting to France reduced Britain's dollar-earning capacity, while importing from France scarcely contributed to Britain's dollar-saving programme. A Board of Trade official made the same point in a wider context: 'we could not look on France as an overriding priority like Argentina'.[17] Argentina had the dollars to pay for British goods and could provide necessary food-stuffs. France, by contrast, lacked dollars to pay for imports, while its luxury exports to Britain were no substitute, as British officials frequently observed, for wheat, steel and meat which could have reduced Britain's dollar payments. It was thus commonly observed in British official circles that France should be more concerned to increase its level of production than to pursue a long-term project like a customs union.[18]

Thirdly, British membership of a European customs union was judged a non-starter in view of its probable adverse impact on national economic management and on major sectors of the British economy. Such a venture would place restrictions on the government's

17. PRO, FO 371/67673, Interdepartmental meeting of officials on Anglo-French economic relations, 8 October 1947. For the Board of Trade's attitude towards British membership of a European customs union see, for example, BT 11/352, Note by the Board of Trade, 26 June 1947, and Board of Trade papers in PRO, FO 371/62552 and PRO, FO 371/71768. See also PRO, CAB 134/244, E.R.(L)(49)260, 22 September 1949. Duff Cooper claimed that the fundamental objection to Anglo-French economic cooperation in Whitehall rested on the view that Britain was richer than France and was therefore likely to be a net loser in any collaborative venture: PRO, FO 371/67674, Cooper to Bevin, 16 October 1947.

18. For Whitehall's scepticism towards the idea of an Anglo-French economic union at this time see, for example, PRO, T 229/207, Hitchman, 'First thoughts on the Monnet discussions', 11 April 1949.

freedom to pursue its own budgetary, planning and exchange policies. This was a particularly unwelcome prospect for a Labour government that set such great store by maintaining national controls. Unlike some of their French counterparts, British policymakers had little or no interest in the idea of a customs union as part of a wider process of national economic planning and modernisation. Rather, there were strong fears, especially at the Board of Trade, that a customs union would have an extremely damaging effect on agriculture and certain manufacturing industries like steel, chemicals and textiles. This protectionist argument, it must be said, did not convince some sections of opinion in the Foreign Office. There it was noted that the Board of Trade had baldly announced that membership of a customs union would mean the decline of British industry in favour of its foreign competitors even before a detailed study of the impact on British industry had been undertaken. At the time, the Board of Trade's attention was focused on the conclusion and implementation of the GATT (1947), whose global emphasis and importance to British commerce overshadowed the idea of regional economic cooperation in Europe.

Finally, the likely effects of a customs union greatly depended on its functions and potential, and this gave rise to a further objection to membership. Treasury thinking was dominated by two views of the form that a customs union might take. One view was that a union which was confined to eliminating only import duties between member states and to establishing a common external tariff was a bogus creation which, as Cripps firmly ruled, could not be contemplated. Such a customs union would have very little direct effect on west European trade, since its members would still be free to use quotas, which would have the same effect as tariffs. The other view was that customs unions had invariably been only impermanent halfway houses which either dissolved or proceeded towards economic union and political federation. Given these stark alternatives, it was therefore necessary, as Cripps expressed the matter in a Cabinet paper of September 1948, to choose between abandoning the customs union idea or moving towards some complete form of European federation.[19] By this time, in fact, British membership of a European customs union was no longer regarded as a practicable proposition.

Meanwhile, a further test of Bevin's original support for some form of union in Western Europe centred on the idea of creating political institutions expressing the collective identity and unity of

19. PRO, CAB 134/219 E.P.C.(48) 78, 7 September 1948.

the region. France took the lead in July 1948 with a proposal for a European Assembly which the BTO powers agreed to consider. Much impetus was given to this proposal by the calls for European political and economic union that had emanated from the unofficial Congress of Europe held at The Hague in May 1948. The French government did not subscribe to the principle of a federalist Europe expressed by some in this gathering. It was nonetheless intent on proceeding beyond the intergovernmental character of the OEEC and BTO, and towards the creation of a more popular institution. What eventually emerged after six months of negotiations within the BTO was the Council of Europe, comprising a Committee of Ministers and a purely consultative Assembly with a greatly circumscribed agenda.

Although this outcome was satisfactory to the British, the negotiations revealed all too clearly their distaste for the idea of institutionalising political union. It was in this context especially that British policymakers were first thrown onto the defensive – there to remain long afterwards – in their support for limited forms of European cooperation. Bevin had considerable reservations about the European Assembly idea.[20] His initial aim was to squash the proposal by highlighting its impracticabilities. Failing this, he was determined to ensure that any organisation caused 'minimum embarrassment', first conceding the case for a Committee of Ministers, then subsequently, and even more reluctantly, accepting the proposal for an Assembly.[21] Support for a federalist Europe on the continent was a source of much concern to Bevin: 'When you open that Pandora's box you'll find it full of Trojan 'orses.'[22] This view was shared by

20. See, for example, PRO, FO 371/73097, Record of a meeting between Bevin, the Minister of State and Kirkpatrick, 24 August 1948: Bevin commented that 'The French were playing politics, and that was a thing we could not do'; PRO, FO 371/73063, Bevin to Attlee, 26 September 1948; PRO, FO 371/73098, Record of a meeting of the Consultative Council of the Brussels Treaty Organisation, 25 October 1948; PRO, FO 371/79262, memorandum by Bevin, 7 January 1949; PRO FO 371/79214, Record of a conversation between Bevin and Schuman, 14 January 1949.

21. Bevin suggested that the Assembly should adopt the 'card vote' system of the British Trades Union Congress, but Dalton reported back from the preparatory conference that 'What sticks most in continental gizzards is our proposal for bloc voting': PRO, FO 371/79214, Dalton to Bevin, 19 January 1949.

22. Bullock, *Ernest Bevin: Foreign Secretary*, p. 659. FO papers at this time were full of critical comments about plans for a European federation. One paper, for example, maintained that 'The mystique of federalism has led too many astray . . .' and that it was necessary to distinguish between 'elaborate Meccano thought structures and the indispensable minimum of political construction which is actually practicable': PRO, FO 371/73099, FO research memorandum, 9 November 1948. See also

Labour leaders at large. Thus Dalton, head of the British delegation to the Council of Europe's preparatory conference, was to describe the federalists as 'conclaves of chatterboxes'.[23] The fact of the matter was that an immediate European political union was at odds with Bevin's emphasis on a gradual, pragmatic, step-by-step approach based on intergovernmental cooperation. In his Western Union speech, he had stressed the difference between the easy exercise of drawing up constitutions for a united Europe and the altogether much harder task of carrying out a practicable programme which took into account realities. Devising constitutional architecture for a federal Europe was, in Bevin's view, not only akin to putting 'the roof on before we have built the building', but also likely to expose serious divisions between the states and to ruin any prospect for west European solidarity.[24]

Certainly the negotiations surrounding the formation of the Council of Europe demonstrated the widening chasm between Britain and its BTO partners. At the same time, there was a growing antipathy in Labour ranks towards the European unity movement. Bevin had launched his Western Union initiative when there was considerable support in the Parliamentary Labour Party (PLP) for British leadership of a 'Third Force' European union between the US and the USSR: in March 1948 a parliamentary motion advocating a democratic federation in Europe received the backing of some 100 Labour MPs. This tide of opinion rapidly receded, however, especially as the Cold War intensified and Marshall Aid became a reality. Significantly, the Labour government and party boycotted the Congress of Europe and increasingly viewed the European platform as a vehicle for right-wing parties.[25] There was great annoyance at the way in which the Conservatives used the European cause for party-political purposes – Churchill's dominating presence being a case in point. Labour's National Executive criticised the Congress of Europe as a forum that had been exploited by

J.W. Young, 'British officials and European integration, 1944–60', in A. Deighton (ed.), *Building Postwar Europe: National Decision-Makers and European Institutions, 1948–63* (1995).

23. The French delegation to this conference was described as 'a team of historical monuments who, after the effort of the inaugural speeches, would be incapable of any further action': PRO, FO 371/73099, Sargent to Harvey, 10 November 1948.

24. Cited in Young, *Britain, France and the Unity of Europe*, p. 112. See also, for example, FO 371/73095, FO Note, 22 March 1948.

25. See J.T. Grantham, 'British Labour and the Hague "Congress of Europe"', *Historical Journal* (1981).

miscellaneous and unrepresentative interests, and in September 1948 issued a pamphlet – *Feet on the ground* – that expressed unqualified opposition to the idea of a European federation.[26]

The changing climate of political opinion in Western Europe also contributed to a diminishing interest in Labour circles in any form of European unity that either went beyond a narrowly circumscribed type of cooperation or upset anti-federalist prejudices. There was no ideological affinity with the reviving conservative forces on the continent in the shape of Christian Democracy. The Christian Democrat parties emerged as the governing party in Italy in 1948 and in West Germany a year later, and also played an influential role in French coalition governments of this period through the Mouvement Républicain Populaire (MRP).

Moreover, there remained in the Labour Party and official quarters a deeply pessimistic view of the condition of the continental states. Thus Sir Edmund Hall-Patch, head of the UK delegation to the OEEC, warned ministers in early 1949: 'Do not put all your eggs in the European basket. It is a pretty shoddy contraption and there are no signs yet that the essential repairs are going to be made.'[27] The mixture of arrogance and condescension that shot through official British attitudes towards the continental European states at large was also well expressed by Hall-Patch on taking leave of his OEEC post in July 1952: 'The Europeans look to us for leadership; they are delighted when we are able to give it; they respond to it in a remarkable manner.'[28] But a headmasterly Britain did not possess an inexhaustible supply of patience or interest in shepherding an increasingly recalcitrant group of European states that aspired to tighter integration.

By the spring of 1949, in fact, the limits of British involvement in the process of European integration were far more clearly established than had been the case when Bevin had first called for some form of union in Western Europe. In policymaking circles at least, a consensus was emerging that Britain must not compromise its independence or dilute its strength by integrating too closely with Western Europe. This conclusion first emerged in the course of an interdepartmental meeting of senior British officials in January 1949:

26. In the following month Bevin emphasised the limited character of Western Union as a basis for European political union when he commented ' "Western Union" was indeed a misnomer; it was rather an association of nations on the lines of the Commonwealth': PRO, CAB 133/88.

27. PRO, FO 371/77999, Hall-Patch to Berthoud, 4 and 16 April 1949.

28. *DBPO*, series II, vol. I, no. 466.

> Our policy should be to assist Europe to recover as far as we can. . . .
> But the concept must be one of limited liability. In no circumstances
> must we assist the Europeans beyond the point at which our own
> viability was impaired. Nor can we embark upon measures of coop-
> eration which surrender our sovereignty and which lead us down
> paths along which there is no return.[29]

A paper by Bevin and Cripps, supporting this view, was approved by
the Cabinet's Economic Policy Committee in the same month, and
a further paper on the economic implications of this assessment
was endorsed by the Cabinet the following October.[30] A line was
thus drawn under a wide-ranging debate in official circles, and the
concept of limited liability established the benchmark against which
to judge the merits of any new schemes for European integration.

29. A. Cairncross (ed.), *Anglo-American Economic Collaboration in War and Peace
1942–1949 by Sir Richard Clarke* (1982), p. 209.

30. PRO, CAB 134/221, EPC (49)6, 25 January 1949; PRO, CAB 128/16, CM(49)62,
27 October 1949.

CHAPTER THREE

'We are not ready': Britain and the Schuman Plan

On 9 May 1950 Robert Schuman, the French Foreign Minister, announced a proposal to place all Franco-German coal and steel production under a common High Authority in an organisation open to the participation of the other countries of Europe. The most distinctive institutional feature of this Schuman Plan, which was primarily the handiwork of Jean Monnet, the head of France's postwar Modernisation and Re-equipment Plan, was a proposed supranational High Authority with powers independent of the governments of member states. The declared political purposes of this ostensibly economic organisation, as expressed in Schuman's original announcement, were to overcome the deep, long-standing conflicts in Franco-German relations, to ensure that war would be 'not merely unthinkable, but materially impossible',[1] and to take the first step towards the creation of a European federation. In the event, the immediate result of this opening chapter in the history of the EC was the signing, on 18 April 1951, of the Treaty of Paris establishing the ECSC, which came into being on 10 August 1952 and comprised France, West Germany, Italy, Belgium, The Netherlands and Luxembourg – the grouping commonly referred to as the Six.

Britain was a conspicuous absentee. It was the supranational dimension of the Plan that ultimately proved to be the formal major obstacle to British membership, and predictably so in view of the Cabinet's decisions in 1949. Yet the politics and diplomacy of this episode involved more than the mechanical application of recently established criteria. There were basic differences of perspective,

1. Cited in P. Fontaine, *A Fresh Start. The Schuman Declaration 1950–90* (1990), p. 44.

priority and policy between Britain and France that surfaced in the period down to 3 June 1950, when it became clear that Britain would not be involved in formal negotiations concerning the Plan.

The initial response of British ministers and officials to Schuman's announcement involved a combination of surprise and incredulity. The Labour government was given no advance notice of the French plan, even though the US and West Germany had been informed of French intentions shortly beforehand.[2] According to Dean Acheson, the US Secretary of State, this lack of prior consultation and suspicions of a Franco-American conspiracy sent Bevin into a 'towering rage'.[3] Bevin was also angered by the timing of Schuman's announcement since it came – significantly so for the French – only three days before Acheson, Schuman and Bevin himself were due to hold talks on Germany. This initial reaction soon gave way to a more considered and also widespread view in official British circles that was summed up by the comment of one senior Foreign Office official to Monnet shortly after the announcement had been made: 'We are not ready; and you will not succeed.'[4] From the British standpoint, the Western international system had developed along satisfactory lines by this time with the Atlantic Pact, the revival of close Anglo-American relations, and the model of Britain as the centre of the three interlocking circles of Europe, the Commonwealth and North America. Furthermore, there seemed little reason to expect or to encourage any new west European organisation beyond the OEEC, the BTO and the Council of Europe. By 1950, in effect, Britain was broadly satisfied with the status quo. Change was sought only in so far as west European organisations could be better dovetailed with the Atlantic community.

From the outset, there were abounding doubts in Whitehall about the seriousness of French intentions. The Plan was perceived as the latest in a series of ambitious French schemes for west European unity since 1945 which, far from being viable, well-conceived projects to solve specific problems, were symptomatic of the internal weaknesses of France. Thus French interest in a European customs union, particularly pronounced following the Marshall Aid offer, had been regarded as little more than window dressing designed to curry favour with the Americans and to ensure that France received the maximum amount of aid. The French proposal for a European

2. *Foreign Relations of the United States* [hereafter *FRUS*] 1950, vol. III, pp. 691–2.
3. D. Acheson, *Sketches from Life of Men I Have Known* (1961), p. 44.
4. Cited in M. Charlton, *The Price of Victory* (1983), p. 122.

Assembly (see Chapter 2) had been largely viewed in London as evidence of a weak French government attempting a European structure in order to hold off its Communist and Gaullist opponents.[5] Moreover, French-inspired attempts in 1949, to create first a Franco-Italian customs union and subsequently a wider union including the Benelux states ('Fritalux'), both ended in failure: in Foreign Office circles the former scheme was dismissed as a facade of aspirations with no construction behind it.[6] What further reinforced British doubts about the French position was the very novelty of the idea that France should embark on such a venture in view of its past record of stubborn resistance to British and American plans for the political and economic recovery of Germany. It seemed unlikely that French fears of a revived Germany could be allayed without a British commitment. If the Plan was to be more than a rhetorical flourish, Britain, as France's senior partner in Western Europe, would have to come to the rescue. As one Foreign Office official put it condescendingly: 'We shall have to do what we can to get the French out of the mess into which they have landed themselves.'[7]

Such a dim view of the Plan's chances of success and of the degree of French commitment, however, was not allowed to stand in the way of a full consideration of the matter. Whitehall undertook an immediate assessment of the strategic, economic and political implications of the Plan. There was a mixed response. The Foreign Office viewed the Plan as a French attempt to take the initiative in determining the pace of Germany's economic recovery and in seeking to control West Germany while granting it equality. There were fears that the Plan might encourage a neutralist, 'Third Force' federated Europe.[8] The Chiefs of Staff welcomed the possibility of a Franco-German rapprochement as a contribution to

5. See, for example, PRO, FO 371/73099, Kirkpatrick, 8 September 1948.

6. PRO, FO 371/78111, Hall-Patch to FO, 24 September 1949. In a report to the the Cabinet's European Economic Cooperation Committee, the Fritalux plan was described as unambitious and unlikely to succeed, though it was acknowledged that the inclusion of Germany (thus incorporating all the founder member states of the EEC) 'might involve serious dangers for us by making Fritalux a more powerful and probably a more exclusive group': PRO, CAB 134/248, 14 January 1950. Foreign Office officials amused themselves by coining different acronyms for these groupings including Benefrit or Benefritz ('unlikely to commend itself') if Germany was included in the grouping: PRO, FO 371/78113, Berthoud, 23 December 1949.

7. PRO, FO 371/85843, Makins, 19 May 1950.

8. For some of the initial reactions to the Plan in Whitehall see, for example, PRO, FO 371/85841, Stevens, memorandum on the French proposal to establish a Franco-German Coal and Steel Authority, 10 May 1950; PRO, FO 371/85843, Jebb to Strang, 11 May 1950. Strang, the Permanent Under-Secretary, considered that there was very little substance to the view that the Plan was likely to make war

the defence of Europe and as a means of facilitating some form of German rearmament which they regarded as a necessity in the longer term. The economics ministries were fearful of a powerful Franco-German coal and steel combine and emphasised the importance of a 'one world', multilateral approach to economic problems.

Whether or not Britain should enter into negotiations and on what terms had yet to be decided. It was expected that more information about the Plan would be made available when Monnet visited London (14–19 May 1950). In the course of meetings with British ministers and officials and in response to requests for further information, however, Monnet acknowledged that there was nothing to hand beyond Schuman's original announcement. He thus confirmed British suspicions that the Plan had been hastily conceived for largely political purposes,[9] and especially to convince the Americans in advance of the Acheson/Bevin/Schuman meeting that France was prepared to take the lead in a form of European integration including West Germany. Monnet was chiefly intent on emphasising three aspects of the Plan: that West Germany *had* to be involved while other states could join if they chose; that all member states had to surrender control of their coal and steel industries to the supranational High Authority; and that all prospective member states had to make a prior commitment to the supranational principle of the Plan before entering into formal negotiations about its details.

It has been argued that such conditions were deliberately designed to exclude Britain from the Schuman Plan negotiations. But this is to assume that the British response was uppermost in the minds of Schuman and Monnet and also that the British were desperate to secure full involvement in negotiations on acceptable terms. The truth is that the French were more interested in the West German rather than the British response. Participation by Britain might rank as desirable, but holding West Germany to the supranational principle was of vital importance. Monnet's overriding concern was to ensure that the British did not negotiate away the fundamental principles of the Plan by the sort of hedging and delaying tactics that they had successfully employed in stymying economic integration within the OEEC. Furthermore, Monnet's earlier discussions with British officials (in 1949) had convinced him that the British

impossible between France and Germany as 'Economists have been saying this kind of thing since Norman Angell, and they are always wrong': PRO, FO 371/89176, Strang, 25 August 1950.

9. See, for example, PRO, FO 371/85842, Makins, minutes of a meeting with Monnet, 16 May 1950.

had little understanding of, and even less sympathy for, his commitment to a single European economy and economic planning.[10] Certainly his plans for large trade deals between the two countries, with a view to an Anglo-French economic union in the longer term, had fallen on stony ground in London. British officials simply did not approach the subject of postwar economic recovery in the same frame of mind as Monnet, who was determined to forge a link between the modernisation of the French economy and the idea of an economically integrated Western Europe. Nor was there any British equivalent to the type of long-term, 'indicative' economic planning and investment embodied in the French Modernisation and Re-equipment Plan supervised by Monnet via the government-controlled Planning Commissariat. The Labour government's declared interest in economic planning scarcely advanced much beyond the maintenance of wartime controls, the programme of nationalisation and the establishment of an Economic Planning Board (1947). Besides, the grim economic conditions of the time – highlighted by the US loan of 1945, the convertibility crisis of 1947 and the devaluation of the pound in 1949 – invariably meant that the requirements of long-term economic planning were swept aside by the imperatives of day-to-day crisis management. Roger Stevens, one of the leading Foreign Office officials who strongly supported British membership of a west European customs union in 1947–8, detected the same preoccupation with the needs of the moment in Whitehall's consideration of this possibility: 'On the whole however the short term complexities and adjustments loom more largely in the minds of departments than the problematical (though generally conceded) long term advantages.'[11]

Although Monnet had failed to provide further details about the Plan, British ministers and officials publicly commended the idea.

10. Monnet was involved in a series of talks with British officials in 1949. See, for example, PRO FO 371/77933, Note of four conversations between Plowden and Monnet, 3–7 March 1949; PRO T 229/207, Hitchman, 11 April 1949; K. Jones, *An Economist among Mandarins: A Biography of Robert Hall (1901–1988)* (1994), pp. 160–1; P. Hennessy, *Never Again: Britain 1945–51* (1992), pp. 378–81.

11. PRO, FO 371/62555, Stevens, 22 December 1947. On his appointment as a junior Foreign Office minister in the Attlee government, Christopher Mayhew requested a briefing paper outlining the government's foreign policy, only to be informed that no such document existed and that 'it was really rather doubtful whether we had a foreign policy in the proper sense at all': cited in *The Guardian*, Hugo Young, 30 July 1998. For different assessments of the process of British foreign policymaking in the early postwar period see, for example, S. Croft, *The End of Superpower: British Foreign Office Conceptions of a Changing World, 1945–51* (1994); R. Edmonds, *Setting the Mould: United States and Britain 1945–1950* (1986).

There was good reason to support the initiative in so far as it signified a more constructive French attitude towards Germany and a
promising first step towards a Franco-German rapprochement. It
was also important to demonstrate positive interest in the Plan in
view of the fact that the US quickly backed it and thereafter played
a key role in ensuring its success. Any suggestion of lukewarm British support for the Plan or, worse still, efforts to sabotage it would
have had a damaging effect on UK–US relations and would have
invited the now familiar charge of British foot-dragging on European cooperation.[12] Moreover, given that American pressure on
Britain to take the lead in further west European integration had
recently relaxed in favour of viewing France as the most likely pacemaker (see Chapter 6), the British could not be seen to jeopardise
a French response to such pressure.[13]

There was, of course, a sharp distinction between publicly welcoming the Plan and supporting full British involvement. Ideally,
ministers wished to be associated with any Franco-German talks, while
reserving their position pending a detailed study of the Plan. The
idea of association without commitment – a characteristic feature
of British policy towards the EC during the 1950s – was endorsed
by the Cabinet's Economic Policy Committee on 23 May on the
assumption that any substantial progress was likely to be slow.[14]
Two days later, however, British calculations were upset by a French
proposal to hold a conference on the Plan comprising those states
prepared to make a prior commitment to its supranational principle. France had managed to obtain West German agreement to the
Plan. This decisive breakthrough meant that Monnet and – despite
fleeting reservations – Schuman were determined to press ahead
with or without British participation. This hardening in the French
position became evident in the course of diplomatic exchanges
between Paris and London in the period 25 May–3 June, all of
which failed to reconcile French insistence on prior commitment
to the supranational principle with the British case for a preliminary meeting of interested states to obtain more details of the likely
workings of the Plan. The imposition of a French deadline – an

12. For American suspicions in this regard see, for example, *FRUS*, 1950, vol. III,
pp. 724–6, US ambassador (London) to Acheson, 8 June 1950, and also p. 740,
Acheson to Certain Diplomatic Offices, 8 July 1950.
13. See, for example, PRO, FO 371/85844, Franks to FO, 29 May 1950.
14. The first meeting of ministers following the Schuman announcement concluded that 'much time would elapse before substantial progress could be made
with this proposal in France or Germany': PRO, CAB 130/60, GEN 322/1st meeting,
11 May 1950.

ultimatum in the British view – brought matters to a head on 3 June when, following its rejection of a British proposal for an Anglo-French ministerial meeting, France announced that the Six would hold a conference on the Plan.[15]

Most accounts of these diplomatic exchanges suggest that this was a case of two governments which did not wish to discuss the question or were talking at cross purposes. From the British point of view, the idea of prior commitment to a principle in the absence of detailed information was comparable to signing a blank cheque. Bevin was particularly irritated by the way in which the French had employed shock tactics to try to bounce him into a decision without sufficient warning and study. At the official level at least, a distinction was made between the supranational principle itself – about which some British officials claimed to be open-minded – and prior acceptance of this principle. Some of the government's critics maintained that this last obstacle might have been overcome by adopting the same escape clause as the Dutch, namely by accepting the Plan's principles while reserving the right to retract this acceptance if it proved impossible to apply these principles in practice.[16] But this did not address the official British position, which was to avoid either acceptance or rejection of the Plan's principles in advance of detailed discussions. It was also argued that there would be far more damaging consequences for the project if Britain entered negotiations and subsequently withdrew than if the Dutch were to do so.

Some contemporary observers, like Sir Oliver Harvey, the British ambassador to France, viewed this episode as symptomatic of a wide difference between British and French modes of thought and diplomatic methods: 'The negotiations were in fact a classic example of the difficulty of reconciling French cartesianism with British empiricism, the French habit of proposing lofty aims and then thinking out the methods of achieving them with the British habit of only advancing step by step.'[17] More important, however, was the

15. See PRO, FO 371/85844, FO to Ankara, 4 June 1950.

16. PRO, FO 371/85852, Rickett to Jay, Note of a meeting of ministers, 21 June 1950.

17. PRO, FO 371/85847, Harvey, 6 June 1950. See also PRO, FO/85850, Harvey to Younger, 16 June 1950. In an earlier dispatch to the FO, Harvey cited the formation of the Council of Europe as an example of how the French maintained that 'the creation of European machinery would stimulate the growth of European consciousness, whereas the British held that until that consciousness had developed the machinery would be useless and probably dangerous': PRO, FO 371/89189, Harvey to FO, 2 March 1950.

fact that French and British national interests were so different at this stage that whatever miscalculations were made on the British side, whether in underestimating the French commitment and the likely success of the Plan or in overestimating the British ability to win support for an alternative scheme at the appropriate time, the outcome would have been the same. To have entered negotiations on French terms would have suggested that the Cabinet's stated position on European integration in 1949 was far more elastic than had been originally intended. Moreover, behind the British stance on the issue of prior commitment to the Plan's principles there existed a decided opposition to participation in a supranational project. This became most apparent as the British set to work on an alternative plan on the basis of a set of proposals devised by Cripps and approved by ministers on 28 June.[18] A central feature of this plan was that it abandoned the idea of a supranational High Authority for an intergovernmental council appointed by and responsible to member governments.

The lack of common ground between Britain and France on the Schuman Plan was most strikingly demonstrated by their contrasting policies and attitudes towards the recovery of Germany, and also by their assessments of the needs and interests of their own heavy industries. In many respects the Schuman Plan clearly exposed a major, and what proved to be an enduring, difference of outlook between Britain and France on the value of European integration in addressing the economic and security implications of a revived Germany. The British did not share the same compelling reasons as the French for viewing European integration and the possible accompanying loss of national sovereignty as an acceptable or necessary price for controlling or accommodating Germany within a new, tightly knit European system. The evolution of British and French policies towards Germany in the early postwar years reflected these very different priorities and emphases.

British policy towards Germany in the period of military occupation (1945–9) was greatly influenced by strategic and financial considerations favouring the political and economic recovery of the three Western occupation zones. From the outset, it was recognised that any attempt to maintain long-term occupation controls over a weakened German economy would have adverse consequences for the European economy at large. A Europe 'chained to the German corpse', as Churchill graphically expressed it, was also likely to assist

18. PRO, CAB 130/60, GEN.322/2nd meeting, 28 June 1950.

the further expansion of Soviet power and influence on the continent. It was, however, the heavy cost of maintaining the British occupation zone – approximately £80 million in 1946 – that cleared the way towards a more systematic commitment to Germany's recovery, first via the economic merger of the UK and US zones in January 1947 and subsequently through largely American-driven plans for the economic recovery and growth of this Bizone. UK–US cooperation in occupied Germany, together with the making of the Atlantic Pact, strengthened British support for a particular approach towards accommodating the new West German state in the international system. By 1950, in effect, the British were convinced that the western alliance system offered the best way to supervise the further recovery of West Germany. This 'Atlantic solution', as Bevin described it, should also serve to allay French fears about a revanchist Germany, especially since the original function of NATO in Western Europe was (in the words of Lord Ismay, the first Secretary-General of NATO) 'to keep the Russians out, the Americans in and the Germans down'.[19] At the time of the launching of the Schuman Plan, therefore, British policymakers saw little or no need to devise a new European mechanism or organisation to control a potentially strong West German state. Existing organisations were considered sufficient for this purpose, the more so as West Germany became a full member of the OEEC and an associate member of the Council of Europe in 1950. Grave doubts about this view of the connection between German and European developments found expression in a US State Department memorandum at this time: 'They [the British] seem to have no concept that the question of the organization of Europe or the West has any bearing on the German question . . . They speak of a step by step approach but seem to ask from the Germans nothing but entry into the Council of Europe.'[20]

By contrast, the French were not only more fearful than the British of a resurgent Germany, but far less convinced of the usefulness of a western alliance solution. They were particularly concerned to avert any future military threat from Germany in view of the three German invasions of France in 1870, 1914 and 1940. On Germany's defeat in 1945, therefore, French policymakers were determined to maintain a weak, divided Germany. Their plans for heavy reparations and controls (the so-called 'French thesis') were combined with schemes for dismembering Germany which echoed

---

19. Cited in Hennessy, *Never Again*, p. 253.
20. *FRUS*, 1950, vol. III, pp. 333–4.

Clemenceau's celebrated comment: 'I like Germany so much that I want as many Germanies as possible.' But these plans failed to come to fruition, as the onset of the Cold War determined the more limited partition of Germany into two states while intensifying American and British determination to hasten the recovery of the Western occupation zones. By 1947, and increasingly so thereafter – particularly in view of its heavy dependence on US aid – France had perforce to align itself more closely with American and British moves towards the formation of a West German state. In the course of this protracted and bitterly contested process, French involvement in the creation of the West German state was assisted by a number of measures, notably the formation in 1948 of the International Authority for the Ruhr, by which the three Western occupying powers and the Benelux states (later joined by West Germany) controlled the production, distribution and prices of the Ruhr's heavy industries. By 1950, however, it was increasingly obvious that this piece of occupation machinery had a doubtful long-term future. The US and the UK, urged on by the new West German government, clearly supported the further dismantling of restrictions on Germany, whether by agreeing to leave the issue of the ownership of the Ruhr industries to be settled by the Germans or by considering the possibility of raising the level of German steel production. In the circumstances, French policymakers faced a critical choice between continuing to mount rearguard actions in the face of heavy American and British pressure or taking matters into their own hands by proposing a direct Franco-German link. This latter option was all the more appealing because of scepticism in French circles about the long-term future of the US commitment to Europe and thus about the British view that the western alliance framework was adequate to contain a revived Germany. The French wanted European controls over Germany's recovery, and the Schuman Plan offered a new and positive approach to achieving this objective. The particular attractions of the Plan were that it reduced the pressure on France to abide by any Anglo-American timetable for the further recovery of Germany and also gave France a more commanding position from which to determine the future development of the still partially sovereign West German state.

The very different interests and resources of Britain and France in the heavy industrial sector also greatly contributed to dissimilar policies. A major concern of French policymakers throughout the early postwar years centred on production and allocation arrangements for the coal, coke and steel output of the Ruhr, Germany's heavy industrial arsenal whose economic capacity and military potential aroused a host of French fears. By 1950 the progressive lifting of economic restrictions on West Germany greatly alarmed French policymakers. They were determined to safeguard much-needed French access to German coal: approximately 40 per cent of the French steel industry's coke requirements were met by imports from Germany. They were also anxious to preserve France's heavy postwar investment in the steel industry against rising German competition. It was feared that as allied controls over the production level and price of German coal were relaxed, France would be able to obtain German coal only on German terms and that the German steel industry would benefit far more than its French counterpart from increased German coal production. It was out of such material considerations that the Schuman Plan was born. Monnet himself, as head of the French modernisation programme, which allocated some 30 per cent of its total investment funds to coal mining and steel, was acutely conscious of the likely adverse impact of Germany's recovery on France's heavy industrial needs and interests. As early as 1947, he was gloomily speculating on likely cutbacks in French steel production as the German steel industry revived and not only absorbed all the coke produced in the Ruhr, but also undercut French steel prices. The doubling of West German steel output in the period 1948–50 accentuated French fears. Indeed, the extent to which this development threatened to undermine France's modernisation programme has prompted the historian Alan Milward to suggest that the 'Schuman Plan was called into existence to save the Monnet Plan'.[21] Such a portrayal of Monnet, less as a disinterested supporter of European integration and more as an active participant in shaping French policy, was foreshadowed in some of the astringent criticisms of the Schuman Plan at the time. In some quarters it was claimed that French rhetoric about European unity merely concealed yet another French attempt to exploit German weakness: 'They say Europe but mean coal', commented one West German SPD deputy who was deeply sceptical of French motives.

It is fair to say that British officials were aware of some of the specific problems that the French were seeking to address via the Schuman Plan. They were also commonly and significantly disposed to regard the Plan primarily in the context of Franco-German relations, rather than in the wider framework of European integration.

---

21. A.S. Milward, *The Reconstruction of Western Europe 1945–51* (1984), p. 475.

A Cabinet paper at the time took the view that the French were seeking an escape from their dilemma by aiming to freeze German steel production at current levels and by ensuring that German steel producers did not create combines in order to obtain German coal at prices over which the French had no control.

Few if any of these considerations amounted to overriding priorities in the case of Britain, which enjoyed a dominant position in coal and steel production as compared with the Six. In 1949 Britain accounted for 48.9 per cent of the total coal production of Britain and the Six combined and 35.5 per cent of total steel production in that area.[22] It was from this strong position that the British government's official working party on the implications of the Plan arrived at its main conclusions on 16 June 1950. It considered that the UK might suffer some but not intolerable disadvantage over a continuing period by staying out of the Plan. There was felt to be a case for some form of international cooperation, especially as postwar shortages of coal and steel were giving way to the prospect of over-supply, but not for a supranational authority to oversee such cooperation. All in all, the long-term prospects for the British coal and steel industries were judged to be good. Certainly there existed none of the fears that had impelled the French to propose the Plan. While the French were concerned about guaranteed access to German coal, the British were primarily intent on ensuring the maintenance of national controls over the distribution of British coal. Since the war there had been pressure on Britain – especially from the US – to export more coal to assist the European recovery. Bevin was a vigorous exponent of the case for doing so in order to maximise British influence, prompting his well-known claim that 'If I had three million tons of coal which I could export . . . I could have a foreign policy'.[23] But it was nonetheless axiomatic – all the more so in view of the coal shortages and three-day working week of 1947 – that domestic requirements should take priority. As the official working party commented: 'we must avoid having to negotiate on the present modest scale of our coal export trade'.[24] Similarly, Britain did not share the same concerns as France about steel and the impact of increased German production and competition on the European market: approximately 60 per cent of total British

22. See PRO, CAB 134/293, FG(WP)(50)38, Working Party on proposed Franco-German Coal and Steel Authority.

23. Cited in M. Blackwell, *Clinging to Grandeur* (1993), p. 91.

24. PRO, CAB 134/293, FG(WP)(50)38. See also PRO, FO 800/493, Record of a meeting of Cabinet ministers with National Union of Mineworkers representatives.

steel exports went to the Commonwealth, while Western Europe accounted for only 5 per cent.

Such considerations found expression in the British domestic politics surrounding the reception given to the Plan. In the first major parliamentary debate on the Plan, on 26 June 1950, both major parties expounded the same conventional wisdom. Cripps for the government and Churchill for the Opposition both acknowledged that membership of a federal Europe was out of the question, not least because it was incompatible with ties and obligations beyond Europe. True, there was some Conservative criticism of the government's handling of the diplomatic exchanges with France. There was also sufficiently strong support for the idea of participating in international consideration of the Plan for the Conservatives to table an amendment to that effect. But this was far from endorsing the supranational principle. In the face of Cripps's argument that no British government could contemplate surrendering control of its heavy industries to a foreign body, the Conservative leadership recognised the dangers of being portrayed as the party prepared to do so. Here electoral considerations entered into play. Labour's parliamentary majority of 146 in the 1945 general election had melted away to five as a result of the February 1950 general election. Another election appeared imminent and was eventually held in October 1951. Labour was quite prepared to capitalise on any suggestion of Conservative willingness to surrender national sovereignty and, had the parliamentary debate gone against the government, one member of the Cabinet, Jowitt, the Lord Chancellor, was convinced that he couldn't think 'of any better issue to go to the country on'.[25]

The government's handling of the issue was widely supported by the Labour Party at large. Strong antipathy towards the idea of British membership of a European federation was particularly apparent on the National Executive Committee (NEC), which produced a pamphlet, *European Unity*, in June 1950. The timing of this publication – some ten days after the conclusion of diplomatic exchanges with France – together with its strident opposition to the prospect of a Labour Britain being corralled into a European supranational authority with a permanent anti-socialist majority, embarrassed the party leadership. Yet both Attlee and Bevin had previously approved its substance, and its main arguments received widespread Labour backing, particularly with reference to retaining

25. Young, *Britain and European Unity*, p. 34.

national controls over the coal and steel industries.[26] No other pair of industries as a basis for European economic integration was more likely to arouse Labour Party passions than coal and steel. Both industries had been singled out as playing an integral role in the party's nationalisation programme of 1945. Coal was the first industry to be nationalised (1946), while the nationalisation of the steel industry (1949) – a more complicated and contested exercise – was to be the government's last major piece of nationalisation. There was thus unquestioning support for the view that Labour had not assaulted 'the commanding heights of the economy' in order to hand over control of coal and steel to a supranational European body. Herbert Morrison, the chief architect of the nationalisation programme, pithily expressed the party consensus on hearing about the imposition of a deadline by France: 'It's no good, we cannot do it, the Durham miners won't wear it.'[27]

Some later accounts of this episode were to criticise the Labour government for its short-sighted, ill-considered view of the possibilities.[28] It was noted, for example, that the formal decision not to participate in the Plan on French terms was taken at a Cabinet meeting held (on 2 June) in the absence of three of its leading figures: Attlee and Cripps were on holiday, while Bevin was in hospital.[29] Yet their ministerial underlings were acting in accordance with their instructions and these, in turn, were ultimately based on a strategic view of the limits of British interest in the process of European integration. There was no compelling imperative to enter into negotiations on French terms. The merits of intergovernmental cooperation, the weaknesses of idealistic schemes for European federation, the desirable balance between European and extra-European interests, and Britain's restricted economic interest in Western Europe all told against any other response and demonstrated the meaning of the concept of limited liability. Certainly there was a basic miscalculation about the prospects for the original Plan which, as it came to fruition, increasingly threw the British

26. Nor did the Foreign Office view the pamphlet as marking a departure from British policy. Strang, the Permanent Under-Secretary, concluded that 'The Labour Party statement, though ill-timed and in places ill-expressed, is in its main thesis along the true line of British policy': PRO, FO 371/89189, Strang, 15 June 1950.

27. Cited in B. Donoghue and G.W. Jones, *Herbert Morrison: Portrait of a Politician* (1973), p. 481.

28. For a recent critical assessment of the Labour government's response to the Schuman Plan see E. Dell, *The Schuman Plan and the British Abdication of Leadership in Europe* (1995).

29. PRO, CAB 128/17, C.M.(50) 34th Conclusions, 2 June 1950.

onto the defensive and involved a constant struggle to achieve some satisfactory form of association – short of full participation – with the collective endeavours of the Six. British exertions in this regard intensified during the early 1950s, as it seemed that the Six were embarking on even more comprehensive schemes for integration.

CHAPTER FOUR

The Case for Association

In the history of Britain's relations with the six Schuman Plan states during the 1950s, the period 1950–54 witnessed British attempts to develop forms of association with the Six that avoided supranational integration, enhanced Britain's self-styled role as the chief sponsor or supervisor of west European cooperation and meshed west European organisations with the western alliance. The successful course and outcome of the Schuman Plan negotiations meant that an opportunity to win support for an alternative British scheme never presented itself. Instead, negotiations for formal links between Britain and the ECSC resulted in the conclusion of a treaty of association in December 1954. This event, unremarkable in itself, was nonetheless indicative of the British preference for the principle of association with the Six that was upheld by both the Labour and Conservative governments of this time.

A striking feature of British policy towards European integration throughout this period was the strong degree of continuity between the Labour government that lost power as a result of the October 1951 general election and the incoming Conservative government under Churchill. In this, as in other foreign policy spheres, there was some substance to the common saying that the only difference between Anthony Eden, the new Foreign Secretary, and Bevin was that the latter dropped his aspirates. At the beginning of his period of office Eden was presented with a Foreign Office brief summarising British policy towards European integration, the principal features of which were a willingness to engage in organisations based on intergovernmental cooperation, to offer encouragement to countries that wished to adopt a supranational approach and to consider methods of associating Britain with European supranational bodies short of full membership.[1] There was also an evident concern to cultivate the idea of an Atlantic, rather than a purely European, community and to incorporate any supranational European body into the larger Atlantic framework. Eden approved the substance of this brief and scarcely strayed from its main guidelines during the course of his foreign secretaryship. His general approach to European cooperation was spelt out at an early stage when he stated in December 1951: 'We want a united Europe . . . it is only when plans for uniting Europe take a federal form that we cannot ourselves take part.' The practical implications of this view were to be seen in his handling of the highly controversial issue of West German rearmament. This was an issue that dominated European international relations and politics throughout this period and also suggested that the Six were about to make a quantum leap towards integration via a supranational European Defence Community (EDC).

The proposal to rearm West Germany first appeared on the Western international agenda in the midst of heightened Cold War tensions following the outbreak of the Korean War in June 1950 and increased fears of a Soviet threat to Western Europe. The US response to these conditions was to present its European allies in September 1950 with a 'one package' proposal involving the dispatch of additional American forces to Europe, the creation of an integrated NATO force under an American Supreme Commander and the rearmament of West Germany. This last item immediately caused a furore throughout Western Europe. In Britain, the Labour government was shocked by the prospect but reluctantly authorised Bevin to accept the 'one package' proposal in principle – largely on the grounds that German rearmament was the price that had to be paid for US assistance and the preservation of close US–UK relations.[2] As some observers have noted, this acceptance in principle scarcely accorded with the formal British objection some months earlier to participating in the Schuman Plan negotiations. Opposition in France, however, was altogether greater and the government there flatly rejected the idea of German rearmament. French dependence on American economic and defence aid made this an untenable position and eventually caused Paris to put up an alternative proposal for a European army in October 1950. This plan, devised by Monnet but named after René Pleven, the current French

1. *DBPO*, series II, vol. I, no. 414.
2. PRO, CAB 128/18 C.M.(50) 59th Conclusions, 15 September 1950.

Prime Minister, sought to apply the Schuman Plan principle of sector integration to the military field. It envisaged the fusing of the defence forces of the member states under a supranational authority. One of the main attractions of this scheme to French policymakers was that it avoided the formation of a new German army under a NATO coalition of national military forces. The European army plan subsequently evolved into the EDC Treaty which was signed by the Six in May 1952, modified by additional protocols thereafter and finally rejected by the French National Assembly in August 1954.[3]

Initial British reactions to the Pleven Plan combined deep scepticism about its viability with considerable concern about its impact on the western alliance. The Plan was widely and correctly perceived as a French device to thwart the immediate rearmament of West Germany on American terms and to establish conditions for such rearmament that delayed its possibility. While the Plan was not publicly rejected by the Labour government, Bevin was nevertheless highly critical of French procrastination at a time when the immediate strengthening of the western alliance was called for. Furthermore, he suspected that the French were attempting to construct a European bloc which, though connected with the western alliance (Britain's preferred instrument for controlling Germany, as noted earlier), would act as a quasi-independent force in international politics. His worst fears centred on the possibility that the European federal concept would gain a foothold in NATO and act as 'a sort of cancer in the Atlantic body' which had to be nipped in the bud.[4] In the event, the matter was not to be so easily resolved. The French were determined to proceed only on the basis of the Pleven Plan, while the Americans, who were initially as sceptical of the Plan as the British, began to see some merit in it. The US and its European allies eventually agreed, in December 1950, to address the German rearmament issue in two sets of negotiations: the first would involve the Western occupying powers in Germany and the West German government with a view to raising West German armed units; the second would be based in Paris and would consider the formation of a European army. At the same time, the US agreed to give immediate effect to the rest of its 'one package' proposal.

3. For a detailed account of the EDC project see E. Fursdon, *The European Defence Community: A History* (1980). For a more recent study of the project in the context of security cooperation in Western Europe during the period 1945–91 see, for example, G. Aybet, *The Dynamics of European Security Co-operation, 1945–91* (1997).

4. *DBPO*, series II, vol. III, no. 115, memorandum by Bevin, 24 November 1950, and no. 119, Bevin to Franks, 29 November 1950.

The European army negotiations, which commenced in February 1951 and were conducted by the Six, proceeded so satisfactorily that no other framework for German rearmament seemed feasible. The Americans were increasingly impressed by the project and remained strongly committed to its success in advancing the cause of European integration. In these circumstances, the British had perforce to encourage the scheme, while at the same time being obliged to clarify their view of Britain's relationship with a European army. During his short period of office as Bevin's successor at the Foreign Office between March and October 1951, Herbert Morrison was particularly intent on shaking off the widespread image of Britain in Europe and the US as an obstacle to European integration. He further aimed to replace Bevin's squally relations with the French over the Schuman and Pleven Plans with a more positive, welcoming attitude to the interest of the Six in further integration. On the European army project, therefore, Morrison expressed the view in September 1951 that Britain wished 'to establish the closest possible association with the European continental community at all stages in its development'.[5] But this begged the question as to what was to be understood by 'the closest possible association', and it was this question that confronted Churchill's Conservative government after the general election of October 1951.

There was considerable optimism among continental supporters of supranational integration that the new Conservative government would adopt a far more accommodating attitude towards their views than its predecessor. This climate of opinion owed much to the way in which Churchill had been a principal standard-bearer for the cause of European unity, most notably in his Zurich speech of September 1946 advocating a United States of Europe, in his commanding presence at The Hague Congress of Europe of May 1948, and in his Council of Europe proposal of August 1950 for a European army. But Churchill's past record in this respect offered no guide to his conduct of policy in office, and hopes of a basic change in British policy were soon disappointed. In any case, his use of the European platform in the early postwar years had served a variety of purposes. Certainly his express concern was to strengthen European morale, to assert British leadership in Europe and – most distinctively albeit controversially among some of his continental

---

5. Cited in S. Dockrill, 'Britain's strategy for Europe: must West Germany be rearmed? 1949–51', in R.J. Aldrich (ed.), *British Intelligence Strategy and the Cold War 1945–51* (1992), p. 208.

audiences – to press the case for the reintegration of Germany in Europe.[6] At the same time, however, his high-profile conduct as European statesman was also influenced by party-political motives, including obvious pleasure at embarrassing the Labour government. This last feature, indeed, was occasionally mixed with elements of schoolboyish mischief-making as when, immediately after The Hague Congress, he organised an impromptu deputation: 'Let us march on Downing Street.'[7] Then, too, Churchill clearly drew a distinction between the case for European unity and the degree of British involvement, as demonstrated by a private comment on his European army proposal: 'I meant it for them, not for us.'[8]

On returning to office, Churchill's order of priorities in the field of foreign policy was clearly established in a Cabinet memorandum of November 1951 which emphasised the consolidation of the Empire and Commonwealth, along with the recreation of the special Anglo-American wartime relationship. Besides these concerns, he plainly intended to utilise his declining years – one Cabinet colleague described him as 'a giant in decay'[9] – to play a leading role on the stage of East–West relations with a view to ending the Cold War. Churchill regarded Europe as a secondary theatre of operations. According to this same memorandum, Europe was viewed as 'a separate closely- and specially-related ally and friend'.[10] This convoluted, ambiguous phraseology was all the more understandable in view of Churchill's pronounced antipathy towards the European army project, which he regarded as impracticable on account of its supranational, or what he labelled 'metaphysical', features. His private comments were even more disapproving. He dismissed the project as 'a sludgy amalgam' and 'a bucket of wood pulp' that conjured up visions of a motley, confused collection of Italian, Dutch

6. In his Zurich speech of September 1946, Churchill declared, 'I am now going to say something that will astonish you. The first step in the re-creation of the European family must be a partnership between France and Germany': W.S. Churchill, *Memoirs of the Second World War*, an abridgement of the six volumes of *The Second World War* (1978), p. 1000.

7. Cited in M. Charlton, *The Price of Victory* (1983), p. 78. For FO scepticism about Churchill's views on European unity in the early postwar years see, for example, PRO, FO 371/67578.

8. Cited in D. Weigall, 'British perceptions of the European Defence Community', in P.M.R. Stirk and D. Willis (eds), *Shaping Post-War Europe: European Unity and Disunity 1945–1957* (1991), p. 94.

9. Cited in A. Adamthwaite, 'Introduction: the Foreign Office and policy-making', in J.W. Young (ed.), *The Foreign Policy of Churchill's Peacetime Administration 1951–1955* (1988), p. 24.

10. PRO, CAB 129/48,C.(51)32, 29 November 1951.

and German privates being drilled by a French sergeant. Unsurprisingly, the US President, Dwight D. Eisenhower, later revealed that he used 'every resource, including argument, cajolery and sheer prayer to get Winston to say a single kind word about EDC'.[11]

The absence of any fresh or more radical thinking by Churchill on British policy towards European integration was revealed in a defining moment of his government's view of the matter shortly after it came to power. The new government's policy towards the EDC was awaited with great interest on the continent as an early indicator of any change of course. There were, however, somewhat conflicting signals. In the course of the same day, 28 November 1951, two Cabinet ministers adopted a markedly different tone in their attitude towards the question of Britain and the EDC. In a Council of Europe speech, David Maxwell-Fyfe, the Home Secretary, set out an agreed Cabinet position that no promise could be given that Britain's eventual association with the EDC would amount to full, unconditional participation. At a press conference immediately afterwards, he nevertheless insisted that this did not mean 'any closing of the door by Britain' and that 'there is no refusal on the part of Britain'.[12] Later the same day, however, at a press conference in Rome, Eden ruled out any possibility of British participation in the EDC and suggested only that there might be some other form of association. Eden's statement alarmed the 'pro-Europeans' in the Cabinet like Maxwell-Fyfe, Harold Macmillan (Minister of Housing and Local Government) and Duncan Sandys (Minister of Supply). It also upset leading Conservative members of the British delegation to the Council of Europe Assembly, including Robert Boothby, who claimed that Eden's announcement had come as a 'shattering blow' to most Assembly members.[13] Unlike Eden, they had been active supporters of Churchill's efforts on behalf of European unity during the 1940s. The significant outcome of this episode was that Churchill backed Eden, who thereafter had an enhanced authority in dealing with all aspects of the EDC. Eden's strategy in handling both Churchill and the 'pro-Europeans' in the Cabinet was to draw a clear distinction between cooperation in Europe and the federation of Europe. In response to criticisms that his Rome statement signified a distinct lack of enthusiasm for European unity – a charge he greatly contested – Eden emphasised the

11. Stirk and Willis (eds.), *Shaping Post-War Europe*, p. 95.
12. Cited in S. Dockrill, *Britain's Policy for West German Rearmament 1950–1955* (1991), p. 86.
13. *Ibid.*, p. 88.

supranational character of the EDC, knowing full well that none of his critics favoured any merger with such a body.

During the first six months of his period of office, Eden supported efforts to achieve the signing of the EDC Treaty. In the process he was determined to ensure that Britain figured as an active sponsor of the treaty, especially since the Americans expected a strong British lead,[14] while any French doubts about the scheme had to be assuaged by expressions of British support. There was great pressure, particularly from the French government, for more defined and binding British links with the scheme. Eden was obliged to respond by explaining what was to be understood by some form of association. He was plainly anxious to avoid full British membership of the EDC and fearful of any major British concession to the EDC states that might be 'the first step on a slippery slope to European federation'.[15] It was at this time that he made his well-known comment that British membership of a European federation was 'something we know in our bones we cannot do', thereby drawing the withering response from Paul-Henri Spaak, one of the EC's founding fathers and a constant thorn in the flesh of British ministers, that 'That's a funny place to have thinking'.[16] Besides steering clear of any British involvement in a federalist Europe, Eden was also on his guard against any agreement with the EDC that involved a new formal British commitment to the defence of Europe or that changed the British military role in Europe as the provider of naval and air power rather than ground forces. It was on this basis that he made limited concessions, first agreeing to enter into a technical association with the EDC and finally, in April 1952, conceding the case for a treaty relationship between Britain and the EDC.[17] These measures facilitated the signing of the EDC Treaty in May 1952.

By then, the prospect of a federated Europe based on the Six and excluding Britain had prompted a major debate in British official circles about the best form of general links between Britain and the Six. Eden and the Foreign Office generally took a relaxed view of possible dangers to Britain resulting from attempts at further integration by the Six. There was no knowing at that time whether even the Schuman Plan would prove workable. Moreover,

14. *FRUS*, 1951, vol. III, part I, pp. 955–7, Acheson to Eden, 8 December 1951.

15. Cited in J.W. Young, 'German Rearmament and the European Defence Community', in Young (ed.), *The Foreign Policy of Churchill's Peacetime Administration*, p. 89.

16. Cited in Charlton, *The Price of Victory*, pp. 159, 182.

17. See S. Greenwood (ed.), *Britain and European Integration since the Second World War* (1996), pp. 56–8.

Franco-German differences were likely to remain a formidable barrier to the formation of a strong union. On balance, therefore, the
Foreign Office saw no need 'to divert the integration movement
from its present course'.[18] Eden acknowledged that Franco-German
divisions served the purpose of maximising British influence on
the continent. He nonetheless concluded that it was preferable to
see France and Germany 'in confused but close embrace, than at
arm's length'.[19] In supporting but not participating in the integration of the Six, it was felt that British efforts should be directed
towards cultivating the idea of an Atlantic community based on
three pillars: the US, the UK (including the Commonwealth) and
continental Europe. By such means, Britain could best reconcile
its extra-European commitments with its responsibilities towards
Europe. It could also ensure that the Six did not develop as an
exclusively European union, but as part of the Atlantic community.
On the specific issue of institutional ties between the Six and Britain (as well as other west European states), Eden proposed that the
Council of Europe should be remodelled so that its institutions –
notably the Committee of Ministers and the Assembly – could become institutions of the Schuman Plan, the EDC and any other
future supranational European organisation.[20] This proposal was
approved by the Cabinet in March 1952 and was subsequently known
as the Eden Plan. It envisaged the Council of Europe as an umbrella body including both the Six and also other states like Britain
that supported the principle of intergovernmental cooperation. It
promised to overcome the emerging division between the Six and
the rest of Western Europe by constructing a halfway house. There
was also the additional advantage of providing a more useful function for the hitherto underemployed Council of Europe, whose
Assembly had become a menacing platform for federalist criticism
of British policy. As summarised by Eden, the proposal allowed the
federalists to federate, gave them something to do and kept Britain
associated.[21] In effect, this was an attempt – comparable to the
earlier development of Bevin's Western Union concept and the
later British plan for a Free Trade Area including the Six – to
preserve British influence on the continent while avoiding full participation in the Six's efforts at integration.

18. *DBPO*, series II, vol. I, no. 414.
19. *Ibid.*, no. 439, Eden to Churchill, 18 March 1952.
20. PRO, CAB 129/49 C.(52)40, memorandum by Eden, 15 February 1952.
21. *DBPO*, series II, vol. I, no. 430, Brief for Secretary of State, 8 March 1952.

Eden's proposal, however, did not go unchallenged in Cabinet. Macmillan criticised the Foreign Office for its shortsighted policy – 'a degree of myopia which a mole might envy' – and especially for its failure to appreciate that a continental federation presented 'grave dangers to our essential interests'.[22] He pleaded for consideration of a viable alternative that preserved the importance of the European idea but reduced the possibility of a European federation. By implication, Eden's architectural designs for Europe were flimsy and, if anything, locked British policy towards Europe into an all-or-nothing mindset. Certainly Macmillan agreed that any continental federation had to be kept within the framework of the Atlantic community and subordinated to the Council of Europe. His main concern, however, was to avoid such a formation in the first place. He therefore suggested that, in the event of the failure of the EDC project, Britain should be ready to put up a scheme for a European Union or Confederation organised on Commonwealth lines. Such an arrangement would allow for British membership and include provisions *inter alia* for linking the European currencies individually or collectively to sterling. This suggestion smacked of some of the ambitious intentions underlying Bevin's original Western Union idea of 1948, and Macmillan conceded that the time might have passed to assert British leadership of Europe in this way. He appealed to Churchill for support, declaring: 'It is no longer a case of choosing between the policies of Marlborough and Bolingbroke, but of combining them.'[23] This was of no avail, however, as Churchill merely referred the matter to Eden. In Cabinet Eden easily countered Macmillan's argument. He stressed that the Six were committed to federal union and likely to remain so whatever happened to the EDC. He also pointed out that the western alliance already provided a model of an association of states in some respects more developed than the Commonwealth, while the idea of linking European currencies to sterling would weaken the sterling area and undermine the imperial preference system.

The Eden Plan was soon overtaken by events. After the signing of the EDC Treaty, the Six concentrated on developing institutions for their own exclusive purposes. The evident need for political institutions to supervise the EDC gave rise to the most ambitious attempt to date to create a European political community. In September 1952 the ECSC Council of Ministers authorised the organisation's Common Assembly to draft a treaty for a European political

22. *DBPO*, series II, vol. I, no. 424.   23. *Ibid.*, no. 437.

community which, as it emerged in March 1953, envisaged a quasi-federal single structure incorporating the ECSC and the EDC. Britain was effectively walled off from these discussions in which some of the prime movers – especially Monnet as President of the ECSC High Authority – were determined to press ahead with arrangements among the Six rather than involve the Council of Europe. While the Eden Plan withered on the vine, it remained the case, of course, that the fate of the European Political Community Treaty ultimately depended on ratification of the EDC Treaty by the parliaments of the Six. It was this issue that principally occupied Eden in the period from May 1952 to the demise of the EDC in August 1954.

Eden's efforts to obtain ratification involved protracted negotiations with the French government, which was itself subjected to mounting opposition to the project. In France, strong resistance to any form of German rearmament was increasingly combined with a rising tide of objections to the loss of national sovereignty involved in EDC membership. The declining influence of the two parties that had been the most vigorous advocates of European integration in French politics – the MRP and the Socialists – meant that a majority for the EDC in the French National Assembly was increasingly unlikely. Schuman's departure from the French Foreign Ministry, in January 1953, was a particularly signal event in this respect, and a relaxation in East–West relations following the death of Stalin in March 1953 and the Korean armistice of July 1953 further assisted the anti-EDC forces. The politics of the Fourth Republic – characterised by a rapid turnover of governments, a weak executive and procrastination on important decisions – meant that no government was prepared to put the treaty to a vote in the National Assembly unless and until certain conditions were met and additional protocols to the treaty negotiated. One such condition, as specified by the government in January 1953, was that Britain should become more closely associated with the EDC. At this time, as before and later, it was clear that the French would not be satisfied by anything less than full British membership of the EDC or, at the very least, a strong British commitment that signified more than a loose form of association.

Eden was initially disinclined to offer much more than an informal promise to develop close political and military contacts between Britain and the EDC. In the face of French pressure for a formal agreement, however, he conceded the case for UK/EDC negotiations for a treaty of association in July 1953. In the negotiations resulting in the draft agreement on this treaty in April 1954, Eden aimed to overcome French doubts about the EDC Treaty and to ensure that Britain was seen to make every effort to facilitate its ratification. It was particularly important to convince the Americans that Britain was an unqualified supporter of the project, all the more so in view of a statement by US Secretary of State John Foster Dulles in December 1953 threatening an 'agonising reappraisal' of policy towards Europe in the event of the collapse of the EDC.[24] Such big-stick diplomacy was counterproductive in seeking to overcome French opposition to the EDC. Nor did it enhance Dulles's standing among British leaders: Churchill described him as the 'only case I know of a bull who carries his own china shop around with him'.[25] Nevertheless, this was a threat that could not be disregarded. It implied at best a possible scaling down of the American commitment to Europe's defence and at worst a full-scale withdrawal from Europe by a neo-isolationist US.[26]

The treaty of association between Britain and the EDC powers demonstrated how far Eden had been prepared to go in modifying his policy since his Rome statement of 1951. It was agreed to maintain British troops on the continent for as long as there was any threat to Western Europe's security and to provide for joint UK–EDC military operations. The most substantial concession, however, was the decision to place an armoured British division in the EDC. This committed Britain to Europe's defence to a greater extent than the US. Indeed, Macmillan, so critical of Eden's earlier handling of the issue and lack of interest in European unity, now feared that France was being offered 'almost everything but marriage'.[27] The principle of association, however, remained intact, and Eden had made enough concessions to ensure that Britain was not singled out for blame in the event of the collapse of the EDC project. But anti-EDC opinion in France was unimpressed by the British preference for association rather than full membership: 'Very pleasant, indeed, to be the guest of honour at the banquet of a society to which you pay no dues', was de Gaulle's caustic comment on this arrangement.[28]

24. *FRUS*, 1952–4, vol. V, part I, p. 868.
25. Cited in *The Times Higher Education Supplement*, E. Liggett, 31 December 1982.
26. For Eden's anxiety about the possibility of an American withdrawal from Europe see, for example, Greenwood (ed.), *Britain and European Integration since the Second World War*, pp. 64–5.
27. H. Macmillan, *Tides of Fortune* (1969), p. 478.
28. Cited in A. Werth, *De Gaulle* (1965), p. 227.

The rejection of the EDC Treaty by the French National Assembly on 30 August 1954 was a major setback for the unity of the western alliance and for the process of Community integration of the Six. It also dealt a blow to the planned restoration of full sovereignty to West Germany via the Bonn Contractual Agreements of 1952, which were to take effect following ratification of the EDC Treaty by the six prospective member states. The situation thus created afforded Eden an opportunity to reassert British leadership in Western Europe after five years of defensive responses to the Six's initiatives. He was well placed to take the initiative because, besides the matter of his diplomatic skills in addressing practical problems, few others were inclined to make an early move. The French, under the leadership of Pierre Mendès-France, were thankful to be rid of the EDC issue; Dulles was appalled by the imbroglio and had no contingency plan; and Churchill immediately took to name-calling – describing the French as 'swine'.[29] Eden was thus primarily responsible for convening a conference in London in September 1954. This was attended by representatives of the Six, Britain, Canada and the US and reconvened a month later in Paris to sign a set of agreements. At the centre of these Paris Agreements lay a British-inspired idea, namely to revive the Brussels Treaty Organisation of 1948 under the new title of the Western European Union (WEU), to enlarge its membership to include West Germany and Italy alongside the founding members (Britain, France and the Benelux states), and to make a British military commitment of four army divisions and one tactical air force. Eden's own version of how this scheme originated was that it came to him suddenly while he was having his Sunday morning bath. This has long since been disposed of as misleading, although federalist opinion on the continent often viewed it, nonetheless, as a strikingly authentic expression of Eden's casual regard for and limited interest in European unity. The more prosaic truth is that a plan of this type had been circulating within the Foreign Office for some time, but had not been publicly aired for fear of jeopardising ratification of the EDC Treaty. Regardless of their origins, though, the new arrangements helped to overcome French fears concerning adequate controls over West Germany. They also broke down French resistance to the admission of a fully sovereign West Germany to NATO. Thus France finally agreed to a NATO-type solution that it had

---

29. Cited in V. Rothwell, *Anthony Eden* (1992), p. 154.

originally opposed in 1950, while Britain made a major military commitment which it had previously so studiously avoided.

The collapse of the EDC and the emergence of the WEU highlight several significant features of British policy towards Western Europe at large and towards the Six in particular at this time. First, the failed EDC scheme confirmed a widespread view in British government circles that French fears of Germany remained as strong as ever and that a federated Europe would break apart on the rocks of Franco-German antagonism. The outcome thus appeared to demonstrate that association with the Six had been the proper policy. This, in turn, contributed to some fundamental British miscalculations when, less than a year after the EDC débâcle, the Six embarked on the 'relaunching of Europe' which culminated in the Treaty of Rome.

Secondly, the organising principle of the WEU – intergovernmental cooperation with a Consultative Assembly – served British interests in turning the tide of federalist opinion and in offering a forum for developing closer relations with the Six. But while the WEU was long to remain Britain's last major diplomatic success in Western Europe, it was not viewed by Eden at least as an instrument for furthering European unity. Rather, it was regarded as a device for solving the specific problem of incorporating a rearmed Germany into the western alliance. How far the WEU had been ushered into being solely to resolve a particular crisis became apparent as it languished in later years for want of any major purpose. Certainly Britain's military commitment to the WEU did represent a milestone in the postwar 'Europeanisation' of British defence policy. Yet it did not amount to a substantial advance on what Eden had already offered via the treaty of association of April 1954. The undertaking to maintain a peacetime military presence on the continent marked a shift away from the traditional and primarily maritime character of British defence strategy in peacetime towards a more land-based, continental presence. This commitment, however, was surrounded by escape clauses that allowed for the removal of military forces assigned to the WEU. These clauses were soon to be activated (in 1957) when British defence strategy placed greater reliance on nuclear weapons than on conventional forces, thereby reasserting Britain's role and capability as a global rather than a European power. It was a commitment, too, that did not affect Britain's singular status as a European power with nuclear capability. As Eden stressed in Cabinet discussions, there was to be no sharing with 'our European partners atomic and thermo-nuclear secrets'.

Finally, British policymakers viewed the emergence of the WEU as the best possible outcome in terms of maintaining the idea of British leadership of the west European bloc in the western alliance and of strengthening the special Anglo-American relationship at the centre of this alliance. Throughout the EDC controversy and its aftermath, Eden was particularly concerned to ensure that the US commitment to NATO remained intact. There were perceived dangers on all sides. It was necessary to support the EDC as a loyal partner of the US. Yet at the same time policymakers feared that the successful introduction of the EDC might result in a scaling down of the US military presence in Europe.[30] It was also clear that the failure of the EDC might lead to a similar outcome. An alternative danger was that, in the absence of a prominent British role in brokering a new agreement, the Americans might be tempted to deal directly with the other west European states, thus bypassing Britain and downgrading its standing as the principal American ally in Europe. It was such considerations that greatly influenced Eden's speedy and successful efforts to find a substitute for the EDC.

30. See, for example, *FRUS*, 1952–4, vol. V, pp. 1225–6, Churchill to Eisenhower, 17 September 1954; *ibid.*, pp. 1292–3, Dulles to Eisenhower, 28 September 1954: Dulles reported Churchill's grave concern at the possibility of retaining British forces on the continent in the event of an American withdrawal – 'we cannot stay there alone without you'.

CHAPTER FIVE

The 'Special Relationship' and European Unity

In the early postwar years the US emerged as the single most significant external influence favouring British participation in an integrated Europe. This influence varied in intensity and often revealed widely diverging views in Washington about the concept of European unity. It was nonetheless the case that the evolution of Anglo-American relations in the period 1945–55 was closely linked to the formulation of British policy towards European integration. British perceptions of, and reactions to, US plans for Western Europe at this time thus provide an important key to understanding the process whereby Britain emerged by the end of this period as a North Atlantic power rather than as a power in a closely integrated Europe. Several general aspects of this 'special relationship'[1] had a bearing on the making of British policy towards Europe.

First, there was the fundamental imbalance of power between the two countries. At the end of the war the US accounted for 50 per cent of total world production, ranked as the world's largest naval and air power and had exclusive possession of the atomic bomb. By contrast, Britain's financial and economic problems and its inability to counterbalance Soviet power in Europe meant dependence on US assistance. The US loan of 1945, the Marshall Aid programme of 1947 and the North Atlantic Treaty of 1949 were all indicative of British weakness and US strength. A major concern of British policymakers in these circumstances was how to utilise US resources to serve British interests: a Foreign Office memorandum

---

1. This description of UK/US relations in the early postwar years became increasingly common after Churchill referred to a 'special relationship of the English-speaking peoples' in his celebrated 'Iron Curtain' speech at Fulton, Missouri in February 1946: P. Hennessy and C. Anstey, *Moneybags and Brains: The Anglo-American 'Special Relationship' since 1945* (1990), p. ii.

prepared in 1944, for example, concluded that Britain should 'make use of American power for purposes which we regard as good'.[2]

Secondly, British policymakers persistently wrestled with the problem of minimising the adverse effects of reliance on the US. The experience of the 1945 loan provided an early postwar object lesson in the difficulties that Britain faced in maintaining its independence and in countering what were regarded as some of the unwanted features of a US-dominated Western world. It was recognised that the bigger and lengthier the dependence on US aid, the greater would be the difficulty in resisting US attempts to influence British domestic and foreign policies. Some of the problems involved in this exercise of seeking American assistance while aiming to preserve the status of an independent world power were most apparent in Europe. Besides encouraging economic recovery and greater security, a notable advantage of US aid to Europe was that more British resources could be devoted to maintaining positions beyond Europe, thus obviating the need for a fundamental review of the mismatch between numerous commitments and limited resources. The forging of close Anglo-American ties was also vital in ensuring that Washington viewed Britain as a power worth saving if the worst happened and Western Europe collapsed. Set against these advantages, however, British policymakers were acutely conscious of a number of dangers. Not the least of these was that the Americans might use aid to pressure Britain into participating in ambitious schemes for European integration. Conventional wisdom in British official circles hardened in favour of the view that, while taking the leadership role in Europe, Britain should not become so integrated with Europe as to jeopardise the possibility or maintenance of a US commitment to Europe. There was particular concern about the dangers of being inveigled into a position of carrying the burden in Europe while a neo-isolationist US withdrew from the continent.

This last possibility was one of the increasingly problematical conditions that faced British policymakers in the immediate aftermath of war, when there was a noticeable distancing in Anglo-American relations. The institutions and close contacts of the special wartime relationship quickly dissolved away, though some informal connections remained intact, notably in the defence and intelligence services. The 'business as usual' attitude of US officials during the 1945 loan negotiations indicated the extent to which the two countries

2. PRO, FO 371/38523, Dudley, 21 March 1944.

were drifting apart. Acrimonious exchanges over the standing of wartime agreements concerning development of the atomic bomb also poisoned relations in the period leading up to the implementation of the US McMahon Act of August 1946 which restricted the exchange of nuclear information between the US and other countries. There was, too, a great deal of mutual antipathy in other spheres. Labour's nationalisation and welfare programmes met with the same suspicion and opposition in the US as did the workings of an unfettered American capitalist system in Labour ranks. Meanwhile, there was little rapport between leading politicians: Attlee described the Truman administration as comprising 'little men', and relations between some of the principals like Bevin and his US counterpart, James Byrnes, were often stormy and at best polite.

In this early postwar period, there were also growing doubts in official British quarters about the Rooseveltian view of a postwar international order based on great power cooperation and global institutions like the United Nations Organisation. This 'one world solution', indeed, seemed to be fast giving way to what Bevin described in November 1945 as three spheres of influence: a US sphere encompassing Latin America, China and Japan; a Soviet sphere incorporating eastern Europe; and a third sphere which left Britain and France with 'a tremendous area to defend and a responsibility that, if it does develop, would make our position extremely difficult'.[3] In this early postwar period, great power relations were characterised far more by UK–USSR than by US–USSR conflicts, ultimately convincing the British at an earlier stage than the Americans that cooperation with the Soviets was increasingly unlikely and that they represented a major threat to Europe. The British were thus impelled to seek new forms of cooperation with the US. The catalyst for this was Britain's financial weakness in 1946–7. This led to the economic merging of the US and British zones in Germany and, more dramatically, to the announcement of an early end to British aid to Greece and Turkey, with an accompanying request for US assistance which was to occasion the enunciation of the Truman doctrine.

The serious turn for the worse in British economic conditions that brought about these changes and culminated in the sterling convertibility crisis of July/August 1947 formed the background against which the Marshall Plan was launched in June 1947. It was

---

3. *DBPO*, series I, vol. III, no. 99, memorandum by Mr Bevin on the Foreign Situation, 8 November 1945.

during the subsequent development of this initiative into the ERP that British policymakers had to deal with the full force of American support for European unity. Whereas, previously, the idea of regional blocs or unity had fallen foul of US interest in global designs and institutions, American backing for European unity now began to gain impetus as a response to the division of Europe and Cold War rivalries. European unity was increasingly viewed in Washington as serving a number of purposes, the most important being to contain the Soviet threat, to control and accommodate a revived Germany, and to facilitate the political and economic recovery of Western Europe. At the time of Marshall's offer of aid, however, these were still undeveloped themes, without a detailed set of policy prescriptions. It was in the wake of this offer – with its minimal conditions that the Europeans should take the initiative and should agree on their requirements – that it became increasingly clear that the US was aiming to develop new forms of European economic cooperation. Indeed, it was quickly trumpeted abroad that the US federal system and large integrated single market was an ideal model for a divided and economically backward Western Europe that segregated '270 million people into 17 uneconomic principalities'.

The speedy British reaction to the Marshall offer and Bevin's key contribution in organising a European response strengthened Britain's position in subsequent negotiations. So, too, did the American view that British leadership in Western Europe was essential for the success of the recovery programme. At the same time, however, Marshall's initiative forced the British to define in more detail than before their policy on closer economic cooperation with Western Europe. This exercise was all the more important as the earliest official exchanges between London and Washington following Marshall's speech revealed serious differences of opinion about the Plan and Britain's aid requirements. These exchanges, on 24–26 June 1947, involved discussions between British ministers and William Clayton, the US Under-Secretary of State for Economic Affairs. Clayton insisted that European integration had to be one of the Plan's objectives in order to win support in Congress. He strongly supported the idea of a European economic federation based on a customs union. A further point of emphasis was that there could be no special piecemeal assistance for Britain outside of the Plan: Britain must be in it as part of Europe or not at all. The British position, forcefully expressed by Bevin, was that Britain, with its empire, should be treated on a different basis from the rest of Europe: Britain was not, Bevin said, 'just another European country'. (He was to make the same point less plaintively three years later, by which time the Americans had conceded as much: 'Great Britain was not part of Europe; she was not simply a Luxembourg.')[4] What was required, in Bevin's view, was an Anglo-American financial partnership and a recognition that dollar aid to Europe was of far less value to Britain than dollar aid to the rest of the world.[5] While finally acknowledging that a special position for Britain was out of the question, British ministers nonetheless warned that the formation of a customs union would present Britain with 'very special difficulties'. Certainly Britain could not do without further dollar aid, as a Treasury study indicated.[6] Yet ministers and officials were determined to oppose the more ambitious American plans for British involvement in Europe, and often privately invoked the defence of national sovereignty argument that had been the formal reason for Soviet rejection of the Marshall offer. They aimed to impress on the Truman administration the distinctive features of Britain's standing as a major player in the world economy.

In conducting this exercise, there was a good deal of confidence among British policymakers about their ability to point the great American 'barge' in a direction that served British interests. Such confidence rested, in part, on not uncommon portrayals of the US as a relative newcomer to the international system. Thus it was perceived as a 'lumbering giant', so incapable of measured responses and diplomatic finesse and so given to rapid mood swings that it evidently required the assistance of a worldly-wise guide like Britain. At the time of the loan negotiations of 1945, a piece of doggerel composed by a British official summed up a widespread view among Whitehall mandarins: 'In Washington Lord Halifax / Once whispered to Lord Keynes, / "It's true they have the money bags / But we have all the brains."'[7]

4. *FRUS*, 1947, vol. III, p. 271; PRO, FO 800/517. See also PRO FO 371/73064, Record of a conversation between Bevin and Marshall, 4 October 1948; PRO, FO 371/78134, Record of a conversation between Bevin and the US ambassador, 26 October 1949.

5. See, for example, *FRUS*, 1947, vol. III, pp. 21–2, British embassy (Washington) to the State Department, 18 June 1947.

6. For initial Treasury reactions to the Marshall Aid offer see, for example, PRO, T 236/782 including a note by Clarke, 'The World Dollar Crisis', 14 June 1947; Cairncross (ed.), *Anglo-American Economic Collaboration in War and Peace*, pp. 168–80. See also PRO, FO 371/62566, minutes of the London Committee on European Co-operation, 5 October 1947. For a graphic description of the Treasury's worst-case scenario in the absence of further aid see P. Hennessy, *Never Again: Britain 1945–51* (1992), pp. 299–302.

7. Cited in R.N. Gardner, 'Sterling–dollar diplomacy in current perspective', *International Affairs*, vol. 62 (1986). See also J. Saville, *The Politics of Continuity: British Foreign Policy and the Labour Government, 1945–46* (1993), pp. 64–7; PRO, FO 371/38523, Dudley, 21 March 1944, 'The essentials of an American policy': Dudley

Reluctant Europeans

In the case of the Marshall Aid offer, there was much nimble footwork in Whitehall to safeguard British interests, especially once it became clear that there was to be no privileged position for Britain and that aid was not to be provided – as the British had initially hoped – in response to national shopping lists. Quickly making a virtue out of necessity, Whitehall concluded that requests for aid had to be made in a European framework led by Britain. It was clearly intended to put Britain at the head of the queue. It was also swiftly appreciated that a multilateral approach might help to minimise the number of strings that might be attached to the pro-vision of aid. This consideration was all the more attractive in view of the fact that one of the conditions emerging from the bilateral loan negotiations of 1945 had resulted in the 1947 sterling convert-ibility crisis. In the event, Britain was to receive some 25 per cent of the total ERP aid, a higher proportion than any other country.

Britain also played a dominant role in shaping the structure of the OEEC, an intergovernmental body devoid of any trace of auto-nomous or supranational elements. In this context, Bevin's Western Union initiative of 1948 served a number of purposes. Among other things, it implicitly signalled to the US that Britain was not only prepared to take the lead in west European unity in response to American pressure, but was also determined to stamp its mark on any project before the US had an opportunity to do so.[8] The Scandinavian countries and Ireland supported this British lead, while the US – often with French support – pressed for a stronger, more integrated body. An American attempt to establish an OEEC secret-ariat with real powers was defeated by the British, who insisted that the OEEC's secretary should be bound by the decisions of the ministerial Council. The British also beat off an American attempt to invest the OEEC with strong political authority by appointing a senior official, rather than a government minister, as head of the UK's OEEC delegation. Similarly, they successfully overturned an American proposal to appoint a politically authoritative Director General for the OEEC: Spaak, the Belgian Prime Minister and a leading light in the European Movement, was the proposed candid-ate for this post.

commented that 'If we go about our business in the right way we can help to steer this great unwieldy barge, the United States of America, into the right harbour'.

8. See, for example, PRO, FO 371/73057, Record of a conversation between Bevin and Bidault, 16–17 April 1948: Bevin argued that the BTO Powers should make their own arrangements as soon as possible in order to ensure that the Amer-icans did not 'tell us what to do'.

Some of the reasons for this cautious British approach to the OEEC have already been discussed in Chapter 2. A further relevant dimension in this context, however, concerns early British assessments of what the Marshall Aid initiative portended in terms of American policy towards Europe. British officials did not view the offer as the beginning of an unstoppable process leading to a further major US commitment to Europe. On the contrary, they saw it as indicative of plans to effect a strategic withdrawal from Europe. The accompanying American pressure on Britain to become part of a closely integrated Europe was perceived as serving the same purpose. The public comments of certain US officials and politicians seemed to confirm such suspicions. According to Paul Hoffmann, the head of the Economic Cooperation Administration (ECA), which supervised the American end of the ERP, the main purpose of the ERP was 'to get Europe on its feet and off our backs'. Such a view greatly alarmed British policymakers, because dollar aid in itself did not tackle the key issue of west European insecurity nor help to relieve Britain of its burden in this field. Disquieting evidence of American intentions came from other sources like Senator Vandenberg, the influential Republican leader, whose declared support for US withdrawal from Europe once it had re-established itself was interpreted by the Foreign Office in October 1948 as 'another danger signal that a federated Western Europe is becoming the battle cry of a new isolationism'.[9] Apart from other considerations, therefore, British reluctance to become involved in an increasingly integrated Europe via the OEEC or any other mechanism was linked to the fear that this would strengthen neo-isolationist opinion in the US.

In 1948–9 there was heavy US pressure on Britain to participate in a more closely integrated Europe. This was accompanied by a volley of criticism from Marshall, Hoffmann and Lewis Douglas, the US ambassador to London, that the British were 'dragging [their] feet', failing to enter 'wholeheartedly into the OEEC work' and demonstrating deep 'anxiety neuroses' over European unity.[10] British handling of these complaints was helped by the absence of a clear consensus in American official circles about the precise form

9. PRO, FO 371/71768, Makins to Kirkpatrick, 11 October 1948.
10. Cited in M.J. Hogan, *The Marshall Plan: America, Britain and the Reconstruction of Western Europe, 1947–1952* (1987), p. 186. David Bruce (US ambassador in Paris) maintained that west European integration was inconceivable without full British participation and that Britain should be given a swift kick in a tender place: cited in J. Gillingham, *Coal, Steel and the Rebirth of Europe, 1945–1955: The Germans and French from Ruhr Conflict to Economic Community* (1991), p. 168.

that European unity should take: words like cooperation, integration, unity and federation were often used interchangeably and imprecisely. In the upper echelons of the Truman administration, moreover, the general commitment to promotion of European economic unity was tempered by a desire to avoid any impression of American coercion. There were also divisions of opinion in Washington over the relative merits of a modest scheme for multilateral trade and payments in Europe or a more radical plan for a common market and monetary union.[11]

The twofold British response to American pressure was to emphasise a positive approach to European cooperation and to try to convince the US administration that Britain, with its global interests, was in a qualitatively different position from the mainland European states. The substance and timing of British statements on European cooperation in this period were greatly influenced by the need to make a good impression on American opinion and especially on Congress, which voted annually on aid appropriations under the four-year ERP.[12] Thus the French proposal of July 1948 for a European Assembly received more sympathetic attention in London than might otherwise have been the case but for the need to avoid incurring American criticism. Similarly, British involvement in the OEEC-based discussions on a European customs union continued long after the Labour government had decided against participation. It was recognised that American support for precisely such a scheme counted against any hasty rejection and also, according to a Cabinet paper of March 1948, underlined the importance of handling the issue as 'good Europeans rather than self-regarding islanders'.[13]

From the British point of view, there were several important breakthroughs in 1949 that both reduced US demands for British

11. For FO assessments of American opinion see PRO, FO 371/73065, FO Research Department paper, 4 September 1948; PRO, FO 371/73074, Franks (Washington) to FO, 13 July 1948; PRO, FO 371/78023, FO to British Embassy (Washington), 8 November 1949.

12. See, for example, PRO, FO 371/73048, Roberts, Note of a conversation with Bevin, 9 February 1948; PRO, FO 371/73064, Bevin to Attlee. See also PRO, FO 371/73100, British embassy (Washington) to the FO, 30 November 1948: the embassy advised the FO that 'the creation – if possible before next Spring – of something which could be *called* Europe, *photographed* as Europe, and *regarded* as Europe might have a tremendous effect on the Senate when it came to the voting of dollars for the second year of the ERP programme'.

13. PRO, FO 371/68940, Report by the UK Delegation to the European Customs Union Study Group, 18–23 March 1948. See also, for example, PRO, BT 11/3883, Wilson to Cripps, 31 May 1948.

involvement in an integrated Europe and also marked a greater American recognition of Britain's standing as a global rather than a European power. The North Atlantic Treaty of April 1949, though initially of symbolic value, transformed the situation by addressing the key problem of Europe's weakness and insecurity. But a more significant development in this respect was the sterling crisis of mid-1949 which originated in a sudden worsening of Britain's dollar deficit and resulted in the devaluation of sterling in September 1949 from \$4.03 to \$2.80. The crisis was managed entirely via tripartite negotiations in Washington involving Britain, the US and Canada. There was no reference to the European states or to the OEEC forum – much to the annoyance of some member states, especially France.[14]

This handling of the devaluation crisis suggested to the British that they had won an important argument in persuading the Americans that Britain's economic problems and interests could not be dealt with exclusively or primarily within a European context.[15] It was equally plain to British policymakers that, as one senior Foreign Office official put it, the Washington talks marked 'a turning-point in the world position of Britain' and that the Americans now regarded Britain as their 'principal partner in world affairs'.[16] In October 1949, in fact, Acheson, the Secretary of State, acknowledged that European integration on supranational lines would have to proceed without full British participation. Acheson himself was an Anglophile who was subsequently demonised by the witch-hunting Senator Joseph McCarthy as 'a pompous diplomat in striped pants with a phoney British accent'. He had a much closer relationship with British leaders than either of his two immediate predecessors, and he believed that American power in the world could be best exercised 'only with the cooperation of the British'. He firmly opposed largely ECA-inspired efforts under Hoffmann to make ERP funds to Britain conditional on a more active British involvement in European integration. At the same time, Bevin and Cripps, who had conducted the devaluation negotiations with the Americans, gained Cabinet support for the view that economic relations with

14. For French criticism see, for example, PRO, FO 371/75591, Record of a conversation between Strang and Massigli (French ambassador in London). Massigli complained that the French government had been 'badly treated' by the British.

15. Franks (British ambassador in Washington) reported that the Americans now seemed to appreciate that Britain 'cannot be expected fully to integrate its economy with that of Western Europe': PRO, FO 371/78023, Franks to FO, 9 November 1949.

16. PRO, FO 371/75594, Makins, 26 August 1949. See also, for example, PRO, FO 371/75590, Franks to FO, 20 September 1949.

Europe had to yield priority to the 'new relationship with America'. Any lingering American hopes of full British participation in European economic integration were further dented in late 1949 and early 1950 during the course of negotiations that resulted in the formation of the European Payments Union (EPU). This venture had originally started as part of an ECA plan for a single integrated market of the OEEC states to overcome the restrictive, bilateral features of the European trade and payments system. Britain joined this scheme, but successfully resisted plans for full inclusion of the sterling area and for the creation of a supranational managing board. It was during this episode that Bevin informed Acheson of British reluctance to act as 'a one-man "clearing house" for ambiguous European plans dreamed up in Washington'.[17]

Throughout the remaining life of the Attlee government and the Churchill government of 1951–5, Britain's European policy was shaped in accordance with the higher priority given to the development of the 'special' Anglo-American relationship. In these circumstances, the aim of British policy, as expressed by Attlee in Cabinet on 30 August 1951, was to foster the idea of an Atlantic rather than a purely European community. It was also felt necessary to avoid closer dependence on the European states on the grounds that this would impair the ability of an independent UK to cooperate with the Americans in playing 'a very special and important role in the free world'. How far the Attlee government was prepared to go in cementing this relationship with Washington was immediately made clear by the scale of the British rearmament programme following the outbreak of the Korean War. British defence expenditure was already increasing rapidly – from an annual average of £600 million in the period 1947–9 to an annual average of £1.5 billion in the period 1949–51 – when Attlee, following a visit to Washington in December 1950, reported to the Cabinet that he had persuaded the Americans to accept Anglo-American partnership as the mainspring of Atlantic defence.[18] The advantages of such a partnership, however, could only be maintained by a still greater British rearmament effort, despite mounting opposition to rearmament in Labour Party ranks which was eventually to lead to the resignations of three ministers in May 1951 – Aneurin Bevan, Harold Wilson and John Freeman – in protest at welfare expenditure cuts in Hugh Gaitskell's budget. In effect, a higher price had to be paid in order

17. Cited in Hogan, *The Marshall Plan*, p. 289.
18. PRO, CAB 128/18, CM(50) 87th Conclusions, 18 December 1950.

to ensure Britain's standing as the loyal lieutenant of the US in NATO and to build on the close Anglo-American defence relationship that had been revived at the time of the Berlin crisis of 1948, with the Anglo-American airlift and the dispatch of US bombers to Britain. It was at this point that Britain took on again its wartime role as 'the unsinkable aircraft carrier' for US forces, as well as trading bases for military aid. The global scale of Cold War conflict by 1950, moreover, considerably muted earlier American criticism of British imperialism. Washington now regarded British overseas bases in particular as extremely useful assets: 'Whenever we want to subvert any place, we find the British own an island within easy reach', commented one US covert operations officer of the time.[19]

Both the Attlee and the Churchill governments recognised that in order to establish a closer and more equal partnership with the US – 'equal in counsel if not in power', in the words of Attlee[20] – it was vital to end British reliance on American aid and to demonstrate British strength. At least two developments served this purpose. First, aid to Britain under the ERP was suspended ahead of schedule at the end of 1950. While US military aid was subsequently provided to assist the rearmament programme, this was reduced to such an extent by 1953 that the Churchill government was far less dependent on American support than had been the case at any time since 1945. Secondly, the successful explosion of a British atomic bomb in 1952 was viewed as a crucial factor in enhancing British status and influence in relations with the US. Harold Macmillan, as Minister of Defence in 1955, expressed a commonly held view that the lack of a nuclear deterrent 'surrenders our power to influence American policy'. Possession of 'the bomb' was regarded as a vital contributor to a greater degree of parity between Britain and the US. This nuclear duopoly at the centre of the western alliance also underlined a qualitative difference between the military capacities of Britain and the continental European states, further reinforcing the view held by many – including Lord Cherwell, Churchill's chief scientific adviser – that without nuclear weapons Britain would be just another European state.

During the first half of the 1950s both Labour and Conservative governments emphasised the importance of the special Anglo-American relationship over and above any European ties. Certainly

19. Cited in A. Danchev, 'In the back room: Anglo-American defence cooperation, 1945–51', in R.J. Aldrich (ed.), *British Intelligence Strategy and the Cold War 1945–51* (1992), p. 225.
20. PRO, FO 800/517/US/50/57, Attlee to Bevin, 10 December 1950.

this relationship was more publicly stressed in London than in Washington, where a British move for a detailed written definition of the special relationship was turned down by Acheson in 1950.[21] During the early 1950s the evolution of NATO represented the most important institutional expression of this relationship. The Americans, followed by the British, dominated the top command posts, while official business between the Western allies was invariably transacted in three stages – the first involving only the British and the Americans, the second including the French and the third extending to the other allies. This procedural arrangement often reflected matters of common Anglo-American interest beyond Europe. As one of the US Chiefs of Staff, Vandenberg, commented during a US/UK Chiefs of Staff session in 1950: 'Don't you think we can meet in the back room for the global business and let the French have their say afterwards in the North Atlantic Treaty Organisation?'[22] This pecking order in an alliance centred on an Anglo-American axis greatly irritated the French and was to have major consequences for both the alliance and British relations with the EC following de Gaulle's return to power in 1958.

Under the Churchill government of 1951–5 every effort was made to maintain and strengthen Anglo-American relations and to utilise the framework of the Atlantic Alliance for the purpose of organising Western Europe. The idea of an Atlantic community having a multitude of uses other than in the field of defence and security was widely and strongly shared by British policymakers.[23] Eden, for one, was a leading advocate of such an approach, showing a marked preference for dealing with European policy as much as possible within the OEEC and NATO, which were Atlantic-orientated organisations (the US and Canada became associate members of OEEC in 1950). This emphasis, together with his efforts – as in the Eden Plan – to avoid a sharp demarcation between the Six and the rest of Western Europe, reflected an attempt to establish Britain as a vital link or intermediary between Europe and the US. But this idea of Britain straddling the European and Atlantic spheres served only to intensify suspicions on the continent that Britain was aiming to thwart further integration by stressing the Atlantic dimension.

21. D. Acheson, *Present at the Creation: My Years in the State Department* (1969), pp. 387–8.

22. Cited in Aldrich (ed.), *British Intelligence Strategy*, p. 215.

23. See, for example, *DBPO*, series II, vol. I, no. 414, FO memorandum, 12 December 1951.

British policymakers, however, were required to tread a difficult path in this respect, all the more so because of the advent to power of the Eisenhower administration in January 1953. Eisenhower himself was not disposed to lecture the Churchill government on the need for Britain to be involved in European integration. His Secretary of State, Dulles, however, was far more critical of the British in this respect, believing that they were fundamentally mistaken in attaching more importance to Commonwealth than to European ties. In these circumstances, London could not be seen to act as a stumbling block to the Six's integration efforts if it wished Britain to retain US favour and the status of second power in the western alliance. As against that, it was concerned to do everything possible to cement the American commitment to Europe. The German rearmament question and the EDC project, as noted earlier, posed acute problems in reconciling these positions. The EDC had to be supported in view of strong US backing for it. Yet British policymakers were also fearful that successful adoption of EDC, with or without British membership, might eventually be used by the US as a convenient pretext for withdrawing its forces from Europe. This was an unappealing scenario, since Britain would then be primarily responsible for the defence of Western Europe in the face of Soviet power and would also be required to act as a counterweight to a rearmed Germany. It was on these grounds that the British much preferred a NATO-type solution to the German rearmament issue, with a rearmed Germany anchored in the wider western alliance.

By 1955, earlier fears, as expressed by Bevin, that the US would treat Britain as 'just another European country', had given way to the reality of a revived 'special relationship'. This development was accompanied by a well-used mantra on the British side, namely that Britain could not become closely involved in an integrated Europe because of this special relationship. In many respects, this was an excuse for a course of action that the British would have taken anyway. Certainly the logic of London's position was never entirely clear to the Americans, and they continued to hold the view that Britain's future lay in an integrated Europe. What they were no longer prepared to do was to press the matter, as they had in the late 1940s, on a country which was, in the words of a State Department memorandum of 1950, 'our principal ally and partner'.[24] This judgement was based in part on a key component of British power

---

24. *FRUS*, 1950, vol. III, p. 870.

and influence in the postwar world: the Commonwealth, which was both the foundation stone of Britain's great power status and a determining factor in British policy towards European integration in this period.

CHAPTER SIX

The Commonwealth Dimension

The Commonwealth represented the main source of British power, status and independence in the world during the early postwar period. There was no other comparable body that encompassed such a large expanse of the globe and that incorporated so many disparate elements in a complex network of historical, cultural, strategic, political, economic, financial and commercial ties. As the focal point of British interests, identity and emotional appeal in the wider world, the Commonwealth commanded the attention of British policymakers and public alike in ways that could not be matched by Europe. It was also the most important external factor limiting the nature and extent of British interest in the early postwar process of European integration. No aspect of Britain's European policy escaped scrutiny without reference to what was perceived as the higher priority accorded to British ties, obligations and interests within the Commonwealth. British policymakers invariably invoked the Commonwealth as an integral part of a seemingly unshakable argument against closer British association with Europe. Why was it regarded as such a major stumbling block?

Several general features of the development of the Commonwealth in the early postwar years account for and convey its compelling attractions in British circles. First, it had survived the war intact, and the principal changes of the early postwar years – most notably the granting of independence to India and Pakistan in 1947 and to Ceylon and Burma the following year – did not fundamentally shake British confidence in the future and importance of the enterprise. In fact, the transition from Empire to Commonwealth at this time, so as to include the newly independent states of India, Pakistan and Ceylon, appeared to demonstrate the British capacity for the promotion of smooth evolution and continuity. Meanwhile, it was widely assumed that Britain's colonies in Africa, Asia and the Caribbean would long remain under direct control as 'backward areas'. Their political and economic development towards independence was envisaged, if at all, as taking place over a very lengthy period of time. The second and largely African process of decolonisation in the period 1957–63 was on a timescale that would have been unimaginable to policymakers of the early postwar years: Morrison, for example, dismissed the idea of granting full self-government to many of the colonies as dangerous nonsense comparable to giving 'a child of ten a latch key, a bank account and a shot gun'.[1]

Secondly, there was a strong consensus of opinion in British politics about the value of the Commonwealth. This was accompanied by a deep sense of pride, further heightened by the common wartime effort. Churchill's strongly held imperialist views were summed up in a memorandum of December 1944 to the Foreign Office: 'Pray remember my declaration against liquidating the British Empire ... "Hands off the British Empire" is our maxim.'[2] Eden scarcely required such a reminder. He himself later described Commonwealth ties as 'sacred' and demonstrated where English loyalties and interests primarily lay in the wider world of the 1950s when he said: 'What you've got to remember is that, if you looked at the postbag of any English village and examined the letters coming in from abroad to the whole population, ninety per cent of them would come from way beyond Europe ... Ten per cent only would come from Europe.'[3] Equally importantly, Labour Party leaders shared the same deep-seated feelings. True, some (Attlee) more than others (Bevin) distinguished themselves from unreconstructed imperialists in the Conservative Party, especially on the question of Indian independence. But they were determined to avoid Conservative charges of a dereliction of duty and convinced that the Commonwealth – described by Dalton as the 'Jolly old Empire' and by Attlee as 'one of the greatest political ventures of all time' – was the indispensable base of British strength and leadership in the world.[4] According to another member of the Attlee government, Emmanuel Shinwell, it could not be abandoned 'for all the tea in China'.[5] The

1. Cited in M. Blackwell, *Clinging to Grandeur* (1993), p. 14.
2. PRO, FO 371/50807.
3. Cited in M. Charlton, *The Price of Victory* (1983), p. 157.
4. Cited in M. Blackwell, *Clinging to Grandeur*, pp. 118–19.
5. Cited in M. Caedel, 'British Parties and the European Situation, 1950–57', in E. Di Nolfo (ed.), *Power in Europe? II: Great Britain, France, Germany and Italy and the*

Labour Party's 1950 pamphlet on European unity accurately summarised a national consensus of opinion in its reference to the strong cultural bonds and emotional ties between Britain and the rest of the Commonwealth: 'In every respect except distance we in Britain are closer to our kinsmen in Australia and New Zealand on the far side of the world than we are to Europe. We are closer in language and in origins, in social habits and institutions, in political outlook and in economic interest.'[6] This profound sense of identification with 'kith and kin' in the white dominions remained in being even as the strategic and economic value of the Commonwealth declined in importance. At the time of the Macmillan government's announcement in July 1961 of its intention to seek terms of entry to the European Community, for example, Harold Wilson, then Shadow Chancellor of the Exchequer, expressed a popular sentimental regard for Commonwealth ties when he observed: 'If there has to be a choice we are not entitled to sell our friends and kinsmen down the river for a problematical and marginal advantage in selling washing machines in Dusseldorf.'[7]

Thirdly, strong bipartisan support for the preservation of the Commonwealth rested on a widespread recognition of its critical importance in maintaining London's standing as the focal point of the world's capital, financial and primary products markets and in offering a lifeline for the struggling British economy in the early postwar years. The Commonwealth was the world's largest trading bloc at a time when approximately 50 per cent of international trade and payments was transacted in sterling. British management of, and dependence on, this system was held to yield a host of advantages. These latter, in turn, had a direct and immediate bearing on Britain's European policy – effectively drawing a line between postwar Britain, whose domestic and foreign economic policies centred on the Commonwealth, and many of the continental European states which looked to European economic integration as the motor of economic growth and trade expansion.

Origins of the EEC, 1952–1957 (1992), p. 321. For the Labour government's policy and attitudes see also J. Darwin, *Britain and Decolonisation: The Retreat from Empire in the Post-War World* (1988), pp. 71–3.

6. *European Unity*, a statement published by the NEC of the British Labour Party, May 1950 p. 4.

7. *H.C.Deb.*, vol. 645, col. 1665. For Macmillan's view of Britain's relations with the white dominions at this time see, for example, his correspondence with Menzies (Australian Prime Minister) in PRO, PREM 11/3644, Menzies to Macmillan, 15 January 1962, Macmillan to Menzies, 8 February 1962.

The most powerful symbols of British economic interest in the Commonwealth, constantly brandished as representing insurmountable obstacles to British involvement in Europe, were the imperial preference system and the sterling area. Imperial preference was a product of the economically depressed early 1930s, when Britain had abandoned the long-standing principle of free trade in favour of protective tariffs. At the same time, preferentially lower tariff rates were introduced on trade within the Commonwealth via the Ottawa Agreements of 1932. This measure strengthened trading ties within the Commonwealth at the expense of trade links with third countries. The system had a marked impact on the pattern and direction of British trade, greatly emphasising the importance of sources of supply and markets beyond rather than within Europe. Britain's trade with the rest of the Commonwealth had long been based on an exchange of British manufactured goods for cheap food and raw materials from other members. This arrangement was regarded as an undoubted benefit. Thus Labour's 1950 pamphlet on European unity declared: 'The economies of the Commonwealth countries are complementary to that of Britain to a degree which those of Western Europe could never equal.'[8] The early operation of the imperial preference system further integrated this well-established trade flow. In the period 1931–7, for example, British imports from the Commonwealth as a percentage of total British imports increased from 24.5 per cent to 37.3 per cent, while British exports to the Commonwealth as a percentage of total British exports increased from 32.6 per cent to 39.7 per cent. This trading pattern was reinforced by wartime exigencies and by immediate postwar trading conditions. By 1950, 47.7 per cent of Britain's total exports went to the Commonwealth, and 41.1 per cent of Britain's total imports came from this source. By contrast, British trade with the Six was on a declining curve in the period 1938–48 when British exports to the Six as a percentage of total British exports fell from 21.7 per cent to 16.7 per cent, while British imports from the Six as a percentage of total British imports declined from 18.6 per cent to 13.1 per cent. Britain's huge trading stake in the Commonwealth was in itself a telling factor against involvement in an exclusively and tightly organised European trading bloc or customs union.

This position was accentuated by the workings of the sterling area. Like the imperial preference system, the sterling area arose out of the economic depression of the early 1930s when Britain formally abandoned the gold standard (1931), under which the value of sterling had been tied to gold and the values of most other currencies had been tied to sterling – then the major international currency. In the resulting division of the international financial system into a number of currency blocs, the sterling bloc (or sterling area as it was called following the outbreak of war in 1939) comprised countries which tied their currencies to sterling and traded heavily with Britain. By 1945, and as a result of wartime developments, the sterling area was comparable to a monetary union. Sterling was its principal reserve currency, and the area's exchange reserves were held in a common pool in London. Britain acted as the area's central banker, overseeing a variety of controls which, among other things, encouraged trade within the sterling area and limited expenditure on dollar-costing goods outside it. In the postwar period this arrangement was the foundation stone of Britain's status as the Western world's second most important economic and financial power, and it was perceived by British policymakers as yielding advantages in the field of international trade and payments that had to be maintained.

The combined effects of the imperial preference system and the sterling area helped to produce a closed economic bloc that became more rather than less entrenched in the early postwar years. This development was most evident in the British response to both European and American pressures for closer British involvement in the process of European economic integration. On the trading front, British policy reflected an overriding concern with global rather than European trading conditions. At the time of the Marshall Aid offer of 1947, for example, the British government unsuccessfully attempted to persuade the Americans that the dollar shortage had to be viewed in a global rather than an exclusively European context. The British argued, in fact, that they would have been able to take more chances in Europe if the US had supported the sterling area and had assumed its full responsibilities as the world's, and not simply Europe's, creditor at this time. Only an increase in the world's supply of dollars, it was urged, could assist in developing Britain's far more important trading links beyond Europe. In the postwar world of the dollar deficit, moreover, there were compelling reasons for Britain, which had long financed its trading deficit with the dollar area by surpluses with the Commonwealth, to expand its trade with the raw material producers of the Commonwealth and thereby earn more dollars. It was in these circumstances, for example, that Malaya – a British dependency – assumed particular

importance as a dollar earner for the sterling area in that it supplied over half of US imports of rubber and virtually all its imports
of tin.[9]

The failure to convince the Americans of the need for a more
global dollar-aid programme in 1947 made the Labour government
all the more determined to repel any attempt, via the OEEC, to
interfere with British trading patterns. There was especially strong
opposition to the idea of British involvement in a European body
dealing with the tariff question. The British view was that tariff
matters had to be considered in a global framework, through the
operation of GATT. Any European treatment of the subject raised
the spectre of a European customs union which, if it were to include Britain, would represent – or so it was felt – a serious threat
to Britain's far more important trading ties within the Commonwealth.[10] The fact that the OEEC in its early years did not deal with
tariff questions was largely due to British leadership of this organisation, and it is significant that the issue of tariffs only appeared on
its agenda as British policy itself underwent some change in the
mid-1950s.

In the early postwar years, the contrast between British emphasis
on commercial and financial ties beyond Europe and the interest
of the Six in economic integration to facilitate trade expansion was
to be seen in British efforts to develop a more tightly knit sterling
area and to make more systematic use of colonial resources. The
importance of sterling area controls was underlined in the aftermath of the sterling convertibility crisis of July–August 1947. The
Labour government promptly tightened restrictions on dollar expenditure out of the sterling area's pool of reserves. Sterling area
countries were not to be allowed to draw on their dollar earnings
from the London pool without British permission. Nor would they
be able to exchange their sterling earnings for dollars since sterling was now not convertible. Further restrictions were introduced
in July 1949 when, as a result of a British initiative, the Commonwealth finance ministers agreed to reduce dollar imports into the
sterling area by 25 per cent as compared with their value in the previous year. This common programme, under the close supervision

9. For the value of the colonies as a dollar earner at this time see, for example,
C.H. Feinstein, 'The end of empire and the golden age', in P. Clarke and C.
Trebilcock (eds), *Understanding Decline: Perceptions and Realities of British Economic
Performance* (1997).

10. For a review of some of the problems involved in reconciling British membership of a European customs union with Britain's Commonwealth trading ties see, for
example, PRO, FO 371/71851, Marten, 14 April 1948.

of Cripps at the Treasury, basically aimed to increase sterling area exports to the dollar area and to cut back on dollar imports by encouraging alternative sources of supplies within the sterling area. A more cohesive sterling area was thus considered vital in assisting Britain's passage towards economic viability and in overcoming the dollar deficit that had led to dependence on American aid.

This determination not only to preserve but to strengthen the sterling area greatly coloured British policy towards financing arrangements for expanding European trade. There was particularly fierce resistance in Whitehall to the idea of the identity and advantages of the sterling area being lost in a European construction. This was most apparent in the negotiations leading up to the formation in 1950 of the European Payments Union (EPU), a multilateral payments system that embraced the OEEC states and sought to overcome the problems caused by bilateral trading accounts and inconvertible currencies in blocking the expansion of intra-European trade. The venture, however, was far removed from an original American plan that was devised by the ECA in October 1949 and aimed at a single European market, with provision for a European monetary union and a European central bank. The American plan fell by the wayside largely as a result of the conditions on which Britain was prepared to allow the EPU to include the sterling area. In effect, there had to be due recognition of sterling's role as an international currency, while the EPU was stripped of any supranational character and of all potential for developing into a European monetary union.

A further indication of the British view that extra-European markets and sources of supply ranked far higher than Europe in assisting postwar recovery and growth was to be found in the more intensive development of colonial resources. In the early postwar years of mounting dollar deficits, the colonies were increasingly viewed as relatively unexploited assets that could be pressed into providing more foodstuffs and raw materials, thereby reducing dollar import payments and boosting dollar earnings. This alluring prospect of greater self-sufficiency and less dependence on US aid prompted the imperialist-minded Bevin to comment that 'if Britain only pushed on and developed Africa, we could have the US dependent on us and eating out of our hand in four or five years' time'.[11]

11. Cited in G. Warner, 'Britain and Europe in 1948: the view from the Cabinet', in J. Becker and F. Knipping (eds), *Power in Europe: Great Britain, France, Italy and Germany in a Postwar World 1945–1950* (1986), p. 35. See also PRO, FO 371/62554, Bevin to Attlee, 16 September 1947.

Certainly the programme of intensive colonial development, or 'new spasm of Empire', undertaken by the Labour government in the period 1947–9 focused much attention on Africa, regarded as a treasure house of undeveloped resources. In the event, this programme – based on the idea of British bulk buying of colonial produce at less than world market prices – fell far short of expectations and resulted in some spectacular failures, like the notorious groundnuts scheme in Tanganyika. It was nevertheless illustrative of the extent to which economic, commercial and financial ties with the rest of the Commonwealth overshadowed Britain's economic links with Europe. In this Indian summer of empire, the programme also demonstrated the extent to which British official opinion still viewed the entire Commonwealth complex as an asset rather than an incubus. It is true that the colonies were becoming costly prizes, adding £195 million to the deficit on the British balance of payments in 1947. It is equally the case that some political figures were far from enamoured by the prospect of indefinitely maintaining a colonial empire which, as Dalton confided to his diary in February 1950, contained 'pullulating, poverty stricken, diseased nigger communities'.[12] Yet there was no general inclination to contemplate a shift away from the Commonwealth towards Europe.

During the 1950s, the Commonwealth dimension was repeatedly cited by British policymakers to account for limited involvement and interest in ambitious schemes for European integration. This emphasis was most pronounced under the Churchill government of 1951–5, one of whose initial priorities was, as Churchill himself put it, 'the unity and consolidation of the British Commonwealth and what is left of the British Empire'.[13] Politicians and officials alike subscribed to the view that the Commonwealth had to take precedence over Europe in the event of any incompatibility. None of the 'pro-Europeans' in the Cabinet dissented from this position. At the Conservative Party conference of 1954, for example, Peter Thorneycroft, the President of the Board of Trade, entered a strong plea for recognising the increasing importance of economic links

12. C. Barnett, *The Lost Victory: British Dreams, British Realities* (1995), pp. 103–4. Opinion polls at the time suggest that the British public was ill-informed about the colonies. According to a government survey (1948), only 50 per cent of the sample could name a single British colony: cited in N. Owen, 'Decolonisation and postwar consensus', in H. Jones and M. Kandiah (eds), *The Myth of Consensus: New Views on British History, 1945–64* (1996), p. 175.

13. PRO, CAB 129/48, C.(51)32, Note by the Prime Minister and Minister of Defence, 29 November 1951.

between Britain and the Commonwealth. Shortly after his criticism of Eden's attitude towards European unity early in 1952, moreover, Macmillan is said to have commented that the only possibility available to Britain was to develop the Empire into an economic unit as powerful as the USA and USSR.[14] Four years later, at the time of the making of the Rome Treaties, Macmillan publicly declared that if it came to a choice between imperial preference and a European customs union, 'We could not hesitate. We must choose the Commonwealth.' By that time, however, there was already a growing body of evidence suggesting that neither the sterling area nor the imperial preference system was an immutable fixture and that the important functions served by both since the early 1930s were being undermined by developments in the international economy during the 1950s.[15]

Economic conditions in the early postwar years, notably the worldwide shortage of raw materials and the existence of a seller's market, lent weight to the view that the Commonwealth placed Britain in a strong position to resume a leading role in the international economy. The Commonwealth provided relatively assured, if not easy, markets for British industry. It also offered guaranteed access to important commodities. During the 1950s, however, these trading patterns were being increasingly undermined by continuing pressure to liberalise the system of international trade and payments inherited from the inter-war period, as well as by the workings of an international economy whose dominant characteristics were sustained economic growth and trade expansion. A further feature of the international economy in the 1950s was that the fastest economic growth and trade expansion were associated with industrial economies which were trading more and more with each other rather than with the rest of the non-industrialised world.

These trends highlighted a marked distinction between Britain and the Six in the 1950s. The Six experienced rapid trade growth in a competitive market. Meanwhile, the bulk of British trade was with more sluggish Commonwealth markets, as became increasingly apparent by the mid-1950s: in the period 1952–6, for example, the value of British exports to sterling area countries increased at a slower rate (13.8 per cent) than to North America (52.5 per cent)

14. Cited in A. Horne, *Macmillan 1894–1956, Volume I* (1988), p. 351.
15. Shortly after his appointment as Prime Minister in January 1957, Macmillan commissioned Whitehall officials to conduct a profit and loss account for all British colonies. See T. Hopkins, 'Macmillan's audit of empire, 1957', in Clarke and Trebilcock, *Understanding Decline*.

and to the rest of the OEEC (30.5 per cent).[16] The very different performances of the British and West German economies in the 1950s illustrate this contrast.[17] During this decade, West Germany's average annual economic growth rate was 6.6 per cent and its booming, European-orientated export trade boosted its share of the total value of world manufacturing exports from 7.3 per cent to 19.3 per cent. Over the same period Britain's annual economic growth rate averaged 2.3 per cent and its share of the total value of world manufacturing exports slumped from 25.5 per cent to 16.5 per cent. For much of the 1950s British policymakers were inclined to view such evidence of faster economic growth and trade expansion as a temporary postwar phenomenon, largely accounted for by continental economies starting from a much lower base than postwar Britain and resuming traditional trading relations. It has been argued that British policymakers should have been more alert to the greater potential of the European market as opposed to the Commonwealth. According to this criticism, there were already clear signs in the early postwar years, and most markedly so by the period 1950–52, when the volume of British exports declined by 5 per cent and West German exports soared by 50 per cent, that the rapid economic growth and high productivity associated with the expansion of intra-Six trade were more likely to improve British economic fortunes than maintenance of traditional Commonwealth ties. British policymakers, however, lacking a crystal ball, were more inclined to base policy on longer-term past trends which suggested that access to raw materials beyond Europe would remain critically important. This view was bolstered by early postwar shortages of such raw materials, and it was not until 1952/53 that market conditions changed, as the price of manufactured goods increased faster than the price of raw materials.[18]

In the buoyant international economic conditions of the 1950s, the sterling area and the imperial preference system, as the products of economic depression and trade contraction in the inter-war period, were both increasingly weakened by internal and external influences. Yet this was a slow, often imperceptible, process that

16. Figures derived from PRO, CAB 129/86, C.(57)65, Note by the Chancellor of the Exchequer. See also The Economist Intelligence Unit, *The Commonwealth and Europe* (1960).

17. For a comparative assessment see, for example, A.S. Milward, *The European Rescue of the Nation-State* (1992), pp. 396–424.

18. See A.S. Milward, *The Reconstruction of Western Europe 1945–51* (1984); C. Wurm, 'Two paths to Europe', in C. Wurm (ed.), *Western Europe and Germany: The Beginnings of European Integration 1945–1960* (1995).

did not immediately or dramatically impress itself on British policy-makers as presenting an unanswerable case for a fundamental reorientation of British foreign economic policy. The gradual withering away of the imperial preference system is a case in point. Under this system, Commonwealth exports to Britain entered duty free or at lower rates than exports from third countries: British exports to the Commonwealth were granted similar concessions. The regime involved a complex mixture of specific duties, which were mainly applied to Commonwealth exports to Britain, and *ad valorem* duties which largely covered British exports to the Commonwealth. The problem of measuring the precise commercial value of these arrangements was compounded by considerable variations in the margin of preference between Britain and other individual Commonwealth states. For example, British exports to Australia, New Zealand and Canada, which accounted for over 80 per cent of total British exports to the Commonwealth (1956), enjoyed larger preferences than those to South Africa and India.[19]

During the 1950s British policymakers gradually came to realise that the days of imperial preference were drawing to a close.[20] Rising world prices eroded the value of specific duties. In addition, Commonwealth countries were increasingly intent on protecting their infant industries from imports of British manufactured goods. As an example, the large Commonwealth market for British steel exports in the early postwar years was threatened not only by American and continental European steel producers, but also by Commonwealth countries like Australia, with its large postwar investment in the industry. The value of imperial preference was reduced by several other developments. The margin of preference was not sufficiently large to impede the penetration of Commonwealth markets by trade competitors like West Germany and Japan, both of which were by now recovering from wartime dislocation: in the period 1953–9, for instance, Britain's share of sterling area markets for manufactured goods declined from 62.4 per cent to 48.2 per cent, while the share of West Germany and Japan increased from 10.7 per cent to 22.9 per cent. Furthermore, Commonwealth countries increasingly complained that their exports to Britain were sold at world prices and did not benefit from the same preferential access

19. *Financial Times*, 20 June 1956.
20. Supporters of imperial preference led by Leo Amery suffered a major blow at the Conservative Party conference of 1954. They were defeated in their attempt to press for a revision of the GATT in order to allow for an unfettered imperial preference system.

as British exports to Commonwealth markets. It was on these grounds that Australia and New Zealand negotiated reductions in their preferential treatment of British exports in 1956–7.

Although aware of the doubtful long-term future of imperial preferences, British policymakers were determined to preserve the system for as long as possible. In the case of British exports to the Commonwealth, for example, a Cabinet paper of 1960 estimated that the average margin of preference, by now less than half its 1948 level of approximately 15 per cent, still had some way to fall before reaching the minimum significant level of 5 per cent. It was believed that even a preference margin of this order over 20 per cent of total British exports was of real psychological value to British industry. Immediately prior to the opening of negotiations for EC membership a year later, moreover, Macmillan advised the British negotiators that retention of Commonwealth preferences was 'very important'.[21]

During the first half of the 1950s at least, the concentration of British trade within the Commonwealth constituted a major barrier to public consideration of a new, more European-focused trading policy. The Commonwealth remained the principal target for British exports, accounting in 1954 for 61 per cent of Britain's iron and steel exports, 95 per cent of its car exports, 52 per cent of its engineering exports (excluding cars) and 49 per cent of its chemicals exports. At the same time, the Commonwealth also continued to play its long-standing role as a source of cheap food and raw materials for Britain: Australia and Canada, for example, supplied 61 per cent of the country's wheat imports in 1955, while Australia and New Zealand provided 60 per cent of its total meat imports.[22] Such substantial proportions meant that in the period 1952–4 trade with the Commonwealth accounted for 47 per cent of British imports and 48 per cent of British exports. This was still far in excess of the comparable figures for British trade with the Six: 12.6 per cent and 19.6 per cent respectively.

The changing role and importance of the sterling area at large in the first half of the 1950s was most noticeable as it gradually shed its earlier character as a closed economic bloc. The tightly organised system of controls of the early postwar years began to dissolve under the impact of economic conditions that weakened the case for maintaining a highly co-ordinated and discriminatory system, whether by management of the area's exchange reserves or by

21. PRO, PREM 11/3560, Macmillan to Heath, 14 September 1961.
22. Figures derived from PRO, FO 371/122030.

restrictions on imports. A landmark event in this respect was the decision taken at the 1952 Commonwealth finance ministers' conference to dismantle restrictions on dollar imports and to accept in principle the idea of convertibility of currencies.[23] Subsequent preparations for the convertibility of sterling (formally achieved in 1958), the growing disinclination of independent members of the sterling area to maintain large sterling balances, and the inability of Britain to perform its traditional role as the sole supplier of investment capital were all signs of a far less cohesive bloc. (There were parallel strategic changes that also betokened a further undermining of the concept of Commonwealth unity, most notably the ANZUS defence pact of 1951 which included the US, Australia and New Zealand but excluded Britain.) While the sterling area was becoming more permeable and less susceptible to British direction, however, it still represented a major market for British goods, accounting for approximately 28 per cent of British exports in 1955 (the difference between Commonwealth and sterling area trade figures for this period is largely explained by Canada's status as a non-sterling member of the Commonwealth).

It was this larger picture that often greatly influenced the policies and attitudes of British ministers and officials whenever the economic value of the Commonwealth was measured in the context of European economic integration. In a recent study of the sterling area during the 1950s, Catherine Schenk concludes that 'In hindsight, Britain's hesitations concerning European integration were perhaps misguided, but the Sterling Area was not the main obstacle to Britain's enthusiasm.'[24] Against that viewpoint, however, others have argued that the perceptions of the politicians of the time do not admit of such a clear-cut conclusion. The sterling area, as an integral part of the Commonwealth complex, instilled in political leaders a preoccupation with the latter's importance which distracted their attention from the process of European integration and made them largely indifferent if not dismissive towards new schemes. How far Commonwealth and other considerations did determine British policy towards further integration by the mid-1950s became clear as the Six embarked on successful negotiations for the creation of the European Economic Community in the period 1955–7.

23. At this conference in January 1952 Australia, Ceylon and South Africa were particularly critical of continuing controls on dollar purchasing and pressed for an early return to convertibility: S. Newton and D. Porter, *Modernization Frustrated: The Politics of Industrial Decline in Britain since 1900* (1988), p. 125.

24. C.R. Schenk, *Britain and the Sterling Area: From Devaluation to Convertibility in the 1950s* (1994), p. 132.

CHAPTER SEVEN

From Messina to Rome

In 1955 the Six set in motion a process that resulted in the signing of the Treaties of Rome (hereafter Treaty of Rome) in March 1957 and the consequent creation of the EEC and the European Atomic Energy Community (EAEC). The initiative for this 'relaunching of Europe' was taken by the foreign ministers of the Six, meeting at Messina on 1–2 June 1955, on the basis of a Benelux memorandum containing both a general plan for a common European market and particular schemes for applying the ECSC model of sector integration to communications and power (including nuclear power). Equally importantly, the Messina conference appointed a preparatory committee which was to meet in Brussels under the chairmanship of the Belgian Foreign Minister, Spaak, to consider these different approaches and to report back to governments. It was agreed that Britain should be invited to participate in this exercise without any of the preconditions that had been attached to the Schuman Plan of 1950. Even so, there was from the outset no great expectation among the Six that Britain was likely to join any resulting organisation, and, in the event, this view was to prove better founded than British assessments of the likely fate of the Messina initiative.

This new movement towards European integration had far more serious and lasting consequences for the British than their earlier aloofness from the Schuman Plan. By its exclusion from the negotiations leading up to the Treaty of Rome, Britain effectively lost the battle for proprietary rights over the concept of European unity, allowed the Six to shape the new communities in accordance with their own interests, and continued to pursue the increasingly outmoded and ultimately unsuccessful idea of association with the Six. On the British side, this outcome was largely determined by general notions of Britain's role in the wider world and a set of assumptions about both the British ability to influence European developments and the Six's capacity to pursue further integration without Britain. These assumptions gave rise to miscalculations at each of the major stages in the British handling of the Messina initiative, notably at the time of the key decision of November 1955 to withdraw from any further involvement in Spaak's preparatory committee and the subsequent launching in November 1956 of a British plan for a Free Trade Area (FTA) including the Six as part of a larger European trading bloc.

The immediate response of British policymakers to the Messina initiative was shaped by the prevailing view that Britain was still one of the three great powers in the world and occupied a pivotal position in the interlocking circles of the US, the Commonwealth and Europe. In addition, there was a widespread opinion that British leadership in Europe – considered the least important of these circles – was assured and that the Six's efforts to pursue European integration scarcely merited serious consideration. Under the newly installed Eden government, following the general election of April 1955, Macmillan made his first major parliamentary speech as Foreign Secretary, placing much emphasis on Britain's 'triple partnership' between the US, the Commonwealth and Western Europe but without reference to the Messina conference.[1] This omission was symptomatic of the extent to which the Messina initiative was perceived in official British circles as an inconsequential undertaking. While the recent defeat of the EDC project appeared to justify scepticism about the idealistic designs of the European federalists, the British role in ushering into being the WEU suggested that Britain now occupied a commanding position in Western Europe. A deep sense of complacency permeated the early reactions of British officials, epitomised by the comment of Gladwyn Jebb, the British ambassador to France: 'no very spectacular developments are to be expected as a result of the Messina Conference'.[2] There were also expressions of a well-entrenched condescension towards the Six whose ECSC, one Foreign Office official observed, had so recently received (via the treaty of association) 'the moral blessing of our association with it'.[3]

---

1. *H.C.Deb.* vol. 542, col. 603.
2. PRO, FO 371/116040, Jebb to Macmillan, 15 June 1955. See also, for example, PRO, FO 371/116040, Ellis-Rees to FO, 15 June 1955.
3. PRO, FO 371/116038, memorandum by Edden, 14 May 1955.

In the first instance, British policymakers confidently believed that divisions within and between the Six would be sufficient to thwart any successful conclusion. No clear consensus had emerged at Messina over the relative merits of general and sector integration. Moreover, the principal authors of the Benelux memorandum – Spaak and Jan Beyen, the Dutch Foreign Minister – were themselves in disagreement. It therefore seemed that a lengthy exercise was in prospect and that any plan for a comprehensive measure of economic integration was the least likely outcome. Such a view owed much to British perceptions of French and West German attitudes. According to Whitehall assessments, France was in no fit state politically or economically to consider membership of a common market: French fears about Germany, about loss of national sovereignty and about exposing the highly protectionist French economy to a revitalised West German economy were held to be as real as they had been during the course of the recent EDC controversy. There were likely to remain major obstacles to French acceptance of anything more than piecemeal sector integration at best, particularly if the forthcoming French general election resulted in a more right-wing National Assembly. Furthermore, early intimations of French support for British participation in the post-Messina negotiations served only to confirm the British view of French weaknesses.

It seemed equally clear to British officials that conflicting views in the upper reaches of the West German government would in all likelihood hamper further integration of the Six. In Bonn there existed a basic division of opinion, first evident at the time of the Schuman Plan but now more publicly exposed, between Chancellor Konrad Adenauer and his Economics Minister and Deputy Chancellor, Ludwig Erhard, the commonly portrayed supervisor of the German 'economic miracle'.[4] The two men were at odds over the value of the Six as a model for integration. They also differed over the relative importance of political and economic reasons for pursuing integration. For his part, Adenauer was influenced above all by strategic and political considerations in his support for Six-based

---

4. See, for example, H.J. Küsters, 'West Germany's foreign policy in Western Europe, 1949–58: the art of the possible', in C. Wurm (ed.), *Western Europe and Germany: The Beginnings of European Integration 1945–1960* (1995); S. Lee, 'German decision-making and European integration: German "Europolitik" during the years of the EEC and Free Trade Area negotiations', in A. Deighton (ed.), *Building Postwar Europe: National Decision-Makers and European Institutions, 1948–63*, pp. 38–54; W.F. Hanrieder, *Germany, America, Europe: Forty Years of German Foreign Policy* (1989), pp. 243–6.

integration. This process, he believed, best advanced West Germany's integration, equality and respectability in Western Europe, safeguarded the democratic system of the infant German state and facilitated close relations with the French. Erhard, on the other hand, disliked the idea of West German involvement in a tightly knit, centrally directed economic grouping of the Six and did not favour over-close relations with what he regarded as a protectionist and inflation-prone French economy. What he favoured was the OEEC model of economic cooperation. In addition, Erhard feared that West Germany's manufacturing exports to non-Six Western Europe would be adversely affected by German membership of a customs union confined to the Six. British officials set great store by this West German commercial interest. While this implied an unlikely defeat for Adenauer at Erhard's hands, it was understandable at a time (1958) when a larger proportion of West German manufacturing exports went to non-Six Western Europe than to the Six: 29.1 per cent compared to 23.4 per cent. Besides these considerations, it was also widely assumed in British official circles that West Germany would prove reluctant to place any limitations on its recently restored full sovereignty.

There were some fatal flaws in these British impressions of the Six's unpreparedness for further integration that revealed a limited appreciation of the political will and community of interests propelling the Messina initiative. The failure of the EDC project was a misleading guide to the future. Indeed, the removal of this contentious issue allowed the Six to return to the process of economic integration that had been at the centre of the Schuman Plan and that had been viewed as a means towards political ends. Then, too, there was a failure to appreciate that France and West Germany might eventually forge an agreement, especially if France was able to negotiate satisfactory terms in return for agreeing to the formation of a common market. In the event, the French were able to achieve their main objectives, most notably commitment to a common agricultural policy, harmonisation of social charges and favourable terms for the association of French overseas territories with the EEC.[5]

One of the most mistaken underlying assumptions on the British side – as evident in the immediate aftermath of the Messina conference as it was to be down to the collapse in November 1958 of the

5. A senior Italian diplomat at the time commented 'Europe cannot organise without France and, to get her in, prices must be paid which may seem exorbitant. As the soldiers say, France has the geography': cited in N. Piers Ludlow, *Dealing with Britain: The Six and the First UK Application to the EEC* (1997), pp. 21–2.

British plan for an FTA including the Six – was the view that the
Messina agenda was primarily an economic affair raising issues that
were best considered in the OEEC forum. What the British did not
fully grasp was that their leadership of the OEEC strengthened the
Six's determination to pursue their own form of economic integration. By the mid-1950s the British had effectively reduced the OEEC
to a nullity as far as further exclusively European economic cooperation was concerned. They had repeatedly refused to consider the
tariff issue in this forum – much to the irritation of the low tariff
states like the Benelux, which felt disadvantaged by the uneven,
partial process of trade liberalisation under the OEEC regime. Furthermore, they had successfully used the OEEC in the early 1950s
to smother a series of plans (the Stikker, Pella and Petsch Plans and
the plan for a European investment bank), each of which aimed for
closer economic integration.[6] Following the end of the ERP in 1952,
moreover, there was manifestly little British interest in revitalising
an organisation which, as Macmillan said in June 1955, was likely to
become 'less and less important'.[7] Certainly key questions of British
economic policy like sterling's convertibility were viewed as matters
for discussion with the Americans and the Commonwealth and not
fit subjects for airing in the OEEC. It continued to be felt, in effect,
that trade and payments issues had to be addressed at the global
level rather than in a regional European body, thereby maintaining
Britain's prominent position in world trade and finance while also
supporting an expansion of multilateral world trade.

The initial formal British response to the Messina initiative
amounted to a holding operation, governed by the view that Britain should associate with the Six but avoid positive commitment to
any plans that might emerge from the Spaak Committee. It was on
this basis that Russell Bretherton, an under-secretary at the Board
of Trade, participated in the Brussels-based Spaak Committee during the period July–November 1955. By the end of this period, the
committee clearly favoured the formation of two new communities
– an atomic energy community and a common market with a customs union as its centrepiece – in preference to the idea of a free
trade area. Meanwhile, Bretherton performed the difficult role of
participant without commitment. At an early stage he concluded
that Britain had the power to guide the committee's conclusions in

6. PRO, CAB 134/1030, no. 19, Ellis-Rees to Macmillan, 11 October 1955.
7. PRO, FO 371/116042, Record of a meeting between Macmillan and officials,
29 June 1955.

almost any direction, but later recalled: 'I don't think anybody in London took any notice.'[8] To some members of the committee Bretherton seemed to personify official British attitudes at large. Spaak noted his 'discreet scepticism', while Spaak's principal assistant, Robert Rothschild, commented that 'Bretherton usually had a rather cynical and amused smile on his face, and he looked at us like naughty children, not really mischievous, but enjoying themselves by playing a game which had no relevance and no future ... And then, one day, he disappeared and never came again. It was very strange.'[9]

The decision to withdraw from the Spaak Committee was taken on 11 November 1955 by the Cabinet's Economic Policy Committee.[10] The advice of Whitehall officials was conveyed via the interdepartmental Mutual Aid Committee, which had established a working party on a common market, chaired by Burke Trend, a senior Treasury official. Trend identified the main arguments against British membership of a common market: the adverse impact on the relationship with the Commonwealth and the colonies; the detrimental effect on the global ('one world') approach to international trade and payments; the likelihood of further integration and perhaps political federation unacceptable to British public opinion; and the removal of protection for British industry against European competition.[11] The report contained many finely balanced arguments and much uncertainty about the weight to be given to imponderable considerations, all the more so in that it sought to gauge the impact of different scenarios – one of British membership of a common market and the other of British abstention from an abortive or successful attempt to form a common market. For example, it was acknowledged that the imperial preference system was declining in importance; but there was a marked difference between recognising the diminishing value of imperial preference and accepting

8. Cited in M. Charlton, *The Price of Victory* (1983), p. 184.

9. P.H. Spaak, *The Continuing Battle: Memoirs of a European 1936–1966* (1971), p. 232; Charlton, *The Price of Victory*, p. 180. See also H. Young, *This Blessed Plot: Britain and Europe from Churchill to Blair* (1998), pp. 71–98.

10. PRO, CAB 134/1226, E.P.(55) 11th meeting, 11 November 1955.

11. CAB 134/1026, M.A.C.(55) 45th meeting, 27 October 1955. See also S. Burgess and G. Edwards, 'The Six plus One: British policy-making and the question of European economic integration, 1955', *International Affairs*, vol. 64 (1988); J.W. Young, ' "The parting of the ways"?: Britain, the Messina Conference and the Spaak Committee, June–December 1955', in J.W. Young and M. Dockrill (eds.), *British Foreign Policy 1945–56* (1989); E.J. Kane, 'Tilting to Europe?: British responses to developments in European integration, 1955–1958', (Unpublished Oxford D.Phil. thesis, 1996).

that British entry into a European customs union would involve the introduction of 'reverse preferences' or discriminatory trading measures against other Commonwealth producers. This last consideration was a major obstacle and remained so, as we shall see, when it came to application for EC membership. Any predictions about future trading patterns, moreover, were complicated by the fact that while the value of British trade with the Commonwealth was approximately double the value of that with the Six, only about half of the former benefited from imperial preference while the whole of the latter was subjected to existing European tariffs. There was little inclination on the basis of these realities to support a major shift in British commercial policy away from the Commonwealth towards Europe. In the event, the stock argument about the political value of the Commonwealth carried all before it. This was both summarised in a 1956 Commonwealth Relations Office report, which stated that the importance of the UK by itself would be 'immensely less than it is while she remains the centre of the Commonwealth', and reinforced by Lord Home, the Commonwealth Secretary, who counselled Macmillan to 'return to our old Conservative policy goal of UK producer first, Commonwealth producer second and foreigner last'.[12] Furthermore, although the Trend Report expressed fears about the impact of common market membership on British industry, its findings did not emerge from any detailed study of the subject: 'Industry has not, of course, been consulted.' The report questioned the pessimistic view of Whitehall departments, all of which predicted losses arising out of common market membership. Yet it failed to substantiate its own conclusion that such gloomy assessments 'tended generally to under-estimate the competitive ability of United Kingdom industry'.[13]

The Trend Report confirmed the conventional wisdom about Britain's European policy and scarcely amounted to the type of major strategic review that had been undertaken in 1947–9. At the official level, the prevailing climate of opinion in the two key departments – the Treasury and the Foreign Office – was against British membership of a common market. Edward Bridges, the Treasury's Permanent Secretary, was in no doubt that even involvement in the Spaak Committee was a 'great pity', while another senior Treasury

12. PRO, T 234/195, 28 June 1956; PRO, FO 371/122034, Home to Macmillan, 3 September 1956. See also, for example, PRO, T 232/432, Crookshank to Butler, 21 September 1955.

13. PRO, CAB 134/1030, M.A.C.(55) 199–200, 'The United Kingdom and a European Common Market', 24 October 1955.

official argued that 'we must not let ourselves be misled by the kind of mysticism which appeals to European catholic federalists'.[14] Meanwhile, Bridges's opposite number at the Foreign Office, Ivone Kirkpatrick, maintained that any European institution founded on a Franco-German axis was bound to collapse and that the Messina initiative was a doubtful if not wrong approach. Whereas in 1947–8 there had been marked differences of opinion between the two departments, there was now a consensus that stifled a full examination of the subject. Indeed, the Trend Report's assessment of the political objections to membership of a common market was limited in its scope in that the Foreign Office judged it unnecessary to consider the eventuality of a common market project proceeding without Britain. According to the Foreign Office, proper handling of the matter would be sufficient to avoid such an outcome. All that needed to be done was to shunt the Messina initiative into the OEEC – a tactical response summed up by Jebb as being to 'embrace destructively'.[15]

At Cabinet level, the decision to withdraw from the Spaak Committee was taken almost as a matter of course. There was no division of opinion and no strong awareness of a momentous divergence between Britain and the Six. Eden was scarcely involved in these proceedings, except to confirm that the right policy was 'to lean towards supporting the OEEC while trying to keep out of the more far-reaching schemes of the Messina powers'.[16] He lacked the experience of, or interest in, economic affairs that might have made for closer scrutiny of the matter. In any case, his attention was principally focused on the larger stage of East–West relations. The fact that the Messina initiative was consigned to sideshow status, attracting only a few sentences in his memoirs,[17] reflected far more pressing priorities, the most important of which was the Geneva 'Summit' of July 1955, the first such East–West meeting since Potsdam. R.A. Butler, the Chancellor of the Exchequer, was an intransigent opponent of any shift in policy, dismissing the Messina initiative as archaeological excavations designed to resurrect the dead body of European federalism and later claiming that the decision to withdraw from the Spaak Committee was taken 'through boredom by the British Government'. Spaak's attempts to advance the cause of European unity in this particular quarter evidently

14. PRO, T 236/6018, undated memorandum to the Chancellor of the Exchequer.
15. A. Horne, *Macmillan, Volume I (1894–1956)* (1988), pp. 351 and 363.
16. Cited in Burgess and Edwards, 'The Six plus One'.
17. A. Eden, *The Memoirs of Sir Anthony Eden: Full Circle* (1960), p. 337.

made little headway: 'I don't think I could have shocked him more when I tried to appeal to his imagination than if I had taken off my trousers', the Belgian observed after one particularly difficult meeting with Butler.[18] As Foreign Secretary, Macmillan was the other key figure who had a hand in taking the decision to withdraw from the Spaak Committee. Certainly his initial reaction to the Messina initiative demonstrated a more flexible and far-sighted approach than that of either Butler or Eden. He wanted Bretherton to have the status of representative rather than observer on the Spaak committee. Nor was he disposed to dismiss Messina out of hand, writing: 'This is our second string – we may need it. The "one world approach" isn't going with a swing at the moment. It may even bankrupt us.' In the end, however, Macmillan supported the decision to withdraw from the Spaak Committee, although he conceded in his memoirs that the Cabinet should have been 'more alert' to the dangers of remaining aloof from Messina and had erred in not recognising the real depth of Franco-German reconciliation.[19] As a recent appointment to the Foreign Office, Macmillan was not in the best position to challenge the widespread antipathy towards European integration that had developed in the department during Eden's tenure of the foreign secretaryship.

In the period December 1955 to March 1957, British policy towards the Six lurched from a blatant attempt to sabotage the common market project to a protracted effort to devise a defensive measure for preserving some form of close association between Britain and the Six. In both cases, strategic assessments of the possibilities were either incorrect and quickly overtaken by events or greatly influenced by the view that adjustment to closer integration of the Six was primarily a matter of modifying British foreign economic policy. Throughout much of this period, the fate of the common market idea still hung in the balance. The Spaak Report, published in March 1956, was approved by the foreign ministers of the Six in May 1956. It was not until February of the following year, however, that the major intergovernmental negotiations were at last completed. That the Spaak Committee had come out in favour of a common market meant that from an early stage British policymakers were on the horns of a dilemma. Peter Thorneycroft, President of the Board of Trade, expressed a widely held view in

18. Charlton, *The Price of Victory*, pp. 182 and 194.
19. H. Macmillan, *Riding the Storm 1956–1959* (1971), p. 69. See also PRO, FO 371/116048, Note by Macmillan, 19 September 1955. For a summary of the 'one world approach' at this time see CAB 21/3323, Note by the Treasury, 'The Collective Approach and Proposals for a Free Trade Area'.

Whitehall when he said: 'On any analysis it seems clear that we cannot afford that the Common Market should either succeed, or fail, without us.'[20] A common market without Britain would involve adverse commercial consequences, together with damaging effects on west European unity and the western alliance. Yet the collapse of the common market project would weaken European solidarity and also place Britain in the dock, since British support – as Whitehall deluded itself into thinking – was considered fundamental to the success of the common market: 'Quite possibly,' added Thorneycroft, 'if we want the Common Market to fail, we need only let it alone.'[21] How to overcome this dilemma was the main problem confronting policymakers following the decision to withdraw from the Spaak Committee.

The initial response was a diplomatic offensive designed to draw attention to the disadvantages of the common market idea. In the event, however, this served only to expose British fears and defensiveness and to intensify suspicions among the Six about British motives. During this period, as Spaak later recalled, the British attitude changed from one of disdainful scepticism to growing fears about the threat presented by a common market: 'Your common market . . . will kill our trade, and we will have to fight against it', Macmillan warned one member of the Spaak Committee in February 1956, thereby indicating the limits of his 'pro-Europeanism'.[22] But British attempts to sabotage the common market at this stage – 'bashing the whole thing in', as one of Spaak's assistants put it – were unsuccessful. The US and West Germany were particularly singled out to assist in this purpose. Thus in December 1955 a Foreign Office memorandum to the UK embassies in Washington and Bonn emphasised the damaging effects of the Six's plans on the political cohesion of Europe and on progress towards freer trade. In the case of both countries, the British underestimated their powerful political motives for supporting European integration. On a visit to Washington in February 1956, Eden was left in no doubt about US support for the Messina venture.[23] This dashed British hopes of convincing the Americans of the extent to which a

20. PRO, FO 371/122034, Thorneycroft to Butler, 23 August 1956.   21. *Ibid.*
22. Spaak, *The Continuing Battle*, p. 232; Charlton, *The Price of Victory*, p. 200.
23. *FRUS* 1955–7, vol. IV, p. 405, Record of a meeting between Dulles and Mayer, 10 February 1956. See also *FRUS*, 1955–7, vol. IV, pp. 362–4, Dulles to Macmillan, 10 December 1955, and PRO, FO 371/116057, Macmillan to Makins, 19 December 1955; P. Winand, *Eisenhower, Kennedy and the United States of Europe* (1993), pp. 80–1; F. Romero, 'Interdependence and integration in American eyes: from the Marshall Plan to currency convertibility', in A.S. Milward, *et al.*, *The Frontier of National Sovereignty: History and Theory 1945–1992* (1993), pp. 165–70.

protectionist European customs union was at variance with the US goal of a non-discriminatory, multilateral trading system. Similarly, the Cabinet Economic Policy Committee's decision of November 1955 to engage the West German government's interest in 'a more realistic policy' towards the common market idea proved fruitless.[24] Adenauer's primarily political interest in European integration was recognised in British official circles. But it was not given sufficient weight: the observation in the Trend Report that 'the Germans are certainly not single-mindedly in favour of European economic integration, other than on political grounds'[25] was very much a case of putting the cart before the horse.

Accompanying these failed attempts to stop the common market project in its tracks, there emerged a British counter-initiative, originally known as Plan G, which proposed the formation of an FTA. The economic purpose and character of this proposal demonstrated the extent to which British policymakers were not attuned to the politics of European integration. The Treasury and the Board of Trade played the leading role in the formulation of the proposal. Input from the Foreign Office was strictly limited, with the result that there was scant regard either for the political aspects of relations with the Six or for continuing French interest in devising structures to control Germany's economic potential. Hence the revealing later comment from a Foreign Office official (a member of the European Economic Organisations department) that 'somewhere along the line, in the course of 1956, we lost sight of the essentially political nature of the problem'.[26] The Treasury had never shared the Foreign Office's confidence that diverting the Messina initiative into the OEEC would suffice to ensure that the common market idea was strangled at birth.[27] In the Treasury's view, a British counter-initiative was required to safeguard British interests if not to neutralise the Six's interest in the common market idea. Such a possibility was already under discussion at the time of the decision to withdraw from the Spaak Committee. However, ministers did not attach much importance to this effort. It was believed that there were limits to the extent to which Britain could offer tariff reductions in a purely European context. In any case, another round of GATT tariff reductions was in the offing. Macmillan's appointment as Chancellor of the Exchequer in December 1955 facilitated consideration of the matter.[28] But progress over the next twelve months was slow, with some evidence of bureaucratic inertia and lack of coordination. In May 1956, for example, the Board of Trade noted that the Foreign Office had failed to crystallise its views on the subject, apparently believing that the Board favoured maintenance of the status quo.[29]

The Board of Trade, in fact, was responsible for much of the groundwork in the development of Plan G. which was finally agreed on by it and the Treasury in July 1956.[30] At the same time, the OEEC set up a working party to study possible forms of association between the Six's customs union and the other west European states. The plan, unveiled by Macmillan in the House of Commons on 26 November 1956, proposed the creation of a free trade area including the Six and the other OEEC states. This was formally approved by the OEEC as a basis for talks in February 1957. By that stage, though, the original idea of a scheme to wean the Six away from the common market idea had been changed into a European construction to incorporate the Six as a single entity. The substance of Plan G was to turn the OEEC into a tariff-free trading bloc for manufactured but not agricultural goods. There was to be no common external tariff against non-members of the FTA, nor any of the other deeper forms of economic integration evident in the common market project. For its authors, the chief merits of this scheme were that it offered safeguards for British manufacturing exports to the Six, while preserving the free entry of Commonwealth agricultural goods into Britain, which amounted to approximately 90 per cent of the total Commonwealth exports to Britain. Furthermore, it maintained national freedom to determine tariffs on imports from non-members of the FTA, and generally upheld the principle of British association with the Six. More broadly still, the scheme held out the prospect of reasserting British commercial leadership of Europe and of safeguarding European cooperation against German hegemony.

All in all, the scheme seemed to offer Britain the best of all possible worlds. As one Board of Trade memorandum concluded: 'We have tried to find a mutually beneficial form of association with the customs union short of full membership, so that we may

28. See for example PRO, T 234/183, memorandum by Macmillan, 6 February 1956.
29. PRO, BT 11/5520, President of the Board of Trade's meeting with officials, 11 May 1956.
30. For recent studies of the origins of Plan G see, for example, J.R.V. Ellison, 'Perfidious Albion? Britain, Plan G and European integration, 1955–1956', *Contemporary British History*, vol. 10, no. 4 (Winter 1996); Kane, 'Tilting to Europe?'

be in a position to influence its policies and to have access to its market without a sacrifice of our economic independence.'[31] This was a not unfair representation of British policy both at the time and also until the Macmillan government decided to seek terms of entry to the EC. The scheme was an understandable defensive reaction to the emergence of a common market of the Six. It also marked a shift in the hitherto keen determination to address tariff matters at a global rather than a regional level. It was unclear from the outset, however, how a scheme that was so tailored to suit British commercial interests was likely to appeal to the Six or why they should endorse an arrangement whereby Britain derived maximum benefit without submitting itself to the disciplines of a common market. British officials generally overestimated both the strength of their bargaining position and the attractions of the plan to the Six. One official report, for example, concluded that the plan would be enthusiastically received by some of the more highly industrialised European countries, and that it would greatly encourage both the European Movement and the supporters of the Messina initiative. The reality was, however, that the exclusion of agricultural trade from the proposed FTA was a major obstacle to its acceptance. This was especially the case since France insisted on the inclusion of a common agricultural policy in the common market project and was ill-disposed to grant favourable access of British manufactured goods to the common market without comparable access of French agricultural goods to the British market. Doubts in British official circles about holding the line on the exclusion of agriculture from the FTA were particularly expressed by Butler, who was always sceptical of the likelihood that the European states would be 'all eager to receive us on our terms'[32] and who now, as later, was fearful of the impact of any change of policy on the Commonwealth and on domestic employment and agriculture. Indeed, the British determination to exclude agriculture – a 'non-negotiable' issue, according to Macmillan[33] – was widely opposed by the other states at the OEEC meeting in February 1957. Its effect was to strengthen both the Six's suspicions about British motives and their determination to hasten the signing and ratification of the Treaty of Rome.

31. PRO, BT 11/5520, 18 December 1956.
32. PRO, FO 371/122033, 9 August 1956. See also PRO, BT 11/5520, Butler to Eden, 15 August 1956.
33. Cited in R. Lamb, *The Macmillan Years 1957–1963: The Emerging Truth* (1995), p. 109.

The formulation of the FTA proposal in 1956 figured only to a very limited extent in the minds of ministers. Their attention was increasingly focused on other aspects of the international scene at this time. In the first instance, the developing crisis in Cyprus, where the British military presence was under threat from Greek Cypriot support for union with Greece, assumed far more strategic importance than the question of British relations with the Six. As Eden tersely observed in June 1956: 'No Cyprus, no certain facilities to protect our oil supply. No oil, unemployment and hunger in Britain.'[34] A month later, the Eden government was plunged into an altogether more serious crisis when President Nasser of Egypt nationalised the Suez Canal, which had hitherto been funded and operated by the British- and French-dominated Suez Canal Company. Anglo-French military action against Egypt between 31 October and 6 November was opposed by the US, whose economic pressure – especially the threat to withhold support for sterling – was instrumental in achieving a ceasefire and a withdrawal of British and French forces from Egypt. This humiliating outcome brought contrasting reactions in London and Paris. The French government, feeling betrayed by the British, was now all the more determined to concentrate its attention on Europe and to conclude agreements for the creation of a common market. The British reaction, however, was to give much higher priority to relations with the US than with Western Europe, and this was most marked as Macmillan, who succeeded Eden in January 1957, identified the restoration of the special Anglo-American relationship as his first priority in foreign affairs. Coincidentally but significantly, Macmillan was in Bermuda holding discussions with Eisenhower when the Treaty of Rome was signed. This confirmation of British priorities was indicative of the extent to which the assumptions of British policymakers in the field of European integration remained intact throughout the period 1955–7. The FTA proposal was but the latest example of an attempt to square the circle between the British preference for cooperation and the Six's interest in integration and also between the global and regional strands in British policy. The signing of the Treaty of Rome and its speedy ratification, however, were to render nugatory not only the British plan for an FTA including the Six, but also the principle of association with, rather than membership of, an integrated Europe.

34. Cited in Horne, *Macmillan*, vol. I, p. 364.

CHAPTER EIGHT

On the Defensive

In 1961 the British Conservative government, headed by Harold Macmillan, decided to seek terms of entry to the EC or, as it was commonly referred to in Britain both then and for a long time afterwards, the Common Market. The intention was that Britain would apply for full membership under Article 237 of the Treaty of Rome rather than associate status under Article 238. Macmillan was later to call this decision 'perhaps the most fateful and forward looking . . . in all our peacetime history'.[1] For the government as a whole, and for Macmillan personally, it represented a radical shift in policy. After all, in November 1956, when Chancellor of the Exchequer in the Eden government, Macmillan had flatly ruled out any possibility that Britain might at some stage enter the common market which was then being discussed by the Six. British membership, he told the House of Commons, would be wholly incompatible with the maintenance of imperial preference.[2] Yet by 1961 he had reached the conclusion that Britain's trade and other links with the Commonwealth need not be an insuperable barrier to membership of the EC and that obtaining such membership was in fact a matter of vital national importance.

For the first year or two of the Macmillan government there was little to indicate the dramatic change that was shortly to take place in British policy towards Europe. During this period, Macmillan, like his predecessors Churchill and Eden, tended to attach less importance to relations with continental Europe than he did to those with either the Commonwealth or the US. He was particularly

1. Cited in N. Beloff, *The General Says No: Britain's Exclusion from Europe* (1963), p. 88.
2. *H.C.Deb.*, vol. 561, cols. 37–8. As late as April 1960 Macmillan told de Gaulle that British membership of the EC 'was unfortunately impossible': PRO, PREM 11/2978, the de Gaulle–Macmillan meeting in London, 5 April 1960.

concerned about the poor state of relations with the Americans. Political and financial pressure from the Eisenhower administration had played a major part in causing the abrupt and humiliating abandonment of the Suez campaign in November 1956, and the episode inevitably left feelings of intense bitterness in London – much of it directed against Dulles, the US Secretary of State. When Macmillan replaced Eden as Prime Minister in January 1957, therefore, his first priority was to repair the damage done to the fabric of the 'special relationship'. In this he was highly successful. Macmillan and Eisenhower had been colleagues during the Second World War and the two men quickly re-established a good personal and working relationship. From the British standpoint, the most tangible benefit of the improved atmosphere that ensued was access to recent advances in missile and nuclear technology. July 1958 saw the repeal of the McMahon Act of 1946 which had placed a ban on the sharing of American nuclear know-how with Britain and other allies of the US. In March of the previous year Macmillan had already secured a useful concession when it was agreed, as a result of his meeting with Eisenhower at Bermuda, that a number of Thor intermediate-range missiles should be stationed in East Anglia under joint Anglo-American control – the so-called dual key system.[3] The meeting in Bermuda marked an important stage in healing the rift between Britain and the US.

The maintenance of a 'special relationship' with the US continued to be a key element in British foreign policy for the remainder of Macmillan's tenure of office (until October 1963). If anything, indeed, the relationship grew even closer after John F. Kennedy became President in January 1961. At the same time, the Macmillan government became increasingly preoccupied with the dilemma of how to respond to the developing EC. Cabinet minutes show that as early as May 1957 ministers were already becoming thoroughly alarmed over the economic and political implications of the progress made by the Six since the signing of the Treaty of Rome. The manifest success of the new Community posed a number of serious problems for Britain and set in train a fundamental reappraisal of existing policy on the question of European integration. The outcome of this reappraisal was the decision to apply for membership of the EC.

As we have seen, when the idea of a fully fledged economic community was first mooted in 1955, the official British reaction

---

3. J. Newhouse, *De Gaulle and the Anglo-Saxons* (1970), pp. 13–15.

was distinctly unenthusiastic. There was a great deal of scepticism about the viability of what was being proposed – not entirely surprising, perhaps, given the recent débâcle over the EDC. This scepticism was combined with a certain amount of hostility towards a development seen as potentially damaging to British economic and political interests. But the predominant sentiment can only be described as one of patronising indifference. When it became clear that the Six intended to press on with the establishment of an economic community regardless of whether Britain chose to cooperate or not, the British government produced an alternative scheme, Plan G.[4] This had been adopted as official policy during the closing stages of the Eden government and was taken over by the Macmillan government in 1957. There can be little doubt that one of its main purposes was to serve as a spoiling tactic – a device for frustrating the proposals put forward by the Six. In essence, as has been seen, the British plan aimed at the creation of a free trade area embracing all of the seventeen members of the OEEC who wished to join. It differed from the proposed EEC in at least three important respects. In the first place, it was purely economic in its scope and intentions. There were no political objectives, and certainly there was no question of furthering political integration. A second major difference was that the British plan contained no provision for a common external tariff. Instead, it was limited to the removal of restrictions on trade between the member countries. Thirdly, it was to apply only to manufactured goods: foodstuffs were specifically excluded from its operation.

The British counter-proposals were blatantly self-interested. Despite this, they were not without appeal to some sections of opinion within the Six, especially in West Germany and The Netherlands. Many German industrialists were favourably disposed towards them, as was Erhard. Against that, there were also powerful critics. Adenauer was extremely hostile. What finally put paid to the British proposals, however, was the determined opposition of the French and, more specifically, of de Gaulle.

In August 1957 Reginald Maudling, the Paymaster-General, was made responsible for conducting the FTA negotiations, assisted by a team of officials drawn predominantly from the Treasury and the Board of Trade and reporting back to a special Cabinet committee. For over a year he bargained with the Six and other interested

4. For the text of Plan G see H. Macmillan, *Riding The Storm 1956–1959*, Appendix One, pp. 753–4. For the evolution and preparation of the Plan see W. Kaiser, *Using Europe, Abusing the Europeans: Britain and European Integration, 1945–1963* (1996), pp. 61–87.

states. He did so, it must be said, without any great skill or sensitivity.[5] This was a consequence perhaps of his relative inexperience in international affairs, but also of his essential lack of interest in the project that he was meant to be promoting. The sticking point, predictably enough, was continuing British insistence on the exclusion of agricultural products from the FTA arrangements. Maudling was initially fairly hopeful of obtaining a measure of support for British policy from Germany, Belgium and The Netherlands. In a memorandum submitted to the Cabinet in October 1957, however, he warned that little could be expected from France, which had secured substantial concessions under the Treaty of Rome.[6] His forebodings about difficulties from that quarter proved to be fully warranted. As Jebb reported from Paris, the French were fundamentally hostile to British proposals for an FTA of seventeen states. There was a marked stiffening in their attitude, moreover, following the collapse of the Fourth Republic in May 1958 and the return to power of de Gaulle after a period of twelve years in the political wilderness. With considerable justification, de Gaulle believed that the FTA plan would be far less beneficial to France than to Britain and he had no intention of allowing it to be implemented.[7] In September 1958 a meeting of EC ministers at Venice agreed that any decisions on the FTA should be taken unanimously. This gave France what amounted to a power of veto and de Gaulle proceeded to use it, with his Minister of Information, Jacques Soustelle, telling a press conference on 14 November that there could be no FTA without a common external tariff and 'harmonisation in the economic and social spheres'.[8] Before taking this dramatic step, which ended all remaining hope of an FTA embracing the Six and the other eleven members of the OEEC, de Gaulle had first made sure that he had the backing of Adenauer by giving an undertaking that France would implement the EC's first tariff reductions in full on 1 January 1959.

Following de Gaulle's veto, the British government continued discussions with those countries that had shown a sympathetic interest in its proposals, most of which had tended to align themselves with

5. Maudling's own retrospective verdict on the FTA negotiations was that they stood little chance of success from the outset: R. Maudling, *Memoirs* (1978), p. 67.

6. PRO, CAB 129/89, memorandum by the Paymaster General, 30 October 1957. See also PRO, CAB 129/92, C.(58)65, memorandum by the Paymaster-General, 21 March 1958.

7. De Gaulle told Dulles in July 1958 that he would never accept the FTA: cited in Kaiser, *Using Europe*, p. 106.

8. Cited in R. Lamb, *The Macmillan Years 1957–1963: The Emerging Truth* (1995), p. 122.

UK views on European cooperation since 1945. The result was the signing of the Stockholm Convention in July 1959, its ratification in November and the establishment of the European Free Trade Association (EFTA), made up of seven countries: Britain, Austria, Switzerland, Portugal, Norway, Sweden and Denmark. This development provided a field day for newspaper headline writers who could now speak of Europe being 'at Sixes and Sevens'.

The aim of EFTA, whose members were popularly and significantly known as the 'Outer Seven', was a strictly limited one: to create by 1970 a free market in industrial goods only. From the outset, the British were lukewarm about the new organisation, regarding it as an interim, second-best solution.[9] David Eccles, President of the Board of Trade until October 1959, spoke disparagingly of 'a climbdown – the engineer's daughter when the general manager's had said no',[10] while Sir Frank Lee, the Joint Permanent Secretary at the Treasury, was equally unflattering in his description of EFTA as a heterogeneous and scattered grouping brought together by 'ties of common funk'.[11] Such initial reservations were amply justified. By its very nature, EFTA could only be of limited economic value to Britain. The markets of the other countries were relatively small. In addition, the tariffs in force in several of them, including Sweden and Switzerland, were already lower than the British. This meant that a reciprocal reduction of tariffs would not work in Britain's favour. Within a short time, therefore, it had become abundantly clear that EFTA could not provide a satisfactory answer to Britain's quest for an enlarged market and a more dynamic economic environment. It was noted that British trade within EFTA was only growing at a relatively modest rate – certainly far more slowly than with the Common Market Six. Between 1959 and 1962, when trading at a tariff advantage with the countries of the Seven and a tariff disadvantage with those of the Six, British exports to the former nevertheless rose by only 33 per cent compared to 50 per cent in the case of the latter.

The British government's motives in negotiating EFTA were mixed and essentially defensive.[12] To some extent it was simply a matter of responding to pressure to do *something* to protect British interests after the dismal failure of its efforts to achieve a much

9. See PRO, CAB 128/34, CC(60)41st Conclusions, 13 July 1960.
10. PRO, PREM 11/2531, Eccles to Macmillan, 14 July 1958.
11. PRO, PREM 11/3133, 'The Six and the Seven', memorandum by Sir Frank Lee, 22 April 1960.
12. Kaiser, *Using Europe*, pp. 101–2.

wider free trade area. As Butler told Macmillan in March 1959: 'If we do nothing we are a sitting rabbit.'[13] There was also concern that, in the absence of an alternative focus of loyalty, some countries, such as Austria, Denmark and Switzerland, might gravitate towards the Six. Thus Maudling warned Macmillan in November 1958 of 'increasing difficulty in keeping our flock together'.[14] But one of the main purposes in forming EFTA was undoubtedly to strengthen Britain's bargaining position in dealing with the EC. The hope was that it would be possible to negotiate some sort of associate relationship between the Six and the Seven.

This hope was soon to be dashed. Throughout the negotiations for a free trade area during 1958, the British had consistently overestimated the strength of their bargaining position. Their policy had been based on two broad, underlying assumptions. The first was that the embryonic EC would probably fail because of basic internal divisions. The second was that, even if it did in fact succeed, it would still be possible for Britain to work out some sort of arrangement with it short of full membership. By early 1960 both these assumptions had been proved false. Far from failing, the EC – which had come into being formally in January 1958 – was forging ahead at an impressive rate: tariff reductions were taking place ahead of schedule; it was thriving economically; and it was displaying a much greater degree of political cohesion than most observers had expected. Nor did the EC show the slightest interest in establishing some form of associate relationship with Britain and the rest of EFTA.

By early 1960, therefore, the options available to British policymakers had narrowed down alarmingly. As a matter of fact, Macmillan and his colleagues faced an extremely simple choice: either to enter the EC on the same terms as the original founders – something that had so far been regarded as anathema – or to remain outside, with all the attendant economic and political risks.[15] Inside the EC, Britain would be in a position to guide and shape the Community; outside, by contrast, it would be largely powerless to influence developments that would unquestionably have a vital effect on British interests.

It must be emphasised that the decision to apply for entry was taken not in a fit of Euro-enthusiasm, but out of a reluctant recognition that it represented the lesser of two evils. Perhaps it would be

13. PRO, PREM 11/2827, Butler to Macmillan, 24 March 1959.
14. PRO, FO 371/134504, Maudling to Macmillan, 27 November 1958.
15. E. Heath, *The Course of My Life: My Autobiography* (1998), p. 209.

something of an exaggeration – though not much – to speak of desperation. But the mood of the government was certainly a sober one. When the matter was discussed by the Cabinet in April 1961, several ministers voiced anxiety about loss of sovereignty, as well as about possible damaging effects on domestic agriculture and the Commonwealth. The overwhelming opinion, however, was that there was no real alternative to going in. It was agreed that there might well be an economic price to be paid in the short term; but in the long run the price of staying out would be a much higher one.[16] Entries in Macmillan's diary around this time indicate an equally bleak assessment of the situation. In July 1960, he noted:

> Shall we be caught between a hostile (or at least less and less friendly America) and a boastful, powerful Europe of Charlemagne – now under French control but later bound to come under German control? Is this the real reason for 'joining' the Common Market (if we are acceptable) and for abandoning (a) the Seven (b) British agriculture (c) the Commonwealth? It's a grim choice.[17]

By the end of 1960 Macmillan had made up his own mind about the answer to this 'grim choice'. He had come to the conclusion that it would be contrary to the national interest to remain outside the EC. On economic grounds, there appeared to be strong advantages in joining and strong disadvantages in failing to do so. For a number of years there had been mounting concern about persistent weaknesses in the British economy. This focused on features like cost inflation, overheating, stop–go cycles and recurrent problems with the balance of payments and sterling. Judged in relation to the past performance of the British economy, the record was not unsatisfactory. What was disturbing was that the economies of Britain's European competitors, and especially those within the EC, were growing with a vigour that made the British economy look distinctly sickly by comparison: in 1958, for example, West Germany overtook Britain as an exporter of manufactured goods. Various explanations were offered to account for Britain's inadequate economic performance, one of the most popular being to attribute it to high wage costs arising from trade union obstructiveness. From the mid-1950s, however, economists were pointing to British trade patterns as a major factor. The argument – which has been broadly accepted by historians – was that Britain's traditional reliance on trade with the Commonwealth had served the country well in the

16. PRO, CAB 128/35 CC(61), 24th Conclusions, 26 April 1961.
17. Cited in A. Horne, *Macmillan, Volume II (1957–86)*, p. 256.

past but was now acting as a brake on its economic growth. The system of imperial preference was no longer as advantageous as it had been: of particular significance in this respect was the Australians' insistence on a major renegotiation of their bilateral preference trade agreement with the UK in 1956.[18] In some of the Commonwealth countries British manufactures were being excluded as part of a drive to protect nascent domestic industries. More generally, Commonwealth markets were simply not expanding at a fast enough rate to accommodate British needs. The areas of real economic dynamism were in Europe where the economies of the Six, and West Germany in particular, were booming.[19] Even though Britain was outside the EC, British trade with its members was increasing at a disproportionately rapid rate. It seemed reasonable to assume that, once inside the EC, this underlying trend would be accentuated.

Macmillan appears to have found this economic analysis convincing.[20] On a number of occasions – notably during the Commons debate of August 1961 on the decision to seek terms of entry, and again during the critical London conference of Commonwealth prime ministers in September 1962 – he laid great stress on the economic benefits to be derived from British membership.[21] It would, he argued, bring access to an enlarged, fast-expanding market. It would also have an invigorating effect on British industry by exposing it to competition – an experience which Macmillan likened to taking a bracing cold shower. The consequences of staying out, on the other hand, would be that Britain would face ever-higher tariffs in vital European markets. A particular cause of concern in this respect was the Six's decision, in November 1959, to accelerate tariff reductions between themselves from July 1960. Indeed, Macmillan was so disturbed by the effect this development might have on British exports to the important West German and Benelux markets that three months before the acceleration was due to take effect he wrote to de Gaulle asking him to halt it.[22]

While such economic calculations undeniably played a part in Macmillan's decision to apply for entry, there is general agreement

18. Kaiser, *Using Europe*, p. 64.

19. See, for example, PRO, FO 371/122025, Working Group on UK Initiative in Europe, final version of report, 20 April 1956.

20. *H.C.Deb.*, vol. 645, cols. 1485–8, 2 August 1961.   21. *Ibid.*, cols. 1488–90.

22. Macmillan also raised the matter during a meeting with de Gaulle in March 1960: PRO, PREM 11/2998, Points discussed with de Gaulle at Rambouillet on March 12–13, 1960. De Gaulle later suggested that Macmillan was perhaps unduly 'pessimistic' about the impact on UK trade of the proposed acceleration in tariff reductions: PRO, PREM 11/3133, de Gaulle to Macmillan, 13 April 1960.

among historians who have studied the matter – including his bio-grapher Alistair Horne – that his motives were primarily political. From the standpoint of party politics, it was hoped to gain an advantage over Labour by presenting the Conservative government as being in touch with modern developments. Macmillan's think-ing was governed above all, however, by the conviction that joining the EC offered the best chance of maintaining and enhancing Brit-ish influence and standing both in Europe and in the world at large. By the beginning of the 1960s there were unmistakable signs of a progressive decline in Britain's international status. This was linked, to some extent at least, with changes taking place in the nature of the Commonwealth. During the 1950s, as we have seen, British pretensions to being a power of the first rank were given some credibility by Britain's position as head of the Commonwealth. This position was seen as a source of strength, conferring both economic benefits and a global influence out of all proportion to the country's size and economic weight. Increasingly, however, de-velopments were taking place which tended to reduce the Com-monwealth's real and perceived value. Economic ties between Britain and the Commonwealth were diminishing in importance from the mid-1950s onwards: by 1961 British exports to the Commonwealth had become less than those to Europe. At the political level, too, profound changes were under way, most notably the second wave of decolonisation which began with the granting of independence to Ghana in 1957. The cumulative effect of these changes was to transform the Commonwealth from a comfortable white man's club into an association in which African and Asian members had an increasingly powerful voice. Nor was that voice always used to Brit-ain's advantage, as was pointed out in the report on 'Future Policy 1960–1970' submitted to the Cabinet in March 1960: 'Politically it [the Commonwealth] can sometimes be more of an embarrass-ment than an asset.'[23] In theory, the Commonwealth should have assisted British diplomacy. All too often, however, the reverse was the case, for the simple reason that many members of the Com-monwealth, especially among the newly independent states, tended to be highly critical of British policies and were not disposed to toe the line laid down by London.[24] The classic case of this was the

23. PRO, CAB 134/1929.
24. In early 1962 Macmillan confessed to Sir Robert Menzies that 'I now shrink from any Commonwealth meeting because I know how troublesome it will be, what-ever the subjects immediately under discussion': PRO, PREM 11/3644, Macmillan to Menzies, 8 February 1962.

wrangle over South Africa, where British attempts to prevent its expulsion from the Commonwealth in the spring of 1961 proved unavailing.

As early as the 1956 crisis over Suez, bitter criticism of British policy by India and other Commonwealth states demonstrated the limits of the organisation's usefulness as a diplomatic tool. But the impact of Suez was, of course, much more far-reaching than that. For the Eden government, and for the British people as a whole, the experience was a sobering, indeed traumatic, one. The manner in which Britain was, in effect, brought to heel by the US provided a graphic illustration of the country's international weakness and vulnerability. Over the next few years there were to be other events that served to drive home the same lesson. These included the scrapping of the Blue Streak missile in 1960 and the collapse of the planned Paris summit in May of the same year, following the shooting down of the American U2 spy plane by the Russians. Macmillan had been the prime mover in arranging this summit and, according to those close to him at the time, its collapse was a shattering setback which did as much as anything to convince him of the weakness of Britain's international position and of the need to strengthen it.[25] In these circumstances, entry to the EC seemed to offer the chance to do that. The assumption here was that Britain would quickly take on a leading role – perhaps *the* leading role – in a Community that was already a conspicuous success and that was clearly destined to be a major political force in world affairs. If it stayed out, Britain would forgo this advantage.

There was also a further risk that worried Macmillan greatly, as it did his Foreign Secretary, Selwyn Lloyd: that the special relationship between the US and Britain would be superseded by one between the US and the EC.[26] The importance that Macmillan attached to the special relationship made him acutely sensitive to American views. And there can be no doubt that one of the factors that greatly influenced him was the knowledge that British entry to the EC was strongly favoured by the US government. During a visit to London in December 1959, Douglas Dillon, the US Under-Secretary

25. Certainly this was the view of Macmillan's private secretary, de Zulueta: cited in M. Charlton, *The Price of Victory* (1983), p. 237. Macmillan himself described the failure of the Paris summit as a 'serious setback to the Government' that was 'bound to be a shock to public opinion': PRO, CAB 128/34, CC(60), 32nd Conclusions, 20 May 1960.

26. For Selwyn Lloyd's concern on this possibility see PRO, PREM 11/2998, initialled paper dated 15 February 1960 and seen by Macmillan. See also PRO, PREM 11/2986, FO paper, 'The Future of Anglo-American Relations', 5 January 1960.

of State, left Macmillan in no doubt of the Americans' lack of enthusiasm for EFTA and their desire for Britain to join the EC.[27] The message was conveyed with equal clarity when Macmillan went to Washington for talks with Kennedy in April 1961. The newly elected President made it absolutely plain that he, like his predecessor, wanted Britain in for a combination of economic and political reasons.[28]

It would be wrong to think that Macmillan was motivated solely by a concern for narrow British interests. By 1960 he had come to feel that British entry was desirable for the sake of the western alliance as a whole. At this time, he was much preoccupied with the need for unity within the alliance. This is reflected in a memorandum – half-jokingly entitled 'The Grand Design' – which he drew up at the close of 1960 and the beginning of 1961 setting out all the economic, political and defence problems facing an embattled free world threatened by communism.[29] Given the current international situation, Macmillan's preoccupation is scarcely surprising. In November 1958 Khruschev had demanded the removal of all Western occupation forces from West Berlin and thereby precipitated a long-running crisis over Germany which culminated in the building of the Berlin Wall in August 1961. Throughout this period East–West relations were severely strained, and in this context Macmillan was understandably anxious to do as much as possible to promote solidarity among the Western powers. British entry to the EC, along with fellow members of EFTA, would heal the rift between the Six and the Seven which he described as a 'canker gnawing at the very heart of the Western Alliance'. It would also, in Macmillan's opinion, lessen the chances of friction between Europe and the US. As long as Britain remained outside the Community, there was a risk that it might develop, at the prompting of de Gaulle, in an anti-American,'third-force' direction. Once Britain became a member, and the sooner the better, its influence and guidance would help to prevent that from happening.

The evolution which took place in Macmillan's thinking about Britain's relationship with the EC between 1958 and 1961 was

27. PRO, PREM 11/2870, Record of a conversation at 10 Downing St, 9 December 1959.

28. PRO, CAB 133/244, P.M. (W)(61) 1st meeting, 5 April 1961. See also PRO, PREM 11/3326, Macmillan to de Gaulle, 13 April 1961; PRO, PREM 11/3554, FO to UK delegation to EFTA, 14 April 1961.

29. PRO, PREM 11/3325, memorandum by the Prime Minister, 29 December 1960 to 3 January 1961 ['The Grand Design'].

paralleled by a similar change of attitude among senior officials at the Treasury, the Foreign Office and the Board of Trade.[30] In the case of the Treasury, this process was closely associated with the appointment of a new man at the top, Sir Frank Lee, who in January 1960 was moved from the Board of Trade to replace Sir Roger Makins as Joint Permanent Secretary at the Treasury. Makins had been fundamentally hostile to the EC. For a time, Lee himself had been fairly unsympathetic, but gradually his outlook had begun to change. As early as 1955 he had submitted a dissenting note to the Trend Committee arguing that the economic advantages of British common market membership outweighed the disadvantages. By 1960 he had become thoroughly convinced that Britain had no alternative but to come to terms with the EC.[31] Lee took the view that for too long British industry had been feather-bedded by excessive reliance on the Commonwealth and the sterling area. Entry into the EC would improve its efficiency by giving it a much-needed dose of stiff competition. Lee was a dynamic and forceful individual, and his views quickly gained acceptance within the Treasury and other parts of Whitehall. Nora Beloff, a journalist for *The Observer* who wrote a book in the early 1960s about Britain's first application to join the EC called *The General Says No*, neatly described the change that took place at the Treasury. In 1959, those advocating entry to the EC were considered within the department to be wildly eccentric; by 1960 it had become a fashionable view; and by 1961 opponents of entry were being dismissed as old stick-in-the muds.[32]

There was a corresponding development at the Foreign Office, and again the process was associated with a change of personnel.[33] The head of the department, the Permanent Under-Secretary Sir Frederick Hoyer-Millar, remained sceptical about the case for British entry. But the 1960s saw the arrival in the Foreign Office from postings abroad of a number of senior officials who were strong advocates of membership. The most prominent of these were Sir Evelyn Shuckburgh, Sir Patrick Reilly, formerly ambassador to Moscow, and Sir Roderick Barclay, who was made special adviser on European trade.

30. For the change of attitude that took place among officials at the economic ministries see Kaiser, *Using Europe*, pp. 109–17.

31. PRO, CAB 134/889, E.S.(55) 8th meeting, 1 November 1955; PRO, PREM 11/3133, memorandum by Sir Frank Lee, 'The Six and the Seven', 22 April 1960.

32. Beloff, *The General Says No*, p. 89.

33. According to Hugo Young, in 1961 the FO was the Whitehall department which showed 'the most enthusiasm for Macmillan's idea' of seeking entry to the EC: *This Blessed Plot: Britain and Europe from Churchill to Blair* (1998), p. 176.

Perhaps the most significant pointer to the shift in Whitehall attitudes was the report produced in 1960 by the interdepartmental committee of senior civil servants chaired by Sir Frank Lee. This committee was instructed to review Britain's stance towards the EC and in its report concluded that there was a strong case for joining it. The Lee Committee was impressed by potential economic benefits to be derived from increased competition and access to a much bigger market. It also expressed concern about the impact on British exports and the balance of payments of the decision taken by the Six in late 1959 to accelerate their programme of tariff reductions. But the committee's findings were based chiefly on political considerations. British membership of the Community, it was argued, would contribute to the political stability and cohesion of Western Europe. In addition, it would avert the danger of a successful EC replacing Britain as the main partner of the US.[34] The available evidence strongly suggests that Macmillan found the Lee Report persuasive. By his own account, Edward Heath was also greatly influenced by it.

Outside official circles, important pressure groups and opinion formers increasingly began to come out in favour of British entry.[35] By 1960 virtually the whole of the press – both serious and popular, Labour as well as Conservative – was supporting it with varying degrees of enthusiasm. Apart from the Communist *Daily Worker*, the only major exceptions were the newspapers controlled by Lord Beaverbrook, the *Daily Express*, the *Sunday Express* and the *Evening Standard*, all of which reflected their proprietor's strident opposition.[36] In business circles, after an initial phase of suspicion in the period up to 1959, there was a growing recognition of the costs of staying outside such a thriving and dynamic market.[37] The Federation of British Industries (FBI) had become a staunch supporter of entry by 1960, and the big companies, such as ICI and General Electric, were particularly in favour. A survey of the top 130 companies carried out by the *Sunday Times* in July 1961 showed opinion to be almost uniformly favourable to membership.[38]

34. PRO, CAB 134/1852, E.S.(E)(60)11 (Final), 'The Six and the Seven: Long Term Arrangements', [Lee Report].

35. For the influence of pressure groups at the time of the first British application for entry to the EC see R.J. Lieber, *British Politics and European Unity: Parties, Elites and Pressure Groups* (1970).

36. *Ibid.*, pp. 218–26.

37. The Lee Report spoke of 'great uneasiness, amounting almost to dismay, among leading industrialists at the prospect of our finding ourselves yoked indefinitely with the Seven and "cut off" by a tariff barrier from the markets of the Six': PRO, CAB 134/1852, E.S.(E)(60)11 (Final).

38. Lieber, *British Politics and European Unity*, pp. 92–8.

The existence of such currents of opinion can only have encouraged Macmillan in his decision to go ahead with an application. During 1960 he took a number of preparatory steps. Leading figures in the Six, especially Adenauer and de Gaulle, were discreetly sounded out about how they would feel if Britain applied. Their responses were considered sufficiently encouraging to justify going ahead. At the same time, Macmillan also moved to strengthen the pro-European element within his Cabinet. In July 1960 there was a reshuffle in which a number of ministers who were well disposed towards the EC were moved to posts which were likely to be of critical importance in any negotiations for British membership: Duncan Sandys was made Minister for Commonwealth Relations; Christopher Soames became Minister of Agriculture; and Edward Heath became Lord Privy Seal and Minister at the Foreign Office with special responsibility for European affairs.

All the indications are that Macmillan himself finally made up his mind on the desirability of applying during the Christmas holidays of 1960. But there were still a number of senior ministers who remained undecided, even hostile. Butler, the Home Secretary, and Lord Hailsham, the Lord President of the Council and Minister for Science, continued to have reservations, while Maudling, now President of the Board of Trade, was convinced as a result of his earlier experience with the FTA negotiations that the French were determined to keep Britain out of the EC. It was not until 22 July 1961 that the Cabinet took a formal decision to open exploratory talks with the Six.[39] Shortly afterwards, on 31 July, Macmillan announced the government's intention to the House of Commons.[40] When his statement was debated at the beginning of August, opposition was surprisingly muted. Fewer than 30 Conservatives abstained on a motion to oppose it and only one registered outright hostility – a right-wing backbencher, Anthony Fell, who had earlier castigated Macmillan as a 'national disaster'.[41]

At the time, Macmillan's parliamentary statement came in for considerable criticism. The main complaint was that it was low-key, lacklustre and ultra-cautious, and that it failed to capture the public imagination or to generate enthusiasm for what could have been presented as a historic challenge to the British people. This was the line taken, for example, by the *Manchester Guardian*, which accused Macmillan of 'backing into Europe'. On the whole, historians have

39. PRO, CAB 128/35, CC(61), 42nd Conclusions.
40. *H.C.Deb.*, vol. 645, cols. 928–31.   41. *Ibid.*, col. 934, 31 July 1961.

echoed this critical verdict. Indeed, they have generally gone further and applied it to Macmillan's approach throughout the abortive negotiations.

It must be said that in some respects Macmillan's caution does appear excessive. After all, as a result of the general election of October 1959 he enjoyed a substantial parliamentary majority which never fell below 90. Nor did his policy towards Europe encounter a great deal of open opposition from within the Conservative Party, whether in Parliament or at the party conferences of 1961 and 1962. On the other hand, Macmillan's hesitancy is not hard to understand. He was convinced that public opinion was at best luke-warm and needed to be nursed along carefully and gradually: the possibility of EC membership had not even been mentioned in the Conservatives' 1959 election manifesto. The Cabinet was far from united on the question: Butler's backing was particularly uncertain until he at last fully committed himself as late as August 1962. The imperialist right wing of the Conservative Party gave every indication that it was going to be troublesome. There was bound to be dogged resistance from members of the Commonwealth. More-over, their complaints that their interests were being sacrificed would in all probability receive a sympathetic hearing from many quarters, not least within Conservative ranks. Equally worrying was the prospect of serious trouble from British farmers and their repres-entatives.[42] There was the risk that the Labour Opposition might gain electoral advantage from the issue. Finally, Macmillan was aware of the imponderables, especially those associated with the attitude of de Gaulle. As he told Heath in July 1961, the forthcoming nego-tiations would hang on two points: whether the French leader, 'becoming more and more Napoleonic and self-centred', really wanted Britain in; and whether, even if he did, it would be possible to work out terms which seemed reasonably fair to all concerned.[43] Under such circumstances, it is not really surprising that Macmillan should have felt the need to proceed with care. However under-standable, though, his tactic of deliberately playing down the signi-ficance of what was being attempted had at least one unfortunate consequence. It raised doubts in the minds of the Six about whether there really had been a fundamental shift in official British attitudes towards the Community.

42. See comments on this point by Butler and Soames: PRO, CAB 128/35, CC(61), 24th Conclusions, 26 April 1961.
43. PRO, PREM 11/3559, Macmillan to Heath, 29 July 1961.

CHAPTER NINE

From Application to Veto

The negotiations for British entry to the EC, which were conducted for the most part in Brussels, were long, complex and difficult: in his memoirs Macmillan likens them to a steeplechase with lots of hurdles. They began in Paris on 10 October 1961 with a formal opening statement by Edward Heath indicating that the British government was willing to accept the fundamental obligations of the Treaty of Rome, the *acquis communautaire*, while seeking special terms for Commonwealth access to EC markets and protection of EFTA's 'legitimate interests'. They then continued until January 1963, when they were brought to a sudden and acrimonious end by a veto from de Gaulle.[1]

The principal British negotiator was Heath, referred to in the popular press as 'Mr Europe'. At one time Conservative Chief Whip, in 1959 he had succeeded Iain Macleod as Minister of Labour before being appointed Lord Privy Seal and Minister at the Foreign Office with special responsibility for European affairs in the summer of 1960. The choice proved to be a good one. Heath was untainted by association with the failed earlier FTA negotiations. Moreover, unlike the man who had handled those negotiations, Maudling, he was known to be sympathetic towards the EC. As early as 1950, indeed, he had displayed a favourable attitude to closer cooperation with the Six when speaking on the subject of the Schuman Plan in his maiden speech in the House of Commons. Heath's positive opening statement of 10 October 1961 made a

---

1. For the 1961–3 negotiations see E. Heath, *The Course of My Life: My Autobiography* (1998), pp. 211–36; W. Kaiser, *Using Europe, Abusing the Europeans: Britain and European Integration, 1945–1963* (1996), ch. 6. For a Whitehall account of the negotiations see PRO, FO 371/171442, 'Draft Report on the Brussels Negotiations: EEC'. See also PRO, FO 371/171449, Dixon to Home, 18 February 1963.

good impression on Britain's putative partners, and he was to conduct the negotiations as a whole with great energy, determination
and skill. He was ably assisted by a high-calibre team which was
headed by Sir Pierson Dixon, the ambassador to France, whose
good relations with de Gaulle would, it was hoped, be a great asset.
Sir Eric Roll of the Ministry of Agriculture, born in Austria and able
to speak seven languages, was Dixon's deputy, while Sir Frank Lee
was put in charge of coordinating the work of all the departments
involved back in London.[2]

From the British standpoint, the negotiations were rendered more
difficult by a number of factors. First, they were conducted amidst a
blaze of publicity and to the accompaniment of leaks and rumours
which Roll later called 'a sort of quagmire of information'.[3] This
was a complication that the Messina powers had been spared during the discussions leading up to the Treaty of Rome. Secondly, the
British government faced something of a 'Catch 22' situation. If it
showed great enthusiasm for entry, there was a danger of not only
alarming domestic opinion but also of encouraging the Six to stiffen
their terms. On the other hand, if it was not enthusiastic enough,
doubts would be raised about the sincerity of its intentions. Thirdly,
the British government was hampered by commitments it had
entered into in June 1961 towards fellow members of EFTA –
although it soon became clear that these were not going to be
allowed to stand in the way of an agreement. Fourthly, Britain was
not negotiating with the EC Commission, speaking for the EC as a
whole. Rather, it was obliged to deal with individual representatives
of each member state, all of whom had particular national interests
to be accommodated. Finally, the Community with which Britain
was negotiating was in the process of constant change and evolution while the bargaining was actually taking place. This was especially true in the case of agriculture, with the French insisting upon
arrangements being concluded before the question of British entry
was settled. The framework of the Common Agricultural Policy
(CAP) was agreed upon in January 1962.

The two issues of substance that proved to be most intractable
were British commercial relations with the Commonwealth and
domestic agriculture. It was inevitable that British acceptance of a
common external tariff would mean an end to the system of imperial preference that had been in operation since 1932. Britain would

2. Heath, *The Course of My Life*, pp. 211–13.
3. E. Roll, *Crowded Hours* (1985), p. 121.

thereby forfeit the benefit of cheap imports of raw materials and foodstuffs from the Commonwealth. That was considered unfortunate but manageable. More serious was the damage that would almost certainly be inflicted upon the economies of many of the Commonwealth countries. Temperate zone foodstuffs – wheat, meat and dairy produce from the white dominions – would be especially badly affected. More specifically, there was general agreement that the loss of unrestricted access to the British market would be economically ruinous for New Zealand, which sent over half of its exports to the UK.[4]

In the run-up to the negotiations for entry, consultation with Commonwealth leaders was intensified. In June 1961 a team of five ministers, including Heath and Sandys, was despatched to all parts of the Commonwealth. Its mission was twofold: to gauge local opinion and provide reassurance. Almost everywhere the reaction was negative.[5] The countries that were most hostile were the old dominions. Keith Holyoake, the Prime Minister of New Zealand, declared that he could not conceive of any way to compensate for the loss of duty-free entry of meat and dairy produce to the UK. Robert Menzies and John Diefenbaker, the Australian and Canadian Premiers, expressed similar fears for the future of their countries' agricultural exports.[6]

Pressure mounted for the summoning of a conference of Commonwealth prime ministers. This presented Macmillan with a tactical dilemma about the timing of such a conference. If it was held before serious negotiations with the Six began, there was the danger that the Commonwealth states would kick up such a fuss and demand such cast-iron guarantees that no agreement would be possible. If, on the other hand, a conference was delayed until after the negotiations were well advanced, Macmillan would be vulnerable to the charge of presenting the Commonwealth with a fait accompli. In the end, by way of a compromise solution, a Commonwealth conference was held in London in September 1962, mid-way through the British negotiations with the EC.

---

4. Kaiser, *Using Europe*, pp. 139–40. New Zealand's Prime Minister, Holyoake, warned Macmillan that loss of access to British markets for his country's agricultural produce would mean economic disaster: PRO, FO 371/158/312, Holyoake to Macmillan, 27 April 1961.

5. PRO, CAB 128/35, CC(61), 42nd Conclusions, 21 July 1961; PRO, CAB 134/1821, EQ(61), 5th meeting of the Cabinet European Economic Association Committee; Heath, *The Course of My Life*, p. 209.

6. M. Camps, *Britain and the European Community 1959–1963* (1964), pp. 345–50.

Throughout these negotiations, the Six – and the French in particular – took an uncompromising line against any special treatment for the old dominions. India, Pakistan and the Caribbean countries were to be allowed favourable terms, in some instances similar to those already granted to French overseas territories. In the case of Australia, New Zealand and Canada, however, the basic position adopted by the Six was that, after a short transition period, they should be treated on exactly the same footing as other non-EC countries. The British government, for its part, fought hard to get the best possible deal for the Commonwealth as a whole. But it was also prepared to make concessions in order to secure entry. In tentative early discussions with the Commonwealth during 1960, there had been promises that existing preferential trading arrangements would be preserved. By the time negotiations actually began in October 1961, however, this position had been modified and watered down: the opening move from Heath was to seek 'comparable outlets' within the EC for products that currently found a market in the United Kingdom. As the negotiations progressed, this precise formula was replaced by one of seeking 'reasonable access'.

Such a retreat naturally gave rise to criticism that the government was selling out the interests of the Commonwealth. Given the emotional commitment that many people in Britain still felt towards 'kith and kin' overseas, this was an extremely damaging accusation. The fact that Commonwealth leaders made their own dissatisfaction plain only added to the Macmillan government's embarrassment. In June 1962 Menzies and John Marshall, the New Zealand Deputy Prime Minister, issued a highly publicised statement in which they attacked arrangements just reached on industrial exports from the Commonwealth.[7] At the Commonwealth prime ministers' conference in September 1962, moreover, Macmillan was given a very hard time all round. The representatives of Ghana, Nigeria and other African states expressed opposition to the idea of being given 'associate status' – something which they regarded as a hangover from colonial days – while Nehru, Menzies and Diefenbaker were generally critical of the way negotiations had gone so far. It was such behaviour that prompted Heath to say he was 'astounded by the ignorance, ill-manners and conceit of the Commonwealth'.[8] In the event, Macmillan achieved his main objective, which was to prevent outright rejection of British policy. Nevertheless, the

7. *Ibid.*, p. 397.   8. Cited in A. Horne, *Macmillan, Volume II (1957–86)*, p. 356.

communiqué issued at the end of the conference failed to disguise the existence of strong differences of opinion.

The obvious dissatisfaction of Commonwealth leaders gave great encouragement to domestic opponents of British entry to the EC. It provided invaluable propaganda material for the Beaverbrook press, for example, while Hugh Gaitskell, the leader of the Labour Party, used it as a stick with which to beat the government. It was from the time of the conference that Gaitskell came out openly against membership on the terms currently on offer.

The other issue which presented grave problems in the negotiations was that of domestic agriculture. Since the 1947 Agriculture Act, British farming had operated on the basis of direct government subsidies, or deficiency payments, to producers in order to guarantee them an adequate livelihood. The system was designed to ensure a stable income for farmers, low prices for the consumer and free entry of cheap foodstuffs from the Commonwealth. It was by no means perfect. Even before Britain's application for entry to the EC, experts at the Ministry of Agriculture were concerned about its high costs and were considering ways in which it might be overhauled.[9] Nonetheless, it was considered preferable by far to the one devised by the Six.[10]

When the British government embarked on negotiations, it did so on the assumption that it would have a hand in shaping whatever agricultural policy the EC eventually decided upon. As we have seen, however, that was not what happened. Instead, at French insistence, the Six reached an agreement on the CAP in January 1962, while negotiations over British entry were still taking place. The new policy involved subsidies from the consumer rather than the taxpayer. It also envisaged the establishment of a European Agricultural Guidance and Guarantee Fund, which was to promote improvements and restructuring, and which was to be financed by levies on imports. These arrangements were ideally suited to the interests of France, but were regarded with intense suspicion in Britain. There were fears about higher food prices and adverse effects on the British farmer. Moreover, it was self-evident that, as a

9. See PRO, PREM 11/3194, Minister of Agriculture to Prime Minister, 22 February 1961. There was also strong pressure from the Treasury for a fundamental change in the subsidy system. See Kaiser, *Using Europe*, pp. 140–42.

10. A further complication for the Macmillan government was its pledge in the 1959 general election not to alter the system set up by the 1957 Agriculture Act for the duration of the next Parliament: *H.C.Deb.*, vol. 645, col. 488, 2 August 1961.

big importer, Britain would pay a disproportionately large share towards the agricultural fund.[11]

From the outset Heath accepted that Britain would eventually adopt the CAP in its entirety. The sticking point was the duration of the transition period. Heath initially asked for between twelve and fifteen years in which to adjust. The Six, led by France, insisted on a much shorter period.[12] What they feared was that Britain would use any time allotted to it not to adapt to Community methods, but to try to reshape them to fit in with its own national requirements.

Agriculture was a peculiarly sensitive issue. It was obviously tied up with the highly emotive question of food prices. British producers had an effective and influential lobby in the shape of the National Farmers' Union (NFU), whose president, Harold Woolley, was an implacable opponent of British membership of the EC.[13] In addition, there were traditionally close links between agriculture and the Conservative Party, with agricultural constituencies being represented overwhelmingly by Conservative MPs. Not surprisingly, therefore, as the Brussels negotiations dragged on during 1962, there was mounting concern within Conservative ranks about what were seen as undue British concessions in this area. The whips reported rumbling discontent among MPs with rural constituencies: the potential electoral dangers were underlined by a shock by-election result in November 1962 in the safe Conservative seat of Dorset South which was lost to Labour because of the intervention of an independent anti-Common Market candidate. In the Cabinet, too, there was mounting anxiety about the way the negotiations on agriculture were going. In August 1962 Christopher Soames, the Minister of Agriculture, warned of 'great trouble from our farmers',[14] and his concerns were shared by Butler, the most senior sceptic about British entry. Butler had represented the predominantly rural district of Saffron Walden for some 35 years and was especially worried about the fate of local tomato growers.[15] He was also uneasy about possible damage to his own position in the constituency, noting in his diary: 'My seat is fundamentally at stake.'[16] Macmillan himself was much preoccupied with the danger of splitting his party over agriculture. The disturbing historical precedent he had in mind was that of 1846, when Sir Robert Peel's repeal of

11. Heath, *The Course of My Life*, pp. 217–18; Kaiser, *Using Europe*, pp. 179–80.
12. Heath, *The Course of My Life*, pp. 218–20.
13. R.J. Lieber, *British Politics and European Unity: Parties, Elites and Pressure Groups* (1970), pp. 83–6.
14. Horne, *Macmillan*, vol. II, p. 353.
15. Lieber, *British Politics and European Unity*, p. 131.
16. A. Howard, *RAB: The Life of R.A. Butler* (1987), pp. 295–6.

the Corn Laws had caused a deep schism in the Tory Party. There were frequent references to the episode in Macmillan's diary. Nor was his unease lessened by periodic speculation in the Beaverbrook press that Butler was poised to lead a revolt against him in defence of British agriculture and the Commonwealth.

During 1962, then, negotiations for entry to the EC took place against a background of considerable difficulty for Macmillan. Commonwealth leaders made little attempt to hide their displeasure. There were critical noises from the farmers. Cabinet waverers felt renewed doubts about the wisdom of British membership. There was growing disquiet among Conservative backbenchers. Polls suggested that public opinion was turning against the idea of entry.[17] More generally, the government was shaken by a run of five bad by-election results in November 1962. Finally, Macmillan's own authority was weakened by his sensational Cabinet reshuffle – the so-called 'Night of the Long Knives' – in July 1962, when Selwyn Lloyd, the Chancellor of the Exchequer, and a number of other senior ministers were unceremoniously dismissed.

There was another development which complicated the British government's negotiating position: a shift in Labour's stance. For a long time the party leader, Gaitskell, remained non-committal. On the one hand, he professed to be in favour of entry in principle; on the other, he insisted upon terms that were patently unattainable. His equivocal posture was largely dictated by the desire to avoid open warfare in a party that was deeply divided on the issue. A section on the right of the party, led by George Brown, the deputy leader, Roy Jenkins, Anthony Crosland and Patrick Gordon Walker, strongly supported entry. Alongside these 'pro-marketeers', however, there were others – predominantly though not exclusively left-wing in outlook – who were fiercely opposed to joining what many of them regarded as a 'capitalist club'. Gaitskell therefore trod warily. Following Labour's devastating and unexpected defeat in the 1959 general election, he had set out to make the party more electable by jettisoning its commitment to nationalisation and unilateral nuclear disarmament. The result had been bitter rows at the 1959 and 1960 annual party conferences. In 1961–2 the wounds were still fresh, and the last thing Gaitskell wanted was another bout of vicious infighting between Left and Right.[18]

17. *Ibid.*, pp. 228–33.
18. L.J. Robins, *The Reluctant Party: Labour and the EEC, 1961–75* (1979), p. 32. For the development of Gaitskell's position during 1962 see B. Brivati, *Hugh Gaitskell* (1996), pp. 404–18; H. Young, *This Blessed Plot: Britain and Europe from Churchill to Blair* (1998), pp. 155–64.

Macmillan, who despised Gaitskell, ridiculed the delicate balancing act he was obliged to perform. At the Conservative Party conference in Llandudno in October 1962 he quoted the words of the Jerome Kern song 'She didn't say yes, she didn't say no' and compared Gaitskell to a Frenchman who had recently sat on a tightrope for 174 hours.[19] As a matter of fact, however, by the time Macmillan was delivering these jibes, Gaitskell had already begun to shift his position. On the eve of the Commonwealth prime ministers' conference in mid-September 1962, he issued a statement against entry on the terms currently available, calling for a general election if the parties were unable to agree about the matter. The doubts evinced by most Commonwealth leaders made a profound impression on Gaitskell, and on 3 October he launched a powerful attack on the government's conduct of the Common Market negotiations at the annual Labour Party conference in Brighton. In the course of his speech, he accused Macmillan of betraying the Commonwealth and jeopardising the independence Britain had enjoyed for 'a thousand years of history'.[20] He also set out five essential conditions for entry to the EC: safeguards for the interests of the Commonwealth, EFTA and domestic agriculture, and the preservation of the British government's right to pursue an independent foreign policy and use national economic planning.[21] In theory, these conditions did not preclude British membership of the EC. Gaitskell's audience, however, rightly appreciated that for all practical purposes the Labour leader was declaring against it. Thus anti-marketeers reacted with enormous enthusiasm, while Brown, Jenkins and other pro-Europeans, normally Gaitskell's closest allies, were visibly upset. It was this phenomenon that caused Gaitskell's wife, Dora, to exclaim: 'Charlie [Charles Pannell], all the wrong people are cheering.'[22]

Labour's growing hostility to entry both hindered and helped Macmillan. On the debit side of the balance sheet, it seriously undermined his claim that the British people as a whole were now fully committed to membership of the EC. In addition, Labour taunts about the government 'negotiating on its knees' further added to the difficulty of reaching a sensible compromise with the Six. On

19. Horne, *Macmillan*, vol. II, p. 354.

20. P. Williams, *Hugh Gaitskell: A Political Biography* (1979), p. 729.

21. The five conditions were set out in the 1962 NEC statement 'Labour and the Common Market': K. Featherstone, *Socialist Parties and European Integration: A Comparative History* (1988), pp. 54–5.

22. R. Jenkins, *A Life at the Centre* (1991), p. 146; Brivati, *Hugh Gaitskell*, pp. 413–16.

the credit side, nothing could be more calculated to cause right-wing Conservative dissidents to rally to the government than the distasteful prospect of being aligned with Labour.

Meanwhile, the Brussels negotiations on Britain's application had been proceeding at a painfully slow rate, progress being delayed in the early stages by the Six's preoccupation with two other matters: the CAP and EC political cooperation. Serious bargaining began in early May 1962. Little headway was made, however, before talks were suspended for the summer break in early August. The British government was later to be accused of making a major tactical error in allowing the talks to drag on and get bogged down in endless haggling over individual agricultural items. Monnet, for example, maintained in his memoirs that a more effective approach would have been quick acceptance of the principle of membership, followed by a period of adjustment from within the EC[23] – the very course that Heath was actually to follow with his second and successful set of negotiations in the early 1970s. Such criticism is not entirely fair. The resort to detailed bargaining was not of British choosing. The Macmillan government's initial hope was that it might be possible to secure a general agreement offering acceptable terms of access for the Commonwealth as a whole. In the spring of 1962, however, the Six rejected this proposition out of hand and Heath was therefore left with no alternative but to hammer out a series of deals for individual countries and products – thereby acquiring (thanks to *Private Eye*) the nickname 'Grocer'. Nor was de Gaulle disposed to help in clearing away obstacles to an agreement. A number of historians have persuasively argued, indeed, that during the summer of 1962 he was engaged in a policy of systematic procrastination that was deliberately designed to prevent a settlement being reached before the summer recess. At the end of July Maurice Couve de Murville, the French Foreign Minister, suddenly produced an entirely new set of proposals for temperate zone foodstuffs, and shortly afterwards he suggested an extremely onerous arrangement for Britain's financial contribution to the EC that could not possibly be accepted.[24]

23. J. Monnet, *Memoirs*, translated by R. Mayne (1978), p. 456. See also PRO, FO 371/158176, Record of a conversation between Lord Gladwyn and Monnet, 8 May 1961. Monnet repeatedly advised Heath that the British government should sign the Treaties of Paris and Rome immediately. For Heath's retrospective reservations about such a strategy see *The Course of My Life*, pp. 213–14.

24. J.W. Young, *Britain and European Unity, 1945–1992* (1993), pp. 79–80; Heath, *The Course of My Life*, p. 222.

Negotiations were adjourned on 5 August 1962. After their resumption in late September, they were dominated by a wrangle over transitional arrangements for British agriculture. The Six, led by France, continued to take a tough line. They rejected the British proposal of an adjustment period of twelve to fifteen years. The most they were prepared to concede was a deadline of 1 January 1970 – the date on which the CAP was to come into full operation. It is not inconceivable that a solution might have been found to this disagreement and to other outstanding questions, such as Britain's contribution to the EC budget. In the event, however, the search for an agreement was brought to a premature end on 14 January 1963 when de Gaulle gave a press conference at which he emphatically ruled out the possibility of British membership of the EC. The French leader was able to make such a bold move partly because his domestic position had been considerably strengthened by a successful outcome to the referendum on constitutional reform of October 1962 and to the National Assembly elections in the following month.

Macmillan had never been in any doubt that de Gaulle's prickly and obstructive attitude represented the greatest obstacle to British entry. Under Article 237 of the Treaty of Rome, any of the Six had the right to block an application for membership. It was therefore essential to gain de Gaulle's consent. Macmillan sought to do this in a number of ways. In the first place, he was not averse to a lavish use of flattery. Perhaps the most conspicuous example of this was the careful attention devoted to the state visit laid on for de Gaulle in April 1960. The ceremonial arrangements were organised on a grand scale, far outshining those for Eisenhower's visit the previous year. Secondly, Macmillan pulled out all the stops to convince de Gaulle of the sincerity of British intentions in applying for membership. In a series of meetings between the two men – in November 1961 at Macmillan's country house, Birch Grove, in June 1962 at the Château de Champs near Paris and in December 1962 at Rambouillet – Macmillan used all his considerable powers of persuasion to that end. He was only partly successful. According to Macmillan himself, the French leader showed 'all the rigidity of a poker without the occasional warmth' at Birch Grove.[25] The talks at Château de Champs went better: evidence from both British and French sources, including the testimony of Couve de Murville, indicates that de Gaulle was genuinely impressed by Macmillan's

25. H. Macmillan, *At the End of the Day 1961–1963* (1973), p. 410.

performance. At Rambouillet, however, his attitude was deeply sceptical.

But Macmillan realised that the surest way to secure de Gaulle's backing was to assist his efforts to develop nuclear weapons. De Gaulle felt excluded from the Anglo-Saxon nuclear club and was determined to equip France with a nuclear capacity of its own – a *force de frappe*. The trouble was that France lagged well behind in the field of nuclear technology. It was not until 1960 that it exploded its first atomic bomb – some three years after Britain's first hydrogen bomb test.[26] Catching up would be a long and costly business, unless a short cut was provided by access to American and British know-how. Macmillan himself was not opposed to information being shared with the French, especially if that served to ease Britain's entry into the EC. The final word rested with the Americans, however, and that was the central problem.[27] When Macmillan broached the possibility of helping France during his visit to Washington for talks with Kennedy in April 1961, the latter immediately poured cold water on the suggestion.[28] This continued to be the Americans' stance throughout 1961–2, not least because they were wedded to a policy of nuclear non-proliferation.

Despite this important constraint on his room for manoeuvre, Macmillan was fairly confident that de Gaulle's reservations about British entry could be overcome: the French would be tough and unhelpful, and they would drive a very hard bargain, but at the end of the day, Britain's application would be successful. Others, including the British ambassador to Paris, Sir Pierson Dixon, took a more pessimistic view. At a relatively early stage in the negotiations, Dixon became convinced that de Gaulle had no intention of letting Britain into the EC.[29] In early autumn 1962 he sent a long despatch predicting a French veto – after France's next general election was out of the way. Ironically, Macmillan's reaction was to minute: 'Interesting but not convincing.'[30]

26. For early French attempts to develop a nuclear capacity see J. Newhouse, *De Gaulle and the Anglo-Saxons* (1970), pp. 15–18.

27. For a detailed study of US/UK relations and nuclear weapons see I. Clark, *Nuclear Diplomacy and the Special Relationship: Britain's Deterrent and America, 1957–1962* (1994).

28. PRO, CAB 133/244, P.M. (W) 1st meeting, Record of a meeting held at the White House on Wednesday, 5 April; PRO, PREM 11/3554, Prime Minister's note on his communication with Kennedy on 6 April 1961; PRO, PREM 11/2311, Kennedy to Macmillan, 8 May 1961.

29. PRO, PREM 11/3775, Dixon to FO, 22 May 1962; Heath, *The Course of My Life*, p. 226. See also PRO, FO 371/164839, Dixon to FO, 1 October 1962.

30. N. Beloff, *The General Says No: Britain's Exclusion from Europe* (1963), pp. 114–15.

One of the main reasons for Macmillan's expectation that Britain would eventually secure entry was his belief that Britain could count on strong backing from the 'friendly five' to counteract the negative influence of de Gaulle. He was particularly hopeful about assistance from Bonn. In this he proved to be mistaken. Certainly there was a great deal of support for British entry within West Germany. Public opinion was overwhelmingly in favour. So too were most members of the government. The key factor, however, was the attitude of Adenauer; and it is clear that Macmillan seriously overestimated the extent to which he was prepared to help by putting pressure on de Gaulle.

By the time of the Brussels negotiations, Adenauer, who had been Chancellor of West Germany since 1949, was in his mid-eighties. On purely personal grounds, he had little reason to feel any warmth towards the British.[31] During the early postwar occupation of Germany he had been dismissed from his post as *Oberbürgermeister* of Cologne by a British officer. He had also been prevented from seeing his dying wife in hospital because of the refusal of another British officer to grant him a travel permit. Personal relations between Adenauer and Macmillan were never easy or relaxed. According to Alistair Horne, Macmillan found the West German Chancellor boring. Horne also suggests that Adenauer probably picked up the lingering mistrust of Germans that Macmillan still felt after his experience of the two world wars. Allied to this clash of personalities were policy differences. In 1957 Adenauer was alarmed when informed that the British government intended to cut back its forces stationed in West Germany. From that point onwards, he had growing doubts about Britain's willingness to stand up to Soviet pressure over Berlin and other German issues. His suspicions were fuelled by Macmillan's trip to Moscow for talks with Khruschev in February 1959. After this – to Macmillan's fury – Adenauer began to speak of the British Prime Minister as an appeaser in the Neville Chamberlain mould.[32] Again, at the time of the crisis over the building of the Berlin Wall in August 1961, Adenauer was bitterly disappointed over what he viewed as a weak response by the British government.

No less significant than the steady deterioration in relations between Adenauer and Macmillan was the progressive improvement

---

31. For Adenauer's dislike of the British and Macmillan personally see Kaiser, *Using Europe*, pp. 95–6, 152–5; J.P.S. Gearson, *Harold Macmillan and the Berlin Wall Crisis, 1958–62: The Limits of Interests and Force* (1998), pp. 123–6; A. Tusa, *The Last Division: Berlin and the Wall* (1996), pp. 105–7.

32. Horne, *Macmillan*, vol. II, pp. 119–20, 129–30, 133–6; Kaiser, *Using Europe*, pp. 152–5.

in those between Adenauer and de Gaulle. The West German Chancellor's initial reaction to de Gaulle's return to power in 1958 had been one of wariness. Not surprisingly, given de Gaulle's record, he was concerned that he might adopt a strong anti-German line. An exchange of visits during 1958, however, removed much of this mistrust and laid the foundations of a Franco-German rapprochement. A vital element in this development was de Gaulle's stance over Berlin. Unlike Macmillan, who sought to reach an understanding with the Russians, de Gaulle took an uncompromising position and in the process gained Adenauer's confidence. By 1962 relations between Bonn and Paris were extremely close. They were cemented by a highly successful state visit to France by Adenauer in July of that year and an equally successful return visit to Germany by de Gaulle in September. The great work of Franco-German reconciliation was well under way and was to come to a climax with the signing of the Treaty of Friendship and Cooperation in Paris in January 1963. Given the overriding importance that Adenauer attached to the Bonn–Paris axis, there was never any realistic prospect that he would exert strong pressure on de Gaulle to lift his veto on the British application. This was even more the case since he himself had by this stage become distinctly cool about British entry to the EC. Certainly he had no intention of refusing to sign the Treaty of Friendship and Cooperation, as some urged him to do.

After the French veto of 14 January 1963, the Brussels talks dragged on for another fortnight. The other five members of the Community, particularly the Benelux countries, were furious at what they regarded as de Gaulle's arrogant action. There was talk of continuing negotiations without France. There were threats of blocking progress on issues that were of importance to France, such as the financing of agriculture, until de Gaulle reversed his decision. But the French refused to budge. Couve de Murville – who had probably received no advance warning of de Gaulle's intention – insisted that there was no chance of reaching an agreement with Britain and at last, on 29 January 1963, the negotiations were brought to a close by a formal French veto.[33]

One obvious question that arises is why de Gaulle chose to torpedo the British application.[34] He himself offered a lengthy list of reasons at his press conference of 14 January. Most of these boiled

---

33. Heath, *The Course of My Life*, pp. 229–34.
34. For an interesting analysis of de Gaulle's motives see Kaiser, *Using Europe*, pp. 193–8.

down to the assertion that Britain was not yet a suitable candidate
for membership of the EC. According to de Gaulle, the Treaty of
Rome had been signed by states with similar economic structures
and commercial traditions. They were developing economically and
socially at roughly the same rate. Britain's history and character
made it completely different. It was insular and maritime. It was
linked by its trade, markets and food supplies to distant countries
throughout the world. It was predominantly industrial and commercial, and its agricultural system was totally incompatible with
that adopted by the EC. De Gaulle doubted whether the British
were ready yet to make the fundamental changes that would be
necessary for them to fit in. In any case, if Britain's application was
successful, others would follow suit and the Community would then
expand to eleven, thirteen or more members. Under the impact of
this expansion, the EC would lose its cohesion and 'in the end
there would appear a colossal Atlantic Community under American
dependence and leadership which would soon swallow up the European Community'.[35]

There is no need to question the sincerity of de Gaulle's views.
The fears and reservations he now expressed publicly at his press
conference were essentially those that he had already repeatedly
conveyed to Macmillan during their various private meetings between
November 1961 and December 1962, and especially at Rambouillet.
There is also a certain irony in the fact that the arguments put
forward by de Gaulle were not dissimilar to those that the British
themselves had used in the past to explain why Britain was so different in character from the rest of the continent as to be unable to
take part in the process of European integration.

At his press conference, de Gaulle laid great emphasis on Britain's close links with the US as a basic impediment to British entry.
What he feared was that, once inside the EC, Britain would see to it
that it developed in ways that were consistent with American goals
and interests. A specific reference was made to the recent Anglo-
American agreement at Nassau, and it has often been suggested that
this was a crucial factor in prompting de Gaulle's veto. Historians
have usually stressed the symbolic importance of this agreement: it
convinced de Gaulle of Britain's subservient dependence on the
US. Rather less attention has been paid to de Gaulle's annoyance at
being let down – as he saw it – by Britain over nuclear cooperation.
The meeting at Nassau took place from 19 to 21 December 1962.

35. Beloff, *The General Says No*, pp. 162–4.

The most important topic of discussion between Kennedy and Macmillan was whether Britain should obtain the submarine-launched Polaris missile to replace the aircraft-launched Skybolt missiles which had been promised to Britain in 1960 but which were now revealed as technically deficient. Immediately before going to see Kennedy, Macmillan had visited de Gaulle at Rambouillet (on 15–16 December) in order to quieten the French President's suspicions. There is some dispute over what was said at Rambouillet.[36] In his memoirs, Macmillan claims that he warned de Gaulle that the US was about to abandon Skybolt. He would explain to Kennedy that if Skybolt was not available Britain must have an adequate replacement, such as Polaris. Otherwise, Britain would have to develop its own system. According to Macmillan, de Gaulle said he 'quite understood'.[37] De Gaulle, however, somehow got the impression – perhaps because Macmillan spoke in French, without the aid of a translator – that if Skybolt collapsed, Britain would decide to work with France on the joint development of a nuclear missile. Under these circumstances, de Gaulle's indignation at the outcome of the Nassau meeting is hardly surprising.

It is clear that Macmillan badly misjudged de Gaulle's reaction to the Nassau Agreement. During the meeting with Kennedy and his advisers, Macmillan was actually asked by the Americans whether the British receipt of Polaris might not cause de Gaulle to block Britain's entry to the EC. Macmillan replied that he had put de Gaulle fully in the picture and had received no indication that Polaris would be an obstacle to British entry.[38]

In addition to the reasons for refusing British entry which de Gaulle set out at his press conference, there was another which was understandably left unsaid. With considerable justification, de Gaulle took the view that it was simply not in French national interests to see Britain become a member. As Maudling had somewhat bitterly remarked to Macmillan some two years earlier: 'The French are sitting pretty and they know it.'[39] The EC was working well. It was tailored to suit French requirements, especially in the field of agriculture, and it was dominated by France. There was a distinct possibility that British entry would have a disruptive effect. At the very

36. For the official British records of the Rambouillet meetings of 15–16 December 1962 see PRO, PREM 11/4230.

37. Macmillan, *At the End of the Day*, pp. 347–8; Horne, *Macmillan*, vol. II, p. 431.

38. PRO, PREM 11/4229, Record of a meeting held at Bali-Hai, The Bahamas at 9.50 a.m. on 19 December 1962; *FRUS*, 1962, vol. XIII, no. 402, memorandum of conversation, Nassau, 19 December 1962, 9.45 a.m.

39. PRO, PREM 11/2678, Maudling to Macmillan, 27 November 1959.

least, it would mean a new challenge to French leadership. Edgar Pisani, the French Minister of Agriculture, made no bones about what was at stake when he explained to European colleagues that no cock likes to share his hens with another, even if the other cock brings six more hens of his own into the pen. Using the same farmyard imagery, Macmillan told Kennedy shortly after the veto that the real reason de Gaulle was determined to keep Britain out of the Community was because he wanted 'to be the cock on a small dunghill instead of having two cocks on a larger one'.[40]

40. Macmillan, *At the End of the Day*, p. 365.

CHAPTER TEN

Ancient Rivalries

In studying a particular aspect of modern Anglo-French relations, it is impossible to ignore the influence of centuries of history.[1] Rivalry between Britain and France stretches back to at least the Hundred Years War. There have obviously been periods since then when relations between the two countries have been friendly. But these have been the exception rather than the rule. In its attempt to maintain a balance of power in Europe, Britain has traditionally thrown its weight against the single strongest state. More often than not that has been France. Indeed, some of the most memorable episodes in British military history have occurred as part of a struggle to prevent the establishment of a French hegemony in Europe – notably in the wars against Louis XIV and Napoleon. Viewed in this long-term historical context, Britain's cooperation with France during the First World War seems almost like an aberration. In fact, there is a celebrated story about a conversation that is supposed to have taken place between the British and French prime ministers, David Lloyd George and Georges Clemenceau, which brings this out. Clemenceau told Lloyd George that he had the impression that as soon as the war ended, Britain had become once again the enemy of France. To this Lloyd George replied: 'Hasn't that always been the policy of my country?'[2]

Even today the traditional animosity lingers on. Whenever French farmers have a grievance about the workings of the CAP or some

1. For the historical background to Anglo-French relations see R. Faber, *French and English* (1975); R. Gibson, *Best of Enemies: Anglo-French Relations since the Norman Conquest* (1995); D. Johnson, F. Bedarida and F. Crouzet, *Britain and France: Ten Centuries* (1980).

2. J. Martet, *Le Tigre* (1930), p. 59; D.R. Watson, *Georges Clemenceau: A Political Biography* (1974), p. 388.

related issue, their instinctive reaction seems to be to take action against imports of British food.[3] There were echoes of this during the 'mad cow' crisis when, in June 1996, protests by French agricultural unions against the level of compensation paid for losses caused by the collapse in beef prices spilled over into anti-British demonstrations, complete with the burning of effigies of John Major and measures to prevent the docking of a ship carrying British passengers at the port of Caen. On the other side of the coin, nothing is more calculated to arouse the xenophobic fury of the British tabloid press than such activities. To take another example, it is hard to believe that Jacques Delors, the President of the EC Commission from 1985 to 1993, would have become quite the hate figure he did to some sections of British opinion if he had not been French.

The point of this preamble is to emphasise the extent to which Anglo-French relations in the 1950s and 1960s, as in other periods, were conditioned at least in part by deep-seated suspicion and mistrust on both sides. Prejudice, as well as rational calculation of national self-interest, played a part in shaping attitudes and policies.

During the late 1950s and throughout the 1960s, France represented the main stumbling block to British efforts to achieve some sort of accommodation with the EC. There can be little doubt that, but for the stance adopted by the French, Britain would have succeeded in obtaining entry to the EC well before 1973. On two separate occasions – in January 1963, as we have seen, and in November 1967 – a British application for membership was vetoed by de Gaulle. This was despite the clear wish of most other members of the EC – especially the Benelux countries – that Britain should be admitted. Some years earlier, in 1958, British proposals for the establishment of an industrial FTA embracing the Six and other members of the OEEC who wished to participate were similarly torpedoed by the refusal of the French government to cooperate. Certainly Maudling, the minister responsible for conducting the negotiations on these proposals, was himself convinced that 'but for the attitude of the French there would be no difficulty in getting agreement', and Macmillan agreed (in March 1958) that 'the main difficulty is with the French'.[4] As in the two later cases, it was de Gaulle who actually applied the veto in November 1958. But

3. Some interesting views on the influence of British membership of the EC on Anglo-French relations are offered in F. Crouzet, *Britain Ascendant: Comparative Studies in Franco-British Economic History* (1990), ch. 14.

4. Cited in R. Lamb, *The Macmillan Years 1957–1963: the Emerging Truth* (1995), p. 114.

even before he had come to power, at the beginning of June of that year, there were already clear signs – as with the Faure Plan of March 1958 – that the British proposals were not acceptable to France.[5]

The prospects for acceptance of the FTA scheme were not enhanced by the generally poor state of Anglo-French relations during the years 1956–8. The deterioration in relations between the two countries evident at that time was partly a consequence of the Suez affair of 1956 and its aftermath.[6] Suez had an adverse effect in at least two ways. In the first place, the French – who had collaborated with Britain and Israel in mounting a military expedition against Egypt – were dismayed and angered by the British decision to abort the operation in response to American financial and political pressure. They were convinced that the Egyptian leader, Nasser, was behind many of their current difficulties in Algeria, and as a result were naturally disappointed at losing an opportunity to topple him from power. Secondly, as has been seen, the rift that Suez caused between Britain and the US led to a determined attempt by the British government to repair the 'special relationship'. After Macmillan succeeded Eden as Prime Minister that became his main foreign policy objective, and relations with Europe were accordingly given a lower priority. Not surprisingly, the overriding importance which Macmillan so obviously attached to close relations with the US and his cosy bilateral discussions with Eisenhower did not create a favourable impression in France.

There were other factors that contributed to a cooling of relations between Britain and France at the time of the FTA negotiations. One was the decision of the Macmillan government to reduce the strength of British military forces on the continent as part of a programme of sweeping cuts planned by Sandys, the Defence Secretary, in 1957. The French were informed of the proposed cutback when Macmillan went to Paris for talks with Guy Mollet, the French Prime Minister, in March 1957 – shortly before his scheduled meeting with Eisenhower in Bermuda. The disclosure produced an unpleasant wrangle between the two prime ministers and between the

5. For French hostility to the British FTA proposals before de Gaulle's advent to power see M. Camps, *Britain and the European Community 1955–1963* (1964), pp. 130–52 *passim*; W. Kaiser, *Using Europe, Abusing the Europeans: Britain and European Integration, 1945–1963* (1996), pp. 94–8; P.M.H. Bell, *France and Britain 1940– 1994: The Long Separation* (1997), pp. 168–9.

6. The impact of the Suez affair on relations between Britain and France is dealt with in Bell, *France and Britain 1940–1994*, pp. 131–58, 163. See also J. Newhouse, *De Gaulle and the Anglo-Saxons* (1970), pp. 7–9; H. Thomas, *The Suez Affair* (1967), p. 154.

British Foreign Secretary, Selwyn Lloyd, and his French counter-part, Christian Pineau.[7] What particularly annoyed the French was that the British decision appeared to be in breach of an undertaking given some three years earlier. As noted in Chapter 4, in 1954, following the collapse of the EDC, the British Foreign Secretary, Eden, and the French Premier, Mendès-France, had negotiated an agreement under which Britain was to keep four divisions and a fighter force on the continent until the end of the century. In return for this commitment, France had waived its objections to German rearmament. Now the British seemed to be reneging on their part of the bargain. Technically speaking, that was not really the case since the 1954 agreement contained a clause permitting modification of the British commitments in the event of balance of payments difficulties – a gaping loophole, given Britain's perennial difficulties on that score. Even so, rightly or wrongly, the French still felt aggrieved.

They were similarly displeased by the negative British reaction to suggestions of changes in NATO designed to give France a greater say in its operation. In September 1958 de Gaulle sent a memorandum to Macmillan and Eisenhower proposing the replacement of NATO's existing command structure by a triumvirate, or 'triple directorate', consisting of the US, Britain and France. In private, Macmillan rejected as 'absurd' the idea that France should be placed on a par with Britain and the US.[8] His official response to the proposal was more diplomatic but no less discouraging for that, and it has been suggested by some historians (such as Miriam Camps) that this reaction made de Gaulle less inclined to cooperate over Britain's FTA plan.[9]

Quite apart from these extraneous factors, the British proposals for an industrial FTA were in themselves highly unpalatable to the French. It was felt, with some justification, that Britain was seeking the economic benefits of association with the Six without being prepared to accept any corresponding political commitments. More specifically, the exclusion of agricultural products from the British scheme robbed it of any real value as far as the French were concerned.

---

7. A. Horne, *Macmillan, Volume II 1957–86* (1989), pp. 31–2.

8. *Ibid.*, p. 109. Macmillan subsequently adopted a more accommodating attitude towards de Gaulle's views on the NATO command structure. See PRO, PREM 11/3325, memorandum by the Prime Minister, 29 December 1960–3 January 1961 ['Grand Design'].

9. M. Camps, *Britain and the European Community, 1955–1963* (1964), p. 171.

This brings out a fundamental difference which lay at the root of much Anglo-French disagreement about the EC. The plain fact was that the economic interests of the two countries were widely divergent, even diametrically opposed. Britain was a predominantly industrial country. It had an efficient but relatively small agricultural sector and relied upon imports of cheap food from the Commonwealth. Thus the sort of economic arrangement that appealed to the British was one that allowed access to the widest possible market for their industrial exports while at the same time permitting the continued importation of Commonwealth foodstuffs. The position of France was totally different. The French were large-scale exporters of agricultural products and their principal aim was to create an enlarged market – including Britain – for those products.[10] From their standpoint, therefore, the British proposals for an FTA in manufactured goods only had nothing to offer. Indeed, protectionist-minded French industrialists were alarmed – at least initially – at the prospect of the domestic market being opened up to foreign competition.

This basic conflict of economic interests was to be a recurring theme in Anglo-French relations throughout the 1960s – and, indeed, beyond. Another recurring theme which first became apparent during the FTA negotiations was the way in which Britain and France both sought to win backing for their respective – and contradictory – policies from the other five members of the EC. Initially, the British were not without hope that it might be possible to enlist allies in their struggle against the French. West German industrialists regarded the British proposals for an FTA as preferable to French ideas of a common market with a highly protectionist external tariff. Their views were shared, moreover, by most of the West German government, including Erhard. Both the West Germans and the Dutch were unhappy with the direction in which the French were then seeking to push the Community's agricultural policy, feeling that it would be far too advantageous to France. Furthermore, the Benelux countries, and The Netherlands in particular, looked upon Britain as a useful counterweight to undue French influence. There was, then, a certain amount of potential support. Nor did the British hold back from seeking to exploit it. Thus Maudling was told by Macmillan to try to get West Germany on his side. Again, when the

10. In 1961 Michel Debré told Macmillan that 'there was nothing that France would like better than to send her agricultural products to the United Kingdom': PRO, PREM 11/3322, official British record of PM's visit to Rambouillet, 27–29 January 1961.

French government collapsed in April 1958 and there followed a six-week period of political instability, Britain attempted to take full advantage of the situation by starting bilateral negotiations with France's partners in an obvious attempt to isolate it. The attempt was not successful.

On the whole, the French showed themselves to be more adept at such manoeuvring. Frank Figgures, the Under-Secretary to the Treasury who was involved in the later stages of the FTA negotiations, wrote the Treasury's post mortem on them and noted that the French 'had us beaten on tactics the whole time'.[11] De Gaulle was particularly skilful in securing the crucial support of Adenauer. In his biography of Macmillan, Alistair Horne writes of the 'seduction' of the West German Chancellor. This is hardly an exaggeration. In the course of two highly successful exchange visits in 1958 de Gaulle exerted all his considerable charm to win Adenauer's confidence. When he visited him at Bad Kreuznach in November 1958, he was lavish in his flattery, praising him as 'a great man, a great statesman, a great European and a great German'.[12] According to the then British ambassador in Bonn, Sir Christopher Steel, it was at the Bad Kreuznach meeting that de Gaulle obtained Adenauer's backing for vetoing the British proposals for an industrial FTA. Over the next few years de Gaulle was to intensify his efforts to forge a closer link with West Germany. A key element in this campaign, as we have seen, was his unyielding verbal stand against Soviet pressure over Berlin. As it was meant to do, this presented a sharp contrast with Macmillan's apparent willingness to discuss and conciliate. Nor was de Gaulle slow to fan Adenauer's suspicions about the British Prime Minister's intentions. His strategy finally paid dividends in January 1963 when Adenauer travelled to Paris to sign the Franco-German Treaty of Friendship and Cooperation, despite de Gaulle's recent veto of Britain's application for entry to the EC.

Clearly, the personality and role of de Gaulle are central to any consideration of Anglo-French relations and the EC during the late 1950s and the 1960s.[13] After a twelve-year period of self-imposed political exile, de Gaulle returned to power at the beginning of June 1958 in response to the need for a settlement of the deepening

11. PRO, FO 371/150154, 10 October 1959.
12. Horne, *Macmillan*, vol. II, p. 112.
13. The most detailed study of de Gaulle available in English is J. Lacouture, *De Gaulle: The Rebel 1890–1944*, translated by P. O'Brian (1990) and *De Gaulle: The Ruler 1945–1970*, translated by A. Sheridan (1991).

Algerian crisis. For the next decade – first as Prime Minister and then (after December 1958) as President of the new Fifth Republic – he exerted a decisive influence on French policy. After an uncertain start, he gradually consolidated his hold on power and by the end of 1962 his domestic political position was unassailable – buttressed by the successful negotiation of a ceasefire in Algeria in the previous March, by the massive backing that he obtained in the referendum of October over the question of popular election of the President, and by sweeping Gaullist gains in the November general election.

De Gaulle's complex and ambivalent attitude towards Britain was largely the product of two main factors: his experience of the Second World War and his tendency to lump the British and the Americans together as 'Anglo-Saxons'.[14] After the capitulation of France in 1940, de Gaulle had found himself in a difficult and in many ways humiliating position. As the self-appointed head of a defeated state, he was based in London and almost wholly dependent on the cooperation and goodwill of Britain and the US.[15] It was a situation in which friction and mutual suspicion were bound to flourish. De Gaulle was a proud and sensitive man who was quick to see slights, whether real or imagined. He believed that he was not accorded the respect and consideration that were his due. He suspected the British of planning to take advantage of French difficulties to extend their own influence in the Middle East. Moreover, he was understandably incensed by President Roosevelt's attempt in 1943 to replace him as leader of the Free French forces with General Henri Giraud. There were faults on both sides. Roosevelt disliked de Gaulle and was certainly heavy-handed and tactless in his dealings with him.[16] But de Gaulle himself – obstinate, unpredictable, opinionated and immensely conscious of his own dignity – was not the easiest person to handle. Churchill famously declared that he had many crosses to bear during the war, but the heaviest by far was the Cross of Lorraine, de Gaulle's personal symbol.

14. For de Gaulle's dealings with the British and American governments from 1958 to 1969 see Newhouse, *De Gaulle and the Anglo-Saxons*.

15. The complex wartime relationships between de Gaulle, Churchill and Roosevelt are treated in detail in Lacouture, *De Gaulle: The Rebel*, parts III and IV. For good brief accounts see E. Barker, *Churchill and Eden at War* (1978); Bell, *France and Britain 1940–1994*, chs. 2 and 3. See also R. Dallek, 'Roosevelt and De Gaulle', in R.O. Paxton and N. Wahl (eds), *De Gaulle and the United States: A Centennial Reappraisal* (1994), pp. 49–60; Newhouse, *De Gaulle and the United States*, pp. 30–32.

16. Roosevelt is supposed to have described de Gaulle as 'the prima donna who wanted to play both Joan of Arc and Georges Clemenceau': cited in P. Galante with J. Miller, *The General* (1969), p. 123.

The war left de Gaulle with a deep sense of grievance rather than gratitude towards his British and American allies. Nor did he find it easy to come to terms with the shame of France's collapse and surrender. The fact that the British had managed to avoid a like fate only rubbed salt in the wound. Macmillan was convinced that this continued to gnaw at de Gaulle and helped to explain his hostility to British membership of the EC. As he told his biographer: 'Things would have been easier if Southern England had been occupied by the Nazis . . . I may be cynical, but I fear it's true – if Hitler had danced in London we would have had no trouble with de Gaulle.'[17]

During the war – as de Gaulle made a point of mentioning to Macmillan at their Rambouillet meeting of December 1962 – Churchill told the Free French leader that if he was forced to choose between him and Roosevelt, he would always choose Roosevelt.[18] The remark left an indelible impression on de Gaulle, who never ceased to regard Britain as a junior partner of the US rather than as a truly European state. Macmillan's assiduous attention to repairing the 'special relationship' after Suez only reinforced his conviction that a Britain inside the EC would serve as a Trojan horse, promoting and protecting American interests. Paradoxically, therefore, the more Kennedy pressed de Gaulle to admit the British, the more the latter was confirmed in the correctness of his analysis and the more determined he became to exclude them.

It would be a mistake to regard the suspicion and dislike with which de Gaulle viewed the 'Anglo-Saxons', and the Americans in particular, as nothing more than a reflection of his own idiosyncratic and quirky outlook. As a matter of fact, his anti-Americanism struck a chord in many sections of French society, where there was an instinctive distaste for what was seen as American cultural and economic imperialism.[19] In the France of the 1960s there was widespread concern about the activities of large American corporations. This was reflected in a book which was published in 1967 – *Le Défi Américain* (*The American Challenge*) – in which the author, Jean-Jacques Servan-Schreiber, a journalist and politician, warned his countrymen of the dangers of US economic penetration of Europe.[20] The

17. Horne, *Macmillan*, vol. II, p. 319.
18. PRO, PREM 11/4230, Record of a conversation at Rambouillet at 12 noon on Sunday 16 December 1962.
19. For French attitudes towards the United States see D. Lacorne (ed.), *The Rise and Fall of Anti-Americanism. A Century of French Perceptions* (1990).
20. R.F. Kuisel, 'The American economic challenge: De Gaulle and the French', in Paxton and Wahl (eds), *De Gaulle and the United States*, pp. 208–12.

closure of Remington's French factory in 1962 had already provided a practical illustration of this danger, in the process provoking a major press campaign against 'dollar imperialism'.

De Gaulle himself looked askance at the hegemony of the dollar, regarding its position as the world's reserve currency as both unacceptably advantageous to the US and inherently inflationary.[21] His resentment against the Anglo-Saxons was also extremely strong in two other areas: nuclear collaboration and NATO.[22] Following the repeal of the McMahon Act in 1958, Britain obtained access to American nuclear know-how. As a result of the Nassau Agreement of December 1962, it was also provided with the Polaris missile. None of this, however, was available to France, which remained outside the privileged, Anglo-Saxon nuclear club. Matters were not helped by a lack of sensitivity for French feelings on the part of the Americans. The French were enraged by a speech by Robert McNamara, the American Defense Secretary, at Ann Arbor, Michigan, in June 1962 in which he condemned all national nuclear forces except those of the US as 'dangerous' and 'lacking in credibility'. Kennedy gave further offence soon afterwards when, at a press conference, he described de Gaulle's nuclear policy as 'unfriendly'.[23]

De Gaulle, for his part, was determined that France should have an independent modern and sophisticated nuclear capacity, partly for reasons of national security, but also as a matter of prestige.[24] Macmillan was prepared to be helpful, especially if it facilitated British entry to the EC. He was hamstrung, however, by the uncooperative attitude of Washington. De Gaulle raised the issue at least twice: during their meeting at the Château de Champs in June 1962 and again at Rambouillet six months later. Both occasions produced serious misunderstandings about what had been said and agreed. Macmillan believed he had made it clear that his hands were tied because of the line taken by the Americans. De Gaulle was equally convinced that he had been offered the prospect of

21. For de Gaulle's critical views on the role of the dollar in the international monetary system see D.P. Calleo, 'De Gaulle and the monetary system: the Golden rule', in Paxton and Wahl (eds), *De Gaulle and the United States*, pp. 239–55.

22. A detailed discussion of de Gaulle's differences with the United States over NATO and nuclear weaponry is to be found in P.G. Cerny, *The Politics of Grandeur: Ideological Aspects of de Gaulle's Foreign Policy* (1980), chs. 7 and 8. See also P. Messmer, 'De Gaulle's defense policy and the United States from 1958–69', in Paxton and Wahl (eds), *De Gaulle and the United States*, pp. 351–7.

23. H. Macmillan, *At the End of the Day 1961–1963* (1973), p. 123; Horne, *Macmillan*, vol. II, p. 330; Newhouse, *De Gaulle and the Anglo-Saxons*, pp. 187–8.

24. For de Gaulle's views on French possession of independent nuclear weapons see Lacouture, *De Gaulle: The Ruler*, ch. 31.

Anglo-French collaboration. His disappointment with the outcome of the Nassau meeting between Kennedy and Macmillan was all the greater, therefore, and doubtless helped to confirm him in his intention to veto Britain's application for entry to the EC.

De Gaulle was equally unsuccessful in his attempts to secure a more important role for France in the NATO command structure, which he believed to be too much under American (and to a lesser extent British) control. As has been seen, as early as 1958 he proposed the establishment of a three-power 'directorate' involving France, Britain and the US. He continued to press for such a change during the early 1960s and finally, when he failed to make any headway, withdrew France from NATO's integrated command structure in April 1966.

As far as de Gaulle was concerned, the Anglo-Saxons' attitude on NATO and nuclear collaboration made a mockery of all their talk of cooperation between the US and Europe – as expressed, for example, in Kennedy's celebrated 'Grand Design' speech of 4 July 1962. De Gaulle's own vision was of a 'Europe for the Europeans' rather than an 'Atlanticist Europe', one which assumed responsibility for its own defence and which was less dependent on the US. In such a vision, there was no place for a Britain still wedded to the idea of a 'special relationship'.

There are two other points worth making about de Gaulle and Britain's relations with the Six. Both of them present paradoxes. The first is that de Gaulle, the man who barred Britain's entry to the EC, at the same time made the prospect of joining more palatable to British opinion by his thoroughgoing scepticism about European integration. Having ridiculed the project for an EDC in the early 1950s, de Gaulle thereafter consistently made it clear that he had little time for the ideas of the more advanced 'Europeans' like Monnet and Spaak or, for that matter, of some leading Gaullists like Michel Debré. Indeed, at a press conference which he held in May 1962 he expressed his opposition to the supranational development of the EC in such strong terms that five ministers in his government felt obliged to resign. During EC discussions on political cooperation in 1961–2 (in the Fouchet Committee), de Gaulle was determined to ensure that such cooperation should be kept at the strictly intergovernmental level. Moreover, as will be seen in Chapter 12, when de Gaulle plunged the EC into a major crisis in 1965 by boycotting meetings of the Council of Ministers, the issue on which he made his stand was the sovereignty of each member state. As Macmillan rightly noted in his diary at the time of Britain's first application, there was in fact a broad similarity between the Gaullist and the British conceptions of how the EC should develop. De Gaulle wanted the kind of Community that Britain would feel able to join, wrote Macmillan, but without the British in: 'L'Europe à l'anglais sans les Anglais'.[25]

The second paradox worth noting is that Britain's application for entry, although unwelcome to de Gaulle, in the event proved to be of considerable benefit to France. The fact that most members of the Six were anxious to see Britain obtain admission gave de Gaulle a great deal of bargaining power. He used it to good effect. In January 1962, for example, he was able to force through an agreement on agricultural policy that was highly favourable to French interests by making its acceptance a precondition of continuing talks with Britain.

So long as de Gaulle remained in power there was clearly no real possibility of British entry to the EC. In 1969 the situation was transformed. De Gaulle's position was badly shaken by the upheaval known as the 'events' of May 1968. In the ensuing elections, which were called in June, the Gaullists and their allies won a resounding victory. The President's own authority, however, had not been fully restored. In April 1969 a referendum was held on a series of proposed constitutional changes. Although the verdict was a 'yes', it was only by a narrow margin, and de Gaulle immediately resigned. With his departure, the main impediment to British membership of the EC had at last been removed.

25. Macmillan, *At the End of the Day*, p. 118.

CHAPTER ELEVEN

Labour's Retreat into Europe

After de Gaulle's rebuff in January 1963, it was to be another four years before Britain again sought entry to the EC. A second attempt was made by Harold Wilson's Labour government in the summer of 1967. The outcome was the same as in 1963: Britain's application was blocked by a French veto. Moreover, the reason offered by de Gaulle was essentially the same as before, namely that Britain was still too heavily involved in extra-European commitments to be a satisfactory member of the Community. There was, though, one important difference this time: in 1963, the veto came after more than a year of tortuous and detailed negotiations; in 1967, by contrast, formal negotiations had not even started when de Gaulle delivered his unfavourable verdict.

The Wilson government's decision to seek British membership of the EC occasioned considerable surprise in many quarters since it seemed to be totally at variance with the predominantly negative stance that Labour had adopted while in Opposition. At the time of Macmillan's application, after a period of ambiguity and equivocation dictated mainly by tactical considerations, the party had moved in a strongly anti direction. As has been seen, at Labour's annual conference at Brighton in early October 1962, Gaitskell had delivered a passionate attack on the government's handling of the Common Market negotiations and set out conditions for entry which were tantamount to outright rejection. His performance had dismayed some of his closest supporters, such as George Brown and Roy Jenkins, who were ardent pro-Europeans. It had been given a rapturous reception by most of the audience, however, and clearly struck a chord in the party at large.

Other leading figures in the Labour Party shared Gaitskell's growing antipathy to the idea of British membership of the EC. These included Harold Wilson, at that time Shadow Foreign Secretary.[1] In January 1963 Gaitskell died suddenly and in the leadership contest that followed Wilson defeated his main rivals, George Brown and James Callaghan. When Labour took power in October 1964, therefore, the new government was led by a man who had started off as a sceptic on the question of British membership of the Community and who had subsequently moved towards a hostile position. Yet within three years of taking office, Wilson had apparently become an enthusiastic convert to the cause. He intended to apply, he told the House of Commons in May 1967, and he would not take no for an answer.

Some of the reasons why Wilson had changed his mind by 1967 will be examined in more detail later in the chapter, but there is a general point which might be made now. There seems to be broad agreement among historians – including C.J. Bartlett and Stephen George – that a key factor was experience of office.[2] It was easy enough while in Opposition to attack the Conservative government's supposedly weak negotiating stance towards the Six and to argue that there was a perfectly satisfactory future for Britain outside the EC. Once in power, however, Wilson faced the same hard economic and political realities that had earlier caused Macmillan to shift his ground. 'As he [Wilson] sees it', Richard Crossman noted in his diary in February 1966, 'the difficulties of staying outside Europe and surviving as an independent power are very great compared with entering on the right conditions.'[3] There was also steady pressure from the Foreign Office, where the Permanent Under-Secretary, Sir Paul Gore-Booth, and Sir Con O'Neill, who had served as UK ambassador to the EC between 1963 and 1965, were strong advocates of British membership.[4] In Whitehall generally, it was now the received wisdom that Britain ought to join the EC. Apart from the Foreign Office, the newly created Department of Economic Affairs (DEA), with George Brown as its political head and

1. See Wilson's Commons speech of 7 June 1962: cited in U. Kitzinger, *The Second Try: Labour and the EEC* (1968), pp. 83–99.

2. C.J. Bartlett, *British Foreign Policy in the Twentieth Century* (1989), p. 119; S. George, *An Awkward Partner: Britain in the European Community* (1991), p. 37.

3. R. Crossman, *The Diaries of a Cabinet Minister, vol. I, Minister of Housing 1964–66* (1975), p. 461, diary entry of 18 February 1966.

4. J.W. Young, *Britain and European Unity, 1945–1992* (1993), p. 88. Alongside Gore-Booth and O'Neill, there was a younger generation of strongly pro-European officials, including Michael Palliser, Michael Butler and John Robinson, who were beginning to move up the Foreign Office hierarchy in the early 1960s. For the influence of what he calls this 'elite regiment' see H. Young, *This Blessed Plot: Britain and Europe from Churchill to Blair* (1998), pp. 172–80, 185–6, 189–90.

Sir Eric Roll as its Permanent Under-Secretary, was a major force in pushing the case for entry.[5]

In the 1960s Wilson presided over two administrations, the first lasting from October 1964 to March 1966 and the second from March 1966 to June 1970. During the first of these the question of Britain's relations with the EC was not a high priority. There were a number of reasons for this. The first and most obvious was that at that stage Wilson had not yet abandoned his own negative attitude towards British membership. Secondly, there were far more urgent matters to be attended to. At the top of the agenda was the government's survival. The general election of October 1964 had left Labour with a precarious overall majority of only five. This was soon whittled down even further. In the general election, Patrick Gordon Walker, the Shadow Foreign Secretary, had been defeated at Smethwick by a candidate playing the race card. Wilson nevertheless appointed him Foreign Secretary and a by-election was duly arranged for January 1965 in the 'safe' Labour seat of Leyton. Unfortunately for the government, the hapless Gordon Walker suffered another defeat. He was replaced as Foreign Secretary by Michael Stewart and the government's overall majority was now down to three. With such a wafer-thin margin, there could be no question of taking a major foreign policy initiative, especially on an issue that was likely to be extremely divisive. The government's over-riding objective at this stage was to hang on to power until it was possible to hold another general election under more favourable circumstances and thereby obtain a comfortable working majority.

In the meantime, there were pressing domestic matters to be attended to, the most urgent of which was the balance of payments deficit that had been inherited from the previous government. On the very day they took office, Labour ministers were informed by the Treasury that there was a predicted deficit of £800 million for 1964 – twice the gloomiest estimate that Wilson himself had made during the election campaign. By today's standards, that might seem a trifling amount, but then it was regarded as catastrophic. Action had to be taken immediately. Devaluation was ruled out, a decision which has since been widely criticised as a profound mistake whose consequences were to dog the government for the remainder of its term. Instead, it was decided – much to the indignation of Britain's EFTA partners – to introduce a temporary import surcharge. This measure brought short-term relief. For the next few years, however,

5. Young, *Britain and European Unity*, pp. 87–8.

until the enforced devaluation of November 1967, the government found itself engaged in a desperate struggle to maintain the parity of the pound.[6]

The government's attention was also absorbed by a number of other domestic issues. There was a major programme of economic and social reform to be implemented, including renationalisation of the steel industry, reintroduction of rent controls and the provision of additional legal safeguards for the trade unions. Pensions were to be increased and prescription charges abolished, and in September 1965 the government unveiled the much-heralded National Plan, the centrepiece of Labour's strategy for reversing Britain's long-term economic decline.

Insofar as the Wilson government *was* interested in foreign affairs in the period 1964–6, its attention tended to be focused on events outside Europe. The biggest challenge was presented by the crisis over Rhodesia, where a white minority was intent on preserving the privileged position that it currently enjoyed. In November 1965 Ian Smith, the Rhodesian Prime Minister, announced a unilateral declaration of independence (UDI). Wilson retaliated by instituting an economic embargo and for the remainder of his period in power was involved in a fruitless attempt to bring the illegal regime to its knees. It would be no exaggeration to speak of Wilson having an obsession with Rhodesia.[7]

In order to make the embargo effective, it was essential to have cooperation from the US. American cooperation was also vital in the fight to maintain the value of the pound. But there was a price to be paid. In return, Lyndon B. Johnson, the American Democratic President, demanded British support for US policy in Vietnam. More generally, the British government was asked to maintain its role east of Suez, patrolling the Indian Ocean and Persian Gulf, keeping a military presence in Malaysia and generally aiding the US in the global struggle against communism. The bargain – at first implicit, later explicit – was struck by Wilson and Johnson during visits to Washington by the former in December 1964 and December 1965.[8]

The role that the US wanted Britain to play east of Suez was not uncongenial to many members of the government, including Michael Stewart, the Foreign Secretary, Denis Healey, the Secretary

---

6. B. Pimlott, *Harold Wilson* (1992), pp. 350–54.
7. For Wilson's struggle to solve the Rhodesian crisis see Pimlott, *Harold Wilson*, pp. 366–81.
8. *Ibid.*, pp. 365–6, 377, 383–8.

of State for Defence, and Wilson himself. As Wilson told the House of Commons in December 1964: 'I want to make it quite clear that whatever we may do in the field of cost-effectiveness, we cannot afford to relinquish our world role – our role which, for shorthand purposes, is sometimes called our "east of Suez" role.'[9] At the same time, the government's east of Suez stance was not without its Labour critics. It came under fire not only from the vast majority of those on the left of the party, but also from some of its pro-European members who saw it as expensive, unnecessary and an obstacle to British entry into the EC. As we shall see, this was the line taken by Brown, who argued passionately that Britain's future lay in Europe.

During his first administration Wilson personally showed little interest in the question of Britain's relations with the Six. The one exception was a number of tentative moves which he made in the spring of 1965 about the possibility of some form of limited industrial free trade association between EFTA and the EC. This was a suggestion which predictably failed to enthuse the Community. In the meantime, other ministers were already beginning to take up positions and the battle lines were being drawn. In June 1965 Douglas Jay (President of the Board of Trade) and Fred Peart (Minister of Agriculture), both of whom were strongly opposed to joining the Common Market, produced a paper on the commercial and agricultural implications of doing so which came to some very gloomy conclusions. At the other end of the spectrum, Stewart, the pro-membership Foreign Secretary, in December 1965 advised Wilson to make an immediate application.[10]

At that stage, Wilson was not keen to have the matter discussed, not least because of the imminence of a general election. With the calling of an election for March 1966, however, the European issue soon became a topic of lively debate. This was inevitable, given the attitude of Edward Heath, the leader of the Conservative Party. As has been seen, Heath, who had replaced Sir Alec Douglas-Home in August 1965, had a pro-European record which went back to 1950 when he had criticised the Attlee government for not responding with greater warmth to the Schuman Plan. Between 1961 and 1963 he had conducted the Brussels negotiations for British entry to the EC with great enthusiasm and determination, and he went into the 1966 election campaign firmly committed to making

9. *H.C.Deb.*, vol. 704, cols. 423–4, 16 December 1964: cited in P. Darby, *British Defence Policy East of Suez 1947–1968* (1973), p. 285.

10. D. Jay, *Change and Fortune* (1980), p. 361; Crossman, *The Diaries of a Cabinet Minister*, vol. I, diary entries of 31 January and 2 February 1966.

a second attempt.[11] Wilson was therefore obliged to define his own position.

As yet, Wilson himself had no particularly strong feelings on the matter. His overriding objective, as so often, was to prevent a split being caused in Labour's ranks. This was reflected in the carefully ambiguous stance he adopted which was designed to satisfy both the pro- and anti-marketeers (the terms commonly applied to supporters and opponents of British membership of the EC during the 1960s and 1970s) within the party. The position that Wilson adopted was strikingly similar to that of Gaitskell in 1961–2. On the one hand, he claimed to be in favour of entry; on the other, he stipulated conditions which in fact stood no real chance of being accepted by the Six.[12] His position was summed up in a key election speech at Bristol on 18 March: 'Negotiations? Yes. Unconditional acceptance of whatever terms are on offer? No.' In this speech, while setting out the potential benefits of EC membership, Wilson insisted that there must be safeguards for continuing imports of cheap food, the interests of the Commonwealth and the right of the British government to pursue an independent foreign policy. Unable to resist a sideswipe at Heath, he accused him of subservience to the French: 'One encouraging gesture from the French Government', he said, 'and the Conservative leader rolls on his back like a spaniel.'[13]

The general election of March 1966 gave Labour an overall majority of 97. The government was therefore now in a position, if it wished, to proceed towards a second application for entry to the Community. Wilson appointed George Thomson, the Chancellor of the Duchy of Lancaster, as the minister to conduct negotiations. He also set up a Cabinet committee to deal with the question. Apart from Wilson himself, this committee represented a mix of supporters and opponents of British membership. Those opposed included Jay, Peart and Healey, the last of whom was subsequently to alter his opinion on the issue several times. The most prominent

11. The Conservatives' manifesto committed them to 'work energetically for entry to the European Common Market at the first favourable opportunity': E. Heath, *The Course of My Life: My Autobiography* (1998), p. 356.

12. Heath, *The Course of My Life*, p. 356; Young, *Britain and European Unity*, p. 91. Labour's 1966 election manifesto, *Time for Decision*, stated that 'Britain should be ready to enter the European Economic Community, provided essential British and Commonwealth interests are safeguarded.'

13. *The Guardian*, 19 March 1966; H. Wilson, *The Labour Government 1964–1970: A Personal Record* (1971), pp. 217–18; Heath, *The Course of My Life*, p. 356. For the full text of Wilson's speech see Kitzinger, *The Second Try*, pp. 108–12.

member of the other camp was Brown. A conspicuous absentee was one of the most ardent pro-Europeans within the Cabinet, Roy Jenkins.[14]

Throughout the remainder of 1966 the government moved closer to a decision to seek membership. Initially, Wilson proceeded slowly and cautiously. He was acutely conscious that the Cabinet and the Labour movement as a whole were deeply divided on the question. In any case, too rapid a conversion from scepticism to enthusiasm about entry would have posed serious problems of credibility. By the spring of 1967, however, the drift towards Europe was gaining a momentum that was virtually unstoppable.

Various explanations have been advanced for Labour's decision to apply for membership. It has been suggested, for example, that Wilson was engaged in a Machiavellian exercise: he knew that there was no chance of securing entry and the application was intended to prove just that. Wilson's biographer, Ben Pimlott, dismisses this interpretation as fundamentally implausible. If that really had been Wilson's intention, Pimlott argues, he would not have become so personally involved in the application in a way that risked exposure to humiliation.[15] Another, more convincing, suggestion is that Wilson – the master tactician and political manipulator – was motivated to some extent at least by calculations of party advantage. He knew that Heath was fervently pro-European and would want to make it a major issue at the next general election. He therefore took action to neutralise a potential Conservative weapon. If the negotiations succeeded, he would gain credit; if they failed, at least Labour could not be accused of not even making an effort. Labour's application for entry has also been seen as a response to the failure of certain key aspects of government policy – in particular, the collapse of its economic strategy. A typical press comment at the time was that the bid to get into the Common Market was little more than 'a desperate "try anything" move to jolt the economy into active life'.[16] In a similar vein, Tony Benn was later to say of the events of 1967: 'We were now looking for a solution to our problems from outside and somehow we were persuaded that the Common Market was the way of making progress.'[17]

14. Pimlott, *Harold Wilson*, p. 434.   15. *Ibid.*, p. 438.

16. *Evening Standard*, Robert Carvell, 11 July 1967.

17. T. Benn, *The Benn Diaries*, single volume edition, selected, abridged and introduced by R. Winstone (1996), p. 171. Harold Wilson had earlier offered a similar analysis in relation to the 1961 application for EC entry, describing it as 'an exercise in economic escapism': *H.C.Deb.*, vol. 645, col. 1653, 3 August 1961.

In 1964 Wilson had successfully presented himself to the electorate as the man who could solve the persistent British problem of
slow economic growth. It was to be done through the coordination
of resources and investment by means of a National Plan. The idea
of such a plan was inspired to some extent by the example of
French postwar indicative planning. In addition, it owed something
to the belief – which nowadays seems incredible – that the Soviet
command economy was performing more efficiently than capitalist
models. There were also echoes of the Attlee government's experiment of 1947, when it had set up a Ministry of Economic Affairs
within the Treasury.

The implementation of the National Plan, which was unveiled
with a flourish in September 1965, was to be overseen by George
Brown at the head of a new super-ministry, the DEA. The targets it
set were highly ambitious: economic growth of 25 per cent over the
next five years, an average of almost 4 per cent per annum. Not
surprisingly, they were never met. From the outset the DEA and the
Treasury viewed each other with intense suspicion. Moreover, their
political masters, Brown and Callaghan, were fierce rivals who had
not long before been engaged in a contest for the Labour Party
leadership. What really brought about the collapse of the National
Plan, however, was the existence of contradictory strands within
government policy. For the National Plan to succeed, it was necessary to provide expansionary conditions. Yet the maintenance of
the value of the pound, which was the chief priority as far as the
Treasury was concerned, required retrenchment. The two goals
were simply incompatible, and attempts to square the circle came
to a disastrous end in July 1966 when a heavy run on sterling compelled the government to introduce a severe deflationary package,
including a freeze on prices and wages. This signalled the effective
end of the National Plan and the prospects of rapid economic
growth. The centrepiece of the government's economic policy lay
in ruins.[18] In the vacuum thus created, entry into the EC was seen
as an alternative route to economic salvation. In psychological terms,
Europe provided a strategic goal and a sense of a crusading mission
previously offered by the National Plan.

There were other factors that prompted the Wilson government
to seek a future for Britain within the EC. One of the most important
was the realisation that a future *outside* it was not all that appealing.
This, in turn, was bound up with growing reservations about the

18. Pimlott, *Harold Wilson*, pp. 360–64, 408–30.

Commonwealth, the special relationship with the US and Britain's east of Suez role.

The Wilson government began with high hopes for the Commonwealth, from both the economic and the political standpoint. Wilson himself was strongly committed to the idea of the Commonwealth, viewing it as a promising interracial community that had an important and distinctive part to play in world affairs. He had an emotional attachment to the old dominions which went back to his youth and which was doubtless not unconnected with a visit he had paid then to a favourite uncle in Australia. He was also interested in the problems of underdeveloped countries, having written extensively about Third World poverty during the 1950s. In the 1964 election campaign, he laid considerable emphasis on the need to develop closer links with the Commonwealth and offered the prospect of a substantial expansion of Commonwealth trade as one of the main answers to Britain's economic difficulties – an echo of his time as a young President of the Board of Trade in the first postwar Attlee government. Attacking the Conservatives for allowing the Commonwealth's share of British trade to fall from 44 per cent to 30 per cent, Wilson pledged himself to reverse this trend. His pledge, however, was not fulfilled. During the mid- and late 1960s trade with the Commonwealth grew at only a modest rate. By contrast, over the same period Britain and the other members of the Commonwealth found themselves trading more and more with the EC.[19]

In political terms, too, Wilson's experience with the Commonwealth proved disillusioning, largely because of the problems created by the Rhodesian crisis. Throughout his period in office Wilson was haunted by the spectre of Rhodesia. The British government came under intense pressure, especially from President Kenneth Kaunda of Zambia and other African leaders, to bring down Ian Smith's illegal regime. From the outset Wilson ruled out the use of force, accepting that the logistical problems involved in such a policy would be enormous. Instead, he relied on the imposition of economic sanctions. In an effort to quieten Commonwealth critics, Wilson was unwise enough to predict, at a conference held at Lagos in early 1966, that these sanctions would bring the rebellion to an end 'in weeks rather than months'. The economic embargo proved a failure, however, and British prestige was thereby dealt a great

---

19. R.J. Lieber, *British Politics and European Unity: Parties, Elites and Pressure Groups* (1970), pp. 261–2. For Wilson's disillusionment on economic relations with the Commonwealth see PRO, CAB 128/42, CC(67)26th Conclusions, 30 April 1967.

blow. The protracted Rhodesian affair also imposed severe strains on the unity of the Commonwealth, which at times appeared to be on the point of breaking up because of the bitter discord that the question generated. In his book *Breach of Promise*, Clive Ponting has suggested that another element in Wilson's growing disenchantment with the Commonwealth was the acceptance by India and Pakistan in 1965 of Soviet rather than British mediation to end their border conflict.[20]

In addition to doubts about the Commonwealth, fundamental questions were also being raised in the second half of the 1960s about Britain's role as joint world policeman with the US. This was in part because of disquiet about escalation of the Vietnam war. Wilson never bowed to pressure to dissociate himself from American policy. He nevertheless refused to send a contingent of UK troops, as Johnson wanted, and was increasingly unhappy at having to defend continuing British support for a war which a growing number within the Labour movement as a whole, as well as within the government itself, found wholly unacceptable. More generally, by 1966 at the latest it was patently obvious that Britain's east of Suez role was simply beyond its financial and military resources. It was no longer a matter of *whether* to withdraw from it but *when*. The strains were self-evident. In February 1966 there were heavy cuts in naval strength, including the decision not to build a new aircraft carrier. The Defence White Paper which announced these cuts highlighted the essence of Britain's dilemma when it declared that there was no point in being a world policeman if you didn't have the resources to fulfil such a role.[21]

The lesson which at least some senior members of the Wilson government drew from these trends and developments was that it was time for a change of direction: a shift away from the 'special relationship', the Commonwealth and a role east of Suez, and towards a future in the EC. This view was strongest among right-wing ministers like Jenkins, the Home Secretary, Crosland, the Education Secretary, and above all Brown. The last-named had long been an enthusiastic supporter of Britain's entry to the EC and by 1966 was utterly convinced that Britain's destiny lay in that direction. More than that, he was supremely confident that the Six were eagerly awaiting British leadership, telling Willy Brandt, then the Foreign Minister of West Germany: 'Willy, you must get us in so we can take

20. C. Ponting, *Breach of Promise: Labour in Power 1964–1970* (1987), p. 205.
21. Cmd. 2901, *Statement on the Defence Estimate, 1966: Part I, The Defence Review.*

the lead.'[22] Brown's impatience to make Britain a member of the EC is brought out clearly in a conversation he had at the height of the financial crisis of July 1966 with Barbara Castle, the Minister of Transport, who was herself a strong opponent of entry. According to the account in Castle's diary, Brown said that he was sick of having to defend the Americans over Vietnam:

> 'We've got to break with America, devalue and go into Europe.' 'Devalue if you like,' I [Castle] said, 'but Europe no. I'll fight you on that.' 'But I believe it passionately, we've got to go somewhere. We can't manage alone.'[23]

The reference in this extract to devaluation may appear somewhat puzzling. What has to be remembered, though, is that in the debate taking place during 1966 the questions of entry to the EC and devaluation of the pound were regarded as being inextricably linked. This is reflected in the label that Wilson applied to Jenkins and Crosland when he described them, with some contempt, as the 'European devaluers'.[24] The reason for this connection was quite straightforward. There was general agreement among British policymakers that before Britain could join the EC it would need to improve its economic competitiveness by devaluing its overvalued currency. This was also the view of the French, as their Prime Minister, Georges Pompidou, and Foreign Minister, Couve de Murville, made clear during discussions in London with Wilson and other British ministers on 7 July 1966.[25]

Brown's wholehearted commitment to entry was an important factor. Certainly that was the opinion of Jay who later claimed that 'the application to join the Market would probably never have been made' if Brown had carried out his threat to resign during the July 1966 financial crisis.[26] As deputy leader of the Labour Party and the most senior minister after Wilson, Brown exercised considerable

22. W. Brandt, *People and Politics: The Years 1960–1975*, translated by J. Maxwell Brownjohn (1978), p. 161.
23. B. Castle, *The Castle Diaries 1964–1976* (1990), p. 75, diary entry of Monday 18 July 1966.
24. Cited in Pimlott, *Harold Wilson*, p. 421.
25. *Ibid.*, p. 414; Young, *Britain and European Unity*, p. 92. For a French account of the meeting see M.N.L. Couve de Murville, *Une politique étrangère, 1958–1969*, part 3 (1971), pp. 416–19. The need for devaluation of sterling before British entry to the EC was a recurring message from French statesmen. See, for example, PRO, PREM 13/922, Record of conversation between Christopher Soames and Couve de Murville in Paris on 24 November 1966; PRO, PREM 13/1476, Reilly (Paris) to FO, 26 January 1967; *ibid.*, Record of a meeting held at the Elysée Palace on Wednesday 25 January 1967 at 4.15 p.m.
26. Jay, *Change and Fortune*, p. 363.

influence over government policy. He was not without serious character weaknesses – including a volatile temperament, an extraordinary capacity for rudeness and an excessive fondness for both women
and alcohol. But despite these flaws he had a strong following
within the Labour movement, reflected in a popular saying of the
time: 'Better George drunk than Harold sober'.[27] In August 1966,
he left the DEA to replace Stewart as Foreign Secretary. This move
was rightly seen, both at home and in the Community, as a clear
indication that the government was in earnest about making a bid
for membership of the EC. At the Foreign Office, Brown teamed
up with strongly pro-EC officials like Sir Con O'Neill, and from this
time onwards the drive towards an application began to accelerate.

On 22 October 1966 the matter was discussed by relevant members of the Cabinet at an all-day meeting held at Chequers.[28] The
morning session was also attended by senior civil servants. One
of these, Sir William Armstrong, the Joint Permanent Secretary at
the Treasury, put something of a damper on proceedings when he
announced that, in his judgement, there could be no question of
applying within the next two years because of the weakness of the
economy. Armstrong added that it would almost certainly be necessary to devalue as a precondition of entry. Ministerial opinion was
sharply divided. Brown and Stewart, who was now Secretary of State
for Economic Affairs, argued that Britain had no real alternative
but to join. It was essential, they insisted, not for economic reasons,
but rather to keep up Britain's international status and its place
at the 'top table'. They were supported by seven other ministers,
including Jenkins and Crosland. Among the eight who spoke on
the other side were Jay, Peart, Healey, Castle and William Ross, the
Scottish Secretary. Crossman, the Lord President and Leader of the
House of Commons, indicated that he, too, was really opposed to
making a bid, but was nonetheless prepared to go along with it
because he thought that in the end it would come to nothing in
view of the attitude of the French: 'the General will save us from
our folly'.[29] Wilson, who refrained from stating his own views, came
up with the suggestion that he and the Foreign Secretary should
together visit each of the capitals of the Six. The idea behind this

27. Pimlott, *Harold Wilson*, pp. 329–31.
28. For a summary of the arguments put forward at the Chequers meeting see
PRO, PREM 13/909, Burke Trend to Prime Minister, 28 October 1966. See also *The
Benn Diaries*, p. 165, diary entry of 22 October 1966; B. Castle, *Fighting All the Way*
(1993), p. 474; Crossman, *The Diaries of a Cabinet Minister*, vol. II, pp. 81–5; Jay,
Change and Fortune, pp. 365–6.
29. R. Marsh, *Off the Rails* (1978), p. 96.

was that they should sound out opinion and convince EC leaders of the seriousness of British intentions.[30]

This suggestion was not well received. Brown, who regarded it as 'a mad idea', joined several other ministers in trying to dissuade Wilson. But the latter was determined to go ahead. Early in November 1966 he was advised by Crossman and John Silkin, the Chief Whip, that there was no major opposition to his proposed course of action within the party, and on 10 November he announced to Parliament that it was the government's intention to enter the EC – provided essential British and Commonwealth interests could be safeguarded. 'We mean business', he declared. Brown's reaction to Wilson's statement was that the 'juggernaut had started to roll, and nothing could now stop it'.[31]

The exploratory probe by Brown and Wilson began with a visit to Rome on 15 January 1967. It then continued until early March. The overall response was not particularly encouraging. In Bonn, for example, where a coalition of Christian Democrats and Social Democrats led by Kurt Kiesinger and Willy Brandt respectively was in power, it was made clear that the West German government was not prepared to exert pressure on the French to let Britain in. It was the French, of course, who would have the final say on whether or not the British application was successful. The crucial meeting with de Gaulle took place in Paris on 24–25 January.[32] Wilson stressed the potential advantage to the EC of British advanced technology and of his own close links with the Soviet leadership. De Gaulle appears not to have been much impressed on the former point. Nor is his lack of any great interest really surprising. Recent experience of Anglo-French collaboration over the Concorde project, characterised by repeated British attempts to withdraw, was not an auspicious omen. Besides, as de Gaulle pointed out, technological cooperation could take place outside the framework of the EC. Whilst not ruling out the possibility of British entry, de Gaulle said that it would not be easy. He expressed particular reservations about

30. G. Brown, *In My Way* (1971), pp. 205–6; Wilson, *The Labour Government*, pp. 380–81. According to Benn, 'Harold was not prepared to let George go alone because he didn't trust George and he thought that George didn't trust him': *Benn Diaries*, p. 165, diary entry of 22 October 1966.

31. *H.C.Deb.*, vol. 735, cols, 1539–40; C. King, *The Cecil King Diary 1965–1970* (1972), p. 95, diary entry of 10 November 1966.

32. PRO, PREM 13/1476, Record of a meeting held at the Elysée Palace on Wednesday 25 January 1967 at 4.15 p.m. A full account of the discussions with de Gaulle is to be found in Wilson, *The Labour Government*, pp. 35–41. For a preliminary assessment of the impression Brown and Wilson had made on de Gaulle see PRO, PREM 13/1476, Reilly (Paris) to FO, 26 January 1967.

the reserve role of sterling, British dependence on the US and the changes that would have to be made in the EC to accommodate Britain. What he proposed was some form of association. It may be recalled that this was what Wilson himself had suggested some two years earlier, in the spring of 1965. Now, however, he dismissed it out of hand as an unsatisfactory substitute for full membership.

During the Paris visit, Brown was engaged in a number of embarrassing incidents of the kind for which he was notorious. As one observer delicately put it, he showed that 'he had more of the human touch than Harold'.[33] As for Wilson, according to Pimlott, the visits as a whole, and the talk with de Gaulle in particular, had an extraordinarily dramatic impact upon him. He now approached the task of securing British entry with something like the fervour of a missionary.[34] His changed mood was noticed by Crossman, who wrote: 'Harold comes back from Paris for the first time determined to enter the Market. Something seems to have happened during the de Gaulle interview which has made him work unreservedly for entry.'[35] Barbara Castle similarly detected a new-found resolve, recording in her diary: 'Harold is straining every nerve to get in.'[36]

After the exploratory probe had been completed, Brown and Wilson presented a report to the Cabinet on 21 March 1967.[37] They admitted that de Gaulle did not want enlargement of the Six and that the other members of the EC were not prepared to take him on. The feeling of the Cabinet, however, was that it was now too late to draw back without suffering a humiliating loss of face.

During April, the question of whether or not to apply was the subject of regular discussion by the Cabinet.[38] There was still opposition. It proved ineffective, however, against the Wilson–Brown front. This was partly because of disunity. Opponents of entry were divided into those, like Jay, who were irredeemably hostile and others, like Healey, whose opposition was of a more pragmatic variety. The most intransigent opponent, Jay, was on the right of the Labour

33. Pimlott, *Harold Wilson*, p. 439; Young, *This Blessed Plot*, pp. 192, 194.

34. Pimlott, *Harold Wilson*, pp. 439–40.

35. Crossman, *The Diaries of a Cabinet Minister*, vol. II, p. 212, diary entry of 26 January 1967.

36. Cited in Pimlott, *Harold Wilson*, p. 440.

37. For the report by Brown and Wilson and the ensuing Cabinet discussion see PRO, PREM 13/478, The Approach to Europe Memorandum by the Prime Minister and Foreign Secretary, March 1967; PRO, CAB 128/42, CC(67), 14th Conclusions, 21 March 1967. For the report given to the Cabinet in January on their discussions with de Gaulle see PRO, CAB 128/42, CC(67), 3rd Conclusions, 26 January 1967.

38. See, for example, PRO, CAB 128/42, CC(67), 26th Conclusions, 30 April 1967. See also Wilson, *The Labour Government*, pp. 387–9.

Party and was thus unable to rally those on the left, like Castle, who shared his views on the Common Market but on little else. Castle was, in any case, a close associate of Wilson and disliked and distrusted Jay. Some of the anti-marketeers believed that the proposed bid would in all probability end in a veto by de Gaulle. Certainly that was the opinion of Healey and Crossman.[39] Under these circumstances, there appeared little reason to put up a fight to the finish or to threaten resignation. In the event, no minister resigned or even threatened to, although Jay later expressed the view that he had made a mistake in not doing so.

With opponents of entry thus in disarray, Wilson, Brown and the pro-entry group were able to carry the day. On 30 April 1967 the Cabinet took a vote on the matter – always a sure sign of an irreconcilable divergence of views – and decided by thirteen votes to eight to apply to join. The decision was announced to Parliament on 2 May. It was then approved by the Commons by 488 votes to 62, with 35 Labour MPs voting against and a further 51 abstaining.

A Cabinet committee was immediately set up, headed by Brown, to work on the terms of entry. On 16 May, however, there occurred a dramatic intervention by de Gaulle who held a press conference at which he applied the so-called 'velvet veto'. In language that was polite to the point of being insulting, the French President explained that Britain was not yet ready to join the EC. British entry would only be possible, he said, when 'this great people, so magnificently gifted with ability and courage, should on their own behalf and for themselves achieve a profound economic and political transformation which could allow them to join the six continentals'.[40]

Despite this grave setback, Wilson remained determined to persevere. On 19 June 1967 he had a further meeting with de Gaulle in Paris. In a vain attempt to sway the French President, he again emphasised that British expertise in the field of technology would be a valuable asset to the EC. He also suggested that France needed Britain in to serve as a counterweight to the Germans. In return, he was treated to a lecture on Vietnam, described by de Gaulle as the greatest absurdity of the twentieth century. The subject was relevant to Britain's application, de Gaulle told Wilson, because of

39. D. Healey, *The Time of My Life* (1989), pp. 329–30; Marsh, *Off the Rails*, p. 96.

40. A substantial extract from de Gaulle's press conference speech of 16 May 1967 is to be found in *Western European Union Assembly, General Affairs Committee Fourteenth Ordinary Session: The British Application for Membership of the European Communities 1963–1968: Brief Prepared by Mr M. van der Stoel, Rapporteur* (Paris, May 1968), no. 39, pp. 55–8.

Britain's continuing special relationship with the US: France still did not know whether or not Britain could act independently of America.[41]

The interview was not a success. Yet curiously enough, when he reported back to the Cabinet, Wilson claimed that the chances of securing entry now seemed brighter than before. Britain's application for membership was tabled at a meeting of the WEU in July. British hopes were finally dashed, however, when de Gaulle formally vetoed the application in November 1967.[42] For the second time in four years, therefore, Britain's attempt to join the EC had been thwarted by the French. Nor did there seem any prospect of a more successful outcome as long as de Gaulle remained in power.

41. For Wilson's record of the conversation sent to George Brown on 21 June, see PRO, PREM 13/1521. See also Wilson, *The Labour Government*, pp. 402–13.

42. *WEU Assembly: The British Application for Membership of the European Communities 1963–1968: Brief Prepared by Mr M. van der Stoel, Rapporteur*, no. 50, pp. 75–7.

CHAPTER TWELVE

Mission Accomplished

In April 1969, less than two years after blocking Britain's second attempt to join the EC, de Gaulle resigned from the French presidency following disappointing results in a referendum on constitutional change. In the ensuing elections for his successor, held in June, Georges Pompidou, who had served as Prime Minister from 1962 until his abrupt dismissal in 1968, won a comfortable victory. These two developments transformed relations between Britain and France. They also opened the way for renewed negotiations with the Six. Before these could begin, however, Wilson was unexpectedly defeated in the general election of June 1970. The successful Conservative leader, Heath, subsequently formed a government and it therefore fell to him to submit a third – and this time successful – application for British entry to the EC. Given his long-standing and unwavering dedication to that objective, this was not inappropriate.

The new Prime Minister came to power fired with a mission to modernise and regenerate the British economy. This was to be achieved by a combination of radical reform of industrial relations and exposure of domestic manufacturing to fierce competition within the EC.[1] For Heath, however, British membership of the EC was never merely a question of economics. It was nothing less than a political crusade.[2] Heath was without doubt the most European-centred of any of the British premiers since 1945. Unlike all his postwar predecessors, he had no interest in the maintenance of a special relationship with the US, deliberately avoiding an early visit

1. J.W. Young, 'The Heath government and British entry into the European Community', in S. Ball and A. Seldon (eds.), *The Heath Government 1970–74: A Reappraisal* (1996), pp. 260–61.

2. J. Campbell, *Edward Heath: A Biography* (1993), pp. xv–xviii; S. George, *An Awkward Partner: Britain in the European Community* (1991), pp. 46–7.

to Washington and steadfastly resisting every attempt by Richard Nixon, the American President, and Henry Kissinger, his Secretary of State, to establish more cordial relations. Nor did he feel any sentimental attachment to the Commonwealth.[3]

Heath's passionate commitment to securing British entry to the EC was both an asset and a disadvantage in the negotiations that were quickly set in train. On the one hand, it provided him with a fund of goodwill in the capitals of the Six which helped to overcome some of the difficulties that inevitably cropped up. On the other, it rendered him vulnerable to the accusation that he was willing to pay any price to fulfil a cherished political ambition. Heath was alert to this danger, and the Conservatives' 1970 election manifesto, *A Better Tomorrow*, stated: 'Obviously there is a price we would not be prepared to pay.'[4] This attempt to pre-empt criticism was not entirely successful. As will be seen, mainly for reasons of internal party politics, the Labour Opposition chose to focus attention on the terms of entry, and throughout the negotiations one of Wilson's most effective tactics was to condemn those obtained by Heath as a sell-out of national interests.

From his first-hand experience of the 1961–3 negotiations, Heath had learnt two valuable lessons. The first was that there was no point in trying to obtain fundamental changes to existing EC arrangements. Thus Heath was now fully prepared to accept the EC as it stood, complete with the CAP and other features which were undoubtedly disadvantageous to British interests. The second lesson was that it was equally futile to try to mobilise the 'friendly five' against France on Britain's behalf – the mistake made by Macmillan and repeated by Wilson in 1967. British membership of the EC would only become possible when the French government was ready to sanction it.[5] One of Heath's first moves after coming to office, therefore, was to open up a private channel of communication with Pompidou via Christopher Soames, the British ambassador to France since 1968, and Michel Jobert, the Secretary-General at the Elysée Palace. Preliminary talks were then held on a possible British application which were so secret that neither the French Prime Minister, Jacques Chaban-Delmas, nor his Foreign Minister, Maurice

---

3. H. Kissinger, *The White House Years* (1979), pp. 932–8; H. Kissinger, *The Years of Upheaval* (1982), pp. 140–41, 189–92; C.J. Bartlett, *'The Special Relationship': A Political History of Anglo-American Relations since 1945* (1992), pp. 130–31; H. Young, *This Blessed Plot: Britain and Europe from Churchill to Blair* (1998), pp. 221–2.

4. Campbell, *Edward Heath*, p. 248.

5. E. Heath, *The Course of My Life: My Autobiography* (1998), p. 364; D. Hurd, *An End to Promises* (1979), pp. 58–9.

Schumann, knew of their existence.[6] France's EC partners were similarly kept in the dark about them.

The atmosphere in Paris had undergone a rapid change since the resignation of de Gaulle. Schumann let it be known that the French government would not exercise a veto if Britain were to apply again. This represented a significant advance and by the end of 1969 the Six had taken a decision in principle to open negotiations. Pompidou played a major part in these developments. He did not share his predecessor's obsessive hostility towards the Anglo-Saxons.[7] There were other reasons, however, why he was inclined to adopt a more favourable attitude towards the idea of British membership of the EC. In the first place, earlier French fears about damaging competition from British industry had largely disappeared since France had by now overtaken Britain as an industrial power. Secondly, the prospect of a substantial British contribution towards the EC budget was not unwelcome once Pompidou had managed to secure an agreement (at the end of 1969) on financial arrangements that were distinctly advantageous to France. Thirdly, it is possible that Pompidou was motivated in part by concern about the current unhealthy state of the French economy. During the early 1960s France had enjoyed a period of rapid economic growth and prosperity. Towards the end of the decade, however, it faced mounting difficulties. In August 1969 the franc was devalued in order to provide the basis for another bout of economic expansion; and in this context the enlargement of the EC through the admission of Britain and other applicants offered an obvious route to bigger markets for French exports.[8] Finally, there was an element of political calculation. In France, as elsewhere, due note was taken of West Germany's growing economic and financial power, reflected most obviously in a steady appreciation of the Deutschmark against the franc. There was also a certain amount of wariness at signs that Bonn was no longer as willing to accept the role of junior partner to France as it had been in the days of the Adenauer–de Gaulle axis.[9] After becoming West German Chancellor at the head of an SPD/FDP coalition in September 1969, Brandt showed from the outset that he was determined to establish a new relationship with

6. Interview with Lady Soames and Donald Maitland, Heath's private secretary, in BBC 2 Television documentary, *The Poisoned Chalice*, part 2.

7. Heath, *The Course of My Life*, pp. 369–70.

8. S. George, *Britain and European Integration since 1945* (1991), p. 20.

9. Young, 'The Heath government and British entry into the European Community', in Ball and Seldon (eds.), *The Heath Government*, p. 265.

the Federal Republic's neighbours in the east – especially the Soviet Union, East Germany and Poland. Such a bold and independent initiative caused some disquiet on the part of the French, and Britain was accordingly seen as a potential countervailing force against an increasingly assertive West Germany.[10] Kissinger was forcibly struck by the French President's preoccupation with his country's traditional enemy at this time, commenting that 'every conversation with Pompidou, no matter how it begins, always ends up by involving the German problem'.

It must be emphasised that Pompidou was not alone among political leaders of the Six in seeing benefits and advantages to be derived from having Britain within the EC as part of a general process of enlargement. In point of fact, there was a widespread feeling in the late 1960s that the EC needed to be strengthened if it was to be capable of protecting its members' interests vis à vis the superpowers. Soviet–US discussions over the Middle East underlined the danger that decisions that were of vital importance to the Europeans might be taken over their heads. The Strategic Arms Limitation Talks (SALT I), in which the Americans and Russians were engaged from 1968 onwards, provided an even starker warning of this risk. Brandt was as conscious as anyone of the necessity of beefing up the EC. In his case, there was an additional factor behind his support for its further development. He was concerned to demonstrate that his new *Ostpolitik* implied no weakening of the Federal Republic's commitment to its Western partners, and the need to provide such reassurance helps to explain his espousal of policies designed to strengthen the EC.

Another point that must be stressed is that the question of British entry was dealt with as only one aspect of a general process of enlarging, consolidating and deepening the EC. During the 1960s de Gaulle's intense hostility to the slightest hint of supranationalism had served to stifle any movement towards closer integration of the Six. His departure from the political scene had a liberating influence and was followed almost at once by a series of important initiatives. After the débâcle over the EDC in 1954 there had been a *relance* of the European idea. The closing months of 1969 saw a second one in which Pompidou and Brandt played a prominent part.

10. D.W. Urwin, *The Community of Europe: A History of European Integration since 1945* (1995), pp. 137–8; J.W. Young, *Britain and European Unity, 1945–1992* (1993), p. 105.

The first public manifestation of this new mood came at a summit meeting of the leaders of the Six held at The Hague in December 1969. At The Hague three important decisions were taken: first, to enlarge the EC by opening negotiations with Britain and the three other countries which had expressed an interest in joining – Ireland, Denmark and Norway; secondly, to move towards full economic and monetary union (EMU) by 1980; and thirdly, to complete the first stage of economic integration.[11] The French were adamant that this last should be achieved before negotiations with Britain began. By 1969 the first stage of economic integration was well on the way to completion. A common external tariff was in place and the CAP was already operating. All that remained to be done was to devise a mechanism for financing the EC budget. Up to that point, the funds for this purpose had been provided on an annual basis by individual contributions from each of the member states. In 1965 the Commission had proposed an automatic funding mechanism by which revenue for the EC would be derived from the levies on agricultural imports and tariff receipts from industrial imports from outside the Community. This proposal, however, was linked to the suggestion that the European Parliament (EP) should be given budgetary powers. As might be expected, de Gaulle regarded this as anathema and had responded by a French boycott of all meetings of the Council of Ministers. The result of this 'empty chair' crisis was that no arrangements were reached on a funding mechanism in 1965 and finance continued to operate on the basis of annual national contributions.[12] Pompidou was determined to get the issue sorted out before Britain entered the EC, calculating that British participation in producing a finance mechanism would in all probability have an outcome that was less favourable to France. He therefore made a prior settlement on financing the EC budget an absolute precondition of opening negotiations with Britain. By the end of December 1969 the Six had reached agreement on the matter. Despite a request from the Wilson government, Britain was not allowed to take any part in the discussions leading up to this agreement. Not surprisingly, therefore, it took little account of British interests. In essence, the arrangements that were adopted followed the lines laid down in the 1965 proposals: the EC's 'own resources' were to come from levies and tariffs on all external imports, plus up to 1 per cent of receipts from Value Added Tax (VAT).

11. Urwin, *The Community of Europe*, pp. 138–9; George, *Britain and European Integration since 1945*, pp. 20–22; Young, *Britain and European Unity*, p. 105.
12. George, *Britain and European Integration*, pp. 18–20.

From the British standpoint, these new arrangements were unfortunate to say the least. They placed Britain at a double disadvantage. In the first place, Britain imported more from outside the EC than any of its prospective partners. It followed that its contribution to the budget would be disproportionately large. Secondly, the bulk of the money raised for use by the EC was devoted to the CAP. Since Britain's agricultural base was relatively small, it stood to gain less than others from the financial resources that were made available. Britain, in other words, would be making a contribution to EC expenditure which was wholly disproportionate to the benefits it received and also to the size of its GDP. This was to be the central problem during the negotiations for entry and, indeed, for many years afterwards.

In a sense, this financial penalty could be viewed as the price that had to be paid for Britain's tardiness in seeking and securing membership of the EC. By the time it managed to obtain entry to the 'club', the original members – and the French in particular – had understandably drawn up rules which suited their own interests. Newcomers like Britain were consequently left with no real alternative but to accept them. In at least two respects, however, the time lag between Britain's first application in 1961 and the third in 1970 could be said to have eased some of the difficulties associated with British entry.

First, the question of ties with the Commonwealth had become less of a problem by the beginning of the 1970s than it had been a decade earlier. During the intervening period, trade between Britain and the Commonwealth countries had continued to decline in relative importance. By 1967 a point had been reached where Harold Wilson was seeking guarantees on only two matters relating to Commonwealth trade: imports of New Zealand meat and dairy products and of Caribbean sugar. These were also the special interests that Heath felt bound to protect.[13]

Secondly, by 1970 the prospect of joining the EC had become somewhat more palatable and less disturbing to British opinion in general because many earlier fears about loss of sovereignty had been substantially lessened. Ironically, much of the credit for this was due to de Gaulle, who throughout the 1960s had frustrated all efforts to promote political integration of the EC. Of particular

---

13. The problem presented by New Zealand was particularly important: Heath, *The Course of My Life*, pp. 373–4. For the negotiations on New Zealand interests see S.Z. Young, *Terms of Entry: Britain's Negotiations with the European Community, 1970–1972* (1973), pp. 167–79.

importance in this respect was the outcome of the crisis that the French leader had precipitated in 1965. As has been seen, the crisis arose from attempts by the Commission to link proposals for provision of the EC's 'own resources' with the granting of budgetary powers to the EP. De Gaulle retaliated by boycotting meetings of the Council of Ministers. Negotiations to resolve the deadlock took place in Luxembourg. In the course of these, the issue of new powers for the EP ceased to occupy centre stage. Instead, attention switched to another question on which the French held strong views – majority voting in the Council of Ministers, the EC's decision-taking body. Under the Treaty of Rome, this would replace the rule of unanimity once the first stage of economic integration was completed. Such a development was not welcome to France and in the end a formula was agreed in early 1966 – the so-called 'Luxembourg Compromise' – by which each member state would retain the right to exercise a veto on any proposal it considered to be a threat to its vital interests. This soon became established as a device for blocking majority decisions on a whole range of issues, thereby offering protection against the possible erosion of national sovereignty.[14]

Fears on this score, however, had still not been completely eradicated by 1970 and were to be voiced with insistent force by the maverick Conservative former minister Enoch Powell. Although a supporter of British membership of the EC at the time of the 1961 application, Powell had subsequently changed his mind and had begun to express opposition to it in 1969. At first he concentrated his attention on the alleged economic disadvantages that Britain would suffer. It soon emerged, however, that his fundamental objection to British entry to the EC was that it would involve a loss of parliamentary sovereignty. This was the theme of his speech to the 1971 Conservative Party conference.[15] The government's response to Powell's challenge was to dismiss the danger of instant federalism and to stress the protection afforded by the Luxembourg Compromise.[16] 'Joining the Community', Heath insisted in the Commons

14. For the 1965 'empty chair' crisis and the resultant Luxembourg Compromise see R. McAllister, *From EC to EU, An Historical and Political Survey* (1997), pp. 31–5; Urwin, *The Community of Europe*, pp. 107–15.

15. *The Times*, 14 October 1971.

16. Cmd. 4715 (1971), *The United Kingdom and the European Communities*. The White Paper stated: 'There is no question of any erosion of national sovereignty; what is proposed is a sharing and enlargement of individual sovereignties in the general interest.' Margaret Thatcher, a junior Cabinet minister at the time, later described this as 'an extraordinary example of artful confusion to conceal fundamental issues': M. Thatcher, *The Path to Power* (1995), p. 209.

in May 1971, 'does not entail a loss of national identity or an erosion of essential national sovereignty.'[17] Fortunately for him, his tactic of playing down the sovereignty question was made easier by a tendency for British opinion to focus on economic issues. In retrospect, however, Heath's critics have frequently complained that he was guilty at best of being 'economical with the truth', at worst of deception.[18]

As indicated earlier, at The Hague conference of December 1969 it was decided to open negotiations with Britain once agreement had been reached among the Six about the EC's 'own resources'. By the end of December the latter problem had been resolved. This cleared the way for tackling the question of enlargement, and on 30 June 1970 – almost immediately after Heath's election victory – negotiations got under way in Luxembourg with an opening statement by the chief British negotiator, Anthony Barber.[19] Within a matter of weeks, Barber had been replaced by Geoffrey Rippon when he himself became Chancellor of the Exchequer, following the death of Iain Macleod. Rippon was aided by Sir Con O'Neill of the Foreign Office, the official head of the British delegation, and John Robinson, one of Heath's assistants during the 1961–3 negotiations.[20] He reported back to a Cabinet committee chaired by Lord Home, the Foreign Secretary, and to Heath personally. As in the early 1960s, the British team was obliged to negotiate in public, with Rippon giving a television interview after each session. In another respect, however, the mechanics of negotiation were this time more favourable. Whereas Heath had had to bargain with all of the Six simultaneously, Rippon was in the fortunate position of being able to deal with the President of the Council of Ministers acting as their representative. In the crucial months of January–June 1971 the presidency was exercised by France.

17. *H.C.Deb.*, vol. 818, cols. 32–3, 24 May 1971; Young, *This Blessed Plot*, pp. 240–43.

18. B. Castle, *Fighting All the Way* (1993), p. 444. The Referendum Party has been especially critical of Heath's 'deceit'. See, for example, the full page advertisement in *The Independent*, 11 January 1997. Heath has always defended himself by drawing a distinction between 'pooling' sovereignty and 'surrendering' it: Heath, *The Course of My Life*, pp. 210–11.

19. For accounts of the negotiations see Heath, *The Course of My Life*, pp. 363–77; U. Kitzinger, *Diplomacy and Persuasion: How Britain Joined the Common Market* (1973); C. Lord, *British Entry to the European Community Under the Heath Government of 1970–4* (1993); Young, *Terms Of Entry*; Young, *This Blessed Plot*, pp. 223–38. The last draws heavily on the Foreign Office's own account of the negotiations, written by Con O'Neill and as yet unavailable to the general public.

20. Campbell, *Edward Heath*, pp. 297, 302–3; Young, *This Blessed Plot*, pp. 224–6.

It was during this period that Heath was to make a decisive personal intervention which gave fresh impetus to talks that were in danger of stalling. Negotiations formally opened at Brussels in late October 1970. During the first few months there was some limited progress. Thereafter, however, the French negotiating stance began to harden and by the spring of 1971 a stalemate had developed. This was broken by a meeting in Paris between Heath and Pompidou on 20–21 May. This meeting, initiated by Heath, prepared by Soames and Jobert and preceded by a magnificent banquet at the British embassy – an interesting case of 'gourmet diplomacy' – was an outstanding success. In the words of Sir Con O'Neill, the two men 'clicked', and after twelve hours of talks, with only interpreters present, Pompidou announced to the press: 'The spirit of our conversations . . . allows me to think that the negotiations will be successful.'[21] Heath had achieved his purpose: the French President had given a clear public signal of his commitment to the success of the negotiations. Although much detailed bargaining lay ahead, a positive outcome was now no longer seriously in doubt.

After the Heath–Pompidou summit, the main oustanding issues in the Brussels negotiations were resolved within a matter of weeks. What were these issues? One important point raised at an early stage of the proceedings by Valéry Giscard d'Estaing, the French Finance Minister, was the position of sterling. Since its devaluation in November 1967 the pound had become much stronger. The French were nevertheless concerned that its role as a reserve currency, together with the existence of the sterling balances, might constitute a barrier to the creation of EMU. It was also felt that the pound's special position was incompatible with the Community's basic principle of equality of status for all member state currencies. The British, for their part, were not prepared to discuss the issue as part of the official negotiations. During the Heath–Pompidou summit, however, an agreement was reached on the matter and on 7 June Rippon offered Giscard d'Estaing an assurance that there would be an 'orderly and gradual run-down of official sterling balances' – though there was no definite commitment as to how or when sterling's world role would finally end. As arranged beforehand by

21. *The Times*, 22 May 1971. Heath, *The Course of My Life*, pp. 364–7, 370–72; P. Whitehead, *The Writing on the Wall: Britain in the Seventies* (1985), p. 61; Young, *This Blessed Plot*, pp. 236–7; Young, 'The Heath government and British entry into the European Community', in Ball and Seldon (eds.), *The Heath Government*, pp. 271–3. For Heath's statement to the Commons on his talks with Pompidou see *H.C.Deb.*, vol. 818, cols. 31–5, 24 May 1971.

Soames and Jobert, the assurance was accepted. Some of France's partners were surprised that such a vague undertaking had been considered adequate. As a former banker himself, however, Pompidou appreciated that an orderly run-down of overseas holdings of sterling was bound to be a long and complicated process. Besides, general instability on the international exchanges during the early part of 1971 and, more specifically, the West German decision in May to float the Deutschmark, set back hopes of any early progress towards EMU and thereby rendered the sterling question less urgent.[22]

Another area of difficulty was the import of meat and dairy produce from New Zealand and sugar from the Caribbean islands. In both cases, matters were complicated by the fact that the imports in question were in direct competition with French products, especially cheese and sugar beet. In the event, the only concession that Heath was able to extract from the Six was that the preferential access to British markets which these Commonwealth exports currently enjoyed should be phased out over a period of four years. This arrangement was not wholly satisfactory and was to be one of the matters renegotiated by Wilson at the Dublin European Council of 1975.

A far more serious problem was presented by acceptance of the CAP and the related issue of Britain's contribution to the EC budget.[23] It was generally acknowledged that the transition from Britain's own agricultural system to the CAP would be an extremely painful process. This was inevitable, given the fundamental differences that existed between the two set-ups. Both involved a substantial element of subsidy. But the similarity ended there. In Britain, farming operated on the basis of deficiency payments. Prices were allowed to find their own level and farmers were compensated for any resultant shortfall in income by means of direct subsidies from the Treasury. The CAP, by contrast, was based on the principle of guaranteed prices which were fixed annually. In the event of prices falling below the agreed level, the Commission intervened to buy up surpluses and place them in storage. If prices were above those prevailing in world markets, farmers who exported their produce were paid a subsidy so as to bring their receipts up to the level they would have got if they had been selling within the EC. Under the

---

22. *H.C.Deb.*, Rippon, vol. 818, col. 1044, 9 June 1971; *ibid.*, Heath, cols. 1235ff., 10 June 1971; Heath, *The Course of My Life*, pp. 374–6; Campbell, *Edward Heath*, pp. 355, 357, 360–61; George, *An Awkward Partner*, pp. 50–51, 55; Young, *Terms of Entry*, pp. 195–209.
23. For a full treatment of this issue see Young, *Terms of Entry*, ch. 3.

British support system, it was the taxpayer who paid the subsidies and prices tended to be low. Under the CAP, the burden of subsidy was borne by the consumer, with the result that prices were generally on the high side. There was never any doubt that British acceptance of the CAP would bring a sharp increase in food prices. A government White Paper of February 1970 estimated that full application of the CAP would mean an increase of 18–26 per cent. A White Paper issued in July of the following year put the figure somewhat lower – at around 16 per cent.[24]

Obviously, the prospect of such a steep rise in the price of food was a highly sensitive issue. Heath was never under any illusion that it might be possible to negotiate fundamental or even substantial modifications to the CAP. It was, after all, such a central element in the life of the EC. The best that could be achieved was to cushion the shock of adjustment by an extended transitional period. After a great deal of hard bargaining, he managed to obtain five years.

So far as the related question of Britain's contribution to the EC budget was concerned, Rippon's opening proposal was for an initial payment of 3 per cent of total contributions, rising to a maximum of 15 per cent over five years and with provision for reviews if the burden became too great. This was dismissed by Pompidou as a good example of the famous British sense of humour. The French countered with a figure of 21 per cent and no relief in the early years. It was eventually agreed that there should be a five-year phasing in period (with provision for a possible two-year extension), by the end of which Britain would be contributing around 19 per cent of all payments towards the budget.[25] Heath seems to have expected that the problem would become less acute as Britain's shifting pattern of trade resulted in its taking a progressively smaller proportion of imports from outside the EC and hence making smaller payments to the budget. But he also pinned his hopes on the establishment of a regional development fund which would afford Britain the opportunity to claw back some of the money that it paid out.[26] Under the existing regime, the bulk of the EC budget was devoted to helping agriculture. What was needed was an equivalent subsidy for depressed industrial areas, from which Britain would

24. Cmd. 4289 (1970), *Britain and the European Communities: An Economic Assessment*; Cmd. 4715 (1971), *The United Kingdom and the European Communities*.

25. *The Times*, 22 January 1971; Heath, *The Course of My Life*, pp. 372–3; Campbell, *Edward Heath*, pp. 355, 357.

26. Heath, *The Course of My Life*, p. 373.

stand to receive substantial amounts. Heath's hopes in this area were to be somewhat disappointed.

In October 1972, before Britain had formally become a member of the EC, the British government took part in a summit meeting of the enlarged Community held in Paris. Here Heath successfully pressed for agreement to the establishment of a European Regional Development Fund (ERDF). Unfortunately for Heath, and for Britain, introduction of this fund was in fact to be delayed for several years.[27] There were a number of reasons for this delay, not least the dramatic deterioration that was soon to occur in world economic and financial conditions. Another factor was the way in which the British government proceeded to antagonise most of its new partners, especially the Germans, who would be picking up the bill for most of the projected spending on regional aid. Long-established members of the EC resented being told by the newcomer that it did not make sense to have Community institutions situated in three different places: Brussels, Luxembourg and Strasbourg.[28] There was also considerable friction over two matters of substance. The first of these concerned progress towards EMU. Following The Hague summit of December 1969, when the Six had committed themselves in principle to the goal of EMU, the EC established a system known as the 'snake in the tunnel', under which the exchange rates of the different currencies were tied together within a narrow band of fluctuations. The new system soon came under enormous strains because of the turbulence on the international exchanges caused by Nixon's decision in 1971 to end the convertibility of the dollar into gold. Britain was a member of the 'snake' only briefly. It joined in May 1972, but by July had been forced out by intense pressure on sterling.[29] The Treasury refused to re-enter without assurances that the West German central bank, the Bundesbank, would underwrite the pound's parity, something which the Germans were not prepared to contemplate without prior agreement on the coordination of economic policies. This disagreement produced a sharp deterioration in Anglo-German relations.

Relations were further damaged by an acrimonious disagreement over energy policy. The quadrupling of oil prices by the Organisation of Petroleum Exporting Countries (OPEC) during and after the

27. Heath, *The Course of My Life*, p. 372; Urwin, *The Community of Europe*, p. 151; George, *An Awkward Partner*, p. 57.

28. George, *An Awkward Partner*, pp. 61–3.

29. P. Stephens, *Politics And The Pound: The Conservatives' Struggle With Sterling* (1996), pp. 2–3; Young, *Terms of Entry*, pp. 192–4.

1973 Arab–Israeli war highlighted the need for a common strategy on energy. Heath took the lead in calling for a united EC stance towards the oil producers. But the Germans, along with the French, argued that this was not enough: it must be accompanied by an agreement on internal energy policy, including a commitment to pool resources in time of crisis. Since Britain was about to become a major oil producer itself and was anxious to keep full control over such an important national asset, this suggestion was not surprisingly rejected.

The souring of Anglo-German relations as a result of these disputes over energy and the 'snake in the tunnel' inevitably had an adverse effect on other areas of policy. In particular, it led to a marked hardening of Germany's attitude over regional subsidies. It was not until December 1974, several months after Heath had left office, that a decision was finally taken to set up the ERDF, and even then the amount made available was much smaller than Britain had sought.[30]

The negotiations for British entry to the EC were brought to a close with a final session in Luxembourg on 22–23 June 1971. The terms were set out in a White Paper issued on 7 July, and at the end of the month the House of Commons was invited to 'take note' of them.[31] The government was not yet ready to proceed to a vote on the requisite legislative measures. Although there was overwhelming Conservative backing for Heath's policy – as was to be shown at the annual party conference in early October – the parliamentary arithmetic was tricky. The government had an overall majority of 25. It could rely upon the support of five Liberals, but their votes would be cancelled out by those of six independents, nationalists and Democratic Unionists. If all Labour MPs voted against, it would only need 21 Conservative rebels to defeat the government.[32] Much depended, therefore, on the line taken by the Labour Opposition, and here the omens were neither particularly good nor easy to read.

Immediately after its electoral defeat in June 1970, Labour had begun to turn against the EC – a shift that was closely associated with the growing strength of the Left. By 1972 most sections of the party were virulently opposed to British membership. This presented

30. Heath, *The Course of My Life*, pp. 500–502; George, *An Awkward Partner*, pp. 64–9.

31. Cmd. 4715, *The United Kingdom and the European Communities*; Heath, *The Course of My Life*, p. 377.

32. For the parliamentary battle to secure passage of the European Communities Bill see Kitzinger, *Diplomacy and Persuasion*, ch. 13.

Wilson with an acute dilemma.[33] Having favoured and applied for entry in 1967, there was clearly a limit to how far he could swim with the tide of party opinion without losing every semblance of credibility. In addition, there was the formidable task of holding together a party that was bitterly divided on the issue. Wilson's answer was to concentrate on the terms. The line that he took was that he was not opposed to entry in principle but would not have accepted the terms that Heath had. Many found this assertion incredible, and the available evidence does suggest that had Wilson won the 1970 general election he would in fact have taken Britain into the EC on pretty much the same terms as Heath did. Certainly that was the view of George Thomson, who had been appointed by Wilson to conduct the negotiations in the expectation of a Labour victory.[34]

Whatever the actual truth of the matter, Wilson's stance placed staunchly pro-European Labour MPs like Roy Jenkins, Shirley Williams, William Rodgers, Roy Hattersley, George Thomson and Harold Lever in a quandary. Many members of the party felt that a vote against the forthcoming European Communities Bill, in conjunction with Powell, Teddy Taylor and other Conservative dissidents, represented a golden opportunity to defeat what Michael Foot termed 'the most reactionary government for a hundred years'.[35] But this was not a view shared by Jenkins and his associates, who regarded support for British membership of the EC as a matter of principle which they were not prepared to sacrifice for party advantage: 'There are some of us', Jenkins told Benn in December 1971, 'who will never vote against entry into Europe.'[36] From the standpoint of the government, the main tactical problem was how to help these potential allies to vote in the desired manner. Heath was initially against permitting a free vote. By mid-October, however, he had been persuaded by Francis Pym, the Government Chief Whip, that this was in fact the best approach, since a three-line whip would not bring die-hard Conservative rebels to heel but would nevertheless add to the difficulties of Labour pro-marketeers.[37]

33. For Labour's swing against the EC and the problems this presented for Wilson see H. Wilson, *Final Term: The Labour Government 1974–1976* (1979), pp. 50–54; Kitzinger, *Diplomacy and Persuasion*, pp. 293–330; Pimlott, *Harold Wilson*, chs. 25 and 26; P. Ziegler, *Wilson: The Authorised Life of Lord Wilson of Rievaulx* (1993), pp. 380–87.
34. Ziegler, *Wilson*, p. 380.   35. Jenkins, *A Life at the Centre*, p. 337.
36. T. Benn, *The Benn Diaries*, single volume edition, selected, abridged and introduced by R. Winstone (1996), p. 238, diary entry of 16 December 1971.
37. Heath, *The Course of My Life*, pp. 378–9; Campbell, *Edward Heath*, pp. 361, 401–2.

In the event, these tactics proved successful and on 28 October 1971 the government won a majority of 112 for approval in principle of Britain's entry to the EC on the terms negotiated. This outcome was only possible, though, because 69 Labour MPs felt sufficiently strongly to defy a three-line whip and vote with the government, while a further twenty abstained. Jenkins and others had originally been assured by Wilson and Robert Mellish, Labour's Chief Whip, that there would be a free vote. They therefore felt a keen sense of betrayal. But they themselves were regarded as traitors by many sections of the Labour movement and came under intense pressure from the whips and constituency activists to vote against the government. This pressure came to a peak during the six-day debate leading up to the vote, when Jenkins in particular was subjected to considerable verbal abuse. Hattersley was so concerned that his colleagues might be manhandled, indeed, that he made contingency plans for his safe exit after the vote.[38] The whole episode left a legacy of deep bitterness within the Labour Party and set the scene for the vicious internecine conflict of the early 1980s.

Having backed the government on the vote in principle, Labour pro-marketeers announced that henceforward they would be following the official party line in the impending legislative battle over the European Communities Bill. Despite this, the measure was passed without a single clause being voted down – though the majority sometimes fell to a dangerously low level. This was made possible in part by continuing, if clandestine, cooperation from Labour pro-marketeers. Opponents of the Bill suspected at the time that these were colluding with the Conservative whips. Their suspicions have recently been confirmed, with revelations in a television documentary that the operation was orchestrated on the Labour side by a backbencher, John Roper, whose meticulous record – in a little red book – of the votes of each sympathetic MP enabled him to organise a rota of abstentions and convenient 'absences' from the Commons at crucial points.[39] In this way, the risk of victimisation was minimised. The other main explanation for the Bill's successful passage was that its opponents were outmanoeuvred. Their original expectation was that the European Communities Bill would contain a vast number of clauses and that there would be endless opportunities to prevent its completion. In the event, however, the number of clauses was restricted to twelve so that proceedings were greatly simplified.

38. Castle, *Fighting All The Way*, p. 449; Jenkins, *A Life at the Centre*, pp. 329–31.
39. Interviews with Francis Pym and John Roper, BBC 2 Television documentary, *The Poisoned Chalice*, part 2. See also Heath, *The Course of My Life*, p. 386.

Even so, the parliamentary struggle lasted for months – until July 1972 – and it finally proved necessary for the government to resort to the guillotine.[40]

The Treaty of Accession was signed in Brussels on 22 January 1972, and on 1 January of the following year Britain became a full member of the EC. Yet there remained a great deal of unfinished business. It is a truism that during the negotiations Heath's basic approach was to secure entry as quickly as possible and sort out any outstanding difficulties from within. No doubt such an approach was unavoidable, since any attempt to accommodate British interests by insisting on fundamental changes in the EC's existing structure would have been fatal to the prospects of getting in. However necessary, though, Heath's negotiating strategy meant that the terms he obtained were far from ideal. This was especially true in the case of Britain's net contribution to the EC budget. From the outset, therefore, it was always probable that attempts would be made to secure a better deal for Britain by some process of renegotiation. As will be seen in the next chapter, Wilson was the first to try his hand at this.

40. Heath, *The Course of My Life*, pp. 383–7; M. Jones, *Michael Foot* (1994), pp. 334–5; Kitzinger, *Diplomacy and Persuasion*, pp. 375–8.

CHAPTER THIRTEEN

Renegotiating 'Tory Terms'

At the time of Britain's accession to the EC in 1973, the Church of Scotland marked the event with a special prayer which included the verse: 'Our God, We are now in the Common Market. Some of us feel that this has been a mistake. Some of us believe that this will bring opportunities for good. Most of us just don't know.' This snapshot impression was a fairly accurate measure of public attitudes towards membership at the time. It was also to hold true for the first ten years of membership under the Labour governments of Wilson (1974–76) and Callaghan (1976–79) and the first two Conservative governments under Thatcher (1979–84). During much of this period the British public was often confused about the objectives and desirability of membership, as the polemical warfare of pro- and anti-marketeers generated much heat but little light on the subject. This was especially the case as the Wilson government undertook a renegotiation of the original terms of entry and as the Labour Party conference subsequently – in 1981 – voted for withdrawal from the EC. British involvement in the EC throughout this period has attracted similar assessments from a number of commentators. Most of these assessments portray Britain as one of the most troublesome and least committed member states, occupying a semi-detached status with a set of policies which consistently sought to minimise both the EC's development and its impact on Britain. In many respects, much of the period 1974–84 was taken up with a lengthy attempt to renegotiate the original terms of entry, formally so under the Wilson governments of 1974–6 and informally so thereafter down to the Fontainebleau Agreement of 1984 on Britain's contribution to the EC budget. Several factors complicated and prolonged this problematical process of adjustment.

First, Britain's relatively late and long-postponed entry into the EC put it at a decided disadvantage when joining an organisation whose member states were already accustomed to a high degree of economic integration that had been greatly assisted by sustained economic growth. The EC's institutions and policies reflected the interests of the Six. France, in particular, demonstrated a keen determination to settle key issues before British entry. In 1961, as has been noted, de Gaulle had insisted on reaching the first set of agreements on the CAP before the first British application for membership of the EC was given serious consideration. Pompidou was equally intent on achieving new arrangements for the financing of the EC in 1970 before attending to the third British application. Neither the CAP nor the new budgetary system suited Britain, with both heading the list of British complaints about the workings of the EC throughout the period 1974–84. A further and related difficulty was that Britain entered the EC with an array of extra-European trading and financial interests and concerns that fitted awkwardly into the EC framework. What further compounded Britain's difficulties was that, as a new member state, it was joining a dynamic organisation with a new-found sense of movement and purpose dating from the summit at The Hague of December 1969.

Secondly, British entry into the EC occurred at a time when the virtually uninterrupted growth in the Western international economy since the early postwar years was beginning to experience a check. The collapse of the Bretton Woods fixed exchange rate system in 1971, together with the quadrupling in the price of oil during 1973–4, meant that British membership of the EC started against a gloomy background which was far removed from the buoyant economic conditions that had fostered the earlier development of the EC. Whereas in the period 1963–72 the annual average growth of Gross National Product (GNP) for the EC and Britain were 4.5 per cent and 2.9 per cent respectively, the EC growth rate slumped to 2.1 per cent and Britain's to 1.2 per cent in the period 1973–82. Meanwhile, there was a marked increase in the rate of inflation: from an annual average of 6.1 per cent for the EC and 7 per cent for the UK in the period 1968–73 to 11.3 per cent and 15.7 per cent respectively in the period 1974–9. The change in British economic conditions was particularly dramatic in the period before, during and immediately after entry to the EC. In 1970 rates of inflation and unemployment were still in relatively low single figures, while there was a healthy balance of payments surplus. By 1975, however, the economy was in the throes of 'stagflation', with inflation running at over 25 per cent, a huge balance of payments deficit, falling production and investment, and rising unemployment. In these circumstances the pre-entry arguments for membership on economic grounds began to look increasingly questionable. This, in turn, added to the difficulties of any attempt to present EC membership in a favourable light.

Thirdly, the domestic political situation in Britain during the period 1974–9 was a major constraint on the way the government dealt with EC business, in that a deeply divided Labour Party held office without a strong parliamentary majority. Following the defeat of the Heath government in the general election of February 1974, Wilson returned to power at the head of a minority Labour government. As a result of a further election in October 1974, Labour was returned to office, but with an overall parliamentary majority of only three seats. This majority eventually melted away in early 1977 when the Callaghan government negotiated the Lib–Lab pact, by which it retained power until 1979. The absence of a strong majority government – an unusual condition in post-1945 British politics, except in the periods 1950–51, 1964–6 and 1995–6 – greatly influenced the government's aims and objectives in the EC sphere. It also meant that the handling of EC issues was largely governed by the balance of forces within the governing party.

The impact of domestic politics and especially of internal party conflicts on the question of EC membership had been particularly pronounced during Labour's period in Opposition after the election defeat of 1970. The party went into Opposition bitterly divided over the issue of EC membership, in much the same way as it had left office in 1951 in discord over the issue of rearmament. The basic division between the pro- and anti-marketeers largely, though not entirely, corresponded to the increasing gulf between right-wing and left-wing opinion in the party. In this respect, EC membership was one of a number of issues that contributed to mounting ideological warfare and sorely tested party unity. The growing ascendancy of left-wing views in the party was greatly assisted by what were perceived as the failings of the Wilson governments of 1964–70 and also by widespread loathing for the economic and industrial policies of the Heath government. The influence of the Left, in turn, contributed to the anti-marketeer majorities that gradually emerged at all levels of the Labour movement. On the left, long-standing antipathy towards the EC was based on a populist/socialist mixture of opposition to the EC as an undemocratic creation of international capitalism and support for the maintenance of national sovereignty and state-centred controls. On the right, EC membership was viewed as an integral part of a reformist, social democratic programme. Both sides approached the issue as a matter of high principle, though there was also much low political manoeuvring related to the future direction, identity and leadership of the party.

The major problem of preserving at least a facade of party unity on this issue was overcome only by undertaking to renegotiate the Heath government's terms of entry and to hold a popular vote on membership. In the making of these manifesto commitments on which Labour fought the February 1974 election, Wilson played a crucial role that employed all his tactical skills and attracted venomous criticism about lack of principle and opportunism. There is little doubt that if Labour had won the 1970 election Wilson would have pressed on with EC membership negotiations and settled for more or less the same terms of entry as the Heath government. He had refused to accept de Gaulle's second veto in 1967 as the last word on the matter. The Labour Party manifesto of 1970 maintained that Britain would be able to stand on its own feet outside the EC if satisfactory terms could not be obtained. But this was a far less attractive prospect to Wilson than it had been six years earlier, when he visualised Britain at the head of a revitalised Commonwealth. Pragmatic calculation rather than deep-seated commitment had always characterised Wilson's view of the EC issue. He did not display the uncompromising attitude of pro-marketeers like Roy Jenkins, for whom EC membership was a matter of national interest transcending party loyalties. Nor did he share the fundamentalist views of inveterate anti-marketeers like Douglas Jay and Peter Shore. As party manager, Wilson was intent on keeping the options open and on limiting damage to the party.[1] This was especially the case in the critical period 1971–2, when his shifting position on the terms of entry and a referendum on EC membership attracted criticism within and beyond the party. Other leading Labour figures at this time, like Callaghan, Healey and Crosland, were equally flexible in their views, while some, notably Benn, underwent a dramatic conversion from a pro- to an anti-marketeer position.

During this period, Wilson complained that he had been 'wading in shit for three months to allow others to indulge their conscience'

1. This form of management often reflected Wilson's view that a 'decision deferred was a decision made': cited in P. Whitehead, 'The Labour governments, 1974–1979', in P. Hennessy and A. Seldon (eds), *Ruling Performance: British Governments from Attlee to Thatcher* (1987), p. 245.

on the question of EC membership.[2] He maintained the distinction between the principle of membership and the terms of entry, successfully defeating party conference motions opposed in principle to membership. By concentrating on the terms of entry and conceding the case for renegotiation, he forged a position that held together the pro- and anti-marketeer factions in the party. He also strengthened his own leadership, which was indissolubly linked to his handling of the EC question. Jenkins effectively scuppered his own ambitions to lead the party by resigning from the position of deputy leader following the Shadow Cabinet's decision in March 1972 to support the idea of a referendum.[3] But Callaghan – who lurked like a pike in the shadows, as Jenkins portrays him[4] – represented the more serious threat to Wilson's leadership. Unlike Jenkins, Callaghan had contacts across the party and served as a reliable weathercock of shifts in party opinion. He also held the view that EC membership or non-membership was of marginal importance in addressing the problems of the British economy. Wilson neutralised the threat from Callaghan by closely shadowing Callaghan's moves on the EC issue, especially his publicly voiced scepticism about EC membership in the spring of 1971 and his early recognition of the possible usefulness of a referendum as a life raft that both sides in the party would one day be happy to scramble aboard.[5]

On returning to power in February 1974, Wilson's immediate priority was to restore domestic peace and, in particular, to settle the miners' strike that had precipitated the election. His principal aim was to prepare the party for a second election in order to achieve an overall parliamentary majority. There was every reason to delay as long as possible any renegotiation of the terms of entry, not least in view of the rising tide of opposition to membership in the party. Although the process of renegotiation formally began in June 1974, Britain's EC partners indicated that no substantial progress could be expected until a majority government was in office.

Wilson was acutely conscious of the dangers involved in any mishandling of the EC issue. In particular, as Pimlott has put it, he

2. Cited in D. Healey, *The Time of My Life* (1989), p. 360.

3. For an account of the Shadow Cabinet's discussion see T. Benn, *Office Without Power: Diaries 1968–72* (1989), pp. 420–21.

4. R. Jenkins, *A Life at the Centre* (1992), p. 310. See also L.J. Robins, *The Reluctant Party: Labour and the EEC, 1961–1975* (1979), pp. 99–101.

5. J. Callaghan, *Time and Chance* (1987), pp. 309–10. See also T. Benn, *The Benn Diaries*, single volume edition, selected, abridged and introduced by R. Winstone (1996), p. 237, diary entry of 11 November 1970.

aimed to avoid a repetition of the nightmare scenario of 1931.[6] He had no intention of playing the role of Ramsay MacDonald at the head of a rump Labour Cabinet acting in defiance of party opinion, upheld only by the support of the Opposition and disastrously splitting the party. The appointment of Callaghan as Foreign Secretary was especially important in this respect: it tied a principal rival and centrist figure in the party to the course and outcome of the renegotiating exercise. There was to be very effective collaboration between the two men – a 'brilliant combination' according to Bernard Donoughue, one of Wilson's personal assistants at the time[7] – both of them competing only in the extent to which they could obscure their real motives and intentions about the renegotiation exercise. On first taking up office, Callaghan adopted an emollient tone in expressing a wish to avoid any confrontation with the other EC states.[8] Shortly afterwards, however, he adopted a harder stand by insisting on the right to propose changes to the EC treaties as an essential condition of continued British membership, as well as the right to withdraw from the EC in the event of failure to achieve satisfactory terms. Meanwhile, Wilson reserved his position on continued membership and played the nationalist card as the stout defender of British interests. He publicly dismissed the EC as a 'shambles' and ridiculed the EC Commission's plans for the harmonisation of regulations, as horror stories of 'Euro beer', 'Euro bread' and so on filled the pages of the British tabloid press. All in all, he generally pioneered a form of highly ritualised Brussels-bashing that was to become the stock-in-trade of later British leaders.

During the period of the Wilson minority government in 1974, the renegotiation exercise was chiefly confined to identifying the substantive issues and thus determining the nature and extent of the operation. Labour's manifesto commitment to a 'fundamental' renegotiation was capable of different constructions in practice, ranging from a largely spurious face-saving effort on the one hand,

6. B. Pimlott, *Harold Wilson* (1992), p. 583.
7. B. Donoughue, 'Harold Wilson and the renegotiation of the EEC terms of membership, 1974–5: a witness account', in B. Brivati and H. Jones (eds), *From Reconstruction to Integration: Britain and Europe since 1945* (1993), p. 194. Callaghan later observed that Wilson gave him the fullest support and that 'our relationship was never closer': cited in Callaghan, *Time and Chance*, p. 300.
8. In his opening statement to the EC's Council of Ministers on 1 April 1974, Callaghan expressed his preference for 'successful renegotiation from which the right terms for continued membership will emerge'. For the text of this statement see J. Mayall and C. Navari (eds), *The End of the Post-War Era: Documents on Great Power Relations 1968–75* (1980), pp. 465–70.

to radical changes in the original terms of entry on the other. Wilson himself had long since learnt the usefulness of employing the slippery concept of renegotiation in order to promise different outcomes to opposing factions in the party. Prior to the 1964 election, for example, he had effectively limited the electorally damaging consequences of Labour's divisions over British possession of nuclear weapons by committing a Labour government to renegotiate the Nassau Agreement of December 1962. Following the election, however, the idea of renegotiation faded away and the agreement was maintained.

There was much less room for manoeuvre over the EC membership question in 1974 than there had been over nuclear weapons in 1964, when the party had just ended thirteen years in the political wilderness. Nevertheless, there was scope for casting aside some of the criticisms of the EC contained in the party manifesto. This might be on the grounds that they were without foundation – as in the case of Labour's commitment to a zero VAT rate on basic items, which did not conflict with EC regulations – or on the grounds that particularly objectionable EC plans had been overtaken by events: an example of the latter was that the EC commitment to create EMU by 1980 was sinking fast under the impact of turbulent economic and monetary conditions. At the same time ministerial experience of the actual conduct of EC business, combined with the influence of Whitehall officials universally supporting continued EC membership, allayed fears in some circles and helped to reduce the list of formal grievances: 'An ounce of practice is worth a ton of theory', commented Callaghan at an early stage in the exercise.[9] Arguably, the key decision taken by the Wilson Cabinet, however, was to renegotiate membership only within the existing EC treaties, thereby avoiding the likelihood of widespread opposition among the other EC states to a British list of treaty amendments. This acceptance of the *acquis communautaire* effectively limited the character of the exercise. It also outmanoeuvred Labour anti-marketeers, for whom the principle and not the terms of entry was the fundamental issue.[10] The anti-marketeers were slow to spot the significance of this decision and were, in any case, under pressure to maintain party unity with an election in the offing. They were thus unable to seize on the best means of ensuring an unsuccessful set of renegotiations resulting in British withdrawal.

9. Joe Haines, Wilson's Press Secretary, believed that support for British membership of the EC in the Foreign Office was so strong and determined at this time that 'no Government of any party could have indefinitely resisted it': cited in J. Haines, *The Politics of Power* (1977), p. 71.

10. J.W. Young, *Britain and European Unity 1945–1992* (1993), p. 121.

Four main issues were finally identified as matter for renegotiation: reform of the CAP; access to the EC for the products of Commonwealth states; state aid to industry and the regions; and Britain's contribution to the EC budget. Many observers did not view this list as presenting insuperable problems. They saw it even less as a basis for justifying British withdrawal from the EC. There is little reason to dispute the view of Donoughue that, apart from the issues of New Zealand food imports and trade relations with the developing world, Wilson himself had no strong opinions on these matters and was prepared to argue any proposition required of him so long as it could be made to conform to the party manifesto. The government, however, attempted to demonstrate the seriousness of the exercise. It argued that the original terms of entry on these four issues were so marked by unsatisfactory assurances that the Heath government had effectively signed a blank cheque.

It proved possible to deal with most of the issues as part of the ongoing business of the EC. Insistence on reform of the CAP – an improbable venture not undertaken until ten years later – was greatly diluted by fortuitous developments that countered domestic antipathy towards the policy. In particular, the government made much of the fact that food prices in the EC were now for the first time below the level of world food prices. In addition, it was argued that other EC states were increasingly accepting the case for putting a ceiling on the cost of the CAP – especially when, in September 1974, Helmut Schmidt, the West German Chancellor, overruled his agricultural minister and rejected an interim price increase for meat that had been agreed by the EC agriculture ministers.[11]

The question of access to the EC for the products of the Commonwealth states offered the Wilson government an opportunity to claim more solid success for the process of renegotiation on at least two counts. First, negotiations on trading relations between the EC and the developing Commonwealth countries – the African, Caribbean and Pacific (ACP) states – were already in progress before Labour returned to power. These resulted in the Lomé Convention of 1975, which also included other developing states that had associate status with the EC. The Convention was hailed as a notable achievement for a progressive, outward-looking British trade policy. It abandoned the system of reciprocal trading preferences and

---

11. C.F. Lankowski, *Germany and the European Communities: Anatomy of a Hegemonial Relation* (1982), pp. 388–9. In 1975 Schmidt described the CAP as a 'mammoth misguidance of economic resources': cited in G. Hendriks, *Germany and European Integration – The Common Agricultural Policy: An Area of Conflict* (1991), p. 121.

allowed the developing states maximum access to the EC market without the requirement of a comparable counter-concession. In addition, the government was able to gain specific concessions, like the guaranteed access to the EC market of up to 1.4 million tons of sugar from the Commonwealth states in the Caribbean. These developments helped to draw some of the sting from the anti-marketeers' common portrayal of the EC as an inward-looking, rich man's club.

Secondly, there was sufficient progress on the question of continued entry to the EC for New Zealand dairy products for Wilson to be able to maintain that he had obtained a better deal than Heath. Where his predecessor had settled for an arrangement extending only to the five-year transitional period ending in 1977, Wilson managed to extract from the Dublin European Council of March 1975 an agreement guaranteeing access for New Zealand butter beyond 1977 and also an undertaking to study the future access of New Zealand cheese. This outcome was scarcely commensurate with the vast and highly publicised amount of time and effort that Wilson devoted to the matter which both wearied and baffled other EC leaders – one of whom, the Belgian Prime Minister, complained that Council sessions had been reduced to the level of auditors of a supermarket chain.[12] But Wilson was determined to play to the domestic gallery on this issue. He claimed a personal interest in the matter, having some 44 relatives in New Zealand; but there were also political dividends to be gained from championing a Commonwealth interest on behalf of an electorate for whom the Commonwealth still represented stronger emotional and kinship ties than Europe.

The Wilson–Callaghan approach to the question of possible EC interference in state aids to industry and the regions was overwhelmingly governed by the internal politics of the Labour Party. Left-wingers in the party were determined to maintain national instruments of control and to advance their case for a large-scale interventionist economic strategy by central government. Thus the EC plan for a European Regional Development Fund, which was implemented in 1975, was immediately viewed with alarm by this body of opinion which included in its ranks Tony Benn, the high-profile socialist and anti-marketeer Industry minister. While not

---

12. Callaghan later recalled that he felt more like a multiple grocer than a Foreign Secretary during lengthy negotiations in Brussels on such matters as standardising a fixed position of rear-view mirrors on agricultural tractors: cited in *Time and Chance*, p. 304.

directly involved in the renegotiations, Benn used his position to such obstructive effect – including the refusal to allow his departmental officials to cooperate in any assessment of EC rules concerning state aids – that Wilson became increasingly exasperated and commented at the time that Benn 'immatures with age'.[13] In the event, Wilson and Callaghan were able to brush aside fears of EC interference. They argued that EC practices and obligations presented no obstacle to a national regional policy. Nor did EC rules threaten the proposals for nationalisation, a National Enterprise Board and planning agreements that flowed from the adoption of 'Labour's Programme 1973'. Some of these proposals, especially nationalisation, scarcely appealed to Wilson. He had vetoed the idea of a controlling state interest in 25 of the country's largest manufacturers, caustically commenting to Benn at this time: 'Who's going to tell me that we should nationalise Marks and Spencer in the hope that it will be as efficient as the Co-op?'[14] (On another occasion, indeed, Wilson expressed the view that ideally he would have liked to have dealt with the issue of nationalisation in the Labour Party in much the same way as Macmillan had held up 'the banner of Suez for his party, while leading the party away from Suez'.)

At least part of Wilson's strategy and tactics in handling the renegotiations was designed to counter, and if possible inflict a defeat on, the Left by concentrating its attention on the EC issue and by conceding the case for a referendum on the renegotiated terms of entry. The Labour Cabinet's decision in January 1975 to hold a referendum followed a lengthy pro-referendum campaign headed by Benn in the expectation of a popular vote against EC membership. This campaign in itself absorbed time and energy that might otherwise have been devoted to pressing for an even more left-wing domestic economic policy. As Donoughue comments: 'Tony Benn's army of the left was diverted from the dangerous fields of British industry onto the deceptively inviting marshes of the EEC. Once committed and trapped there, Mr Benn was blown up by a referendum of the British people.'

The final and most substantive issue in the renegotiations was the British contribution to the EC budget. At this time calculations concerning the full British contribution to the budget belonged to the realm of guesstimates in view of the five-year (or possible seven-year) phasing-in period. There was no disputing, however, that it

13. Wilson also dismissed Benn's White Paper on industrial policy as 'sloppy and half-baked': cited in Whitehead, 'The Labour Governments, 1974–1979'.
14. P. Ziegler, *Wilson: The Authorised Life of Lord Wilson of Rievaulx* (1993), p. 394.

would be disproportionately large in relation to Britain's share of the EC's GNP. In his handling of this issue, Wilson was determined to ensure that any settlement represented a marked improvement on the original terms of entry, met the British case for cash rebates and allowed him to reap maximum political advantage from success in a hard and prolonged diplomatic battle. Heath had accepted an assurance to the effect that the EC would be impelled to find equitable solutions in the event of an unacceptably high British contribution to the budget. Wilson managed to obtain a formula specifying the criteria that had to be met in order to qualify for a rebate. A member state applying for a rebate had to be a net contributor to the budget, had to have an economic growth rate not exceeding 120 per cent of the EC's average and had to be experiencing a balance of payments deficit. Besides these criteria, there was a complex mechanism for determining the amount of rebate. This was to be broadly based on the gap between a state's gross payments to the budget and its share of the EC's average GNP, but with provisions for setting a ceiling on any rebate. This extremely complicated arrangement scarcely aroused the interest of the British public and subsequently proved to be an irrelevant paper scheme.[15]

More importantly, the protracted wranglings over the issue served the purpose of projecting the image of Wilson as a tough campaigner – especially during the Dublin European Council, where he appeared to dominate proceedings and insisted on finalising the package of renegotiated terms of entry. It was widely assumed beforehand that the terms already agreed were satisfactory and that Wilson and the majority of his Cabinet would recommend acceptance. Indeed, Wilson announced a football result at the start of his post-Council news conference, as if to confirm that the nailbiting atmosphere before the Council meeting had been a charade and that he had always expected to reach an acceptable settlement.[16] But his passage towards this successful conclusion was greatly assisted by the two principals – Helmut Schmidt, the West German Chancellor, and Giscard d'Estaing, the French President. Schmidt was

15. The scheme was regarded as a major improvement by Wilson but as a minor adjustment by Giscard d'Estaing: cited in P.M.H. Bell, *France and Britain 1940–1994* (1997), p. 228. For further details concerning the ceiling on any rebate see Mayall and Navari, *The End of the Post-War Era*, p. 517.

16. In a Commons debate on the terms of the settlement a fortnight after the Dublin European Council, Wilson commented that 'the Government cannot claim to have achieved in full all the objectives that were set out in the manifesto on which Labour fought': cited in K.O. Morgan, *The People's Peace: British History 1945–1989* (1990), p. 364.

particularly influential in supporting the British case on the EC budget and in brokering talks between Wilson and Giscard d'Estaing. It is possible, however, that the massed ranks of anti-marketeers at the Labour Party conference addressed by him in November 1974 contributed to his later view that perhaps de Gaulle had been right after all in vetoing British membership. Giscard d'Estaing proved flexible, especially on the budget question, but Wilson had to pay the price of agreeing to a French proposal for direct elections to the EP which stored up trouble for another day. Wilson emerged with a package of renegotiated terms which, though scarcely representing a substantial advance on the original terms of entry, were sufficient for him to recommend a vote for continued membership in the referendum of June 1975. While the Cabinet voted sixteen to seven in support of these terms, Labour Party opinion as a whole registered majorities against them. In the critical Commons vote of 12 April 1975, the package failed to command majority support within the PLP: 137 voted for, 145 against. A fortnight later, a special Labour Party conference rejected the terms by 3.724 million votes to 1.986 million votes. This was roughly the same two to one margin as that by which the electorate was to support them in the referendum of June 1975.

The outcome of the referendum did not lead to any major change or fresh start to British policy within the EC arena. But the clear rejection of the left-wing anti-marketeers' views did afford Wilson an opportunity to make changes to the Cabinet, including the transfer of Benn from Industry to Energy. This move reflected Wilson's irritation with Benn's conduct during the renegotiations and the referendum campaign. It was also intended to end Benn's ability as Industry minister to press for a more interventionist economic strategy. The new appointment did not diminish Benn's obstructive attitude towards EC business, which was carried to the point of proudly claiming that an EC Council of Energy Ministers was delayed while he attended a local Labour Party meeting.[17] More generally, the government pursued a minimalist approach to the EC, betraying neither great interest in nor marked antipathy towards EC initiatives. The establishment of the ERDF in 1975 did not produce the sizeable benefits that had been expected on the British side at the time of the Heath entry negotiations. The Fund's initial resources – £540 million over a three-year period – were largely

17. Cited in S. George, *An Awkward Partner: Britain in the European Community* (1991), p. 96.

determined by West German unwillingness to finance a larger deal and by the fact that the CAP consumed some 80 per cent of the EC budget, thus leaving limited resources for other common policies.[18] The Wilson government demonstrated no interest in the longer term future and financing of the initiative. It ensured that Britain received its full allocation of the total funds (28 per cent), but attracted criticism in EC circles for failing to abide by the principle of financing projects that were additional to any that were to be funded nationally.

On the more vital question of energy policy at this time, the Wilson government pursued a distinctive line that put it at odds with the other EC states and further reinforced the image of Britain as a disagreeable partner. In the wake of the quadrupling of the price of oil and in the absence of a coordinated EC energy policy, there emerged efforts to ensure that the EC states acted as a single entity at the international conference on energy that was held in Paris in December 1975 to provide a forum for discussions between the oil producers and the oil consumers. The Wilson government was determined to ensure that Britain's North Sea oil reserves, which first came ashore in 1975, did not come within the scope of EC legislation. It was thus initially opposed to any idea of a common EC stance on energy and insisted that, at the very least, as an oil-producer state Britain should have separate representation at the Paris conference. This demand for special status, first expressed by Callaghan in February 1975, was strongly resisted by the other EC states. Schmidt made a forceful intervention, not least by indicating that West Germany – as the EC's paymaster – was disinclined to allow the British to benefit from EC funding while they were at the same time refusing to accept the principle of solidarity. Wilson was ultimately forced to retreat from the demand for separate representation in return for the assurance that Callaghan should be offered an opportunity to make a brief statement at the Paris conference.[19] In the event, Callaghan's unduly lengthy statement annoyed the other EC states. He expatiated on the failure of the EC to formulate a common energy policy, while shamelessly ignoring

18. Schmidt, the West German Chancellor, was very sceptical about the value of the ERDF and dismissed it as a device for redistributing finance 'clothed in a pair of bathing trunks with "regional policy" painted on them': cited in S. Bulmer and W. Paterson, *The Federal Republic of Germany and the European Community* (1987), p. 202.

19. George, *An Awkward Partner*, p. 104. See also *The Times*, R. Vielvoye, 19 December 1975. French government sources complained that Callaghan had departed from the EC's agreed mandate: cited in *The Times*, 19 December 1975.

the extent to which his own government was responsible for this failing. All in all, the episode scarcely enhanced Britain's EC credentials, even if it was a necessary part of playing to a domestic gallery.

The renegotiation exercise, culminating in the 1975 referendum, was a major triumph for Wilson. Even his detractors regarded it as such. One contemporary commentator noted that Wilson had had three objectives: 'to keep his party in power and in one piece and Britain in Europe'.[20] He had managed to achieve each of these objectives. He had kept the Labour Party together, despite the absence of majority support for the terms at all levels of the Labour movement outside the Cabinet. To be sure, the party's divisions did not dissolve away in the wake of the referendum. In the view of some scarcely disinterested observers like Jenkins, moreover, the handling of the EC question by the Labour leadership in the 1970s did more to cause the party's disasters of the 1980s than any other issue. Wilson had also obtained a result via the referendum that gave popular legitimacy to British membership of the EC. While the use of the referendum was wholly dictated by Labour Party politics, the result nevertheless lent some substance to the view, as expressed by Donoughue, that 'Mr Heath had taken the British Establishment into Europe. Harold Wilson took in the British people.'[21] What failed to emerge through this episode was any positive view of how Britain intended to shape the EC's future. Nor did the referendum result signify a fresh start in the making of British policy as an EC state.

20. Cited in Pimlott, *Harold Wilson*, p. 659.
21. Brivati and Jones (eds), *From Reconstruction to Integration*, p. 205.

CHAPTER FOURTEEN

'Full-hearted Consent':
the 1975 Referendum

Heath entered the 1970 general election pledged to resume negotiations for entry to the EC. Negotiations began in June 1970. In
January 1972 the Treaty of Accession was signed, and on 1 January
1973 Britain became a member of the Community. Throughout
this period the issue of whether it was in British interests to join the
EC was the subject of a vigorous, sometimes acrimonious, debate.
Nor did the debate end in 1973. On the contrary, it intensified,
coming to a climax at the time of the national referendum on
British membership in June 1975.[1] The aim of this chapter is to
examine the main forces on the pro- and anti-market sides, the
organisations they formed in the run-up to the 1975 referendum
and the various arguments they deployed.

A convenient starting point might be to look at the stances
adopted by the major political parties. So far as the Liberals were
concerned, they remained consistent in their advocacy of British
membership. They had come out strongly in favour in the late
1950s and throughout the 1960s and 1970s, under the leadership
of Jo Grimond and his successor, Jeremy Thorpe, continued to be
the most unequivocally pro-European of the three main parties.

The two other parties were divided, Labour bitterly so. During
the negotiations for entry in the early 1970s, Heath had to contend
with a small right-wing faction of anti-marketeers within the Conservative Party. This was reflected in the Commons vote on the
principle of entry of 28 October 1971, when a substantial minority
of 39 Conservative and Unionist MPs voted against the government, leaving Heath dependent upon Labour and Liberal support

---

1. The two most detailed studies of the 1975 referendum are D. Butler and
U. Kitzinger, *The 1975 Referendum* (1976) and P. Goodhart, *Full-Hearted Consent: The
Story of the Referendum Campaign – and the Campaign for the Referendum* (1976).

or abstentions to carry the measure. Once entry had been accomplished, however, such dissent tended to die down. Thus in April 1975 only eight Conservative MPs voted against continuing membership of the EC on the terms renegotiated by Wilson.

The schism within Labour's ranks was far more serious, and at times during the period 1970–74 came close to tearing the party asunder. The issue itself aroused strong passions among both the pro- and anti-marketeers within the party. But what made the dispute particularly poisonous and damaging was that it was inextricably bound up both with the question of the Labour leadership and with an ideological battle between Left and Right. As was indicated in the previous chapter, Labour's electoral defeat in 1970 was followed by a strong upsurge of anti-European feeling within the movement as a whole. Part of the explanation for this lay in a reflex hostility to government policy. The Conservative government was applying for membership of the EC: therefore Labour would oppose it as a matter of course. The fact that the European cause was strongly identified with Heath personally only reinforced this natural tendency, since the Conservative leader was cordially disliked by many Labour people who regarded his policies, especially those towards the trade unions, as harsh and regressive. At the same time, Labour's growing dislike of the EC was also linked with the party's strong shift to the left after 1970. It is true that not all anti-marketeers were necessarily left-wingers. Douglas Jay, to take one obvious example, was both a passionate opponent of British entry and on the right of the party. Broadly speaking, however, it was among left-wingers, people like Barbara Castle, Michael Foot and Ian Mikardo, that hostility to the EC was to be found. In left-wing circles the EC was routinely dismissed as a 'capitalist club', and it was felt that entry would rule out the adoption of socialist policies by a British Labour government.

Labour's swing to the left was partly a result of disillusionment with the Wilson governments of 1964–70. It was also a product of the industrial strife generated by the Heath government's 1971 Industrial Relations Act. The 1970s saw a pronounced growth in the influence of the Left at constituency level and on the NEC. The Left also occupied a dominant position in the trade union movement. The two largest unions, the Transport and General Workers' Union (TGWU) and the Amalgamated Union of Engineering Workers (AUEW), were led by prominent left-wing figures, Jack Jones and Hugh Scanlon respectively, both of whom were fervent anti-marketeers. This had important policy implications, since the system of block voting at party conferences conferred enormous influence on the most powerful trade union leaders. At the Labour Party conference at Blackpool in October 1970, a resolution calling for outright opposition to British entry to the EC was only defeated by the narrowest of margins. As the negotiations in Brussels proceeded, Labour attitudes hardened further, and a special party conference on the Common Market, held at the Central Hall, Westminster, in July 1971, came out definitely against entry on the terms then available.

Wilson had no real alternative but to go along with this trend. But his situation was an extremely delicate one. What he had to prevent at all costs was a decision by the party to oppose entry in principle. Given that he himself had applied to join only three years previously, such an outcome would have rendered his personal position completely untenable. It would also have caused an open split within the PLP where there were over 100 MPs who supported British membership of the EC. As a device for keeping a deeply divided party together, Wilson took the line that the terms obtained by Heath – the 'Tory terms' – must be renegotiated and then submitted to the people for approval. It was not made clear at first precisely what form the proposed popular consultation would take. Initially, Wilson was not attracted by the idea of a referendum. When Benn suggested it to him in November 1970, shortly after the annual party conference at Blackpool, he dismissed it out of hand. Gradually, however, he came to see its usefulness as a way of preventing an open split in the party.[2]

At the time Benn first broached the matter with Wilson, he was still in favour of British membership and therefore did not look upon the holding of a referendum as a means of frustrating entry. After 1971, however, as his views underwent a complete change, that was precisely how he began to think of it. According to Benn's biographer, Jad Adams, the referendum issue also possessed appeal for him as a device for marginalising the 'social democratic' element within the Labour Party.[3]

At first, it proved difficult to gain any significant support. When Benn raised the possibility of a referendum with the NEC in December 1971, for example, he failed to obtain a single vote for it – with

2. T. Benn, *The Benn Diaries*, single volume edition, selected, abridged and introduced by R. Winstone (1996), pp. 236–7, diary entry of 5 November 1970; P. Ziegler, *Wilson: The Authorised Life of Lord Wilson of Rievaulx* (1993), pp. 381–7. Benn had tried to interest Wilson in a referendum as early as September 1969: *The Benn Diaries*, p. 214.

3. J. Adams, *Tony Benn* (1992), p. 330.

the exception of his own.[4] The first real indication of solid Labour interest came in March 1972, during the passage of the European Communities Bill through the House of Commons. The government was currently experiencing considerable difficulty in getting the measure through, with its majority at times falling as low as four. Labour therefore saw an opportunity to cause it great embarrassment and possibly even defeat it by supporting a proposed amendment by a staunch Conservative anti-marketeer, Neil Marten, calling for a consultative referendum before British membership took effect. When the Shadow Cabinet discussed the tactics to be pursued in mid-March, the vote was eight to four against supporting the Marten amendment. On 22 March, however, Benn persuaded the NEC – in the absence of Wilson, Jenkins and Callaghan – to ask the Shadow Cabinet to reconsider. The result was that the earlier decision was reversed on 29 March, Wilson, Healey and Ross having changed their minds in the interim. It was decided by eight votes to six that there should be a whipped Labour vote in support of the pro-referendum amendment. This decision provoked the resignation of Jenkins, Lever and Thomson from the Shadow Cabinet, and when the Conservative amendment (which was defeated by 49 votes) was moved on 18 April around one-fifth of Labour MPs either abstained or failed to turn up.[5]

By the time of the 1974 general elections, Labour was firmly committed to consulting the people through the ballot box. In neither its February nor its October manifestos, however, was it specified whether that would be done by means of a referendum or through a general election.[6] It was not until 23 January 1975 that it was announced in the Commons that there would be a consultative referendum by June of that year at the latest.[7]

The decision to hold a referendum met with a mixed response. Some regarded it as a welcome extension of the British people's democratic rights; in other quarters, however, it was portrayed as a dangerous constitutional innovation which posed a threat to the sovereignty of Parliament. The conventional wisdom, backed up by opinion polls, was that a majority of the public was opposed to

4. R. Jenkins, *A Life at the Centre* (1992), p. 342; Ziegler, *Wilson*, p. 382.
5. *The Benn Diaries*, pp. 254–7, diary entries of 16 March, 29 March and 18 April 1975; Jenkins, *A Life at the Centre*, pp. 341–8; Goodhart, *Full-Hearted Consent*, pp. 44–59; U. Kitzinger, *Diplomacy and Persuasion: How Britain Joined the Common Market* (1992), p. 392.
6. For the actual wording of the manifesto commitments on consultation see Goodhart, *Full-Hearted Consent*, pp. 75, 80.
7. *H.C.Deb.*, vol. 884, cols. 1745–50.

membership and would reject it if given the chance. Not surprisingly, therefore, the idea of holding a referendum was overwhelmingly popular with anti-marketeers. For the same reason, pro-marketeers tended to disapprove of it. There were some notable exceptions: Shirley Williams, for example, instinctively sympathised, according to Jenkins.[8] It is interesting to note, moreover, that Jenkins's own initial hostility began to abate in late 1974 as opinion polls indicated that the public mood was becoming more pro-market.

But attitudes were determined not solely by calculations concerning the likely outcome. Important constitutional principles were also held to be at stake. Within the Labour Party, support for a referendum was fully in keeping with the emphasis currently being placed on participatory democracy. Many people, including Foot and Benn, believed that the Wilson governments had gone wrong because they had lost touch with grassroots opinion. Allied to this belief in the need for greater consultation was an uneasy feeling that on this particular vital issue the British people had not been given an adequate opportunity to express their views. In the lead-up to the 1970 election, Heath had declared that Britain would only go into the EC with 'the full-hearted consent of Parliament and the people'.[9] It was widely felt that this undertaking had not been honoured. In the election all three party leaders – Heath, Wilson and Thorpe – had supported entry. As a result, it was argued, the electorate had been deprived of a real choice. Referenda about enlargement of the EC had been held in France, Denmark, Ireland and Norway. Why should the British people not be allowed a similar opportunity to make their views known?

Opponents of the referendum maintained that it was setting a dangerous precedent. Jenkins, who was in any case utterly contemptuous of Wilson's motives for calling for one, warned that future referenda might be used to obstruct progressive measures such as race relations legislation. He was also concerned that this particular referendum would be extremely divisive and would split the Labour Party from top to bottom.[10] At a more fundamental level, he endorsed the thesis advanced by Edmund Burke in the eighteenth century, that MPs were representatives, not delegates, and must be allowed to exercise their own judgement. This was also

8. Jenkins, *A Life at the Centre*, pp. 341, 347.

9. E. Heath, *The Course of My Life: My Autobiography* (1998), p. 362; D. Butler and M. Pinto-Duschinsky (eds), *The British General Election of 1970* (1971), p. 105; Goodhart, *Full-Hearted Consent*, p. 25.

10. Jenkins, *A Life at the Centre*, pp. 243–4. See also Jenkins's resignation letter to Wilson: cited in Goodhart, *Full-Hearted Consent*, pp. 47–50.

the official line taken by the Conservative Opposition, with Geoffrey Rippon denouncing referenda as 'wholly contrary to our constitutional practices'. When the matter was debated in the Commons on 11 March 1975, the newly elected party leader, Margaret Thatcher, pointed to the constitutional difficulties that could well arise if, for example, the vote went against the government's recommendation.[11]

Despite strenuous Conservative opposition, the Referendum Bill was passed in late April 1975. By then, as has been seen, the promised process of renegotiation had been completed. The Labour Cabinet was badly split on whether or not to accept the renegotiated terms. In the end, a vote was taken and a minority of seven ministers voted against acceptance: Tony Benn, Michael Foot, Barbara Castle, Peter Shore, John Silkin, William Ross and Eric Varley.[12] As an indication of just how deep the divisions were, it was agreed that for the duration of the referendum campaign ministers on both sides of the argument should be free to air their views. As a result, the public was treated to the extraordinary spectacle of members of the same government openly disagreeing with each other on a major policy issue. The precedent for this highly unusual arrangement was that of 1931, when ministers in Ramsay MacDonald's National Government had been permitted to express conflicting views on the contentious question of Protection.[13]

After the Dublin European Council of March 1975, the way was clear to hold a referendum and the date was fixed for 5 June. Before it could take place, however, there were many details to sort out about how to organise what was, after all, a major constitutional experiment.[14] Should the validity of the outcome be made conditional on a minimum turn-out or majority? Should the question put to the electorate have a preamble explaining the government's recommendation? How should the question itself be worded? This last point was of the utmost importance, as was clearly demonstrated by an exercise conducted by the polling organisation NOP in February 1975 in which a series of differently worded questions produced widely different outcomes.[15] After much consideration, the following wording was adopted:

11. *H.C.Deb.*, vol. 888, cols. 310–14, 11 March 1975.
12. H. Wilson, *Final Term: the Labour Government, 1974–1976* (1979), p. 103; Pimlott, *Harold Wilson*, pp. 655–6.
13. *H.C.Deb.*, vol. 884, col. 1746; Wilson, *Final Term*, pp. 98–9.
14. The detailed arrangements for the Referendum were set out in Cmd. 5925 (February 1975), *Referendum On United Kingdom Membership of the European Community*.
15. Butler and Kitzinger, *The 1975 Referendum*, p. 60. Polls carried out by Gallup at around the same time produced similar results: *The Daily Telegraph*, 24 January 1975.

The Government have announced the results of the renegotiation of
the UK's terms of membership of the European Community.
DO YOU THINK THAT THE UK SHOULD STAY IN THE EURO-
PEAN COMMUNITY (COMMON MARKET)?[16]

Another vital matter was how the referendum campaigns should
be funded. In the event, it was decided that there should be a
government grant of £125,000 to each of the two main organisations responsible for conducting the 'pro' and 'anti' campaigns.
The government would also provide for the free distribution of the
official leaflet put out by each side – a service estimated to be worth
between £750,000 and £1 million. No upper limit was set on the
amount to be spent, and information about all donations above
£100 was to be made public. As we shall see, the absence of any
ceiling on expenditure proved to be an enormous advantage to the
pro-marketeers, who had access to much greater financial resources
than their opponents.

On each side, the referendum campaign was orchestrated by
an umbrella organisation. The body responsible for coordinating
the activities of the pro-marketeers was called Britain in Europe.
Its counterpart in the other camp was the National Referendum
Campaign.[17]

The activists behind the establishment of Britain in Europe came
mainly from two existing pro-European organisations, the more
prominent of which was the European Movement. This had been
founded as far back as 1948 and was committed to federalism. Its
headquarters were at the aptly named Europe House, which was
situated in the National Liberal Club. On the eve of the referendum campaign, it had a full-time staff of 25. Once the campaigning
got under way, the number was greatly expanded, and over six
million of its leaflet, *Out of Europe – Out of Work*, were distributed.
The other group involved in the establishment of Britain in Europe
was the European League for Economic Cooperation, a body which
had played an active role in promoting the case for British entry
into the EC during the 1970–71 negotiations. One of its joint presid-
ents was Geoffrey Rippon, the chief negotiator at that time. Another
was the Labour MP Geoffrey de Freitas, but the club was still felt to
have too much of a Conservative/City image, and to counter that
impression a number of Labour MPs were elected or co-opted to

16. Cmd. 5925.
17. For information on the rival umbrella organisations see Butler and Kitzinger,
The 1975 Referendum, chs. 4 and 5; Goodhart, *Full-Hearted Consent*, ch. 8.

membership, including George Thomson, Harold Lever, Dickson Mabon and David Marquand. The Liberal Chief Whip, David Steel, was also a member. It was at meetings of the European League for Economic Cooperation that plans were worked out for the formation of an umbrella organisation that would assume overall responsibility for the conduct of the 'yes' campaign.

This new organisation – Britain in Europe – was launched in March 1975. At the same time, a sister organisation, the Labour Campaign for Britain in Europe, was set up to work under its auspices. Shirley Williams became its president and it contained 88 Labour MPs, 21 Labour peers and 25 trade union officials. The Labour Campaign for Britain in Europe worked closely with a voluntary group of trade unionists, known as the Trade Union Alliance for Europe. This was presided over by Victor Feather, the former General Secretary of the Trades Union Congress (TUC), and its headquarters were located in a building provided by the white-collar trade union, the Association of Professional, Executive, Clerical and Computer Staff (APEX), whose president, Roy Grantham, happened to be strongly pro-European.

From the outset, great care was taken to ensure that Labour, and for that matter the Liberals too, were given adequate representation in Britain in Europe. The intention was to present a cross-party image. Roy Jenkins was chosen as chairman. He shared overall direction of the campaign with William Whitelaw, and the chief Liberal representative was David Steel. From 10 May 1975 onwards, Britain in Europe organised nightly rallies in major cities. Here again care was taken that the participating speakers were drawn from all three main parties.

The 'yes' campaign derived its support from what might be termed the political mainstream: the Liberals, the right of the Labour Party and virtually the whole of the Conservative Party. The highly efficient Conservative Party machine was put at its disposal and proved to be a big asset. Of the leading Conservative politicians, the one who campaigned most actively on the pro-market side was Heath. The new party leader, Thatcher, who had been elected in place of Heath in February 1975, whilst being a supporter of British membership, played a distinctly low-key role in the proceedings.[18] So, too, did the Labour leader, Wilson. Both he and Callaghan, the Foreign Secretary, declined to become involved with

18. M. Thatcher, *Path to Power* (1995), pp. 334–5; Jenkins, *A Life at the Centre*, p. 402; Lord Beloff, *Britain and European Union: Dialogue of the Deaf* (1996), p. 81.

Britain in Europe and made speeches infrequently. In part, this reflected their relative coolness towards Europe when compared with more ardent advocates like Jenkins. But it also stemmed from a desire not to aggravate existing divisions within the Labour Party.[19]

Besides having backing from the bulk of the political establishment, the 'yes' campaign was also buttressed by support from various influential pressure groups, including a number of pro-market trade unions such as APEX, the Union of Shop, Distributive, and Allied Workers (USDAW), the National Union of Railwaymen (NUR) and the Union of Post Office Workers (UPW). The NFU, which had been hostile to British membership of the EC in the early 1960s, had by the mid-1970s come to realise that British farmers stood to benefit considerably from the CAP and mounted a strong campaign in favour of staying in. More important still was backing from most sections of industry. The overwhelming feeling among industrialists was that being in the EC made good business sense. A survey of the chairmen of major companies carried out by *The Times* in April 1975 indicated that 415 out of 419 respondents favoured membership.[20] Individual companies and the Confederation of British Industry (CBI) campaigned actively for a 'yes' vote. The most tangible help was the finance made available by business and the City. When the details of campaign donations were later declared, it became clear that the pro-marketeers had received substantial amounts from most big companies, including ICI, Cadbury/Schweppes, Marks & Spencer, Shell, Ford and Rank.[21] Last, but by no means least, there was the press. With a few relatively unimportant exceptions, newspapers of all political persuasions supported the pro-European case. In the early 1960s the *Daily Express* and the *Sunday Express*, under the influence of their proprietor, Beaverbrook, had taken a staunchly anti-Common Market line. By the time of the referendum, however, they too were in favour of British membership.

The forces operating under the umbrella of the National Referendum Campaign were far more disparate and wide-ranging than those represented by Britain in Europe. They spanned most of the political spectrum, ranging from the Tribune group on the left of the Labour Party to other groups on the extreme right. An

19. Jenkins, *A Life at the Centre*, pp. 415–16; Pimlott, *Harold Wilson*, p. 659; K.O. Morgan, *Callaghan: A Life* (1977), p. 426.

20. *The Times*, 9 April 1975.

21. For details of expenditure by both sides of the campaign see Cmd. 6251 (October 1975), *Referendum on U.K. Membership of the European Community Accounts of Campaigning Organisations.*

application to be involved from the National Front was rejected out of hand. There were, however, other rather dubious fringe organisations such as the National Council of Anti-Common Market Associations, which was linked with a former air marshal of ultra-right-wing views.

The National Referendum Campaign comprised two main elements, both of which were intensely suspicious of each other: the Common Market Safeguards Committee and Get Britain Out. The former had been established in 1970 with the inveterate anti-marketeer Douglas Jay as its chairman, and had been responsible for organising much of the publicity against British entry during 1970–72. Get Britain Out was a direct successor of Keep Britain Out, which had been formed at the time of the first British application to join the EC in the early 1960s. After Britain became a member, logic dictated a change of name. During the February 1974 general election, Get Britain Out provided Enoch Powell with a platform for his celebrated speeches urging Conservative voters to vote for Labour because of its opposition to entry on the terms negotiated by Heath. There was some concern that Labour and trade union activists might be alienated because of the presence of Powell, and to counteract this danger prominent left-wing trade unionists like Jack Jones and Clive Jenkins of the Association of Scientific, Technical and Managerial Staffs (ASTMS) were enlisted into the organisation's activities.

Get Britain Out and the Common Market Safeguards Committee decided that it was essential to have some organisation to coordinate anti-market activity, and in January 1975 they formed the National Referendum Campaign for that purpose. In its founding statement the new body set out its basic aims as being to restore the British Parliament's exclusive right to pass laws and impose taxation binding upon citizens of the UK, and also to re-establish the power of the UK to trade freely – especially in the case of food – with any country in the world. As we shall see, these were two of the dominant issues debated during the referendum campaign.

The chairman of the National Referendum Campaign was Neil Marten, whose anti-market views had led him to refuse office in the 1970 Heath government. The rest of its executive committee was made up of a curious blend of Labour anti-marketeers like Barbara Castle, Michael Foot, Peter Shore and Douglas Jay; Conservative backbenchers like Ronald Bell and Richard Body; and representatives of the three parties that had come out unequivocally in favour of a 'no' vote – the Scottish National Party (SNP), Plaid Cymru and the United Ulster Unionists. As can be seen, this was quite a mixed bag. This was reflected also in the various affiliated organisations, among them the Anti-Common Market League, the British League of Rights, the Yorkshire-based British Business in World Markets, the Labour Safeguards Committee, Conservatives Against the Treaty of Rome and the Liberal 'No' to the Common Market Campaign.

In terms of organisation, the National Referendum Campaign was no match for Britain in Europe. It was far less professional and possessed a full-time staff of only seven, compared to the 140 or so on the payroll of its rival. At the root of this disparity was lack of finance.[22] Most of the funds donated to the National Referendum Campaign came from trade union sources, and it must be said that the unions were not over-generous. The largest contributor, the TGWU, gave £1,300. No other union donated more than £100. Apart from the grant of £125,000 from the government, the National Referendum Campaign raised a total of less than £9,000. This was in stark contrast with the sum of almost £2 million at the disposal of Britain in Europe.[23]

A further handicap for the 'no' campaign was its lack of support from the press. It was backed by the Communist *Morning Star*, *Tribune*, the newly formed cooperative, the *Scottish Daily News*, the *Dundee Courier and Advertiser* and the *Spectator*. With these ill-assorted exceptions, the press was solidly behind the 'yes' campaign.[24] What was more, the chronic shortage of funds from which the National Referendum Campaign suffered meant that it was unable to afford large-scale newspaper advertising. Even in television presentation it was at a severe disadvantage. Each side was provided with the facilities to mount four short documentary programmes to put its case. The National Referendum Campaign spent only £2,500 on its four slots; Britain in Europe's effort was on a far bigger scale, involving the hiring of an American film and public relations expert, Charles Guggenheim, and expenditure of £105,000.[25]

The sheer diversity of the organisations involved in the 'no' campaign inevitably made it an unwieldy coalition of interests. Nor did the different elements involved always see eye to eye with each other. Not surprisingly, many from the Labour camp were wary and

22. Beloff, *Britain and European Union*, pp. 81–2; J. Callaghan, *Time and Chance* (1987), p. 325.

23. B. Castle, *Fighting All the Way* (1993), p. 474.

24. Butler and Kitzinger, *The 1975 Referendum*, p. 108; Goodhart, *Full-Hearted Consent*, pp. 147–8.

25. Jenkins, *A Life at the Centre*, p. 408; Butler and Kitzinger, *The 1975 Referendum*, pp. 197–200; Goodhart, *Full-Hearted Consent*, pp. 128–9.

suspicious of Powell, while Benn, for his part, refused to share a public platform with *any* Conservatives. Powell, now an Ulster Unionist MP, and Benn were by far the two most striking figures on the 'no' side. Yet polls showed that their impact on voters was generally a negative one. Both were widely regarded as extremist in outlook and even cranky. Powell's luridly expressed views on race and immigration – notably his notorious 'rivers of blood' speech of 1968, which caused his dismissal from the Shadow Cabinet – had served to discredit him in the eyes of many people. Moreover, his sensational recommendation that Conservative supporters should vote Labour in the 1974 general elections had been neither forgotten nor forgiven. Benn was subjected to a sustained campaign of ridicule and vilification in the press, where he was routinely portrayed as a dangerous, wild-eyed fanatic.

In the course of the referendum debate, the two sides traded arguments in innumerable speeches up and down the country and in the three official leaflets which were issued in the last week of May. These leaflets were called *Why You Should Vote Yes, Why You Should Vote No* and *Britain's New Deal in Europe*. The last-named, put out by the government, set out a case which was essentially along the lines of that published by the 'yes' campaign.[26]

Inevitably, there was some attempt to resort to scare tactics, and some of the arguments were plainly silly. Thus some pro-marketeers sought to discredit the 'no' campaign by pointing out that it was supported by the National Front and the Communist Party. Others spread alarmist stories about the prospect of food shortages and rationing if Britain withdrew from the EC. On the other side, there were dire warnings that the Europeans were scheming to get their hands on Britain's oil and fish stocks. The left-wing Labour MP Eric Heffer even predicted the reintroduction of conscription if Britain was misguided enough to stay in.

There were, of course, more serious arguments. In the first place, anti-marketeers dismissed Wilson's renegotiation as nothing but a hollow sham dictated principally by considerations of Labour Party politics. The modifications that had been secured, they claimed, were far from being the fundamental ones he had set out as his objective. Pro-marketeers countered by insisting that substantial changes had in fact been achieved, especially on the question of Britain's budgetary contribution.

---

26. For the text of the three official leaflets see Butler and Kitzinger, *The 1975 Referendum*, pp. 290–304.

Secondly, there was disagreement over the impact of EC member-ship on the regions. According to the 'no' camp, the consequences would be disastrous for their employment prospects. British gov-ernments would be prevented from trying to stem the market-led drift of economic activity to the south and to the continent, and the chief sufferers would be Scotland, Wales and many parts of the north of England. Pro-marketeers denied this, claiming that Britain would not only retain its right to pursue its own regional policy, but would also benefit from the newly established ERDF. It was prob-ably no coincidence that this point was underlined by the announce-ment of EC grants to the National Coal Board and to the Ebbw Vale steelworks shortly before the date of the referendum.

Thirdly, the two sides made competing claims about the attitude of the Commonwealth. At the end of April 1975, Wilson returned from a conference of Commonwealth prime ministers in Jamaica bearing a unanimous endorsement of British membership of the EC. In addition, both of the two official leaflets favouring member-ship contained quotations from various Commonwealth leaders expressing the view that Britain should stay in. Against that, the anti-marketeers claimed that such sentiments did not accurately reflect the opinion of ordinary Commonwealth citizens, and a poll was accordingly commissioned which showed that the majority of New Zealanders would prefer Britain to pull out.[27]

In general terms, the 'yes' campaign sought to portray a grim future for Britain if it left the EC. Christopher Soames, one of two Britons on the Commission, stated: 'Frankly, it's damn cold out-side.'[28] A similar message was conveyed by Roy Jenkins, who spoke of Britain being led into 'an old people's home for faded nations',[29] as well as by the official 'yes' leaflet, with its talk of being 'alone in a harsh, cold world'. Anti-marketeers dismissed such forebodings as defeatist and insisted that Britain would be far better off outside the EC, both economically and politically.

The two issues that dominated the campaign debate were pos-sible loss of sovereignty and the likely consequences of member-ship for the British economy. The 'no' campaigners alleged that if Britain remained in the EC it would gradually lose its political independence and in the end be absorbed into a federal Europe.

27. Cmd. 6066 (1975), *Commonwealth Heads of Government Meeting Kingston, Jamaica, 29 April–6 May 1975 Final Communiqué*; Wilson, *Final Term*, p. 107; Butler and Kitzinger, *The 1975 Referendum*, p. 162.

28. Butler and Kitzinger, *The 1975 Referendum*, p. 183.   29. *Ibid.*, p. 183.

'What you are being asked to decide', Benn declared, 'is whether you want Britain to be self-governing and independent, or whether you want to be under Commissioners you cannot remove.'[30] The 'yes' campaigners replied that there was no question of rule by Brussels bureaucrats. Important decisions were taken by the Council of Ministers, and if necessary a veto could be exercised under the Luxembourg Compromise. In any case, sovereignty was not simply a matter of dry, abstract theory. What counted was how British interests could best be protected, and in an increasingly interdependent world Britain simply could not afford to stand alone.

The sovereignty issue was highlighted by Powell and also by Foot, who was only able to play a limited role in the campaigning because of a recent operation.[31] Opinion polls indicated, however, that 'bread and butter' questions about prices, living standards and the economy loomed far larger in the minds of most voters. The economic debate was a complicated one, and what made it more complicated still was the difficulty of disentangling the various factors responsible for the current parlous state of the British economy. Britain's entry into the EC in 1973 coincided with the beginning of a severe downturn in the world economy, brought on by President Nixon's devaluation of the dollar and imposition of a 10 per cent surcharge on imports in 1971, followed by the quadrupling of oil prices in 1973–4. In the case of Britain, the position was further aggravated by the coalminers' strike and the resultant three-day working week of 1974. In the twelve months to May 1975 consumer prices rose by 25 per cent. Moreover, by May unemployment had reached 850,000, compared to under 500,000 at the end of 1973. There was an acute deterioration in the balance of payments, and the pound had slumped to an all-time low. Not unnaturally, the anti-marketeers attempted to place the blame for these developments on British entry to the EC. Shore argued that Britain's balance of payments difficulties stemmed from a huge deficit with the original Six, while Benn, the Secretary of State for Industry, made the startling claim that membership of the Community had cost Britain 500,000 jobs. The stinging response from Roy Jenkins was to say publicly: 'I find it increasingly difficult to take Mr Benn seriously as an economics minister.'[32]

30. Robin Day 'phone-in', 27 May 1975: cited in Butler and Kitzinger, *The 1975 Referendum*, p. 177.
31. M. Jones, *Michael Foot* (1994), pp. 376–8.
32. Goodhart, *Full-Hearted Consent*, pp. 160–63; Jenkins, *A Life at the Centre*, pp. 410–11.

By far the most sensitive of the economic questions under debate was the price of food. Here the pro-marketeers enjoyed a stroke of luck in that the enormous increase in international commodity prices that had taken place over the past two years meant that by 1975 food prices within the EC were no higher – and in some cases actually lower – than on world markets. According to pro-marketeers, the rise in world food prices was no mere accident. It was the result of a long-term growth in demand and offered a salutary warning that the days of cheap food were gone for good. What mattered now was security of supply. It followed that Britain, as a country that could not feed itself, would be safer in the EC, which was almost self-sufficient in food.

This interpretation was challenged by anti-marketeers like Castle. They insisted that artificially high food prices were an inbuilt feature of the CAP and were the price of propping up inefficient continental producers. As long as Britain remained in the EC, it would have to subsidise the growing beef and butter mountains and wine lakes. Outside, it would be free to buy at the lowest world prices. Castle herself became involved in one of the more lighthearted episodes in the campaign, the 'Battle of the Shopping Baskets'. As a publicity stunt, she purchased a basket of food in London costing just over £4 and then went on a trip to Brussels to buy identical items at a cost of nearly £7. The point of this exercise was to provide a practical demonstration of what lay in store as British prices were brought up to EC levels. Her plan backfired, however, when Britain in Europe got wind of it, sent a woman to Oslo to do some shopping of her own and proved conclusively that the price of food was even higher in Norway, whose people had voted to reject membership of the EC in an earlier referendum.

In the course of the referendum campaign, public opinion began to swing strongly towards a 'yes' vote, and by May 1975 it was fairly clear what the outcome would be. As expected, it was a decisive endorsement of British membership. On a high turnout of almost 65 per cent of the electorate, 17,378,581 voted for Britain to remain in the EC and 8,470,073 against – in percentage terms, 67.2 per cent for and 32.8 per cent against. As Wilson pointed out, it was a bigger majority than any government had received in any general election.[33] There were some regional variations in the overall national pattern. Support for staying in tended to be strongest in the south-east of England, weaker in the north and weaker still in Scotland:

33. *The Times*, 6 June 1975.

only in Shetland and the Western Isles were there majorities against. To some extent, these local differences reflected the regional strengths and weaknesses of the two main political parties. The 'yes' vote was higher among Conservative electors than among their Labour counterparts, though even in the case of the latter the 'antis' were in a minority – something usually explained by rank-and-file loyalty to Wilson. Whether the size of the majority was indicative of any great enthusiasm for British membership of the EC is open to serious doubt. At the time, the electorate's verdict was described by *The Guardian* as 'Full-hearted, wholehearted and cheerful hearted'.[34] Most historians, however, have concluded that the outcome owed more to caution and conservatism than to positive feelings towards the EC. In the words of Butler and Kitzinger, in their detailed study of the referendum: 'the verdict ... was unequivocal but it was also unenthusiastic. Support for membership was wide but it did not run deep.'[35]

As far as the Labour Party was concerned, the referendum was not the triumphant resolution of an intractable problem that it appeared to be on the surface. One of Wilson's main reasons for holding the referendum had been to prevent an irreparable split in Labour ranks. In the short term, that purpose was certainly achieved. In the longer term, however, as Jenkins had feared, far from healing party divisions, it served to aggravate and widen them. Agreed Cabinet guidelines on behaviour during the referendum campaign had deprecated personal attacks upon colleagues.[36] Such niceties, however, had not always been scrupulously observed. Much more damaging was a tendency on the part of leading Labour pro-marketeers to discover, in the course of cross-party campaigning, that they had a great deal more in common with sections of the Conservative and Liberal parties than with the Labour Left.[37] This loosening of the bonds of party loyalty that Jenkins acknowledges in his memoirs was to have catastrophic consequences for Labour unity in the early 1980s and played a major part in the formation of the breakaway Social Democratic Party (SDP) in 1981.

34. *The Guardian*, 7 June 1975.
35. Butler and Kitzinger, *The 1975 Referendum*, p. 280.
36. Wilson, *Final Term*, p. 105.   37. Jenkins, *A Life at the Centre*, p. 424.

CHAPTER FIFTEEN

Semi-detached: the Callaghan Government and Europe

In March 1976 Wilson unexpectedly and voluntarily announced his retirement from office, claiming that he had long since planned to do so on reaching the age of 60. He was succeeded by Callaghan, an older man whose leadership ambitions had been virtually extinguished but whose wide ministerial experience as Chancellor of the Exchequer, Home Secretary and Foreign Secretary, together with his skills as a party manager, made him the obvious successor. Callaghan had few illusions about the magnitude of the problems confronting him. In the midst of deepening economic gloom, he had reportedly mused aloud at one Cabinet meeting in November 1974: 'When I am shaving in the morning I say to myself that if I were a young man I would emigrate. By the time I am sitting down to breakfast I ask myself, "Where would I go?"'[1] Callaghan's government was to be dominated by the politics of economic recession and by the continuing problem of managing a deeply divided governing party: at his last party conference as leader, Wilson wryly observed that the party had never previously demonstrated such united support for the manifesto or such diversity in its interpretation. This diversity was thrown into even sharper relief by the sterling crisis that engulfed the Callaghan government in its first nine months of office and marked out 1976, along with 1949, 1967 and later 1992, as a notable year in the post-1945 history of sterling crises.

Callaghan's 'baptism of fire' as Prime Minister occurred immediately after he took up office, as the continuing problems of high inflation, a large balance of payments deficit and, above all, an historically high Public Sector Borrowing Requirement (PSBR)

1. Cited in A. Morgan, *Harold Wilson* (1992), p. 471.

amounting to 9.6 per cent of GDP finally sent sterling into a free fall on the international money market. In the period March–September 1976, massive sales of sterling reduced its value by 26 per cent. By September, the government's unsuccessful efforts to stop sterling's slide were dramatically exposed as Healey, the Chancellor of the Exchequer, was forced to make a hurried change in travel plans at Heathrow Airport in order to return to the Treasury as sterling continued to plummet on the foreign exchanges – 'the lowest point' in his chancellorship.[2] In the circumstances, only an IMF loan to Britain was sufficient to shore up the pound. The US, as the prime mover in the IMF, largely determined both the size of the loan (£3.5 billion) and also the accompanying conditions that were settled in December 1976. The British government agreed to reduce its planned public spending by £2.5 billion over the next two financial years. It also arranged to sell off £500 million of the government shares in British Petroleum in order to further cut the PSBR. In the event, no more than half of the stand-by credits were drawn on by the government and freedom from IMF controls – 'Sod off Day', as Healey put it – occurred earlier than scheduled.

The impact of this package on government spending, combined with earlier cuts announced in the 1975 and 1976 budgets, resulted in the largest reduction in public expenditure in any single year since 1945: 2.4 per cent in 1976/77 rising to 6.9 per cent in 1977/78. At the time of the 1975 budget, one Cabinet minister, Crosland, crisply announced the end of an era: 'The party's over.'[3] Left-wing opinion in the party was particularly outraged by cuts that undermined manifesto commitments and evoked memories of 1966. At the Labour Party conference during the course of the crisis, Callaghan signalled the new emphases of the times by declaring that the country could no longer seek to spend its way out of recession: Keynesian economic management was in retreat and monetarism in the ascendant, as counter-inflationary policy and curbs on public expenditure took precedence over the problem of rising unemployment.[4]

2. D. Healey, *The Time of My Life* (1989), pp. 429 and 433. At the height of this sterling crisis, Healey addressed the Labour Party conference in Blackpool, dramatising the occasion by announcing that 'I have come from the battlefront' and warning angry delegates that the government was committed to 'very painful cuts in public expenditure . . .': cited in M. Jones, *Michael Foot* (1994), p. 401.

3. S. Crosland, *Tony Crosland* (1982), p. 295.

4. The substance of Callaghan's message was that Keynesian economic management was resulting in higher rates of inflation and unemployment: 'We used to think that you could just spend your way out of recession and increase employment

The course and outcome of the 1976 sterling crisis connected with and illuminated the real, albeit limited, interest of the Callaghan government in the EC. IMF assistance ensured that the crisis was handled in the context of the wider Western international economic system rather than in an exclusively European framework. This approach suited Callaghan's priorities and preferences in the world at large, not least because of his strong 'Atlanticist' inclinations over and above any European ties. In his first major speech as Foreign Secretary in 1974, he had been particularly critical of the Heath government for allowing its European commitment to weaken Anglo-American relations.[5] At the same time, he had called for a greater degree of cooperation between Europe and the US in order to counter the view – evident in some of the fractious EC–US exchanges during the 1973 'Year of Europe' – that EC unity was best forged in opposition to the US. In 1976, as in previous sterling crises, the British authorities looked to direct dealings with the Americans to resolve the crisis. Any suggestion that the EC states, either collectively or individually, might serve a useful function in this respect was as unthinkable to some members of the Callaghan government as the idea of fully engaging the OEEC states in managing the devaluation of sterling in 1949 had been to the Attlee government. At a particularly important point in the IMF loan negotiations, for example, Schmidt sent an envoy to London, Karl Otto Pöhl, a senior Bundesbank official. The reception from Healey was frosty: 'What do you want here? This is our business.'[6] But West German intervention to make the IMF conditions less burdensome was welcomed by Callaghan. He was to enjoy a better working relationship than Wilson had with Schmidt and other EC leaders. He was also far less disposed than Wilson to parade his nationalist credentials.

The government's handling of the sterling crisis also registered a defeat for left-wing, anti-EC opinion within the Labour Party which, while still reeling from the referendum result, took the view that the result signified little more than a temporary truce. The Left's

only by cutting taxes and boosting government expenditure . . . it only worked by injecting bigger doses of inflation into the economy followed by a higher level of unemployment at the next step . . .': cited in D. Kavanagh and P. Morris, *Consensus Politics: From Attlee to Major* (1994), p. 42.

5. *H.C.Deb.*, vol. 870, cols. 859–64. See also K.O. Morgan, *Callaghan, A Life* (1997), p. 413.

6. K. Burk and A. Cairncross, *'Goodbye Great Britain': The 1976 IMF Crisis* (1992), p. 90.

response to the sterling crisis – as well as to the general abandonment through this period of socialist prescriptions formulated by the party during the 1970–74 period in Opposition – found expression in the 'alternative economic strategy'. This strategy, principally devised by Benn, envisaged the imposition of import and exchange controls in order to reverse the relative decline of British manufacturing industry, reduce the balance of payments deficit and avoid the public spending cuts of an IMF prescription. The Cabinet, however, was so unimpressed by this protectionist view of Britain as a siege economy that it refused to undertake a study of the strategy. It took the view that such a regime was at odds with the increasing integration of world trade and investment, and was furthermore bound to re-open the question of British membership of the EC. This was precisely one of the advantages of the strategy, in Benn's view, in that it was incompatible with the EC's customs union and would ultimately facilitate British withdrawal from the EC. Certainly there were EC provisions allowing a member state to take protective measures in the event of a currency crisis. But the full panoply of controls advocated by Benn went far beyond temporary emergency actions and was likely to encounter strong opposition from Britain's EC partners.

While Callaghan was determined to maintain British membership of the EC, he did not regard the EC as the principal or exclusive instrument for addressing the problem of continuing economic recession at the international level. His major contribution in this respect – a paper entitled 'International initiative on growth and currency stability' (March 1978) – was based on the premise that Europe and the US had to work in tandem in order to pull the Western economies out of recession. Apart from Callaghan's personal inclination towards Atlantic cooperation,[7] this initiative also expressed the long-standing British preference for dealing with the strategic issues of international economic cooperation in such a way as to ensure US involvement and to emphasise the importance of Western international economic institutions like the IMF and the OECD. This was not an approach that commended itself to other EC leaders, especially Schmidt – a strong critic of the leadership failings of the Carter administration – and Giscard d'Estaing. Both men took a dim view of the American failure to maintain the value of the dollar since the collapse of the Bretton Woods fixed

---

7. For Callaghan's strong support for Atlantic cooperation see, for example, *H.C.Deb.*, vol. 870, cols. 859–62 and 864.

exchange rate system, and were now increasingly disposed to develop an EC scheme for promoting monetary stability.

Throughout its period of office, the Callaghan government was so subjected to domestic political constraints that it had limited room for manoeuvre in the conduct of its EC policy. The public expenditure cuts resulted in deep divisions within the Labour Party. The gulf between government and party was most evident in a key party institution like the NEC, where Callaghan – later describing some members of this body as viewing themselves as an 'alternative Government' – generally failed to command a majority for government policies. Anti-EC opinion was in the ascendancy, with a majority against membership on the NEC and with a party conference vote in 1976 of two to one against the introduction of direct elections to the EP. Such conditions left an increasingly beleaguered government open to pressure to adopt a minimalist approach to the EC in order to assuage at least some of the party's opposition to the government's economic policy. The problem of party management was made more acute by the loss of a parliamentary majority and the emergence of the Lib–Lab pact, by which the strongly pro-EC Liberals extracted a government commitment to introduce legislation providing for direct elections to the EP. The parliamentary arithmetic alone thus forced Callaghan into a delicate balancing act that scarcely made for strong British leadership in EC affairs.

The dominant Franco-German axis in the EC throughout this period also weighed heavily against the possibility of exercising the type of British leadership that had been frequently advanced as one of the reasons for EC membership. Throughout the period 1974–81, there was a particularly close working relationship between Schmidt, the West German Chancellor, and Giscard d'Estaing, the French President.[8] This had first developed in the course of their earlier dealings as finance ministers, was strengthened as a result of a shared and generally pragmatic view of the EC and of wider international developments, and was assisted by the institutionalised forms of cooperation under the Franco-German Treaty of Friendship and Cooperation (1963). During this period Franco-German agenda-fixing in the European Council often irritated other EC leaders. So, too, did the frequent preface to Schmidt's Council speeches: 'The President and I feel'. This formidable partnership meant that strategic management of the EC was not based on an

    8. D.L. Bark and D.R. Gress, *A History of West Germany: Democracy and its Discontents 1963–1991* (1993), pp. 297–8. See also H. Simonian, *The Privileged Partnership: Franco-German relations in the European Community, 1969–1984* (1985), pp. 275–306.

informal triumvirate or *directoire* comprising Britain, France and West Germany, as had been widely expected at the time of British entry. As often as not, Callaghan was a spectator rather than a key player, and it was a matter of common observation that the Franco-German partnership effectively relegated Britain to an unduly low status.

This low-profile posture held out some advantages in the domestic setting, as some of the earlier economic arguments supporting British entry to the EC seemed increasingly open to question. The performance of the British economy, and most especially the weak trading record with the rest of the EC throughout this period, were major obstacles to presenting EC membership in a favourable light. Under the Callaghan government, the transitional period to the full operation of EC rules came to an end with a growing body of evidence easily marshalled by anti-marketeers to demonstrate the adverse effects of membership. The most obviously damning evidence was the phased increase in Britain's net contribution to the EC budget from £111 million in 1973 to £1.184 billion in 1980, by which time Britain was the largest net contributor, although ranking only seventh out of the nine EC states in GNP per capita. Public perceptions of the advantages of membership underwent dramatic changes in the circumstances: the EC's regular Eurobarometer polls of British opinion over the period 1975–81 registered a fall in support for the view that EC membership was a 'good thing' from 47 per cent to 24 per cent, and an increase in support of the view that it was a 'bad thing' from 21 per cent to 48 per cent.[9] The laggardly growth rate of the British economy during the period 1973–9 – averaging 0.5 per cent per annum (excluding North Sea oil production), according to Treasury figures – made a mockery of earlier pro-marketeer claims that membership of a large, buoyant market would galvanise the economy and serve to arrest its long-term relative decline.

There was, of course, much room for speculation that continued to fuel the debate about the economic pros and cons of membership. Pro-marketeers insisted that Britain's economic performance would have been worse still but for membership.[10] In particular,

9. Office for the Official Publications of the European Communities, *Europe as seen by Europeans: European polling 1973–86* (1986).

10. For an introductory guide to academic assessments of the economic impact of EC membership on Britain see A. Scott, 'Internal market policy', in S. Bulmer, S. George and A. Scott (eds), *The United Kingdom and EC Membership Evaluated* (1992). For a detailed discussion of the impact of EC membership on Britain in the 1970s and early 1980s see, for example, C.D. Cohen, *The Common Market: Ten Years After* (1983) and A.M. El-Agraa, *Britain within the European Community* (1983).

they argued that membership had helped to shield Britain from the worst effects of soaring world commodity prices in the period 1974–6. They further maintained that the country's relatively low economic growth rate – just over half the EC average[11] – and its trade deficit with the EC in the period 1973–9 were part of a longer-term pre-1973 trend. According to this analysis, to attribute the post-1973 economic malaise to the impact of EC membership was to mistake the symptom for the fundamental cause – the long-standing lack of competitiveness of British industry in international markets.

Opponents of EC membership, however, concentrated their fire on the extent to which the EC accounted for an increasing proportion of total British trade – 43.8 per cent in 1980 compared with 30.9 per cent in 1972 – in ways that benefited the rest of the EC rather than Britain.[12] The substance of this argument was that the mounting deficit in Britain's visible trade since 1973 was proportionately greater with the EC than with the rest of the world. In the period 1973–7, for example, Britain's trade deficit with the EC accounted for some 59 per cent of its total trade deficit. This figure far exceeded the amount of British trade with the EC as a proportion of total British trade. While food accounted for part of this deficit, it was evident that British manufacturers were failing to penetrate the EC market as effectively as the manufacturers of other EC states were invading the British market. The balance of trade in road vehicles between Britain and the rest of the EC is a case in point: in the period 1975–7 the British deficit in this sector increased from £64 million to £464 million, and British exports to the rest of the EC as a proportion of British imports from the rest of the EC fell from 89 per cent to 70 per cent. Anti-marketeers within the Labour Party quickly seized on such evidence to claim that EC membership had resulted in a loss of British manufacturing jobs,[13] further reinforcing the Bennite case for protectionist measures. This view was pressed all the more forcefully as the rate of unemployment rose from 3 per cent in 1973 to 6.2 per cent in 1977 – then the highest recorded figure since 1945.

Against this background, the proposals for direct elections to the EP and for a European Monetary System (EMS) clearly revealed

11. OECD (1970–80) *Main Economic Indicators.*

12. For British trade figures during this period see *Trade and Industry,* 24 November 1978; *Annual Abstract of Statistics* (1980).

13. See, for example, a pamphlet issued by the Labour Common Market Safeguards Committee, *The Common Market: Promises and Reality* (1976).

the cautious and often heavily qualified EC policy of the Callaghan government in the face of Labour Party opposition to the acceptance of any new obligations. The Treaty of Rome had made provision for direct elections to the EP (or European Assembly, as it was known at the time). The Council of Ministers had repeatedly failed to act on this matter, however, and the EP therefore continued to consist of nominated representatives of the member states' national parliaments. In the wake of The Hague summit's attempts to revive the EC, and especially with the successful completion of enlargement, there was growing pressure to introduce direct elections. This had considerable support in the EP itself, which viewed direct elections as a means of enhancing its legitimacy. A breakthrough occurred in December 1974 when the EC heads of government agreed in principle to proceed to direct elections. As we noted earlier, Wilson had acquiesced in this largely French-inspired initiative in order to win French support in the renegotiation exercise. In September 1976 the EC leaders (via the recently designated European Council) further agreed to ensure that national parliaments completed the required legislation so as to allow the first set of direct elections to be held in the spring of 1978.

Callaghan was prepared to abide by Wilson's earlier undertakings. But he was not favourably disposed to the idea of direct elections and was even less inclined to treat the matter as an urgent necessity. His top priority was to nurse the Labour Party through the deflationary consequences of the sterling crisis and not to expend political capital on a divisive secondary issue. In Cabinet there was a two to one majority in support of direct elections legislation, yet this majority did not amount to a strong, principled commitment. Pro-EC opinion in the Cabinet was greatly weakened by the departure of Jenkins in September 1976 for the post of President of the European Commission, a loss that was not mourned by the anti-marketeers. At the same time, opposition to EC membership in the Cabinet was strengthened by the influential figure of Michael Foot, who had closely challenged Callaghan for the leadership and whose left-wing credentials were viewed by the latter as an important means of undermining the Left's vigorous opposition to the government's economic policy. Party opinion at large was also a persuasive factor counting against any hasty treatment. NEC and party conference opposition to direct elections was mainly based on the view that a directly elected EP was bound to acquire more power and thus propel the EC in a federalist direction. This argument did not sit easily with earlier criticism of the EC as an undemocratic body. Nor did it take cognisance of the fact that some of the principal movers in favour of direct elections, notably Giscard d'Estaing, were equally opposed to federalist designs and viewed a directly elected EP as a substitute for one with real powers.

The government's difficulties on the direct elections issue were compounded by the terms of the Lib–Lab pact of March 1977, by which Callaghan agreed to introduce the direct elections legislation and to take full account of the Liberal Party's commitment to a system of proportional representation.[14] There was no EC requirement for this last feature, and Callaghan himself was a confirmed opponent of such a measure. But proportional representation was a vital necessity for the Liberals, who were likely to win few if any of the 78 British seats in the EP on the Westminster system of single-member constituencies and the first-past-the-post principle. After much delay, reflecting its crablike approach to the issue, in June 1977 the government introduced a Bill implementing direct elections, with provision for proportional representation. In the event, however, the Commons rejected proportional representation in December 1977, with a majority of Conservative and Labour MPs voting against – Labour's divisions accounting for the fact that the government had allowed a free vote. Prevailing opinion in both major parties was primarily influenced by a keen determination to maintain the British electoral system and by an accompanying fear that to embrace the principle of proportional representation for EP elections would ultimately call into question the democratic credentials of the British electoral system. This fear was all the greater because of the widespread use of proportional representation among the EC states.

Given this verdict and the need for further time to allow a boundary commission to draw up constituencies to operate on the British electoral system, Callaghan was obliged to inform the other EC governments that Britain – alone in this respect – was not in a position to hold the first direct elections as scheduled. Thus the first direct elections had to be put back until June 1979, and this episode further strengthened the image of Britain as a recalcitrant member state. If the government was not prepared to risk its survival by more vigorous advocacy and prosecution of the case for direct elections, with or without proportional representation, it was evidently not out of tune with the instincts of the British electorate,

14. For the terms of the Lib–Lab pact see D. Steel, *Against Goliath: David Steel's Story* (1989), pp. 129–30.

the large majority of whom did not vote in the first direct elections for the EP. The British turnout for the 1979 election was 32.6 per cent, compared with turnouts of over 60 per cent in the other EC states (with the exception of Denmark, where the figure was 47 per cent).[15]

The origins of the EMS in 1978 further underlined British exceptionalism in EC affairs.[16] The EMS arose out of a West German initiative that was launched by Schmidt at the Copenhagen European Council of April 1978 and rapidly assumed the appearance of a weighty Franco-German enterprise. It was principally designed to create a 'zone of monetary stability' in the EC and to replace the existing arrangement of floating currencies that had emerged in the aftermath of the collapse of the Bretton Woods fixed exchange rate system in the early 1970s. From the outset, the proposed EMS was clearly more modest in scope than the earlier plans for an EC economic and monetary union, not least because it made no provision for a European central bank and a single currency. Less clear at the time of its inception, however, was the extent to which this initiative was markedly different from the 'snake' system that had been envisaged as the first stage towards monetary union but which had subsequently collapsed into a Deutschmark (DM) zone. The main feature of the EMS, as finally settled at the Brussels European Council of December 1978, was the Exchange Rate Mechanism (ERM). This device linked the currencies of the member states and placed limits on the extent to which each currency was permitted to fluctuate against other currencies in the system. To assist this purpose, the European Currency Unit (ECU) was introduced, the value of which would be determined by a basket of currencies of the EMS states and against which each currency was to have a central rate. These central rates, in turn, provided the basis for a parity grid comprising each pair of currencies in the system and permitting each pair of currencies to fluctuate within a margin of plus or minus 2.25 per cent. There was provision for automatic intervention by the central banks in order to ensure that a pair of currencies operated within this margin. This use of a parity grid system rather than a basket system based on the performance of a single currency in relation to the ECU was a matter of considerable

15. Office for the Official Publications of the European Communities, *Steps to European Unity* (1987).

16. For the origins of the EMS see, for example, K. Dyson, *Elusive Union: The Process of Economic and Monetary Union in Europe* (1994); B. Connolly, *The Rotten Heart of Europe: The Dirty War of Europe's Money* (1995).

debate at the time, the weak currency countries viewing the latter as preferable.

A key aspect of the EMS proposal was its West German author-ship at a time when the country had not only emerged as Europe's economic superpower, but also presented a model – *Modell Deutsch-land* – of sustained economic growth, price stability, low unemploy-ment and balance of payments surpluses. This record was in marked contrast to the high inflation, high unemployment and low growth of some of the other EC states. Schmidt was particularly impressed by the case for a fixed but adjustable exchange rate regime in the EC. He saw it as a means of promoting a more stable monetary environment for West Germany's large stake in intra-EC trade, accounting for 26.4 per cent of total intra-EC exports in 1987. More importantly, he regarded it as an instrument for dealing with the impact of the falling value of the dollar on West German prices at home and abroad: the value of the dollar against the Deutschmark had fallen by 75 per cent in the period 1972–9 and fell by as much as 12 per cent in the critical period October 1977–February 1978, when Schmidt finally decided to take the initiative. It was envisaged that a greater degree of European monetary cooperation would increase the attractiveness of other European currencies and thus take some of the pressure off the Deutschmark, which had become a refuge for holders of the fast-depreciating dollar. For the other EC states, however, the central question posed by the EMS, as in the earlier operations of the 'snake', was whether or not they could afford to enter a system in which the Deutschmark was the bench-mark currency in all but name and which involved tying themselves to the low inflation and highly competitive disciplines of the West German economy. More precisely, there surfaced the question of which country – a strong currency country like West Germany or a weak currency country like Britain – was to take corrective action in the event of major exchange rate fluctuations. Was the Bundesbank, the emblem of West German economic success since 1945, to give unlimited support to any EMS currency that found itself in trouble, or was the onus to be on the weak currency country to take the appropriate deflationary action? Alternatively, were there to be 'sym-metrical obligations', with parallel reflationary and deflationary measures being undertaken by strong and weak currency countries respectively?

The initial British response to the Schmidt initiative was support-ive of the idea of monetary stability. From the outset, however, Callaghan was mainly intent on postponing a decision. What he feared was that a British decision to stay out of the ERM might prompt a run on the pound – an understandable concern in view of the 1976 sterling crisis and his own traumatic experience as Chancellor at the time of the 1967 devaluation. Early confidential discussion of Schmidt's plan demonstrated a characteristically British willingness to participate in top-level deliberations but without any commitment to the exercise. At the Copenhagen European Council meeting, for example, Callaghan had agreed with Schmidt and Giscard that detailed proposals should be considered by a small working group comprising a nominated adviser from each of the three states: Schulmann (West Germany), Clappier (France) and Couzens (Britain). In the event, it was a Schulmann–Clappier paper that was forwarded to the next meeting of the European Council. Couzens, for his part, occupied the role of a sceptical bystander and lacked any political backing from London, thus cutting a similar figure to Bretherton at the time of the post-Messina negotiations in 1955. As on past occasions, France aligned with Germany rather than Britain, in this case largely because Giscard d'Estaing was determined to preserve the Franco-German relationship as the EC's pacemaker and also because he viewed the maintenance of a strong franc (*franc fort*) via EMS membership as a useful external discipline for the French economy.

Callaghan's political agenda in 1978 was increasingly dominated by the next general election and by the fate of the government's incomes policy that was to be put to the test in the 1978/79 'winter of discontent'. There was no inclination to allow yet another European issue to expose government and party divisions and, in that respect, Schmidt's initiative was an unwanted complication at an inopportune moment. In any case, the initiative was viewed as irrelevant to what the government saw as the major requirements, most notably a plan to pull the Western economies out of recession and, more parochially, an EC willingness to address the problem of Britain's contribution to the EC budget. Several telling considerations weighed against full British membership of the EMS, reflecting not only the balance of opinion in the Labour Party but also a wider domestic consensus.

In the first place, the timing of the Schmidt plan coincided with the unveiling of Callaghan's scheme for a joint Euro-American effort to rejuvenate the Western economies. The prospect of a tightly organised European monetary bloc did not commend itself to Callaghan if it was likely to jeopardise the possibility of cooperation with the Americans. Callaghan needed no reminding from one senior Treasury official who, in Sir Humphrey Appleby mode, reportedly commented on the possibility of putting sterling in the ERM: 'But it is very bold, Prime Minister. It leaves the dollar on one side. I do not know what the Americans will say about it.'[17]

Secondly, and more generally, British interests in the wider international economy suggested that there was no compelling reason to sink sterling in an exclusively European construction. Unlike any other EC state, Britain had overseas financial and commercial interests that were still more heavily concentrated in North America and the Commonwealth than in Europe. This consideration, together with sterling's role as an international currency, meant that City opinion focused attention on the wider world economy – especially on the sterling–dollar exchange rate – and betrayed little interest in, or support for, the inclusion of sterling in an exclusively EC monetary framework. Nor was there any strong demand from British industry for a more stable monetary regime to facilitate intra-EC trade. Earlier support for EC membership among British industrialists was now less in evidence, partly due to growing disenchantment with Brussels bureaucracy and plans for harmonisation and partly reflecting the extent to which the EC market was not of overriding importance for British exports. A smaller proportion of Britain's manufacturing exports (38.8 per cent) went to the EC than was the case with all of the other EC states except Denmark: the comparable figures for France, Italy and West Germany (in 1986) were 47.5 per cent, 51.4 per cent and 47.5 per cent respectively. In 1987, intra-EC trade accounted for only 49.1 per cent of total British trade. This was well below the EC average of 58.6 per cent and ranked second lowest, next to Denmark (48.52 per cent). Long-standing trading patterns, in effect, marked Britain off from the more EC-centred commercial activities of the other member states.[18] British industry's doubts about the value of full membership of the EMS were also echoed in the Conservative Shadow Cabinet. There were still vivid memories of the Heath government's disastrously short-lived attempt in 1972 to put sterling in the 'snake': John Nott, then a Treasury minister and now the Shadow Trade Minister, was particularly opposed to repeating the experience.

Thirdly, there was a decidedly negative response in government quarters as the full implications of the Schmidt plan became apparent

17. Cited in G. Radice, *Offshore: Britain and the European Idea* (1992), p. 105.

18. This difference was even greater in the early years of British membership of the EC. See, for example, Office for Official Publications of the European Communities, *Annual Abstract of Statistics* (1980) and *The Economy of the European Community* (1982).

in the course of negotiations. True, the Foreign Office supported EMS membership on strategic and economic grounds – predictably so, in Healey's view, in that the Foreign Office favoured anything that included the word 'European'.[19] Elsewhere in Whitehall, however, and especially in the Treasury, there was a far more influential body of opinion that focused on the probable deflationary consequences of tying the value of sterling to the Deutschmark in the EMS. The Treasury's reading of the situation was greatly influenced by the relatively poor performance of the British economy as compared with the other major EC economies. During the period 1974–8, Britain's annual output had grown by only 0.25 per cent, compared with 1.5 per cent in the case of Germany and Italy and 2.5 per cent in that of France, while the British rate of inflation during the same period had averaged over 18 per cent as compared with 10 per cent in most other EC economies and 5.5 per cent in West Germany. This economic record, and especially the accompanying slide in the value of sterling against the Deutschmark, did not augur well for the consequences of full EMS membership. The government would be required to take deflationary measures in order to keep sterling in the ERM, thereby adversely affecting growth and employment. According to Treasury estimates, the inclusion of sterling in the ERM would mean a progressive increase in its value of 6 per cent by the end of 1979 to 20 per cent by the end of 1981, with an accompanying reduction in GDP of 1 per cent in 1980 and as much as 5 per cent in 1981. In the event, sterling's value on the money markets rose sharply in the period 1979–81 as a result of its petrocurrency status and the doubling in the price of oil in 1979/80 in the wake of the revolution in Iran in January 1979. These developments brought the worst economic recession since 1945, greatly accelerated the process of deindustrialisation and prompted Healey to comment later that a strong sterling in the ERM would have required massive intervention by the weaker EMS currencies and that 'Far from paying a price to get Britain in, the other members of the European Community would have paid a lot to keep us out'.[20] In the circumstances of 1978, however, full British membership of the ERM was perceived as abandoning the one instrument that British governments had used to adjust British prices in the international economy – devaluation. Certainly Callaghan and Healey were determined to ensure that any decision to withhold sterling from the ERM was not interpreted in this light.

19. Healey, *The Time of My Life*, p. 439.   20. *Ibid.*, p. 439.

Thus Callaghan informed Schmidt that his government's priority was fighting inflation and, without any trace of irony, voiced his doubts about EMS in view of the divergent inflation rates of the member states.

Finally, there was no substantial support in the Cabinet or in the Labour Party at large for full membership of the EMS. In Cabinet, any initial interest in full membership of the EMS dissolved away. This was partly because an early attempt to make British member-ship of EMS conditional on a satisfactory settlement of Britain's net contribution to the EC budget[21] proved unacceptable to the other member states and, more importantly, because it became apparent that the actual workings of the EMS were unlikely to serve British economic interests. There were sharply opposing but clearly minor-ity views on the subject. Harold Lever, Callaghan's economic adviser, favoured full membership of the EMS. Benn, the most vociferous opponent, argued that EMS membership would lead to the further deindustrialisation of Britain. He also expressed the view that Britain could stop the venture in its tracks by exercising a veto – an idea which one of his ministerial colleagues later described as 'for the birds'.[22] But the bulk of Cabinet opinion, including pro-Europeans like Edmund Dell, the Secretary of State for Trade, was less partisan and took the view that, on balance, there was little to be gained and much to lose from placing sterling in the ERM. Dell himself later commented that the most striking contrast during the EMS nego-tiations was between the continental conviction that politics should have priority over economics and scepticism in London as to whether in the long run this was really possible[23] – an observation no less applicable to some aspects of Britain–EC differences long before and long after this particular episode. Healey concluded that the proposed scheme was little more than a reincarnation of the 'snake', with a 'European' element that was largely a matter of political window dressing. In effect, the Germans were trying to persuade the other weaker European currency countries to serve as a lead balloon on the Deutschmark. Callaghan took the same view and knew that he 'could not travel fast' in EC affairs due to opposi-tion in the Labour Party.[24] There was considerable hostility to EMS

21. For the UK's gross and net contribution to the EC budget in the period 1973–8 see Cmd. 7405, *The European Monetary System.*

22. E. Dell, 'Britain and the Origins of the European Monetary System', *Contemporary European History*, vol. 3 (1994).

23. *Ibid.*

24. J. Callaghan, *Time and Chance* (1987), p. 493. See also Morgan, *Callaghan*, pp. 614–16.

membership at the 1978 Labour Party conference, largely on the grounds that such a move represented a direct assault on national economic sovereignty and marked a further stage on the road to a federal Europe. Any remaining doubts in Callaghan's mind about the inadvisability of full membership of the EMS were here swept away. Shortly afterwards, following Cabinet discussions in November–December 1978, it was formally decided to withhold sterling from the ERM – the centrepiece of the EMS – but to participate in the other aspects of the system, including arrangements for the partial pooling of member states' gold and foreign currency reserves to create the ECU.[25] This meant that the EMS could be introduced as an EC scheme, but with Britain as the only member state spurning full membership – Italian and Irish reservations being overcome by West German financial assistance.

In relaying this decision to the other EC leaders in December 1978, Callaghan sought to minimise the significance of the decision and to avoid the impression that this was a question of being for or against the EC. As on previous and also later occasions in similar circumstances (the Major government's opt-out from the single currency, for example), it seemed that the British government was intent on maximising the advantages of association with an EC initiative while avoiding full commitment. It was entirely in keeping with this mentality that the Callaghan Cabinet agreed that, if the EMS was to be set up as an EC scheme, it had to be devised in a way acceptable to Britain and to meet several British requirements. The first of these was that 'the door must be left open to the UK to join at any time it wished, and there must be scope to amend the scheme to make it more acceptable'.

By the end of Callaghan's period of office, the problematical process of adjustment to EC membership was still in evidence. Callaghan himself was clearly aware of the value of membership, but his wider, 'Atlanticist' preferences limited his interest in the dynamics of EC development. There were major constraints on the government's room for manoeuvre, especially its minority status, its preoccupation with economic difficulties and its inability to convey to much of its own party and the public at large the benefits of EC membership. In these circumstances, it was not possible to advance beyond a generally defensive and highly qualified approach to EC affairs.

25. For Callaghan's Commons statement on the decision see *H.C.Deb.*, vol. 959, cols. 1421–1422.

CHAPTER SIXTEEN

More U-turns: Labour and the EC in the 1980s

Labour's defeat in the general election of May 1979 marked the beginning of a prolonged period of frustrating opposition, most of it spent while Margaret Thatcher was in power. During Thatcher's eleven-year premiership, between 1979 and 1990, the party's official stance on Europe – always subject to periodic shifts – evolved through two contrasting phases. In the years immediately following the election, there developed within the Labour movement as a whole powerful currents of hostility to continuing British membership of the EC. This led to the adoption of a policy favouring negotiated withdrawal at the earliest opportunity. From the mid-1980s, however, a new and more positive mood began to emerge. At first the change was gradual, but it later gathered pace until by the end of the decade Labour had come to be generally regarded as far more 'Europhile' (the expression replacing 'pro-market') than the Conservatives. To such an extent had the parties' customary roles been reversed, indeed, that the Labour leadership found itself subjected to opponents' taunts that it was the 'poodle' of Brussels. These developments, as will be seen, were partly a consequence of changing circumstances within the EC as a whole. But they were also intimately connected to the dynamics of domestic politics and, in particular, to Labour's own internal battles.

As in 1970, albeit this time in a much more rancorous atmosphere, the electoral setback of 1979 was followed by an exhaustive inquest and bitter recriminations over responsibility for what had gone wrong. Those on the left of the Labour Party were quick to lay the blame on the deflationary policies pursued by Callaghan, Healey and other ministers in response to the 1976 IMF crisis and, more specifically, on the late government's doomed attempt to impose a third phase of incomes policy – with a rigid 5 per cent limit – on a trade union movement which was manifestly deter-mined to reject it. It was this ineptitude, it was claimed, that had in January 1979 precipitated the disastrous 'winter of discontent' – the period of industrial strife, with its television images of rubbish uncollected and dead unburied, that had done so much to damage Labour's standing with large sections of the electorate. Right-wingers offered an entirely different interpretation of events. They were equally convinced that the main cause of Labour's misfortune had been trade union irresponsibility.[1]

These conflicting explanations for the downfall of the Callaghan government underlay much of the ferocious infighting that charac-terised Labour politics during the early 1980s.[2] But the divisions ran deeper still and were rooted in divergent ideas about the nature of accountability and democracy. The experience of Labour's period in office between 1974 and 1979 had persuaded many on the left that there must be fundamental changes in the organisation and structure of the party. According to those who took this view, suc-cessive Labour governments had reneged on election promises and failed to implement socialist policies because they, along with the body of MPs on whose support they rested, were too remote from the rank and file. What was needed, therefore, was to devise means for making those at the top more accountable to ordinary party members. Such notions had been current since the early 1970s when disillusionment with the Wilson administrations of 1964–70 had prompted the formation of the Campaign for Labour Party Democracy (CLPD). It was only after the shockwaves of 1979, how-ever, that they began to make real headway, vigorously promoted by a variety of left-wing bodies such as the Labour Coordinating Committee, Militant (a Trotskyite splinter group pursuing the tactic of 'entryism') and, most important of all, the CLPD. By 1981 most of the constitutional objectives of these organisations had been achieved, largely as a result of decisions taken at a special confer-ence held at Wembley in January of that year. Among the changes introduced were mandatory re-selection of MPs by their local con-stituency associations and an end to the monopoly enjoyed by the PLP over election of the party leader: henceforth the choice was

1. J. Adams, *Tony Benn* (1992), p. 394. It must be said that Healey was later to admit that the 5 per cent norm had been a tactical blunder: D. Healey, *The Time of My Life* (1989), p. 462.

2. For Labour's internecine warfare during the early 1980s see H. Pelling and A.J. Reid, *A Short History of the Labour Party* (1996), ch. 11; B. Castle, *Fighting All the Way* (1993), ch. 19; R. Jenkins, *A Life at the Centre* (1992), ch. 28; M. Jones, *Michael Foot* (1994), pp. 436–8; K.O. Morgan, *Callaghan, A Life* (1997), ch. 29.

to be made by an electoral college in which representatives of the trade unions would have 60 per cent of the total vote, with representatives of the PLP and of the local constituencies sharing the remaining 40 per cent equally. These reforms were not carried through without fierce, if unavailing, resistance from the Manifesto Group and others on the right of the party.

The Left's success in pushing through these constitutional changes was paralleled by, and reinforced, the leftward drift of Labour policies in the early 1980s. Unilateral nuclear disarmament and an extension of state control of the economy were soon adopted as the official party line. What is more relevant to this study, the 'lurch to the left' – as unsympathetic observers described it – resulted in a reorientation of policy on Europe. At the party conference held at Blackpool in October 1980, a motion from Clive Jenkins calling for withdrawal from the EC to be included in the next manifesto was carried by 5 million to 2 million votes.[3] This policy was endorsed at the 1981 conference and Labour duly entered the general election of 1983 firmly committed to it. *A New Hope for Britain*, its manifesto, stated that Labour would 'open immediate negotiations with our EEC partners, and introduce the necessary legislation, to prepare for Britain's withdrawal from the EEC to be completed well within the lifetime of the Labour Government'.[4]

Two of the main driving forces behind all these developments were Foot and Benn. Following Callaghan's announcement of his resignation as party leader in October 1980, Foot had defeated Healey in the ensuing election for his successor, an outcome which further strengthened growing left-wing influence within the party.[5] During his period in office in the late 1970s, Foot had displayed a zeal in helping to enforce the government's incomes policy that had shocked and pained some of his usual political allies.[6] His performance in that respect, however, was not indicative of a general shift in his political agenda. He remained an enthusiastic advocate of unilateral nuclear disarmament and nationalisation. Nor had there been any abatement of his long-standing antipathy to British membership of the EC.[7] He therefore welcomed and gave wholehearted backing to Labour's newly stated aim of negotiations for

3. Castle, *Fighting All the Way*, p. 527; K. Featherstone, *Socialist Parties and European Integration* (1988), p. 63.
4. Pelling and Reid, *A Short History of the Labour Party*, pp. 169–70.
5. Jones, *Michael Foot*, pp. 453ff; Morgan, *Callaghan*, pp. 719, 723–4.
6. Castle, *Fighting All the Way*, pp. 508, 527–8.
7. Pelling and Reid, *A Short History of the Labour Party*, p. 164.

immediate withdrawal. Benn likewise warmly approved of this latest about-turn on Europe, as well as the other policy and organisational changes currently taking place. It could scarcely have been otherwise, indeed, since he, more than anybody, was responsible for bringing them about.

The early 1980s represented the high point of Benn's influence within the Labour movement. He had always been an able and persuasive communicator. Now he emerged as the kind of inspirational leader that the Left had lacked since Aneurin Bevan was at the peak of his powers. Although never a member of the CLPD, Benn was closely associated with its activities and rightly seen as the principal architect of the reforms to 'democratise' the Labour Party.[8] In addition, he played a leading role in reshaping policy over a wide range of issues, including Britain's relations with Europe. After the 1975 referendum, his initial reaction – unlike that of some in the 'no' camp, such as Ian Mikardo – had been to accept the result. The people had voted to stay in by an overwhelming majority, he explained, and he would abide by their verdict. Within two years, however, he had changed his mind, announcing in July 1977 that he no longer regarded the outcome of the referendum as binding.[9] This was the prelude to a renewed attempt to secure Britain's withdrawal from the EC. As long as he served (as Secretary of State for Energy) in a Cabinet which favoured British membership, his efforts to that end were necessarily restricted, confined to frustrating and obstructing colleagues' attempts at cooperation with other EC governments. Once in Opposition, however, he embarked upon a full-blooded campaign which quickly achieved the desired objective.

Not surprisingly, Labour's abrupt reversal after 1979 of its stance on the EC caused intense dismay to the pro-European section of the party. As early as August 1980 David Owen, William Rodgers and Shirley Williams wrote an open letter to *The Guardian* protesting against the party's decision, at the prompting of the left-dominated NEC, to support withdrawal from the EC without even holding another referendum.[10] Over the next few months their disillusionment on the matter was to reach such a pitch that it helped to precipitate their departure from the party to which they had devoted all their political lives. They were accompanied by Roy

8. Castle, *Fighting All the Way*, pp. 504–5. See also Adams, *Tony Benn*, pp. 403–6.

9. *The Benn Diaries*, single volume edition, selected, abridged and introduced by R. Winstone (1996), diary entry of 5 June 1975, p. 319; D. Butler and U. Kitzinger, *The 1975 Referendum* (1996), p. 273; Jenkins, *A Life at the Centre*, p. 509.

10. *The Guardian*, 1 August 1980.

Jenkins, the final member of the so-called 'Gang of Four' who signed the Limehouse Declaration in late January 1981 before going on to form the Social Democratic Party (SDP) two months later.

Four years earlier, in January 1977, Jenkins had taken up the post of President of the European Commission, disappointed by Callaghan's refusal to offer him the foreign secretaryship on the grounds that everything he did would be 'regarded with deep suspicion by the anti-marketeers on our benches'[11] and generally unattracted by the prospect of remaining in a government with whose policies he felt increasingly out of sympathy. From Brussels, he had followed developments in the Labour Party with mounting anxiety and distaste. It would be wrong to suggest that either he or the others who eventually found it impossible to stay in the party were influenced solely by their views on Europe. They were deeply unhappy with the general thrust of recent policy changes – including the commitment to unilateral nuclear disarmament and more nationalisation – and regarded Foot's victory in the 1980 leadership contest as a recipe for disaster. They were also outraged by the alterations made to the party's constitutional arrangements which served to enhance the power of the trade union block vote and local party activists at the expense of MPs: it is not without significance that the formation of the SDP came almost immediately after the Wembley special conference. Nevertheless, the accounts provided by the 'Gang of Four' themselves leave no doubt that their inability to accept a policy based on leaving the EC was a crucial determinant in persuading them that they must seek a political future outside the Labour Party.[12]

The defection of a substantial body (29) of Labour MPs to the newly established SDP during 1981–2 necessarily had significant implications for the balance of forces within the party they left behind. As might be expected, those who switched their allegiance – among them David Marquand, Robert Maclennan and Michael Thomas – had belonged to the right-wing, pro-European section of the Labour Party. Their departure therefore placed the anti-Europeans of the Left in an even stronger position than before. More than that, those like Healey and Hattersley, who had shared the defectors' fears about the direction in which Labour was moving but had chosen to carry on the fight from within the party, now found

11. J. Callaghan, *Time and Chance* (1987), p. 399.
12. See, for example, D. Owen, *Time to Declare* (1991), pp. 66–7. For Owen's account of the developments leading up to his departure from the Labour Party see *ibid.*, chs. 19–23.

themselves in an unenviable situation. By setting up a rival political organisation which appeared to pose a real threat to Labour's hopes of ever forming a government again, the Social Democrats had put themselves beyond the pale in the eyes of many former colleagues. They were seen as 'traitors' who had already let the party down in 1971–2 by helping to secure the passage of Heath's European Communities Bill and who had now committed the ultimate act of treachery by deserting the movement to which they owed whatever political success they had enjoyed. In such a climate of intense suspicion, it became difficult for Labour MPs whose views were not dissimilar to those held in the SDP to voice them openly for fear of raising speculation that they too were about to decamp. Indeed, expressions of support for British membership of the EC – an identifying feature of the SDP – came to be seen almost as a mark of disloyalty.[13]

In the period following the formation of the SDP, the Left's ascendancy within the Labour movement seemed assured, based upon possession of a majority on the NEC and strong backing in the trade unions and local constituencies. From late 1981, however, it was progressively eroded. The first indication of this tendency was Benn's defeat by Healey in the contest for deputy leader, held at Brighton under the new electoral college arrangements, at the end of September. Although the margin of the defeat could scarcely have been narrower – 49.754 per cent to 50.426 per cent – for Benn personally and for the Left as a whole it nevertheless represented a heavy psychological blow from which they never really recovered, checking the apparently irresistible momentum that they had been building up since 1979 and offering much-needed encouragement to their opponents. Nor did the damage end there, for Benn's decision to mount a challenge for the deputy leadership proved to be deeply divisive for the Left. From the outset, there was a substantial section of the Tribune group who regarded the whole business as an unwelcome distraction from the main task of attacking the government. The fact that Benn announced his intention to stand several months before an election could take place meant that Labour energies were consumed by a protracted bout of electioneering and internal wrangling. At a time of soaring unemployment and inner-city riots there were many on the moderate left as well as on the right of the Labour Party who viewed such self-absorption as intolerable. There was also disquiet over the manner

13. Featherstone, *Socialist Parties and European Integration*, p. 64.

in which Benn conducted his campaign, and more especially over his refusal to repudiate unequivocally attempts by assorted anarchists and other extremists to break up meetings addressed by Healey.[14] By the time the election was due a number of Tribunites had already distanced themselves from the Benn camp. These included Neil Kinnock, who had roundly criticised Benn in *Tribune* for encouraging a personality cult and had made it clear that he had no intention of voting for him. In the event, Kinnock voted for John Silkin in the first ballot and then abstained in the second – a course of action which infuriated committed Bennites like Tony Banks.[15]

In a number of respects, then, the 1981 election for the deputy leadership served to divide and weaken the Left, driving a wedge between what came increasingly to be known as its 'hard' and 'soft' components – the former being represented by the Campaign Group. As far as Benn himself was concerned, the episode was followed by further setbacks and a perceptible waning of his influence.[16] In the general election of June 1983, he lost his seat in Bristol and was therefore unable to take part in the leadership contest that was held the following October after Foot's resignation. Nor did he regain a place in the Commons until 1985 when he won a by-election at Chesterfield. In the meantime, the other bases on which his power had rested were gradually crumbling. The merging of the Home and International departments of the NEC, as part of Kinnock's thoroughgoing reorganisation of the party, deprived him of the influential post of chairman of the Home Policy Committee, which he had used as a sounding board for many of his radical political ideas. Those ideas themselves, moreover, no longer commanded the same degree of acceptance within the Labour movement as they had in the early 1980s. Like their author, they were treated with increasing scepticism and mistrust. A telling indication of Benn's declining popular appeal was provided by his performance in the annual election for the constituency section of the NEC: by 1985 he had slipped to third place in a poll which he had topped in every previous year since 1974.[17]

The slide in Benn's own political position was matched by that of the Left as a whole. As early as the 1981 party conference, the

---

14. Adams, *Tony Benn*, pp. 409–12.

15. *Tribune*, 18 September 1981; Adams, *Tony Benn*, pp. 415–17; Castle, *Fighting All the Way*, p. 530.

16. For Benn's declining influence within the Labour movement after 1983 see Adams, *Tony Benn*, ch. 35.

17. Castle, *Fighting All the Way*, p. 576.

latter's grip on the party machine had been substantially weakened when it lost five seats on the NEC to representatives of the Right, and the process continued the next year with the loss of two more seats.[18] It was after the electoral defeat of June 1983, however, that a reaction against left-wing influence and policies began to build up a head of steam. From the Labour standpoint the election was an unmitigated disaster. The result was far worse than that of 1979, which itself had been regarded as dreadful. The party won fewer seats than at any time since the rout of 1935 and only managed to hang on to second place by the skin of its teeth, obtaining 27.6 per cent of the total vote compared to 25.3 per cent for the Liberal–SDP Alliance. Labour had been severely punished for its chronic disunity. But the electorate's verdict also represented a decisive rejection of the programme offered by the 'hard left' or 'Bennite' wing of the party. The 1983 election manifesto, famously described by Gerald Kaufman as 'the longest suicide note in history', faith-fully reflected such a programme, calling for unilateral nuclear disarmament, more nationalisation, a restoration of trade union rights and withdrawal from Europe. This time, then, there could be no dispute over where the responsibility for Labour's defeat rested, or about the steps that needed to be taken to improve the pro-spects for success in the next election. The scene was set for yet another reversal of policy over Europe.[19]

The chastening events of the summer of 1983 brought a change of Labour leadership, a radical overhaul of party organisation and a major reappraisal of all areas of policy. Following Foot's resigna-tion, Kinnock was chosen to succeed him at the October 1983 party conference. The election of Hattersley as his deputy completed the 'dream ticket' – a balanced combination which, it was hoped, would help to heal the party's self-inflicted wounds. As a Tribunite and a protégé of Michael Foot, with whom he enjoyed something akin to a father–son relationship, the new leader had strong ties to the Labour Left. As has been seen, however, during the early 1980s he had become increasingly disenchanted with the activities of the 'Bennites', regarding them as a profoundly disruptive force. In addi-tion, one of the main lessons he drew from the 1983 election was that it was imperative to dispel the widespread public perception that Labour was dominated by the 'loony left'. That meant con-fronting organisations like Militant head on, something which he

18. Pelling and Reid, *A Short History of the Labour Party*, p. 167.
19. *Ibid.*, pp. 169–71.

did in spectacular fashion at the 1985 conference where he mounted
a fierce attack on Derek Hatton, the deputy leader of the Liverpool
Labour group.[20] It also necessitated the abandonment of certain
left-wing policies which were popular with party activists but deeply
distrusted by voters at large. Soon after becoming leader, Kinnock
launched a general policy review, starting with a polling exercise
called 'Look and Listen' and the appointment of seven groups,
manned by representatives of the Shadow Cabinet and the NEC, to
examine what changes might be required. The process of reshaping policy was a comprehensive one, embracing such matters as
unilateral nuclear disarmament, the rights and responsibilities of
trade unions and Britain's relations with the EC. It was to take
many years and to meet with stiff opposition from critics who argued
that the party was sacrificing its principles to the pursuit of power.
Kinnock showed considerable ruthlessness in carrying it through,
however, and his conviction as to the vital importance of attuning
Labour policies more closely to the wishes of the electorate was
only strengthened by another defeat in the 1987 general election.

In the case of some of the changes that occurred, Kinnock
seems to have felt genuine reluctance to discard policies to which
he had long been passionately committed. This was certainly true
with regard to unilateral nuclear disarmament. By his own account,
however, he had no regrets whatever over the decision to drop the
party's existing stance on Europe. Support for withdrawal, he later
said, was 'one thing I was glad to be rid of'. Even before the 1983
election, he had entertained serious reservations about it, his own
instinct being 'We're in. We are staying in. That's it. Now let's get
on with the next chapter.'[21] Fear of adding to Foot's difficulties had
persuaded him to toe the party line. As soon as he assumed the
leadership, however, he began to press for the adoption of a different policy. From 1983 onwards, indeed, he became increasingly
enthusiastic about Britain's role in the EC, a development which
was to lead eventually to his appointment as European Commissioner for Transport in 1995. According to Barbara Castle, who
declared herself 'startled' by Kinnock's change of heart, for him
'European unity had become an emotional crusade'.[22]

Kinnock's 'conversion' to the cause of Europe was symptomatic
of a general trend within the Labour movement as a whole during

20. *Ibid.*, pp. 176–7.
21. Interview in BBC 2 Television documentary, *The Wilderness Years*, part 3. See
also N. Ashford, 'The political parties', in S. George (ed.), *Britain and the European
Community: The Politics of Semi-Detachment* (1992), pp. 128–9.
22. Castle, *Fighting All the Way*, p. 545.

the second half of the 1980s. The beginning of a change of emphasis was discernible as early as the 1983 party conference, which endorsed without a vote an NEC statement that there could be no question of leaving the EC during the lifetime of the next Parliament and that Labour policy must therefore be to fight inside it for 'the best deal for Britain'.[23] As a sop to anti-marketeers, the statement added that the option of pulling out had to be retained. Even so, it represented a clear departure from the uncompromising call for withdrawal contained in the recent election manifesto. Over the next few years Labour continued to retreat from its earlier hard-line anti-European stance. By the 1987 general election, the policy of withdrawal had been abandoned, and in the 1989 European elections Labour fought on the basis of a solid commitment to closer cooperation with Britain's EC partners.[24]

There are a number of explanations for this fundamental change of sentiment.[25] In part, it reflected a gradual and final acceptance by the broad mass of the party that there was no realistic alternative to remaining in the EC and, further, that British membership brought benefits as well as disadvantages. The process of accommodation operated at different levels. Labour local councillors who were hard-pressed by central government financial constraints were gratified to discover that there were generous EC grants available to fund a variety of economic projects. At the same time, trade union suspicions about British involvement with the EC tended to lessen as a result of collaboration with European colleagues in the European Trade Union Confederation (ETUC).[26] In addition, at least some of the Labour representatives in the EP came to believe as a result of first-hand experience that many of the negative stereotypes that had coloured Labour thinking about the EC were not entirely justified. It is true there was no uniform pattern. A number of the Labour MEPs, including Derek Enwright and Brian Keys, needed no convincing, being from the outset ardent pro-Europeans. At the other extreme were those like Alf Lomas and Richard Balfe, members of the hard-left Campaign Group, whose dislike of the EC

23. *Ibid.*, p. 539.

24. Pelling and Reid, *A Short History of the Labour Party*, pp. 177, 180.

25. For Labour's evolution in a pro-European direction see J. Grahl and P. Teague, 'The British Labour Party and the European Community', *Political Quarterly*, 59 (1988), 72–85; Ashford, 'Political parties', in George (ed.), *Britain and the European Community*, pp. 129–30; H. Young, *This Blessed Plot: Britain and Europe from Churchill to Blair* (1998), pp. 477–88.

26. A. Butt Philip, 'British pressure groups and the European Community', in George (ed.), *Britain and the European Community*, p. 160; S. George, *Britain and European Integration since 1945*, p. 81.

was unalterable. There was, however, a third category: Labour MEPs who began their stints in a sceptical or even hostile frame of mind, but whose attitude began to soften in an atmosphere rendered more congenial by the dominant position enjoyed by the Socialist group at Strasbourg. The most prominent example of these was Barbara Castle. She had campaigned vigorously against British membership of the EC at the time of the 1975 referendum but had nevertheless decided to stand in the 1979 EP elections – the first direct ones – after her dismissal by Callaghan from the post of Social Services Secretary. Her subsequent contacts with European statesmen, members of the Commission and fellow MEPs undoubtedly had a mellowing influence.[27] Here there is a certain irony. Before his appointment as President of the European Commission, Roy Jenkins used to say, only half-jokingly, that he kept his 'European faith burning brightly by never visiting Brussels',[28] and certainly his four-year stay there proved to be in many ways a dispiriting and frustrating one. For Castle, by contrast, proximity to the inner workings of the EC tended to improve her opinion of it. There was never any question of being uncritical: she continued to attack her pet aversion, the CAP, and was adamantly opposed to British entry into the ERM because of its federalist implications. On the other hand, she did develop a more sympathetic understanding of the desire for European unity felt by Britain's partners. She also became convinced that, despite their grumbles, the British people had come to accept membership of the EC as part of their way of life and that a second referendum would produce an even bigger majority for staying in than in 1975.[29]

Party-political considerations were another factor helping to nudge Labour in a pro-European direction from the mid-1980s. A number of historians have suggested that it felt the need to move closer to the stance adopted by its main rival for the anti-Conservative vote, the staunchly pro-European Liberal–SDP Alliance.[30] At the same time, the inherently adversarial nature of British politics meant that it adopted almost as a reflex action the opposite policy on Europe to that of the Conservatives. This natural tendency was accentuated not only by Thatcher's own combative style and the visceral dislike that she provoked in many of her political opponents, but also by Labour's belief that the electorate was losing patience with the kind

27. Castle, *Fighting All the Way*, p. 446.   28. Jenkins, *A Life at the Centre*, p. 446.
29. Castle, *Fighting All the Way*, pp. 526, 532–3.
30. See, for example, Ashford, 'Political parties', in George (ed.), *Britain and the European Community*, p. 129.

of abrasive approach to Britain's EC partners that it had broadly approved during the struggle to secure a budget rebate in the early 1980s. There were good reasons for thinking that Europe was becoming a political liability for the government and for the Prime Minister in particular. From the time of the signing of the Single European Act in January 1986, Thatcher found herself increasingly at odds with her EC colleagues and almost totally isolated in her dogged rearguard action against the Social Charter, EMU and deeper integration. This produced a widespread feeling that she was overplaying her hand and that her continuing truculence was having a detrimental effect on the national interest. Equally damaging to the government's cause was mounting evidence that Thatcher's views on Europe were not shared by some of her most senior colleagues. Her determined resistance to British entry into the ERM led to barely disguised disagreements with successive chancellors and foreign secretaries and, eventually, to the resignations of Nigel Lawson and Geoffrey Howe in October 1989 and November 1990 respectively. Not surprisingly, the Labour Opposition sought to capitalise on this dissension and, in order to exploit dissatisfaction with Thatcher's tactics to the full, tended to play up its own pro-European credentials. The result was a certain amount of electoral success, at least in the EP elections. In the 1989 European elections, which the Conservatives contested on a platform of outright hostility to Brussels, Labour presented itself as being more constructive in its attitude to the EC. Its reward was to win forty-five seats, thirteen more than the Conservatives.[31]

Quite apart from calculations of electoral advantage, however, Labour was becoming increasingly attracted to many aspects of the economic and social policies being offered by the Commission and the majority of EC governments from the mid-1980s. The evolution of these policies, which was closely associated with the renewed drive for deeper integration at that time, came when Labour (as has been seen) was engaged in a full-scale review of its own policies and therefore receptive to new ideas. The hard-left's so-called 'alternative economic strategy', the main features of which were domestic economic expansion, nationalisation, and controls on imports and foreign exchange, had been thoroughly discredited by its hostile reception in the 1983 general election. François Mitterrand's lack of success in attempting to apply a similar prescription in France between 1981 and 1983 also cast grave doubt on the feasibility of

---

31. Pelling and Reid, *A Short History of the Labour Party*, pp. 180–81.

such an approach.[32] In the policy void thus created, Labour began
to show greater interest in closer economic cooperation with Britain's EC partners. In pointed contrast to Margaret Thatcher, Kinnock
and his front-bench economic team, led by John Smith, became
staunch advocates of British entry to the ERM, seeing it as a valuable
weapon in the battle against inflation which was again reaching
worrying levels in the late 1980s, following wholesale credit deregulation in 1986 and Lawson's tax-cutting budget of 1988.[33]

More appealing still to Labour was the 'social market' philosophy
embraced by the European Commission and most of the EC governments. Certainly it appeared infinitely preferable to the economic
policies currently being pursued by the Thatcher government. By
the second half of the 1980s little was to be heard in British Labour
circles of the former staple complaint that the EC was a 'capitalist
club'. On the contrary, the legal protection, working conditions
and welfare provisions enjoyed by workers in France, Germany,
Italy and other member states were now an object of envy. This was
especially true as far as the trade unions were concerned. Demoral-
ised and weakened by persistently high unemployment, a declining
membership, recently enacted curbs on their activities and their
exclusion from the corridors of power, they looked to the Social
Charter of May 1989, with its programme of minimum rights for
workers and citizens, as a shield against the harshness of market
forces. Equally, they had come to regard Jacques Delors, the President of the EC Commission and the main inspiration behind the
Charter, almost as a surrogate champion for the British worker at a
time when the trade union movement and the Labour Opposition
in Parliament seemed unequal to the task.[34] The fact that Delors
was the *bête noire* of Thatcher, who denounced the rather modest
provisions of the Social Charter as 'Marxist', only enhanced his
popularity in the eyes of British trade unionists and no doubt contributed to the enthusiastic reception he was given when setting out
his vision of the future for European workers in his celebrated
speech to the TUC congress at Bournemouth in September 1988.[35]

32. George, *Britain and European Integration since 1945*, p. 81; J.W. Young, *Britain and European Unity 1945–1992* (1993), pp. 153–4.

33. P. Stephens, *Politics and the Pound: the Conservatives' Struggle with Sterling* (1996), p. 80.

34. See Butt Philip, 'British pressure groups and the European Community', in George (ed.), *Britain and the European Community*, pp. 161–2.

35. *The Guardian*, 9 September 1988. A leading trade unionist, John Monks, later commented, 'We'd bought the whole lot that Jacques Delors was offering . . .': cited in J. Sopel, *Tony Blair: The Moderniser* (1995), p. 112.

By the late 1980s, then, both the industrial and the political wings of the Labour movement had moved away completely from the intense hostility to British membership of the EC which had been characteristic of their attitude at the beginning of the decade. More than that, Europe had ceased to be the deeply divisive issue for Labour that it had so often been in the past. Instead, as will be seen in later chapters, it was the Conservatives for whom it was a potent source of discord.

CHAPTER SEVENTEEN

'Megaphone Diplomacy': Thatcher and the EC, 1979–1984

Between 1979 and 1990 there were three administrations headed by Margaret Thatcher: the first from May 1979 to June 1983, the second from June 1983 to June 1987 and the third from June 1987 until her fall from power in November 1990. During this eleven-year period the influence of Thatcher herself was overwhelming. She had an unusually dominant personality and her personal opinions and prejudices played a major part in shaping British policy on Europe, as on other matters both foreign and domestic. It is clear that some of her Cabinet colleagues and elements of the Whitehall establishment were not always in full agreement with her views or with the idiosyncratic methods she employed for conducting foreign relations. There was a great deal of friction in particular with the Foreign Office. In the early 1980s the Foreign Secretary, Lord Carrington, and his deputy, Sir Ian Gilmour, were driven to despair by Thatcher's intransigent stand over Britain's contribution to the EC budget. Again, from the mid-1980s onwards, there was growing tension between Thatcher and Sir Geoffrey Howe over Europe, which was to culminate first in his removal from the Foreign Office in July 1989 and then in his resignation from the government in November of the following year.

These differences were as much about style as content. The Foreign Office approach was to proceed by patient diplomacy and accommodation. It was based upon the recognition that successful negotiations depend upon give and take and a willingness to make reasonable concessions. Such an approach was completely alien to Thatcher. It smacked of weakness and a lack of resolve in defending British interests. Equally, her own preferred method – which has been variously described as 'megaphone' or 'handbag' diplomacy – appalled and disturbed the Foreign Office, which was accustomed to a smoother and more civil performance by British leaders and which was usually left to repair the damage after the Prime Minister's set-piece battles with EC colleagues.[1] It is interesting to note in this connection that Schmidt and Giscard are supposed to have referred to Thatcher as a rhino and to Carrington as her zookeeper. One of Thatcher's great strengths, as well as one of her weaknesses, was a total inability to see the other side's point of view. She simply set out her demands and then refused to budge, whatever the pressure and however isolated she became. There has been considerable debate over how effective such tactics actually were. Some have argued that her exceptional assertiveness and tenacity achieved results. On the question of Britain's contribution to the EC budget, for example, her stubbornness eventually obtained a rebate mechanism which yielded some £1 billion p.a. – a substantial advance on the original offer of £350 million. In the opinion of others, however, Thatcher's refusal to compromise was often counter-productive. According to this line of argument, her obduracy only stiffened the attitude of other heads of government and made it more difficult to reach a sensible agreement. Sir Robert Armstrong, who was Cabinet Secretary at the time, has criticised her tactics[2] – as have a number of historians. Among others, Stephen George has suggested that the financial offer accepted at the Fontainebleau European Council in June 1984 did not represent much – if any – of an improvement on that made at Brussels a few months earlier (in March), which Thatcher had rejected as wholly inadequate.[3]

Thatcher's abrasive negotiating style was, in part, simply a reflection of her personality. She was a forceful and combative individual who positively relished disputes with her Community counterparts. In fairness, though, it should also be pointed out that her notorious prickliness was to some extent a response to the way in which she was treated initially by Schmidt, the West German Chancellor, and Giscard d'Estaing, the French President. Both men had been in power since 1974. By 1979 they were well-established, senior figures within the EC and tended to deal with the recently elected British Prime Minister as though she were an interloper. The fact that she was a woman probably did not help matters.[4] There had

1. For Thatcher's prejudices about the Foreign Office see I. Gilmour, *Dancing with Dogma: Britain under Thatcherism* (1992), pp. 226–7; H. Young, *This Blessed Plot: Britain and Europe from Churchill to Blair* (1998), pp. 314–18.

2. Interview in BBC 2 Television documentary, *The Poisoned Chalice*, part 3. See also R. Jenkins, *A Life at the Centre* (1992), pp. 494–508 *passim.*

3. S. George, *Britain and European Integration since 1945* (1991), p. 57.

4. C. Tugendhat, *Making Sense of Europe* (1986), p. 122.

been a strong Franco-German axis since the time of de Gaulle and Adenauer in the early 1960s. This was reinforced by close personal ties between Schmidt and Giscard, who were in the habit of constantly consulting each other on policy matters.[5] As has been seen, between 1976 and 1979 Callaghan had been made to seem like something of an intruder.[6] It is hardly surprising, therefore, that his successor should have had a similar experience.

In the case of Giscard at least, there was an additional element of personal dislike. Relations between him and Thatcher were always cool, and the French President – who was notoriously snobbish and haughty – made little attempt to hide the fact that he regarded her as socially inferior: he dismissed her contemptuously as 'la fille d'épicier', the 'grocer's daughter'.[7] One first-hand British observer, Christopher Tugendhat, a former Conservative minister and a European Commissioner during the early years of the first Thatcher administration, laid at least some of the blame for the acrimonious tone of the early discussions on Britain's contribution to the EC budget on the alleged failure of Giscard and Schmidt to adopt a more welcoming attitude towards Thatcher. Others who were also qualified to speak from direct personal experience – Carrington, Sir Michael Butler, the British ambassador to the EC between 1979 and 1985, and Roy Jenkins, who was President of the EC Commission from 1977 to 1981 – have expressed a similar opinion. According to Tugendhat, the French and German leaders showed a complete lack of statesmanship in not making a more serious effort to find a prompt solution to the British problem. By making a 'derisory' offer at the Dublin European Council in November 1979, they effectively drove Thatcher into a corner and provoked her into taking up a more unyielding stance than she might otherwise have done.[8]

Having said this, it is evident that there was also an element of political calculation behind Thatcher's hectoring and aggressive dealings with the rest of the EC. Thus Gilmour has persuasively claimed that she deliberately prolonged the crisis over Britain's budgetary contribution, hoping to use it to boost her flagging

5. For Thatcher's intense resentment of the close collaboration between Giscard and Schmidt see G. Urban, *Diplomacy and Disillusion at the Court of Margaret Thatcher: An Insider's View* (1996), p. 25.

6. Jenkins, *A Life at the Centre*, p. 460. For a different interpretation in which emphasis is placed on the cordiality of Callaghan's relations with both Giscard and Schmidt see K.O. Morgan, *Callaghan, A Life* (1997), pp. 591–2.

7. Cited in H. Young, *One of Us: A Biography of Margaret Thatcher* (1990), p. 187.

8. Tugendhat, *Making Sense of Europe*, pp. 120–22.

political standing at home. In May 1980 she was extremely reluctant to endorse an agreement that Gilmour and Carrington had reached at Brussels. Gilmour was in no doubt about her motives. In his memoirs he writes:

> To my mind there was only one explanation for the P[rime] M[inister]'s attitude ... the grievance was more valuable than its removal.
>
> Not for the last time during her term of office, foreign policy was a tool of party politics. However badly things were going in Britain, Mrs Thatcher could at least win some kudos and popularity as the defender of the British people against the foreigner. Hence a running row with our European partners was the next best thing to a war; it would divert public attention from the disasters at home. Her attitude was, of course, inflaming British antagonism to the Community, but that did not worry her at all; it probably pleased her.[9]

Gilmour is not the most impartial of witnesses. As a leading 'wet' within the first Thatcher government, he was basically out of sympathy with most aspects of policy being pursued by it and was soon dismissed (in September 1981). But others have also commented on Thatcher's use of the European issue as a way of distracting attention from domestic difficulties and drumming up popular support at home. In his biography of Thatcher, *One of Us*, Hugo Young argues that at a time of enormous problems for the government in the early 1980s, when its popularity had sunk to a desperately low point and when the country was in the grip of a devastating recession, it served the Prime Minister's interests well to be seen putting up an heroic defence of national interests against the eight other members of the EC.[10] Stephen George similarly maintains that the harsh line employed by Thatcher at that time – with her talk of 'getting back our own money' – was largely determined by domestic political considerations.[11]

When Thatcher formed her first government in the summer of 1979, it was widely, if mistakenly, assumed that her advent to power would bring a marked improvement in Britain's relations with her EC partners. Labour had been in office for the previous five years and was considered – with much justification – to be less pro-European than the Conservatives. A new Conservative government, it was thought, would mean a more positive attitude towards

9. Gilmour, *Dancing with Dogma*, p. 240.   10. Young, *One of Us*, pp. 189–90.
11. S. George, *An Awkward Partner: Britain in the European Community* (1991), pp. 162–3.

the EC. What this broad analysis failed to take into account was that some Conservatives were less enthusiastic than others about British membership of the Community. This was certainly true of Thatcher when compared with her predecessor Heath. The contrast between the two was brought out clearly during the 1975 referendum campaign when Heath played a much more active and wholehearted role than Thatcher for the 'yes' camp. Heath was a committed European of long standing. He regarded the successful outcome of his negotiations for British entry into the EC as the crowning achievement of his political career. Thatcher, on the other hand, was basically a sceptic on the matter. In that respect, indeed, her attitude was closer to that of Wilson and Callaghan than to that of Heath. Christopher Soames aptly summed up her approach when he described her as 'an agnostic who continues to go to church'.[12] Like de Gaulle, she was frankly contemptuous of the more visionary prophets of European unity. She envisaged the development of the EC as being limited to cooperation between independent nation states and was adamantly opposed to any moves in the direction of the dreaded 'F' word, 'federalism'. She was determined to prevent any erosion of parliamentary sovereignty and deeply suspicious of all attempts to enhance the power of the Brussels bureaucracy, which she routinely referred to as the 'Belgian Empire'.

There was another crucial difference between Heath and Thatcher. This lay in their divergent approaches to the 'special relationship' with the US. Heath, who always considered relations with the EC the key element in British foreign policy, made little effort to develop a close rapport with President Nixon or with Kissinger, his chief foreign policy adviser. Kissinger formed the opinion that Heath felt little emotional attachment to the US, and Heath himself spoke in terms of a 'natural' rather than 'special' relationship – a small but significant distinction.[13] In the early 1970s, during Heath's premiership, certain tensions developed between the US and the Europeans over financial and economic questions and, in particular, over how to respond to OPEC's dramatic increase in oil prices. Heath's general reaction to these difficulties was to align himself with the other European states. This tendency was reinforced by his suspicion that Kissinger was trying to play the

12. Cited in Young, *One of Us*, p. 185.
13. See H. Kissinger, *The White House Years* (1979), p. 937; *Years of Upheaval* (1982), pp. 140–41; C. Hill and C. Lord, 'The foreign policy of the Heath government', in S. Ball and A. Seldon (eds), *The Heath Government 1970–74: A Reappraisal* (1996), pp. 305–8.

Europeans off against each other. When Heath visited Washington in December 1971, he made it clear it was now the practice to establish a common European position in the first place and then – and only then – to fit this in as far as possible with the interests and wishes of the US.[14]

It is impossible to imagine such a statement about Britain's order of priorities emanating from Thatcher. Her natural instinct was to place collaboration with the US before that with Britain's EC partners. In this respect, it is interesting to compare Thatcher's dealings with the American administration with the way in which she treated her fellow European leaders. She had not the slightest compunction about engaging in bitter public rows with the rest of the EC. By contrast, it is hard to point to a single instance of a public disagreement with Washington. There were certainly occasions – as at the time the US invaded the Commonwealth island of Grenada in 1983 without giving London advance notice – when Reagan received a scorching rebuke from Thatcher.[15] But this was always administered behind the scenes. In public, Thatcher was always careful to maintain an impression of Anglo-American solidarity.

Throughout her period in office, the maintenance of close relations with the US was regarded as a prime foreign policy objective. In 1979 one of her first foreign policy acts was to visit Washington and pledge her support for President Carter's strong stance against the Soviet Union following its invasion of Afghanistan. With the replacement of Jimmy Carter by Ronald Reagan in January 1981, Anglo-American relations entered upon a new and exceptionally cordial phase. From their first meeting in London in 1975, Thatcher and Reagan established an immediate rapport which later developed into a firm personal friendship during the 1980s. Their mutual admiration was cemented, moreover, by a common ideological bond. Both were dedicated to a policy of free-market economics, cutting taxes and pushing back the role of the state. They were also united by a shared commitment to the containment of international communism. By the time she became Prime Minister, Thatcher had already acquired the nickname of the 'Iron Lady' because of her strident Cold War rhetoric. Reagan, too, was to make his own hostility to the Soviet Union unmistakably clear when he described it as the 'evil Empire'.

14. Campbell, *Edward Heath: A Biography* (1993), pp. 336–7, 342–3.
15. M. Thatcher, *The Downing Street Years* (1993), pp. 328–32; G. Howe, *Conflict of Loyalty* (1994), pp. 325–6; G. Shultz, *Turmoil and Triumph* (1993), ch. 20; Young, *One of Us*, pp. 347–8.

Thatcher made a point of being the first European political leader to meet the newly elected Reagan when she visited Washington in February 1981. In the course of her visit, which was a great public relations success, she came out in support of Reagan's new scheme for the creation of a Rapid Deployment Force for use in the world's trouble spots. This set a pattern of broad support for American policy – even when it proved to be deeply unpopular in many other quarters. In the early 1980s it was agreed to allow the stationing of Cruise missiles in the UK, as a counter to the Soviet intermediate-range SS-20 missiles. There was backing for Reagan's Strategic Defence Initiative, or 'Star Wars' defensive system, in the mid-1980s.[16] Most important of all, in 1986 the Thatcher government permitted American F111 bombers to operate from the British base of RAF Lakenheath to carry out raids on Libya in retaliation for the Libyan leader Colonel Gaddafi's alleged involvement in the bombing of a West Berlin discotheque frequented by Americans.[17] The favours were not all one-sided. In 1982 Britain obtained the promise of an updated version of the Trident missile to replace Polaris on extremely generous terms. In the same year, US assistance in providing satellite intelligence and fuelling facilities on Ascension Island made an invaluable contribution to Britain's victory over Argentina in the Falklands War.[18]

Inevitably – as over the 1983 Grenada episode – there was the occasional disagreement and friction. Despite such tensions, however, on the whole relations between London and Washington remained extremely harmonious and cordial. What were the implications of this for Britain's relations with the EC during the 1980s? In general terms, it could be said that the exceptional closeness of the link between Thatcher and Reagan tended to revive doubts in some European minds about the wholeheartedness of British commitment to membership of the EC. Such doubts were, of course, long-standing. In the period before Britain became a member, there had been considerable scepticism about whether Britain was really willing to downgrade the 'special relationship'. For de Gaulle this had been a key factor in his veto of the British application, with Britain being regarded as a potential Trojan Horse for the Americans. By

16. Thatcher, *The Downing Street Years*, pp. 463–9.

17. *Ibid*, pp. 239–43; Gilmour, *Dancing with Dogma*, pp. 328–32; Howe, *Conflict of Loyalty*, pp. 504–7; Young, *One of Us*, pp. 474–6.

18. Thatcher, *The Downing Street Years*, pp. 244–8; G. Smith, *Reagan and Thatcher* (1990), p. 84; S. Woodward, *One Hundred Days* (1992), pp. xviii, 126; Gilmour, *Dancing with Dogma*, p. 251.

actually joining the EC in the early 1970s, Britain had apparently decided to make cooperation with Europe its first priority. But the manner in which Thatcher went out of her way to emphasise the crucial importance of the US connection seemed to place a question mark over this assumption.

During the 1980s there were several issues on which Britain found itself ranged on the same side as the Americans in opposition to the views of its European partners. Thatcher was the only European leader to support the bombing of Libya in 1986: the rest were highly critical. Whereas F111 bombers were given permission to operate from British bases, the French government was not even prepared to let them overfly its territory.[19] Another area where Britain found itself in the same camp as the Americans and at odds with its EC partners was over the question of South Africa. Most of the Community wanted to see the imposition of economic sanctions as a means of compelling Pretoria to dismantle apartheid. Thatcher and Reagan, on the other hand, were strongly opposed to the adoption of such a measure and in the mid-1980s worked together to frustrate a series of international moves to apply sanctions.[20]

At the same time, it would be wrong to suggest that there was always a convergence of British and American policies. Thatcher was not an uncritical supporter of everything Reagan did. Where she felt that European – and, more specifically, British – interests were likely to be adversely affected by actions taken by Washington, she was not slow to object. On at least two important policy matters Thatcher aligned herself with the rest of the EC to resist American proposals. The first concerned economic measures against the Soviet Union in the early 1980s. Following the Soviet invasion of Afghanistan in December 1979, President Carter introduced a number of sanctions, including an embargo on the export of high-technology goods to the eastern bloc countries and a partial ban on grain sales to the Soviet Union. These sanctions received backing – with varying degrees of enthusiasm – from the members of the EC. The Community's attitude underwent a sharp change, however, when the new Reagan administration tried to step up the pressure on Moscow by putting a stop to a project for piping natural gas from Siberia to Western Europe. Washington was hostile to this project in any case, viewing it as an unwanted boost to the Soviet economy. It therefore placed a ban on the supply of all gas and oil technology

19. Howe, *Conflict of Loyalty*, p. 506.
20. Thatcher, *The Downing Street Years*, pp. 512–16.

to the Soviet Union. In addition, it extended the ban to foreign subsidiaries of US companies and to foreign companies making American products under licence. If implemented, these restrictions would have meant the end of the Siberian gas project, and that, in turn, would have had extremely damaging consequences for various European companies involved in the consortium responsible for laying the pipeline. Not surprisingly, therefore, there were strong protests. The EC countries formed a common front on the matter. Even Thatcher, who had approved the earlier sanctions devised by Carter, drew the line at Reagan's proposal. She was strongly influenced, no doubt, by the fact that the British company John Brown Engineering was a major participant in the project and stood to lose a great deal from its cancellation.[21]

Another event which caused the British government to draw closer to its EC partners in opposition to American policy was the meeting between Reagan and the Soviet leader Mikhail Gorbachev at Reykjavik in 1986. One of the main topics discussed was disarmament, and Reagan, allowing himself to be carried away by the prospect of a sensational agreement, contemplated the complete elimination of strategic nuclear weapons. Gorbachev was also interested, but would only consent if Reagan agreed to halt all further development of his cherished Star Wars programme. In the event, this stipulation proved to be an insurmountable obstacle and no agreement was reached. Even so, America's European allies were aghast at the cavalier manner in which Reagan had made proposals affecting their security without even bothering to consult them. Deprived of the protection of nuclear weapons, Western Europe would have been left dangerously exposed to the conventional-force superiority of the Warsaw Pact. The fact that Reagan appeared oblivious to this consideration was naturally a source of great alarm. Thatcher was as concerned as anybody and obtained assurances from Reagan that NATO's strategy would continue to be based squarely on nuclear deterrence.[22]

If one examines the eleven years of Thatcher government as a whole, it is possible to see three broad phases in British policy towards the EC. First, there was the period from 1979 until the Fontainebleau European Council of June 1984. The second phase lasted from Fontainebleau to the Luxembourg European Council

21. George, *An Awkward Partner*, pp. 138–41.
22. G. Howe, *Conflict of Loyalty* (1994), pp. 522–4; Thatcher, *The Downing Street Years*, pp. 470–72; Young, *One Of Us*, pp. 479–81.

of December 1985, at which agreement was reached on the Single European Act. Finally, there was the period between December 1985 and Thatcher's fall from power in November 1990. It was during this last period that difficulties and differences arose between Britain and the other members of the EC about the practical implications of the Single European Act.

The first phase – with which the rest of this chapter will be concerned – was dominated by attempts to secure a substantial reduction in Britain's contribution to the Community's budget. The issue provoked a bout of what David Sanders has termed 'megaphone haggling'.[23] A series of temporary arrangements was negotiated for the early 1980s. But it was not until the summer of 1984, after five years of acrimonious wrangling, that agreement was at last reached on a permanent rebate formula.

The British Budgetary Question, alternatively described by Roy Jenkins as the 'Bloody British Question',[24] was a problem that Thatcher had inherited and one that Callaghan would have had to address if he had won the 1979 general election. Britain's belated accession to the EC inevitably meant that some of the arrangements that it was obliged to accept were tailored not to its interests, but to those of the original Six. During the negotiations of the early 1970s, as seen in Chapter 12, Heath had not been greatly concerned about the precise terms of entry. His strategy had been to get in first and sort out any difficulties afterwards. As a result, the terms he had obtained were not wholly satisfactory. This was especially true in the case of Britain's disproportionately large contribution to the EC budget. Between 1974 and 1979 Wilson and Callaghan had attempted to negotiate a more favourable deal. They enjoyed only limited success, however, and it was therefore left to the incoming Thatcher government to resolve what was a highly contentious issue.

Apart from West Germany, Britain was in 1979 the only net contributor to the EC budget. Its net payment for that year was approaching £1 billion and was set to become larger still as the transition period ended in 1980 and the costs of the CAP continued to grow. On current calculations, Britain would soon be paying a bigger net contribution than West Germany, despite the fact that it had a much smaller GDP: the actual figures for 1980–81 were £1.184

23. D. Sanders, *Losing an Empire, Finding a Role: British Foreign Policy since 1945* (1990), p. 159.
24. Jenkins, *A Life at the Centre*, p. 491.

billion and £750 million respectively. Thatcher believed this situation to be fundamentally unjust and, in characteristic fashion, set about changing it without delay. She announced her intentions in a speech in October 1979, declaring: 'I cannot play Sister Bountiful to the Community.'[25] The matter was raised at the European Council in Strasbourg, where it was agreed that a report should be prepared for the next European Council, which was due to be held in Dublin in November. In the light of subsequent developments, Thatcher's stance at the Strasbourg meeting was in some ways deceptively moderate: she agreed, for example, to drop the threat to veto farm price increases made earlier in the year by David Owen, the Foreign Secretary in Callaghan's government. On the other hand, there were also warning signals. According to a later account by Roy Jenkins, Thatcher complained that Giscard had cheated her over the agenda, by dealing with the EMS first instead of the budget question. She spoke 'too shrilly and too frequently' and soon got involved in disagreeable exchanges not only with Giscard and the premiers of Ireland, Denmark and The Netherlands, but also with Schmidt, whose support was vital to her. 'Mrs Thatcher', Jenkins writes, 'had thus performed the considerable feat of unnecessarily irritating two big countries, three small ones and the Commission within her opening hour of performance at a European Council.'[26] Worse was to come at Dublin. Schmidt let Jenkins know beforehand that he was prepared to be helpful in negotiating a settlement, provided Thatcher adopted a less hectoring approach. There was little prospect of that, however, given the low opinion that she had already formed of her EC colleagues. 'They are all a rotten lot', she confided to Jenkins in late October. 'Schmidt and the Americans and we are the only ones who would do any standing up and fighting if necessary.'[27]

At Dublin, Thatcher demanded the whole of 'our money' back and dismissed out of hand, as only 'one third of a loaf', the offer of a rebate worth some £350 million. As far as Giscard, Schmidt and the others were concerned, the question had already been settled during the Wilson renegotiations. They were irritated by Thatcher's reference to the EC's 'own resources' as though they belonged to individual member states. Moreover, they were offended by the way in which she subjected them to a relentless harangue, lasting

25. Winston Churchill Memorial Lecture, 18 October 1979: *The Guardian*, 19 October 1979.
26. Jenkins, *A Life at the Centre*, p. 495.   27. *Ibid.*, p. 496.

several hours, over dinner: the reaction from a bored and angry Schmidt was to pretend to be asleep. Not surprisingly, no agreement was reached, and Giscard and Schmidt only consented to further discussion of the question at the next European Council on the clear understanding that Thatcher would act in a 'spirit of genuine compromise'.[28]

In January 1980 Howe, the Chancellor of the Exchequer, and Gilmour, the Lord Privy Seal and Minister at the Foreign Office, toured the EC capitals seeking the basis for a deal. Since they had no authority to consider a settlement which would yield less than Britain's full net annual contribution to the EC budget – 1.5 billion ecus – their mission was fruitless. At the Luxembourg European Council of 27–28 April, however, there appeared to be a real possibility of an agreement. Schmidt, who had had a productive meeting with Carrington at Jenkins's British home in February, proposed that Britain's net contribution for 1980 should not be allowed to exceed the average for 1978 (the figure for which was very low) and 1979. In order to make the proposal more attractive, Giscard further suggested that the net amount to be paid out by Britain in 1981 should be the same as in 1980. In effect, Britain would be receiving an annual rebate of some £760 million for the two years 1980–81. This offer represented a significant advance on that made in Dublin. Carrington recommended acceptance, as did Thatcher's two senior advisers, Sir Robert Armstrong, the Cabinet Secretary, and Sir Michael Palliser, formerly the UK ambassador to the EC and now the Permanent Under-Secretary at the Foreign Office. To the surprise of most observers, however, Thatcher rejected it.[29]

Substantial progress was made at the Brussels Council of Ministers on 29 May 1980. Karl von Dohnanyi, the German Minister for European Affairs, devised an ingenious variant on the Luxembourg formula. Carrington was favourably impressed and, after an all-night negotiating session, an agreement was finally reached at 6 a.m. As before, however, Thatcher was not easily persuaded. When Carrington and Gilmour took the terms of the projected deal to Chequers, they were received coldly: according to Gilmour, indeed, they could not have got a more hostile reception if they had been the bailiffs – or even Heath making a social call accompanied by

28. *Ibid.*, pp. 498–9. See also Gilmour, *Dancing with Dogma*, p. 235; Thatcher, *The Downing Street Years*, pp. 80–82.

29. R. Jenkins, *European Diary 1977–81* (1989), pp. 592–3; Gilmour, *Dancing with Dogma*, p. 236.

Delors (Thatcher's bogeymen). Gilmour's strategem for overcoming Thatcher's opposition was to leak details of the Brussels agreement to the press in such a way as to have it presented as a triumph for the Prime Minister – thereby making it difficult for her to disown it. Thatcher also came under heavy pressure from the Cabinet, with Howe giving Carrington strong support and the latter threatening resignation. In the event, she reluctantly acquiesced.[30]

An arrangement on Britain's budgetary contribution was thus in place for the next two years. In June 1982 another temporary deal – this time for one year – was negotiated by Francis Pym, who had just become Foreign Secretary following Carrington's resignation over his handling of the Falklands crisis. What was needed, however, was a permanent solution to a problem that was continuing to sour relations between Britain and its EC partners, taking up an inordinate amount of time and diverting attention from other important matters. In the longer term, the advent to power of new leaders in France and West Germany – with François Mitterand taking over from Giscard in May 1981 and Helmut Kohl replacing Schmidt in October 1982 – was to assist the process of reaching an accommodation on the issue. During 1982 and 1983, though, there were no signs of a breakthrough. On the contrary, attitudes seemed to be hardening on both sides. In May 1982 Peter Walker, the Minister of Agriculture, unsuccessfully attempted to veto the annual increase in EC farm prices;[31] in June 1983 Thatcher told the European Council at Stuttgart that she would not agree to a resolution of other issues until the budgetary dispute had been permanently settled; and in December 1983 Mitterand took an equally tough stance at the Athens European Council, insisting that the aim of the meeting should be to agree on another temporary arrangement rather than a permanent formula.[32]

By early 1984, however, Mitterand was intent on disposing of what he had come to see as an intolerable distraction from the current drive for deeper integration of the EC with which he was increasingly preoccupied. After France assumed the presidency of the EC in January, he made a determined effort in that direction. He immediately announced his intention to ensure that all aspects of the budgetary problem were settled by the time of the March

---

30. Gilmour, *Dancing with Dogma*, pp. 237–41.

31. J.W. Young, *Britain and European Unity, 1945–1992* (1993), p. 142.

32. Thatcher, *The Downing Street Years*, pp. 337–8; George, *An Awkward Partner*, pp. 150, 153.

European Council in Brussels and then set off on a round of visits to other EC heads of government. Although Mitterand's stated deadline was not met, the Brussels European Council of 19–20 March saw a considerable narrowing of the gap between Britain's position and that of the rest, particularly the French. It was agreed that there should be an increase in the proportion of VAT revenues allocated to the EC. In addition, Thatcher made a major concession on the contentious issue of how to calculate any rebate that Britain might obtain. The British government had so far always maintained that the tariffs and agricultural import levies that it paid over to the Community should be counted as part of Britain's gross contribution to the budget. This argument, however, had never been accepted by the other EC governments, which insisted that tariffs and levies were not national contributions, but were simply being collected on the EC's behalf. The French now sought to reconcile these conflicting viewpoints by means of a formula on VAT contributions that was to apply only to member states which in the previous year had paid more in VAT contributions than they had received from the budget by an agreed amount – that amount to be determined later. Thatcher accepted this formula as a basis for negotiation. But further progress was halted by a maladroit intervention from Kohl, who proposed a flat-rate rebate of 1 billion ecus annually between 1984 and 1986 which the British rejected.[33]

By the time of the Fontainebleau European Council of 25–26 June 1984, there remained few outstanding points of substance to be resolved, and the settlement that was reached there closely followed the lines laid down in Brussels three months earlier. Agreement was reached without too much difficulty on a rebate of 1 billion ecus for 1984. Making arrangements for subsequent years proved rather more troublesome. Kohl and Mitterand initially had in mind an annual rebate equivalent to 60 per cent of the difference between Britain's VAT contributions and its receipts for 1985 and each year thereafter. Thatcher wanted 70 per cent and sought to play the French and Germans off against each other. Her efforts to arrange a private meeting with Kohl, however, were rebuffed. A meeting between Thatcher and Mitterand brought an increased offer first of 65 per cent and then of 66 per cent – in cash terms, slightly more than 1 billion ecus. A further element in the overall package was a definite increase in VAT revenues from 1 per cent to 1.4 per cent of the national total, with the possibility of another one – to 1.6 per cent – in 1986.[34] This was scarcely consistent with Thatcher's current efforts to impose tight limits on EC expenditure which will form one of the themes of the next chapter.

34. Howe, *Conflict of Loyalty*, pp. 401–2; Thatcher, *The Downing Street Years*, pp. 542–4; Young, *This Blessed Plot*, pp. 322–4; D.W. Urwin, *The Community of Europe: A History of European Integration since 1945* (1995), p. 188.

CHAPTER EIGHTEEN

Fatal Attraction: Thatcher and the Single European Act

Besides resolving the long-running dispute over Britain's budget rebate, the Fontainebleau European Council also took a number of decisions that were to have profound consequences for the EC's future political development. One of the most important of these was the appointment of an ad hoc committee of personal representatives of the heads of government, chaired by an Irishman, James Dooge. The Dooge Committee's remit was to examine the question of institutional reform.[1] Its final report, which was considered by the Milan European Council in June 1985, recommended far-reaching changes, including greater powers for the Commission and the EP and a substantial extension of majority voting in the Council of Ministers in order to streamline decision-making. These recommendations became linked to other proposals currently being canvassed for the creation of a 'single market', and the eventual outcome was the Single European Act (SEA) of December 1985. The Thatcher government viewed these developments with considerable suspicion and, as the full implications of the SEA began to emerge during the latter half of the 1980s, Britain was to become embroiled in increasingly acrimonious clashes with most of the other EC states.

In the period immediately following the Fontainebleau European Council, however, the British government appeared to adopt a more positive and cooperative attitude on EC matters than it had done previously. In addition, there was a marked improvement in its relations with other members of the EC. Apart from the

---

1. D.W. Urwin, *The Community of Europe: A History of European Integration since 1945* (1995), pp. 224–5; J.W. Young, *Britain and European Unity 1945–1992* (1993), pp. 148–9.

elimination of the budget rebate question as a bone of contention, there were a number of other reasons for this.

First, there was no longer any need for Thatcher to provoke or deliberately magnify disagreements with Britain's EC partners for the purpose of boosting her domestic popularity and diverting attention from the government's economic difficulties. In the general election of June 1983, the Conservatives had secured an increased parliamentary majority on the back of victory in the Falklands War. By 1984, moreover, the worst of the recession was over and the economy was beginning to recover. Secondly, there was the enlargement of the EC through the admission of Greece in January 1981, followed by Spain and Portugal in January 1986.[2] In the larger Community of twelve, there was obviously a greater diversity of interests than before, with the result that the British government's chances of finding some support for its viewpoint were correspondingly increased. To put it simply, the risk of total isolation was diminished. It was noticeable, for example, that on the important issue of institutional changes affecting majority voting in the Council of Ministers and the powers of the EP, Greece and Denmark were to be found taking a similar line to Britain.[3] Thirdly, a change of political leadership in France and Germany during 1981–2 saw the advent to power of two men with whom Thatcher was able to establish a better personal rapport than had been possible with their predecessors. Her relations with Giscard d'Estaing and Schmidt had been frosty from the outset. Nor had matters been helped by early, disagreeable wrangles over the British budget contribution. Although it would be an exaggeration to say that either Mitterand or Kohl ever developed any great warmth of feeling towards Thatcher, there was at least an element of grudging admiration.[4] Besides, there did not exist between the new French and German leaders – at least at this stage – the very close personal relationship enjoyed by Giscard d'Estaing and Schmidt which had served to exclude others, including the British Prime Minister. Finally, with time and experience of EC politics Thatcher and her colleagues began to develop a better 'feel' for working the system. In the

2. M.J. Dedman, *The Origins and Development of the European Union 1945–95: A History of European Integration* (1996), pp. 127–8.

3. S. George, *An Awkward Partner: Britain in the European Community* (1990), p. 152.

4. For Thatcher's relations with Kohl and with Mitterand who for a time found her fascinating see H. Young, *This Blessed Plot: Britain and Europe from Churchill to Blair* (1998), pp. 319–21. Some interesting information on Kohl's complex attitude towards Thatcher became available in May 1998 with the release of an assortment of secret German documents on the unification of Germany. See *The Times*, 1 June 1998.

early 1980s Thatcher's automatic preference had been to adopt a confrontational approach; by the mid-1980s she appeared to have realised that this was not always the best way to obtain results. In particular, in cases where other countries shared British doubts and reservations about proposals being made, she showed a greater willingness to allow them to lead the opposition. In that way Britain managed to safeguard its interests without incurring the odium of being seen as awkward and obstructive.

For various reasons, then, the period immediately following the Fontainebleau agreement of 1984 saw a marked reduction in friction between Britain and its partners. Even so, differences persisted, not least over British efforts to curb the remorseless growth of the EC budget which on several occasions during the 1980s brought the EC to the verge of insolvency. The root problem was the CAP, which was extremely expensive and absorbed a large proportion of the total budget. In point of fact, between 1979 and 1986 expenditure on the CAP actually fell as a proportion of the total – from 75 per cent to 65 per cent. But this was largely a consequence of fortuitous movements in world food prices. The underlying problem remained. It was aggravated, moreover, by the accession of new member states requiring heavy subsidies: Greece, Spain and Portugal.

During the early 1980s, Thatcher's attacks on the wastefulness of the CAP and her threats to block increases in farm prices had been used as tactical weapons in the battle to secure a satisfactory budget rebate for Britain. That does not mean, however, that her campaign to impose tighter control on EC expenditure ceased when that objective had been achieved in 1984. Budgetary restraint was a matter on which Thatcher personally had exceptionally strong feelings. She had learnt the virtues of thrift and frugality from her shopkeeper father, and the importance of balancing the books, of living within one's means, occupied a central place in her political philosophy. If this applied to domestic politics, it applied with even greater force in the context of the EC where she saw what she regarded as British money being 'squandered' for the benefit of foreigners.[5]

The British strategy for getting the budget under tight control was to set strict limits on the growth of spending. This was to be linked to a radical reform of the CAP – the main cause of rising costs. At the Fontainebleau European Council it had been agreed that there should be guidelines on expenditure which ensured

5. I. Gilmour, *Dancing with Dogma: Britain under Thatcherism* (1992), pp. 232–4.

that outlays on agriculture rose at a slower rate than spending as a whole.[6] Almost at once a crisis developed on this very question. The money allotted for 1984 was due to run out in November, i.e. before the end of the financial year. The Commission proposed to deal with the impending shortfall by means of a supplementary budget of 2 billion ecus. But Britain objected and suggested that there should be spending cuts instead. Eventually – in September – the British government agreed to a supplement of 1 billion ecus. In return, however, it insisted that there must be strict guidelines to check the future growth of the budget. These guidelines were laid down at the Dublin European Council in December 1984. There it was stipulated that a ceiling should be set on the budget on 1 March each year. The significance of this date was that it came before that on which EC agriculture ministers met to negotiate the level of farm prices. In effect, the intention was to impose cash limits on the amount to be spent on the CAP.[7]

Despite this provision, there was another crisis over the budget in 1987. This resulted in the adoption of a further package of measures at a meeting of heads of government held in Brussels in February 1988. Once again Britain agreed to an increase in overall resources only on condition that it would be accompanied by binding agreements to restrict the production and price levels of surplus agricultural products such as milk, beef and cereals.[8]

Throughout all these tortuous negotiations over the budget between 1984 and 1988, British tactics conformed to a common pattern. Initially, the government took the line that it could not possibly agree to any increase in spending. Then at length, after a great deal of argument, it finally acquiesced – in return for tighter curbs on the amount devoted to agriculture. As Peter Riddell has aptly observed, the procedure was a 'messy and negative' one.[9] It was also a recipe for discord between Britain and its partners.

From the mid-1980s onwards there developed a far more fundamental divergence between Britain and a majority of other EC members. This arose from differing reactions to proposals for a greater degree of economic and political integration. After a prolonged period of EC paralysis following the enlargement of 1973, the

6. Urwin, *The Community of Europe*, p. 188; Young, *Britain and European Unity*, p. 148.

7. George, *An Awkward Partner*, pp. 159–61.

8. *Ibid.*, pp. 189–90; G. Howe, *Conflict of Loyalty* (1994), pp. 522–3; M. Thatcher, *The Downing Street Years* (1993), pp. 728–37.

9. P. Riddell, *The Thatcher Era and its Legacy* (1991), p. 193.

middle years of the 1980s saw yet another relaunch of the European idea similar to those that had occurred in the mid-1950s and late 1960s.[10] This was associated with certain key individuals, especially Mitterand and Delors. Between 1981 and 1983 the French government sought to tackle unemployment and economic stagnation by a policy of nationalisation and increased state spending – what was dubbed the 'Socialist experiment'. By the spring of 1983, however, it was obvious that these measures were not working, and Mitterand was forced to change course.[11] This failed attempt to 'go it alone', it has been argued, demonstrated to the French President the importance of economic interdependence, the value of the EC to French economic well-being and the desirability of deeper integration.[12] At the same time, the appointment of Delors as President of the Commission in 1985 brought to the Community a vigour and a sense of purpose that had been lacking under his predecessor, Gaston Thorn of Luxembourg. Delors, a French Socialist who had recently proved himself to be a highly effective finance minister, was a strong advocate of greater unity within the EC and quickly showed that he possessed the toughness and political skill to push through measures to achieve that objective.

There were other factors at work. The drive to closer economic and political union stemmed to some extent from worries about Reagan's tough stance towards the Soviet Union.[13] But it also reflected widespread fears that Europe was in danger of being left behind by the dramatic advances being made by Japan and the US in computing, robotics, telecommunications and other high-technology industries. At one level, Europe's response to this challenge was to embark upon a major programme of technological cooperation – the so-called Eureka programme, which originated in an initiative from Mitterand in 1985.[14] It was increasingly felt, however, that more needed to be done to fashion the EC into a more effective economic and political unit by eradicating remaining barriers to the free working of the internal market and by improving the decision-making procedures. As early as 1981, a plan was formulated by the foreign ministers of West Germany and Italy,

10. For the relaunch of the mid-1980s see C. Grant, *Delors: Inside the House that Jacques Built* (1994), pp. 61–90.

11. P.A. Hall, 'The evolution of economic policy under Mitterand', in G. Ross, S. Hoffman and S. Malzaher (eds), *The Mitterand Experiment: Continuity and Change in Modern France* (1987), pp. 54–8; Grant, *Delors*, pp. 50–60.

12. Young, *This Blessed Plot*, p. 321; Young, *Britain and European Unity*, pp. 146–7.

13. George, *An Awkward Partner*, pp. 140–41, 151.

14. *Ibid.*, pp. 142–3, 166, 200–201.

Hans-Dietrich Genscher and Emilio Colombo, which aimed to achieve greater political cohesion through revision of the Treaty of Rome and the enactment of a new European Act. This led on to the adoption of the so-called 'Solemn Declaration on European Union' by the heads of government at Stuttgart in June 1983. Not long afterwards, in February 1984, the EP adopted a Draft Treaty on European Union proposed by Altiero Spinelli, an Italian federalist.[15]

The Thatcher government viewed this drive towards greater unity with distinctly mixed feelings. On the one hand, it strongly disapproved of any changes which might have the effect of weakening British sovereignty. It was therefore adamantly opposed to suggestions that the powers of the Commission should be strengthened and also to the introduction of a greater element of majority voting at meetings of the Council of Ministers. On the other hand, it saw considerable merit in some of the other ideas currently under consideration. Thus it strongly supported the removal of all hindrances to the free movement of goods, capital and labour. Its attitude here was influenced by a combination of political ideology and considerations of national self-interest. The elimination of commercial restrictions was obviously fully in accord with the government's staunch adherence to free-market economics. But it was also hoped that Britain's air transport and financial service industries – believed to be leaders in their field – would derive great benefits from the establishment of unfettered competition.[16] Another area in which the Thatcher government welcomed moves towards closer cooperation was foreign policy. European Political Cooperation (EPC) represented an attempt to extend the principle of harmonisation to foreign affairs. The Thatcher government consistently took the lead in pressing for its further development. It is not hard to see why. By espousing EPC with great enthusiasm, it obtained some protection at least from the charge of being wholly negative towards the development of the EC. In addition, there was no question of any surrender of sovereignty. The basis of EPC was close cooperation between independent governments – a formula that was always likely to appeal to any British government.

The Thatcher government's thinking about moves towards closer economic and political union was set out in a discussion paper which it submitted to the Fontainebleau European Council of June

15. Urwin, *The Community of Europe*, pp. 221–4.
16. Thatcher, *The Downing Street Years*, pp. 552–3.

1984. The document, entitled *Europe – The Future*, maintained that the best way to deal with the technological gap opened up by Japan and the US was to sweep away impediments to trade within the EC. Measures were suggested to simplify and speed up customs procedures and other formalities which were hampering trade. So far as constitutional change was concerned, though, the paper had very little to offer. There was a modest proposal for codification of existing procedures for political cooperation. In addition the paper emphasised the importance of retaining the national veto.[17] The British government liked to portray this particular contribution to the debate about the EC's future as a positive one. It claimed to be offering progress on the basis of sensible and practicable reform, as opposed to the more fanciful programmes emanating from the Commission and other quarters. It is possible, however, to view the British paper in a somewhat different light. At the time of the Fontainebleau European Council there was considerable talk, especially from Mitterand, about the possibility of a 'two-speed' Europe and of pressing on with desirable changes without Britain if necessary.[18] Against such a background, the proposals put forward at Fontainebleau can be seen as an essentially defensive tactic – an attempt to avoid complete isolation and to divert the general enthusiasm for political integration and institutional reform into channels that were more congenial to Britain.

In the period after Fontainebleau, the Thatcher government continued to fight a rearguard action against the drive for institutional change. But it was in a difficult position. There was powerful pressure from the Commission whose new President, Delors, insisted that it would not be possible to create a single market without the necessary political reforms to override national interests. Moreover, Britain was in a clear minority in its refusal to accept a greater degree of political integration. France, Germany, Italy and the Benelux countries were all enthusiastic supporters. Only Greece and Denmark shared the reservations felt by Britain, as became clear at the Milan European Council of June 1985.

At Milan, where the main item on the agenda was the Dooge Committee's report, it was agreed in principle to establish by 1992 a fully integrated internal market. Thatcher acknowledged that this would mean abandoning the veto in certain areas and was prepared

---

17. 'Europe – The Future', *Journal of Common Market Studies*, 23 (1984), pp. 74–81. See also Howe, *Conflict of Loyalty*, pp. 407–9.
18. Young, *This Blessed Plot*, p. 324; Young, *Britain and European Unity*, p. 148.

to accept that. What she was opposed to was the establishment of an intergovernmental conference (IGC) to consider a wide range of institutional reforms and a possible revision of the Treaty of Rome in order to carry them through. Thatcher was under the impression that this could only be done on the basis of unanimity. In the event, however, Bettino Craxi, the Italian Prime Minister, who was chairing the session, called a vote – the first time ever in a European Council – and a majority approved the IGC, with only Britain, Denmark and Greece voting against.[19] This was the first of several miscalculations by the British Prime Minister.

The IGC took the form of regular sessions of EC foreign ministers receiving reports from two working parties, one of which dealt with EPC and the other with revision of the founding treaties. It met during September and October 1985 and its proposals formed the basis of the SEA, which was agreed at the Luxembourg European Council in the following December. The SEA's central objective was to reach a single internal market by the end of 1992 through the eradication of all impediments to free movement of persons, capital and goods. This was only one aspect, however, of a measure which involved such matters as EPC and large-scale institutional change. Although the powers of the EP and the Commission were only marginally increased, the SEA entailed a substantial extension of qualified majority voting (QMV) in the Council of Ministers: unanimity would still be required, though, in respect of such matters as the accession of new members, the enunciation of new principles and treaty amendments. The text of the SEA referred to the goal of improving living and working conditions. It also incorporated general commitments to eventual European unity and further development of the EMS. All these elements contained the potential for massive strides towards economic and political integration. Moreover, the creation of a genuine single market, as soon became clear, would in itself have all sorts of implications for national policy in many areas relating to commercial activities, notably taxation, employment law, welfare provisions and border controls.[20]

Despite this, the SEA was accepted by the British government. Equally surprisingly, it was approved by the House of Commons with a minimum of opposition. Among those who voted for its acceptance, indeed, were Conservative backbenchers like William

19. Thatcher, *The Downing Street Years*, pp. 548–51; Howe, *Conflict of Loyalty*, p. 409; Urwin, *The Community of Europe*, pp. 226–8.

20. Howe, *Conflict of Loyalty*, pp. 454–7; Thatcher, *The Downing Street Years*, pp. 551–7; Urwin, *The Community of Europe*, pp. 230–34.

Cash and Peter Tapsell, who were later to be among its bitterest critics on the grounds that it represented an intolerable erosion of national sovereignty.[21] Their subsequent explanation for their acquiescence – that they trusted Thatcher's judgement – is perhaps understandable.[22] What is more puzzling is the attitude of Thatcher herself, and it is interesting to speculate on her motives for going along with the SEA. It is possible that she felt unable to offer further resistance to the growing momentum for political integration. As she later wrote:

> The pressure from most other Community countries, from the European Commission, from the European Assembly, from influential figures in the media for closer cooperation and integration was so strong as to be almost irresistible.[23]

Another likely explanation is that she wholly underestimated the seriousness of intent behind yet another in a long line of vague, ambitious commitments to the goal of European unity. That would certainly be consonant with her tendency to dismiss enthusiasm for political integration as 'airy fairy nonsense'. Given her desire to achieve a single market, subscribing to what she regarded as meaningless declarations no doubt seemed a small price to pay. In her memoirs, she claims to have been misled and betrayed by duplicitous EC partners.[24] Some of her closest confidants at the time, including Charles Powell, her foreign policy adviser, have echoed this charge. They have also alleged that Thatcher was badly misinformed by Foreign Office advisers about what precisely was involved in the SEA. This has been denied, however, by one of the officials concerned, Sir Michael Butler, according to whom Thatcher insisted on having every line of the Act explained to her. Another official has said that she boasted of having read it in minute detail.[25] Certainly it does seem implausible that a politician who was famed for her mastery of briefs should have been unaware of what she was signing up to.

Whatever the truth of the matter, as the full implications of the SEA became clearer, Thatcher dug in her heels – even on such basic and central issues as the removal of national border controls

21. Young, *This Blessed Plot*, pp. 334–5.

22. Interviews in BBC 2 Television documentary, *The Poisoned Chalice*, part 3.

23. Thatcher, *The Downing Street Years*, pp. 547–8.

24. *Ibid*, pp. 555–6; M. Thatcher, *The Path to Power* (1995), p. 473.

25. Interviews with Powell, Butler and Williamson in BBC 2 Television documentary, *The Poisoned Chalice*, part 3; Young, *This Blessed Plot*, p. 336.

and harmonisation of taxes. Removal of border controls, she claimed, would make it impossible to check terrorism and drug trafficking. Her stated objection to having a uniform rate of VAT throughout the EC was that it would mean taking away from the British Parliament the power to determine levels of taxation. There was also concern about the impact on prices of ending Britain's zero VAT rate on a range of essential items. In June 1985 Lord Cockfield, the British Commissioner who had been given the task of making practical preparations for the single market, produced a plan for harmonising rates of VAT. The British government opposed it, arguing that VAT should be allowed to find its own level through the operation of market forces. Cockfield was regarded as a traitor who had 'gone native' since his appointment to the Commission. His punishment was not to be renominated. Instead, he was replaced by Leon Brittan in 1989.[26]

As the Commission proceeded to produce further plans for the EC's future development – notably the Social Charter of May 1989 and the Delors Report of the previous month on EMU – Thatcher reacted with mounting suspicion and hostility. Her mistrust was focused to a considerable extent on the person of Delors, who was nominated for a second term as President of the Commission in 1988. In fact, there developed between Delors and the British Prime Minister something approaching a personal feud.[27] Delors had his own vision of what the SEA entailed. He insisted that it was not simply a question of sweeping away obstacles to a free internal market: the creation of a single market must be accompanied by full economic and monetary union. There must be a greater role for the Commission and the EP, as well as the provision of comprehensive welfare measures throughout the EC. As might be imagined, such notions were anathema to Thatcher who saw them as a blueprint for federalism, a diminution of national sovereignty and the establishment of a centralised European superstate dominated by Brussels. Delors expounded his views in a number of highly publicised speeches. In July 1988 he told the EP that in ten years' time 80 per cent of economic, financial and social legislation affecting members of the EC would emanate from Brussels. Thatcher was infuriated and in a radio programme (*The Jimmy Young Show*)

26. Grant, *Delors*, pp. 67–70; Urwin, *The Community of Europe*, pp. 236–7; Howe, *Conflict of Loyalty*, p. 535; Thatcher, *The Downing Street Years*, p. 547.

27. For the Thatcher–Delors relationship see Grant, *Delors*, pp. 87–90; Young, *This Blessed Plot*, pp. 326–7; Thatcher, *The Downing Street Years*, pp. 547, 551, 558–9, 742.

criticised his remarks as grossly exaggerated and 'over the top'.[28] Delors's speech to the TUC annual conference at Brighton two months later, in which he spoke of the need to protect workers' interests,[29] produced an even stronger retort. Addressing an audience at the College of Europe in Bruges on 20 September, Thatcher denounced the idea of a 'European superstate' and condemned Delors's projects as 'creeping back-door Socialism'. Although the speech was based on a Foreign Office draft, it had been substantially rewritten by Charles Powell and undoubtedly represented the Prime Minister's authentic feelings. Howe, the Foreign Secretary, was aghast when he first saw the amended version.[30]

In her Bruges speech, Thatcher poured scorn on many of the policies advocated not only by Delors but also by most EC governments. She spoke out against centralised direction of the economy, saying: 'We have not successfully rolled back the frontiers of the state in Britain, only to see them reimposed at a European level, with a European super-state exercising a new dominion from Brussels.' In addition, she complained bitterly about the proposed new social dimension. New regulations to safeguard workers' interests would, she argued, make the European economy less flexible and competitive. Similarly, harmonisation of social benefits would impose a cost handicap on European industry. But the centrepiece of the speech was its strident assertion of the crucial importance of the individual nation. Europe would be stronger with 'France as France, Spain as Spain, Britain as Britain, each with its own customs, traditions and incentives'. It 'would be folly to try to fit them into some sort of identikit European personality'.[31] At the time, the press fastened onto this part of the Bruges speech as its most significant aspect. More recently, however, a number of historians, such as Stephen George, have sought to modify this view, pointing out that it represented only a small part of the whole.[32] Of course, historians have a duty to challenge accepted interpretations. In this instance, however, such tortuous textual analysis fails to convince, and it is difficult to avoid the conclusion that the original interpretation was closer to the mark.

The views that Thatcher expressed at Bruges and elsewhere caused strained relations with Britain's EC partners. They also occasioned

28. Grant, *Delors*, p. 88; The Jimmy Young Show, BBC Radio 2, 27 July 1988.
29. *The Independent*, 9 September 1988.
30. Young, *This Blessed Plot*, pp. 348–50; Howe, *Conflict of Loyalty*, pp. 536–8.
31. *The Times*, 20 September 1988; Thatcher, *The Downing Street Years*, pp. 744–5.
32. S. George, *Britain and European Integration since 1945* (1991), p. 60.

mounting disquiet at home. In the early part of the decade, her strident defence of British financial interests had clearly struck a chord with domestic opinion. By the late 1980s, however, there were signs that she was losing touch with the public mood. Her attitude towards the EC seemed to a growing number of critics to be narrow, blinkered, outdated and contrary to Britain's own long-term interests. In July 1990 Nicholas Ridley, the Secretary for Trade and Industry, was forced to resign following publication in *The Spectator* of an indiscreet interview in which he referred to monetary union as 'a German racket designed to take over the whole of Europe', to the French as 'poodles' of the Germans and to the EC commissioners as 'unelected, reject politicians'.[33] The fact that he was widely – and probably correctly – assumed to be uttering Thatcher's own thoughts was symptomatic of the depth of unease that had grown up about her attitude towards Europe.[34] Misgivings had already begun to surface even in the ranks of the normally loyal Conservative Party, and these were greatly strengthened by the party's disastrous performance in the European elections of June 1989 following a campaign fought on a platform of outright hostility to Brussels.

Dissatisfaction with Thatcher's European policies – not least among Cabinet colleagues – was to play a significant part in her fall from power. It is, of course, difficult to separate out the EC issue from the many other strands of discontent at that time. The poll tax was proving to be a political nightmare. After the euphoria generated by Nigel Lawson's 1988 tax-cutting budget, there were justified fears that the economy was becoming dangerously over-heated. Above all, there was growing criticism of the Prime Minister's personal style, which was widely viewed as autocratic and uncaring. What ultimately sealed Thatcher's political fate was the sense that she had become an electoral liability rather than an asset. Her stance towards the EC was nevertheless a major reason for her loss of support within the Conservative Party and more generally. Moreover, it was an EC issue – membership of the ERM – that was the immediate cause of her terminal difficulties.

---

33. *The Spectator*, 12 July 1990.

34. Ridley's interviewer, Dominic Lawson, wrote in the *Spectator* article: 'Mr Ridley's confidence in expressing his views on the German threat must owe something to the knowledge that they are not significantly different from those of the Prime Minister.' See also Howe, *Conflict of Loyalty*, pp. 632–3; G. Urban, *Diplomacy and Disillusion at the Court of Margaret Thatcher: An Insider's View* (1996), p. 153; P. Stephens, *Politics and the Pound: The Conservatives' Struggle with Sterling* (1996), p. 102.

Like her predecessor, Callaghan, Thatcher was against British entry to the ERM – though she had described the other's decision in December 1978 not to take sterling in as 'a sad day for Britain'.[35] In accordance with her free-market principles, she favoured a floating exchange, believing that fixed rates were inherently un-workable. As she put it: 'There is no way in which one can buck the market.'[36] By the mid-1980s, however, several of her Cabinet colleagues had come to the conclusion that going into the ERM would enhance economic stability and provide a more effective weapon against inflation than control of the money supply. This was certainly the view taken by Nigel Lawson, the then Chancellor of the Exchequer, and on 13 November 1985 a meeting of senior ministers and the Governor of the Bank of England, Robin Leigh-Pemberton, was held to discuss his proposal for entry. At this meet-ing there was an overwhelming majority in favour of entry. Only John Biffin, the Leader of the House of Commons, spoke against it. The rest, including Norman Tebbit, the Conservative Party Chair-man, argued for going in. William Whitelaw, then Lord President of the Council and Leader of the House of Lords, summed up, saying that the Chancellor of the Exchequer, the Foreign Secretary, Howe, and the Governor of the Bank of England all supported it and that was good enough for him. Thatcher retorted that it was not good enough for her and that if the government decided to go in, it would have to do so without her.[37]

This episode marked the beginning of a protracted bout of min-isterial wrangling, with the Prime Minister effectively exercising a veto until 1990.[38] Unable to take sterling into the ERM, for a number of years Lawson did the next best thing, pursuing a policy of 'shad-owing the Deutschmark' – that is, acting as though the pound was actually inside by keeping it at a fixed rate against the West German currency. In the spring of 1988 Thatcher openly blamed this policy for stoking up inflation, and from that time onwards differences between Prime Minister and Chancellor became increasingly pub-lic. The quarrel was inflamed by the embarrassing intervention of Professor Alan Walters, Thatcher's personal economic adviser, who has been described by 'an anonymous mandarin' as the man who

35. *H.C.Deb.*, vol. 959, col. 1424, 6 December 1978.
36. Cited in Thatcher, *The Downing Street Years*, p. 703.
37. Howe, *Conflict of Loyalty*, pp. 449–50; N. Lawson, *The View from No.11* (1992), pp. 497–500; Stephens, *Politics and the Pound*, pp. 48–51. Thatcher's account of the meeting is brief and uninformative: *The Downing Street Years*, p. 697.
38. For a brilliant account of Thatcher's increasingly desperate rearguard action against entry into the ERM see Stephens, *Politics and the Pound*, chs. 3–7.

'provided her [Thatcher] with the algebraic equations for her flat-earth economics'.[39] Walters not only ridiculed the ERM as a 'half-baked idea', but also claimed that the Prime Minister agreed with him.[40] Not surprisingly, Lawson found the situation intolerable and on 26 October 1989 he resigned.

But that was not before he and Howe had obliged Thatcher to soften her opposition to British membership of the ERM at the Madrid European Council of June 1989. On the eve of her departure for Madrid, at what Thatcher later called 'an ambush' and 'a nasty little meeting', the Chancellor and the Foreign Secretary threatened to resign unless she agreed to change her current stance. The loss of two such senior figures would have been politically disastrous and Thatcher therefore reluctantly capitulated. Prior to Madrid, Thatcher had stuck to the formula that the pound would go in 'when the time was right'. At Madrid, more precise conditions were laid down. Sterling would enter the ERM when other states had removed exchange controls and restrictions on movement of capital, when real progress had been made in freeing the internal market and, finally, when the UK's inflation rate was significantly lower and much nearer to the average of the ERM states. Although a Downing Street spokesman later claimed that there had been no change of policy, the truth was that it was now a question of when, rather than whether, entry took place.[41]

Despite her enforced climbdown, Thatcher remained unhappy about the prospect of membership of the ERM. She rightly saw it as a preliminary step towards full EMU, complete with a single currency and a European central bank, with the loss of sovereignty that that entailed. In October 1990, however, she was persuaded of the need to go in by the joint efforts of John Major, who had replaced Lawson as Chancellor in October of the previous year after a three-month spell at the Foreign Office, and Douglas Hurd, who had become Foreign Secretary as part of the same Cabinet reshuffle. Major's attitude towards entry to the ERM had undergone a bewildering series of changes in the course of the past decade.[42] In the early 1980s he had been in favour of it as an essential part of the government's anti-inflationary strategy. By 1987, however, when he was Chief Secretary to the Treasury, he was opposed, inclining

---

39. *Ibid.*, p. 129.   40. *Financial Times*, 18 October 1989.
41. Thatcher, *The Downing Street Years*, pp. 710–13; Howe, *Conflict of Loyalty*, pp. 576–84; Lawson, *The View From No.11*, pp. 928–34; B. Anderson, *John Major* (1992), pp. 150–51.
42. See Anderson, *John Major*, pp. 120–32.

to the view that the ERM was not workable and that the only proper way to tackle inflation was by adopting the correct domestic policies. The process of his reconversion began during his brief period as Foreign Secretary – when he became aware of the drawbacks of Thatcher's approach to the EC – and was completed during his first few months as Chancellor. By the beginning of 1990, he was firmly committed to securing British entry at the earliest opportunity. In alliance with Hurd, he set about persuading Thatcher, whose continuing resistance was now the last remaining obstacle. For various reasons the two held a strong hand. They were both on better terms with Thatcher than Howe and Lawson had been. Moreover, their leverage was increased by the fact that she could not afford to risk any further resignations after the ministerial musical chairs of 1989. Besides, Thatcher's opposition was weakening. She was by this stage almost totally isolated on the question, and the resignation of Ridley in July 1990 removed an important anti-ERM voice from the Cabinet. Finally, the economic and financial situation seemed to demand a change of policy. By the spring of 1990 the government's anti-inflation policy was in tatters, destroyed by the boom of the late 1980s. Interest rates were at a higher level than at any time since 1981 and the pound was dangerously vulnerable to speculative pressure.[43]

At a key meeting with Major on 13 June, Thatcher agreed that Britain would join the ERM subject to certain safeguards, and over the next few months Prime Minister and Chancellor held a series of highly secret meetings to discuss arrangements for going in. Hurd was not involved. Indeed, he was not informed of the date of entry until 24 hours before the decision was announced. Thatcher finally gave her consent at a meeting of 4 October with Major and officials from the Treasury and the Bank of England. Phillip Stephens gives an account of this meeting in his brilliant study *Politics and the Pound*, and from this it appears that it had two extraordinary features. First, Thatcher appeared to be principally concerned with how the news should be released to the press – thus giving substance perhaps to Gilmour's jibe that she was the 'mistress of irrelevant detail'. Secondly, she insisted that the right to determine interest rates must remain with the British government, not seeming to realise that this would not be possible.[44] Nobody saw fit to disabuse her. The decision to join was announced after the markets had closed on Friday 5 October and membership took effect from the following Monday. It is no exaggeration to say that this decision and its timing were dictated almost entirely by domestic political considerations. Sterling went in at too high a rate – DM2.95 – and at a time when inflation was well above the ERM average. What the government was interested in was securing a cut in interest rates – and mortgage rates in particular – before the Conservative Party conference, and it was felt that this could only be done without endangering the value of the pound if it was in the ERM and backed by the resources of the Bundesbank. It is significant that the announcement of entry was accompanied by a cut in bank rate from 15 per cent to 14 per cent.

Even after entry, Thatcher remained deeply sceptical. This was reflected in highly critical comments about monetary union during and after the Rome European Council of October 1990 and in her defiant rejection of Delors's plans to bring it about – 'No, no, no',[45] she exclaimed in the course of parliamentary exchanges on the Rome meeting. These remarks, in turn, prompted the resignation of the long-suffering Howe from his position of Deputy Prime Minister at the beginning of November. In his resignation speech of 13 November – later described by Thatcher as 'a mixture of bile and treachery'[46] – Howe attacked Thatcher's whole attitude to Europe, dismissing her vision of a continent that was 'positively teeming with ill-intentioned people, scheming, in her words, to "dissolve our national identities", to lead us "through the backdoor into a federal Europe"'.[47] It was a devastating critique from a politician not noted for his biting invective and it played a major part in precipitating a challenge to her leadership of the Conservative Party and her subsequent resignation on 22 November 1990.

45. *H.C.Deb.*, vol. 178, col. 873, 30 October 1990; Howe, *Conflict of Loyalty*, pp. 643–4.

46. Thatcher, *The Downing Street Years*, p. 840.

47. *H.C.Deb.*, vol. 180, cols. 461–5, 13 November 1990; Howe, *Conflict of Loyalty*, pp. 665–7.

CHAPTER NINETEEN

'At the Heart of Europe'?

On no other question were the Conservatives more divided during the early 1990s than Europe, the issue sometimes referred to as the party's 'San Andreas Fault'. By the time John Major became Prime Minister, dissension over the EC had already contributed to the resignation or enforced departure of several senior ministers, including Michael Heseltine, Leon Brittan, Nigel Lawson, Geoffrey Howe and Margaret Thatcher. It was soon to claim the scalp of another, the Chancellor, Norman Lamont, and posed a constant threat to Major's leadership between 1990 and 1997. The new Prime Minister was fully aware of the dangers that internal party differences on Europe presented to himself and to party unity. He was faced with constant reminders of the fact, not least from highly publicised interventions by his predecessor. Especially during the early part of his premiership, before he had begun to establish his own authority with the unexpected general election victory of April 1992, Major was haunted by the spectre of Thatcher.[1] Her powerful presence and continuing popularity with the party rank and file acted as a constraint on his room for manoeuvre. Even as late as 1997, her occasional speeches, carefully timed to achieve maximum effect, served as shots across the bow, reminding Major of the legacy that she had bequeathed to him on Europe as on other matters.

If Thatcher's views on Europe were easy enough to place, those of her successor were more problematical. From the outset, commentators found it difficult to decide whether he belonged to the Eurosceptic or Europhile wing of the Conservative Party. It might be said that this reflected a more general ambiguity in Major's political stance. As the favoured candidate of the departed leader,

1. A. Seldon, *Major: A Political Life* (1997), pp. 252–5.

275

he was understandably seen by many as the true heir of the
Thatcherite faith – 'dry' on economic matters and sceptical on
Europe. But there were others who claimed that he stood for a
return to the 'One Nation' brand of Toryism which Thatcher had
ostentatiously rejected and was later to ridicule at the time of Emma
Nicholson's defection to the Liberal Democrats in late 1995 as 'No
Nation Toryism'.[2] It is arguable, indeed, that a general inability to
identify Major with any particular section of the Conservative Party
was one of the main reasons for his success in the 1990 leadership
contest against Hurd and Heseltine. This capacity to straddle the
warring factions was to be sorely tested in succeeding years.

Preventing open warfare in a Conservative Party bitterly riven
over both Europe and the related issue of Thatcher's recent demise
was not the only challenge facing Major when he became Prime
Minister. Another urgent claim upon his attention was the need to
repair the damage inflicted on Britain's relations with its EC partners during the previous decade. Whereas Thatcher had gloried in
confrontation and being in a minority of one, it was her successor's
intention to adopt a more conventional and cooperative style of
diplomacy. Instead of being isolated and embattled, Britain would
henceforth be 'at the very heart of Europe'.[3] It was not without
significance that Major uttered these words during an early visit to
Chancellor Kohl in March 1991, for he was particularly concerned
to improve relations with Bonn. These had suffered badly in the
course of 1989–90 as a result of Nicholas Ridley's injudicious
off-the-record comments in the summer of 1990, leaked reports
of a controversial seminar at Chequers involving an exchange of
views on the German national character between Thatcher, Charles
Powell and a number of specialists in German history, and above all
Thatcher's ill-judged attempts to frustrate the great achievement
of Kohl's political life, the unification of Germany.[4] To Major the
advantages of being on better terms with the most powerful state
in the EC seemed self-evident and, unlike Thatcher, he set out to
establish a close personal rapport with the head of the German
government. This, together with a more conciliatory approach to

2. The Keith Joseph Memorial Lecture, 11 January 1996: *The Independent*, 12 January 1996.

3. *The Times*, 12 March 1991; Seldon, *Major*, pp. 166–7.

4. For the Chequers seminar see G. Urban, *Diplomacy and Disillusion at the Court of
Margaret Thatcher: An Insider's View* (1996), pp. 118–59; H. Young, *This Blessed Plot:
Britain and Europe from Churchill to Blair* (1998), pp. 359–61. See also the account by
Norman Stone, a participant, in *The Sunday Times*, 27 September 1998.

negotiations, was to yield dividends at the Maastricht European Council of 9–10 December 1991.[5]

The arrangements agreed at the Dutch town of Maastricht were based upon the work of two parallel IGCs – one concerned with the creation of EMU and the other with furthering political union.[6] As we have seen, these had been set in motion despite fierce opposition from Thatcher, and preparations for them to begin, in December 1990, were already well advanced when Major became Prime Minister. Although Major's negotiating style was less acerbic than that of his predecessor, the actual substance of his policy on the EC's future development involved no great elements of discontinuity – hence the witticism of Ruud Lubbers, the Dutch Premier: 'Mrs Thatcher without the handbag'. Like Thatcher, Major regarded the forthcoming IGCs as undesirable but unavoidable. Like her, he favoured the creation of the single market but was resolutely opposed to surrendering the national veto, an increase in the use of QMV or any other measures seen to be promoting the development of a federal structure. Like her, moreover, he accorded a higher priority to the widening of the EC than to its deepening[7] – the calculation here being that the inclusion of Austria (which had already officially applied for entry in July 1989), Sweden and other members of EFTA, followed by that of the numerous former Communist states of central and eastern Europe, would act as a brake on the drive for political integration. This approach was diametrically opposed to that of the French and German governments which, backed by the Commission, insisted that enlargement must be postponed until not only the single market but also the European Union had come into being. Nor was that the only respect in which British objectives differed from those of the UK's principal EC partners. For his part, Mitterand was determined to press ahead with EMU as a way of controlling Germany's financial might. Despite some concern about opposition from the Bundesbank and domestic public opinion, Kohl, too, was strongly committed to this goal. He was also a fervent advocate of a much greater degree of political integration, calling for a substantial extension of QMV, as well as greater

5. Seldon, *Major*, pp. 164–6, 246.

6. For the discussions and negotiations leading up to Maastricht see C. Grant, *Delors: Inside the House that Jacques Built* (1994), pp.181–210; R. Pryce, 'The Treaty negotiations', in A. Duff, J. Pinder and R. Pryce (eds), *Maastricht and Beyond: Building the European Union* (1994), pp. 36–49; Seldon, *Major*, pp. 242–4.

7. For a statement of Major's negotiating position on the eve of Maastricht see *H.C.Deb.*, vol. 199, cols. 269–81, 20 November 1991.

powers for the Commission and the EP. Such a programme was wholly unacceptable to Major. He therefore went to Maastricht resolved to resist and keep to a minimum any moves towards closer political union. Quite apart from his own convictions on the matter, he could not afford to acquiesce in anything that might produce an outcry in Conservative ranks, especially since a general election could not be delayed for more than a matter of months.

There is some debate over how successful Major's Maastricht strategy was. As his jubilant reaction of 'game, set and match' suggests, his own view was that the outcome of the negotiations represented a decisive victory for British diplomacy and a severe check to federalist aspirations.[8] This verdict has been endorsed by some historians, including John Young, who has written that Major, with the aid of a sympathetic German Chancellor, 'pulled off something of a coup'.[9] Others, however, have reached a different conclusion, arguing that Maastricht resulted in a somewhat messy compromise rather than complete acceptance of British desiderata.[10] This difference of opinion rests essentially on conflicting interpretations of the extent to which the new treaty – which provided for the creation of a European Union (EU) – was intended or likely to extend the scope of supranational institutions and procedures. The complexity, even ambiguity, of many of its provisions makes the evidence on this question hard to assess.[11] On the one hand, it is clear that federalist hopes were not fully realised and that this was due in no small measure to opposition from the British delegation. In response to objections from that quarter, an intended reference in the first article of the treaty to 'a federal goal' had been dropped.[12] The principle of 'subsidiarity' was accepted. Furthermore, the second and third of the three 'pillars' in the projected Union's complicated political structure – those for Foreign, Security and Defence Policy and for Justice and Home Affairs – were based squarely on

8. The celebrated phrase 'game, set and match' was uttered by a spokesman rather than Major himself. It nevertheless accurately reflected his own views. See S. Hogg and J. Hill, *Too Close to Call* (1995), p. 157, n. 7; Seldon, *Major*, p. 248; Young, *This Blessed Plot*, p. 432.

9. J.W. Young, *Britain and European Unity: A History of European Integration since 1945* (1995), pp. 162–3. Seldon similarly presents the outcome of Maastricht as a personal triumph for Major: *Major*, pp. 248–9.

10. See, for example, R. Pryce, 'The Maastricht Treaty and the new Europe' and A. Duff, 'The main reforms', in Duff *et al.* (eds), *Maastricht and Beyond*, pp. 10–11, 19–20; Young, *This Blessed Plot*, pp. 388–9.

11. For an analysis of the Maastricht Treaty see Duff *et al.*, (eds), *Maastricht and Beyond*, chs. 6–8.

12. Major, *H.C.Deb.*, vol. 201, col. 276, 18 December 1991.

intergovernmental decision-making on the EPC model.[13] On the other hand, there were equally certain aspects of the treaty that were distinctly unpalatable to Major because they were designed to foster closer integration. It was envisaged, for instance, that 'joint action' and the adoption of 'common positions' in the security field might eventually lead on to 'a common defence policy'. The EP was to be given increased powers, including a limited right of legislative partnership with the Council of Ministers – something the British had consistently sought to prevent. Above all, for the first time the Maastricht Treaty set out not only the objective of EMU, but also the timetable and means by which it was to be achieved. This was something that Major was simply not prepared to accept and, reviving an idea that he had first put to Thatcher when Chancellor in April 1990, he negotiated a special opt-out arrangement whereby Britain would be allowed to defer a commitment to participation in the third and final stage of EMU until the government and Parliament had made 'a separate decision to do so'. A refusal to subscribe to the Social Protocol signed by Britain's eleven partners – more usually known as the Social Chapter – led to the negotiation of a similar opt-out.[14] As can be seen, then, Maastricht was not the unqualified victory that Major claimed.

The Treaty on European Union was signed in Maastricht on 7 February 1992. For it to come into effect, it had to be ratified unanimously. In some of the countries concerned, however, the process of ratification encountered serious obstacles, and it was not until October of the following year that the whole business was completed.[15] In Britain, the passage of the necessary legislation, in the shape of the European Communities (Amendments) Bill, proved to be a lengthy and tortuous affair – in sharp contrast to what had happened with the SEA, which had been pushed through Parliament in 1986 swiftly and without too much detailed scrutiny. The government's greatest problem was dissent from among its own supporters. Initially, that appeared to present only a minor threat. In the parliamentary debate on the outcome of the Maastricht European Council, held on 18–19 December 1991, criticism from the Conservative benches was generally muted.[16] This was somewhat misleading, however, for what had happened was that the imminence

13. *Ibid.*, col. 277.   14. Seldon, *Major*, pp. 246–8.

15. For an account of the process of ratification see Duff *et al.* (eds), *Maastricht and Beyond*, pp. 53–68.

16. Only seven, including Tebbit and Biffen, voted against the government's bill, with three abstentions.

of a general election had inevitably caused the party to close ranks. The debate had revealed some suspicion and unease on the part of Conservative speakers like Norman Tebbit, Sir Peter Tapsell and Sir Teddy Taylor,[17] and over ensuing months such feelings were to proliferate and intensify in response to developments both at home and abroad. The general election of April 1992 brought into the Commons a new intake of Conservative Eurosceptics such as Iain Duncan-Smith and John Townend. It also reduced the government's overall majority from 88 to 21 (shortly down to 18), thereby further strengthening the hand of potential anti-Maastricht rebels.[18] There were soon renewed doubts about Major's personal authority. In addition, Conservative backbenchers were becoming increasingly restive about the failure of the promised economic recovery to materialise. What was of particular relevance to the fate of the Maastricht Treaty was that some of them were already beginning to see a direct connection between the continuing recession and British membership of the ERM. In the words of Phillip Stephens, 'Europe and the economy were becoming inextricably and explosively entangled'.[19]

The change of mood wrought by these various developments was manifested as early as May 1992 when 22 Conservative MPs voted against the European Communities (Amendment) Bill on its second reading, the biggest Conservative revolt on Europe since the debate on entry to the EC some twenty years earlier. Such anti-Maastricht sentiment was soon to be given a boost by two other developments: the Danish referendum and sterling's ignominious exit from the ERM.

In September 1992 a referendum held in France resulted in approval of the Maastricht Treaty by an extremely narrow margin. This '*petit oui*' was demoralising enough for the treaty's supporters. Several months earlier, however, they had been dealt a far weightier blow when the Danes had rejected the treaty, also by a narrow margin, in their referendum of 2 June. The impact of this event, in Britain as elsewhere, was dramatic and immediate. It provided critics of Maastricht with a psychological lift and renewed hope. At the same time it strengthened the case for a British referendum, for which Thatcher – along with an ill-assorted group of bedfellows,

17. *H.C.Deb.*, vol. 201, cols. 322–7, 330–32, 358–60, 18 December 1991.
18. Seldon, *Major*, pp. 285–6.
19. P. Stephens, *Politics and the Pound: The Conservatives' Struggle with Sterling* (1996), p. 199.

including Norman Tebbit, Nicholas Ridley, William Cash, Tony Benn and Paddy Ashdown, the leader of the Liberal Democrats – had already been pressing for some time.[20] Denouncing Maastricht as 'a treaty too far', Thatcher hailed the result of the Danish referendum as a triumph for democracy and renewed her call for the British people to be given a similar chance to make their feelings known. More than that, she demanded that ratification of the treaty should be halted.[21] Her views chimed in with those of many Conservative MPs, 70 of whom on 3 June signed an early day motion asking for a 'fresh start' in the government's policy on Europe (the origin of the Fresh Start Group). Even within the Cabinet there was some feeling that the vote in Denmark must mean a rethink about the Maastricht Treaty, with Michael Howard, the Environment Secretary, Peter Lilley, the Social Security Secretary, and Michael Portillo, the Chief Secretary to the Treasury, reportedly saying that consideration might be given to abandoning it.[22] Major disagreed. He was proud of what he had achieved at Maastricht and reluctant to risk a new set of negotiations in which it might prove impossible to resist French and German pressure for a more integrationist agenda. Besides, to have disavowed a treaty which he had so recently proclaimed as a great personal triumph would have been extremely damaging to his political credibility, already at a low level. Thus, with support from Kenneth Clarke, the Home Secretary, and Michael Heseltine, the President of the Board of Trade, Major was determined to press on with the process of ratification, although accepting that it could not be completed until after the Danish government had secured a favourable verdict in a second referendum.[23]

His resolve was further tested, however, by the crisis that arose over sterling and the ERM in September. The strains which precipitated this crisis stemmed from the Bundesbank's insistence on maintaining high interest rates in order to counter the inflationary pressures resulting from German unification. This caused difficulties for Germany's EC partners, forcing down the value of their currencies towards the permitted floor within the ERM and preventing them from reducing their own interest rates as a means of stimulating economic recovery. One possible solution to this difficulty was a general devaluation of all other currencies against the

---

20. Tebbit and Thatcher had been pressing for a referendum since November 1991. See *The Independent*, 16 November 1991; *H.C.Deb.*, vol. 199, cols. 293–8, 20 November 1991.

21. Interview on BBC 1 Television, *Breakfast with Frost*, 28 June 1992.

22. Stephens, *Politics and the Pound*, p. 205.   23. Seldon, *Major*, pp. 294–6.

Deutschmark. The British government was prepared to go along with that. The problem was that the French government was not, partly because of its commitment to a *franc fort* policy and partly because of concern for the effect such a move might have on the forthcoming referendum. As both Major and Chancellor Norman Lamont made clear, they were opposed to a general devaluation which did not include the franc. They also rejected with scorn the idea of devaluation of sterling alone. Nor would they countenance withdrawal from the ERM, insisting that British membership was absolutely central to the government's macro-economic strategy. In the absence of any practicable alternative, they were obliged to fall back on ringing declarations of their determination to do whatever was needed to maintain sterling's parity. The markets were unimpressed, however, and on 16 September, 'Black Wednesday', sterling was forced out of the ERM by intense speculative pressure which drove it below its floor of DM2.7780.[24]

This calamitous sequence of events, followed by further turbulence within the ERM, provided Conservative opponents of Maastricht with powerful ammunition with which to attack it. Having consistently argued that EMU – the centrepiece of the treaty – was a wholly unrealistic goal, they could now claim that the ERM fiasco offered a salutary warning of what would happen if the EU persisted in its efforts to move towards a single currency. In the aftermath of 'Black Wednesday', they stepped up their campaign against the treaty. Major's response was to raise the stakes by making passage of the crucial so-called 'paving' motion a question of confidence and threatening to call a general election if it was defeated – a potent weapon, given the government's current unpopularity. This tactic brought some intending rebels into line. As against that, it enabled the Labour Opposition – now led by the strongly pro-European John Smith – to vote against the measure without undue loss of credibility, on the grounds that what was at stake was the survival of the government rather than the Maastricht Treaty. As a result, the motion was approved by a majority of only three on 4 November 1992, with votes by the Liberal Democrats saving the day. Nor was that the end of the government's parliamentary travails, for during the next nine months a nucleus of around 50 Conservative backbenchers continued to fight a dogged rearguard action, with Cash, a leading member of the Eurosceptic Bruges Group, playing a prominent role. These dissidents were not averse to collaborating with

24. Stephens, *Politics and the Pound*, pp. 208–55 *passim*.

Labour, and on 22 July 1993 a revolt by 23 of them led to a humiliating defeat for the government on a Labour amendment to annul Britain's opt-out from the Social Chapter. The following day, however, the government won a comfortable victory on a 'no-confidence' motion, and this cleared the way for Britain to ratify on 2 August 1993. In the meantime, the Danes had voted in favour of the treaty in a second referendum (on 18 May), and in late October the whole process of ratification was formally completed in Brussels.[25]

Although the Maastricht Treaty provided a blueprint for the development of the EU, it nevertheless left ample scope for disagreement among its signatories about what direction the latter ought to take, with the British government remaining determined to keep decision-making as far as possible on an intergovernmental basis and the German, French and most other governments, together with the Commission, seeking to incorporate an additional element of supranationalism. The hybrid nature of the treaty reflected these contradictory approaches and in itself guaranteed continuing controversy about the full implications of what had been agreed. The fact that it had been agreed to hold another IGC in 1996 for the purpose of reviewing the treaty was also bound to generate a lively debate about the future of the EU, as the governments and other interests concerned bargained, manoeuvred and prepared their negotiating positions.[26]

25. For the parliamentary struggle over the Maastricht Treaty see D. Baker, A. Gamble and S. Ludlam, 'The parliamentary siege of Maastricht 1993: Conservative divisions and British ratification', *Parliamentary Affairs*, (January 1994); Seldon, *Major*, pp. 338–42, 386–9.

26. Article N of the Maastricht Treaty provided for it to be reviewed in 1996: A. Duff, *Reforming the European Union* (1997), p. 5.

CHAPTER TWENTY

Opting out: the Maastricht Treaty Review

By the time the rolling IGC was launched in Turin in March 1996, the British government had already set out the line it intended to take in a White Paper whose very title – *A Partnership of Nations* – offered a clear indication of the approach favoured by London.[1] The French government had similarly issued a policy statement, while the European Commission had produced its own plans for the EU in a paper entitled *Reinforcing Political Union and Preparing for Enlargement.*[2] None of these documents contained any real surprises, reflecting for the most part ideas that had been expressed frequently over a number of years. The German government, for its part, refrained from publishing any paper of its own. Its policies were so well known, however, that they did not need to be put in writing. At their centre was the German Chancellor's passionate commitment to closer political union, a commitment rooted in his traumatic personal experience of the Second World War. The war had cost the life of his brother and implanted in Kohl a deep aversion to German nationalism. His concern to prevent its revival led him, as it had Adenauer, to seek to bind Germany into a tightly integrated European political structure, and a logical extension of this was his determination to push ahead with those elements of the Maastricht Treaty that would assist that process. In furtherance of that aim, he consistently advocated a substantial extension of QMV, progress towards a common defence and foreign policy, and an increase in the powers of the EP so as to reduce what was

---

1. Cmd. 3181 (March 1996), *A Partnership of Nations: the British Approach to the Intergovernmental Conference 1996.* The official British line for the IGC was also set out by Rifkind, the Foreign Secretary, in a Commons statement of 12 March 1996: *H.C.Deb.*, vol. 273, cols. 785–9.

2. *The Independent*, Sarah Helm, 20 February 1996.

termed the 'democratic deficit' within the EU. Such objectives were basically incompatible with those of the British government. Equally, the proposals emanating from the European Commission found little favour in London, envisaging as they did greater powers for the Commission's President, the use of QMV in defence, foreign and justice policies, and an end both to opting out from the Social Chapter and to the use of national vetoes – even in the case of fundamental changes to EU rules. The approach adopted by the French government was somewhat closer to that of the British and appeared to offer at least some possibility of compromise. Thus on the same day that the French government released a formal state- ment of its negotiating position for the IGC (14 March 1996), the Prime Minister, Alain Juppé, made a statement declaring his faith in the principle of the nation-state[3] – a credo in close harmony with British official thinking. In the formal statement itself, more- over, there were several proposals which would not have sounded amiss coming from the Major government, including downgrading of the roles of the EP and the Commission. On the other hand, the French stance on QMV, defence policy and enlargement of the EU differed substantially from that of the British.[4]

The overall position, therefore, was that the Major government – like its predecessor – found itself largely out of step with its principal partners, as well as the Commission, on questions vitally affecting Europe's future. As was repeatedly made clear, not least in *A Partnership of Nations*, it had no intention of relinquishing the right to veto fundamental changes to the EU. Nor was it prepared to accept the introduction of QMV into such highly sensitive areas as defence and foreign policy. In a jingoistic speech to the Con- servative Party conference in October 1995, Portillo, the Defence Secretary, stridently rejected the idea of a European army and central command structure.[5] The message from Major, Hurd, his Foreign Secretary, and Hurd's successor, Malcom Rifkind, was more meas- ured but essentially the same.[6] There was also strong resistance to suggestions from Bonn and Paris that the WEU should be placed under the political control of the EU. As Major told the Assembly of the WEU in February 1996, in the opinion of the British govern- ment that would be to 'put institutional tidiness and the illusion of progress before Europe's security needs'. There would be practical

3. *Ibid.*, Mary Dejevsky, 15 March 1996.   4. *Ibid.*
5. *The Times*, 11 October 1995.
6. For Rifkind see *H.C.Deb.*, vol. 273, col. 787, 12 March 1996.

problems because the two organisations were based upon separate treaties and memberships. Furthermore, giving the EU a military role would serve to arouse Russian fears and add another obstacle to the accession of the former Warsaw Pact states.[7] In the realm of foreign affairs, the British response to French and German pressure for a single European voice was generally negative. Both Kohl and Jacques Chirac, who had succeeded Mitterand in the spring of 1995, believed that the ineffectiveness of the EU's response to civil war in Bosnia and to the confrontation between Greece and Turkey in early 1996 had clearly demonstrated such a need. The British government was not entirely convinced. In its White Paper for the IGC, however, it did make some attempt to accommodate its partners' wishes by accepting the idea of an EU foreign affairs spokesman. At the same time, it emphasised that such a figure must be 'fully answerable to the Council of Ministers, representing the views of member states, not deciding them'.[8]

Another point on which the White Paper set out a distinctive British policy goal was reform of the European Court of Justice (ECJ). The ECJ, which sat in Luxembourg, was the highest tribunal of the EU. It provoked much distrust in Conservative circles, where it was widely viewed as a powerful instrument for extending the influence of Brussels through 'political' judgements. Moreover, its unpopularity was compounded by a tendency on the part of many critics to confuse it with the Strasbourg-based European Court of Human Rights, the institution which operated under the aegis of the Council of Europe and which caused an explosion of Conservative anger in 1995 when it condemned Britain for the SAS killing of three members of the IRA in Gibraltar.[9] In March 1996, the ECJ provoked similar outrage with its ruling that Spanish trawlermen, using British-registered trawlers which they had purchased, were legally entitled to a share in the quota allotted to Britain under the EU Common Fisheries Policy (CFP). This judgement, denounced as 'quite crazy' by Tony Baldry, the Fisheries Minister, prompted the Major government to include in its White Paper a demand both for changes in the CFP in order to prevent so-called 'quota hopping' and for curbs on the powers of the ECJ.[10] At the very time the

7. *The Independent*, Christopher Bellamy, 24 February 1996.

8. Cmd. 3181, *A Partnership of Nations.*

9. For British government reverses at the hands of the European Court of Human Rights see *The Guardian*, Michael White, 2 April 1996.

10. *The Independent*, Katherine Butler, 6 March 1996; Cmd. 3181, *A Partnership of Nations*; *H.C.Deb.*, vol. 273, col. 786, 12 March 1996.

White Paper was being issued, the ECJ delivered a preliminary judgement on working hours which reinforced the government's determination to clip its wings. The government had opposed the introduction of an EU directive limiting the working week to 48 hours, claiming that such a measure would impose heavy costs on employers and thereby undermine the competitiveness of member states. It believed that there was no obligation to apply the directive in Britain since it came under the Social Chapter. There was great indignation, therefore, when the ECJ ruled that this was not the case and that the directive was in fact a health and safety matter and, as such, both applicable to Britain and subject to QMV. It was felt that Britain was being compelled to accept the 48-hour limit by sleight of hand, and Major told the Commons: 'It is precisely because of legislation like this and stupidities like this that the EU is becoming uncompetitive and losing its jobs to other parts of the world.'[11] The ECJ's preliminary judgement was subsequently confirmed, and the British government suffered an additional reverse in July 1996, when the court rejected its contention that the worldwide ban on British beef exports imposed by the EU was illegal.

There were at least three other respects in which the British government had a standpoint which placed it at odds with its French and German counterparts and, indeed, most other EU governments. First, it insisted on retaining Britain's opt-out from the Social Chapter. This was useful in the context of domestic party politics, since it enabled the Conservatives to claim that an election victory for Labour, which was committed to abrogating the opt-out, would result in British industry being burdened with a mass of regulations and additional costs. Such an allegation was part of a general campaign to portray the Labour Opposition under John Smith and his successor, Tony Blair, as a party of Eurofanatics whose willingness to subordinate national interests to the goal of a United States of Europe made it unfit to govern.[12] As a matter of fact, this was a caricature. The Labour Party had its own Eurosceptics, including Tony Benn, Peter Shore, Dennis Skinner, Ken Livingstone, Denzil Davies, Diane Abbott and the rest of the 50 MPs who in late March 1996 signed a 'Europe Isn't Working' statement calling on the party leader to rule out British involvement in a single currency. Nor was

11. *H.C.Deb.*, vol. 273, col. 782, 12 March 1996; *The Independent*, Donald Macintyre and Colin Brown, 13 March 1996; Barrie Clement and Katherine Butler, 13 March 1996. See also *The Guardian*, Hugo Young, 21 March 1996.

12. See, for example, Major's attack on John Smith as 'Monsieur Oui, the poodle of Brussels': *H.C.Deb.*, vol. 240, col. 134, 22 March 1994.

Blair a committed federalist. In many ways, indeed, his approach to the EU was extremely cautious, not least in his insistence that a decision on participation in the monetary union must be postponed until it was clear whether it would serve British interests. However that may be, Labour's announced intention of ending the Social Chapter opt-out was seen by the Conservatives as a weakness to be exploited. But quite apart from such tactical considerations, the Conservative leadership regarded the Social Chapter as pernicious – a 'European jobs tax', as Major described it[13] – and its attachment to the opt-out was strongly influenced by the conviction that Britain derived substantial benefits from it. Inspired by a vision of Britain as the 'Hong Kong of Europe', the Major government aimed at creating an economic environment characterised by labour flexibility, low production costs and minimal regulation, and in that scheme of things there was no place for the Social Chapter. Indeed, ministers took great pride in the advantage that British industry was said to enjoy over its EU competitors – reflected in a disproportionate share of inward foreign investment – because of the special opt-out status that had been obtained. It is worth noting that little thought was given as to how this situation could be reconciled with the notion of a 'level playing field' throughout the EU.

Secondly, the British government had every intention of postponing until the last possible moment its decision on whether or not to take part in EMU. Of the other members of the EU, only the Danes took a comparable line, having secured special arrangements for themselves at the Edinburgh European Council of December 1992.[14] Under the Maastricht Treaty, EMU was to be achieved in three stages – along the lines recommended in the 1989 Delors Report. In the first stage, currencies would be aligned with each other in the ERM. The second stage, which was to get under way in January 1994, would see the establishment of the European Monetary Institute, the precursor of a European Central Bank (ECB). In the third and final stage, scheduled to begin in 1997 or 1999 at the latest, a single currency would be created, the operation of which was to be supervised by the ECB.[15] Further details were filled in at the Madrid European Council of December 1995, where it was decided that the new currency should be called the euro and that

13. Speech to the Midlands Institute of Directors in Birmingham, 19 January 1996: *The Independent,* John Rentoul and Colin Brown, 20 January 1996.

14. A. Seldon, *Major: A Political Life* (1997), pp. 348–51.

15. A. Duff, *Reforming the European Union* (1997), p. 26; P. Stephens, *Politics and the Pound: The Conservatives' Struggle with Sterling* (1996), pp. 307–8.

the third stage would definitely start on 1 January 1999 and be completed by 2002 when the new coins and notes came into circulation.

Having negotiated an opt-out deal at Maastricht, Major was determined to make the fullest use of it. Throughout the period 1993–7 he refused to commit Britain to EMU. Indeed, the shattering experience of 'Black Wednesday' made him unwilling to contemplate even the preliminary step of sterling's re-entry to the ERM. On 1–2 August 1993 the ERM had come close to complete collapse and had only been saved by a widening of the currency fluctuation bands from 2.25 per cent to 15 per cent. This episode had convinced Major that it suffered from fundamental flaws and that it would be extremely unwise to allow sterling to enter the revamped exchange rate system unless these were first remedied.[16] Until September 1992, along with his Chancellor, Norman Lamont, he had preached the virtues of British membership of the ERM as an indispensable aid for controlling inflation. Thereafter, however, his attitude underwent a complete volte-face. In Conservative circles, and especially among Eurosceptics, 'Black Wednesday' soon came to be celebrated as 'White Wednesday' – the day when the British government had gained release from the shackles of an overvalued currency and excessively high interest rates. This was a view to which Major himself was increasingly inclined, the more so since sterling's departure from the ERM was followed by a distinct upturn in the British economy.

If Major entertained serious doubts about the viability of the ERM, he was more doubtful still about the prospects for a single currency. However, while fairly sure in his own mind that the whole EMU project was doomed to failure, he was nevertheless unwilling to rule out from the outset the possibility of British participation. This policy of 'wait and see' received strong backing from the Foreign Secretary, Hurd, who was no great enthusiast for a single currency, and also from Clarke, Lamont's successor as Chancellor from June 1993, who was. It was the product of various factors. In the first place, there was a natural desire to postpone making a difficult decision. The British government had until December 1997 to give formal notice of its intentions regarding EMU. That being so, it seemed foolish to announce before then that Britain would definitely not be participating – especially since such a move would inevitably produce friction with the other EU states, exacerbate

16. Duff, *Reforming the European Union*, p. 46; Stephens, *Politics and the Pound*, pp. 288–9.

Conservative divisions and alienate the party's Europhiles, including such influential figures as Clarke, Hurd and Heseltine. As the
allotted deadline approached, it should become clearer whether it
was in the national interest *at that particular time* to take part in the
EMU. In the meantime, it was by no means inconceivable that the
British government might be spared the need to make any decision at all if, as Major anticipated, the plans for EMU fell apart
under the combined force of economic and political pressures. At
Maastricht, Kohl had insisted upon the adoption of strict criteria
for participation in EMU: a budgetary deficit of no more than 3 per
cent of GDP, a maximum public debt ratio of 60 per cent of GDP,
exchange rate stability, and low rates of inflation and unemployment.[17] These criteria had seemed reasonably attainable at the time.
They were based upon the assumption of an expanding European
economy, however, and as the other EU states followed Britain into
prolonged recession in the early 1990s they were increasingly viewed
in many quarters as unrealistic. In these circumstances, it was not
entirely fanciful to surmise that by 1997–8, in addition to those
countries which had no great desire to join EMU, like Britain and
Denmark, there would be others – including Belgium, Italy, Spain,
Portugal and Greece – which would not qualify to do so. A final
and critical element in Major's calculations was his belief in the
crucial importance of continuing to play a part in the process of
shaping EMU. By stating categorically that it would not adopt the
single currency, the British government would effectively forfeit the
opportunity to influence negotiations which would have a vital bearing on the national interest.

A third point of disagreement between the British government
and its French and German partners was the prospective enlargement of the EU, though it must be said that this was an issue on
which Bonn and Paris did not altogether see eye to eye.[18] In January 1995 Austria, Sweden and Finland joined the EU, taking its
membership up to fifteen. Their admission necessarily entailed
institutional changes. These paled into insignificance, however, compared to the comprehensive overhaul that would be needed to
accommodate the many other countries seeking to become members. The queue was a long one, with the so-called 'Visegrad' states
– Poland, Hungary, the Czech Republic and Slovakia – at its head.

17. For the Maastricht criteria, which were deliberately stringent at the insistence
of Theo Waigel, the German Finance Minister, see Duff, *Reforming the European
Union*, pp. 25–6, 30–32.
18. For a discussion of differing British, French and German attitudes towards
enlargement see *The Independent*, Perry Anderson, 29 January 1996.

To admit all or most of the applicants would mean a virtual doubling of the membership and enormous administrative difficulties, and the central challenge facing the EU was to implement the necessary large-scale changes without in the process undermining its own coherence.[19] Responses to this challenge varied. As far as the French were concerned, the question of enlargement was low on their list of priorities. Indeed, their initial inclination under Mitterand was to favour a general association between Eastern and Western Europe outside the framework of the EU. When they did set out a position in their formal statement for the IGC in the spring of 1996, it was to insist that there must be firm decisions on reforming the EU's existing institutions before negotiations could begin on acceptance of new members.[20] The Germans, while much keener to proceed with enlargement – especially where Poland was concerned – nevertheless agreed with the French about the importance of linking it to radical institutional reform. They were convinced that without a substantial streamlining of the decision-making machinery, through the extension of QMV and other measures, an enlarged EU would simply be unworkable. By contrast, the British, who were fervent advocates of incorporating new members as soon as possible, argued that institutional reform was not a matter of urgency and should be delayed until after enlargement had taken place. Speaking at Leiden University in September 1994 and looking ahead to the forthcoming IGC, Major reiterated the familiar refrain that widening the EU should come before deepening it. He also expounded another theme which occupied a central place in official British thinking about the EU's future: the need for greater flexibility to take account of the organisation's growing size and diversity.[21]

According to the Major government, old integrationist ideas, with their emphasis on rigid harmonisation on all fronts, were simply not appropriate for a body of fifteen disparate states and would give rise to intolerable strains when the EU was expanded. Far better, it was suggested, to allow each member to decide for itself the particular areas in which it wished to pursue a policy of integration and the rate at which it did so.[22] This 'variable geometry' or 'multi-speed' approach, which was developed in the first instance by Hurd, was embraced with great enthusiasm by Major and figured

19. For the implications of enlargement see *ibid.*; G. Avery and F. Cameron, *The Enlargement of the European Union* (1998), ch. 8.
20. *The Independent*, 15 March 1996.
21. The second William and Mary Lecture: *The Daily Telegraph*, 8 September 1994.
22. *Ibid.*

prominently in the Conservatives' 1994 European election campaign and in the government's IGC White Paper. The reaction
from most of Britain's partners and the European Commission,
however, was predominantly hostile, at least to begin with. Their
main anxiety was that the British government was principally concerned to obstruct progress by the rest of the EU. In January 1996,
Kohl warned that Britain, as the 'slowest ship in the convoy', would
not be permitted to hold the others back.[23] His warning was echoed
by the Commission in its document *Reinforcing Political Union and
Preparing for Enlargement*, which insisted that the EU 'must not be
condemned to progress at the pace of its slowest member'. In another barb directed at Britain, the Commission went on to call for
an end to 'Europe à la carte' in which individual members felt free
to pick and choose which policies they signed up for and opted out
from. More disturbing from the standpoint of the British government was the fact that the Commission's blueprint for reform envisaged the emergence of a two-speed Europe in which Britain would
be permanently consigned to the slow lane.[24] The French government's formal negotiating position for the IGC likewise touted the
idea of a multi-speed EU, with France and Germany in the fast
lane; and the possibility that this might, indeed, occur was a matter
of growing concern to British policymakers. What they feared was
Britain's exclusion from an influential inner core dominated by the
French and the Germans.

To sum up, during the three years between the ratification of
the Maastricht Treaty and the start of the 1996 IGC Britain, while
not completely isolated, was nevertheless out of step with most other
EU countries over a whole range of important issues. This presented serious problems for Major who, throughout this period,
was engaged in an extraordinarily difficult balancing act. In his
dealings with other political leaders, he was primarily concerned to
block any moves towards closer integration. At the same time, he
had to convince Britain's partners that his government's role was
not purely negative and that it had a vision for the EU which was
just as valid as theirs and a great deal more realistic. This was a task
that required great diplomatic and political skill. It was much complicated, moreover, by the need to take a line which would both
maintain the fragile unity of the Conservative Party and allay the
fears of its Eurosceptic wing that national sovereignty was being
inexorably eroded.

23. *The Independent*, Sarah Helm, 20 February 1996.   24. *Ibid.*

CHAPTER TWENTY-ONE

Eurosceptics versus Europhiles

Major was highly vulnerable to pressure from the Eurosceptics in his party for a number of reasons. Not the least of these was the general weakness of his own position as leader. To a considerable extent Major suffered from comparison with his predecessor. Many Conservatives continued to feel unhappy, even guilty, about the way Thatcher had been ousted. There was widespread nostalgia for the firm leadership that she had provided. This was accompanied by constant sniping at a 'grey' man who was generally felt to lack the charismatic qualities that she had displayed in abundance. Throughout the period 1993–6 there were bouts of speculation – usually associated with dissatisfaction about his supposed lack of firmness over Europe – that Major was about to be forced out.[1] Major himself eventually became so exasperated by such speculation that on 22 June 1995, a week after a particularly disagreeable meeting with Eurosceptics chaired by Sir Michael Spicer, he sensationally announced his resignation in order to flush out a challenge.[2] His victory over John Redwood in the ensuing contest gave him only a brief respite, however, and in early 1996 there was a fresh crop of rumours about his possible replacement.

Another factor contributing to Major's difficulties in coping with Eurosceptic critics was his small and dwindling parliamentary majority. From a figure of 21 immediately after the 1992 general election this was gradually whittled away over the next four years, partly because of defections – Alan Howarth to Labour and Emma Nicholson to the Liberal Democrats – but mainly because of an unbroken run of by-election defeats. These culminated in the loss

---

1. See, for example, *The Daily Telegraph*, 3 April 1994.
2. A. Seldon, *Major: A Political Life* (1997), pp. 561–71.

of Staffordshire South-East in April 1996, as a result of which the government was left with an overall majority of only one. The uncertain progress of the Northern Ireland peace talks taking place at the time cast doubt over how far the government could rely upon the votes of the Ulster Unionist MPs.[3] More troublesome still was indiscipline within the ranks of its own supporters. The principal offenders in this respect were the Eurosceptics, eight of whom were deprived of the Conservative whip at the end of November 1994 because of their refusal to vote for the imposition of VAT on fuel, one of the measures introduced in order to fund the increase in EU resources agreed at the Edinburgh European Council two years earlier. Along with Sir Richard Body, who resigned the whip in support, the 'whipless eight' – Teresa Gorman, Christopher Gill, Nicholas Budgen, Tony Marlow, Richard Shepherd, Teddy Taylor, Michael Cartiss and John Wilkinson – continued to harry the government over its policy on Europe. Freed from party discipline, indeed, they proved to be even more of a nuisance than before, and in April 1995 the government finally backed down and restored the whip to them without the conditions it had previously insisted upon.[4] Body, for his part, only agreed to take the whip again in January of the following year.[5]

The 'whipless eight', who continued to coordinate their activities, were only one element in the Conservative Eurosceptic camp. Operating alongside them was a broad collection of pressure groups such as the Bruges Group, the No Turning Back Group, the Fresh Start Group, the '92 Group, the European Research Group and the European Foundation. Initially at least, their membership was not particularly large. What they lacked in numbers, however, they more than made up for in obsessiveness, energy and flair for publicity. Their views on Europe had a strong following among Conservative activists in the constituencies, and they also attracted growing support from within the parliamentary party.

Major found the Eurosceptics a heavy cross to bear. Some, like Cash, were without interest in, or hope of, ministerial preferment and therefore impervious to the usual blandishments and strong-arm tactics of the Whips' Office.[6] Others posed a threat because of

3. On 5 May 1996 during an interview on BBC Radio 4's *On the Record*, John Taylor, the deputy leader of the Ulster Unionists, warned that the government could not rely on his party to keep it in power.

4. Seldon, *Major*, pp. 511–12, 522–3, 544–6; P. Stephens, *Politics and the Pound: The Conservatives' Struggle with Sterling* (1996), pp. 317–18.

5. *The Independent*, 18 January 1996.

6. For Cash's contemptuous refusal of offers of junior ministerial positions see H. Young, *This Blessed Plot: Britain and Europe from Churchill to Blair* (1998), p. 394.

their seniority. Within the Cabinet itself were several ministers who made no secret of their Eurosceptic sympathies, conducting a form of guerrilla warfare against the official line through a combination of coded messages and open dissent. At the time of the government's difficulties over ratification of the Maastricht Treaty in 1992–3, the ministers most prominently associated with such activities were Howard, Lilley, Portillo and Redwood – the 'bastards' as Major called them in one of his periodic fits of exasperation, not realising that he was speaking into a live microphone at the time.[7] In subsequent years, other members of the Cabinet, including Stephen Dorrell, the Secretary of State for Health, also began to speak the language of Euroscepticism, partly in response to the general shift in the Conservative Party's centre of gravity, but also in an attempt to strengthen their challenge for the leadership in the event that electoral defeat would precipitate Major's downfall. On the available evidence, indeed, it seems clear that by 1995–6 the Eurosceptics constituted a majority in the Cabinet. They were also strongly represented at junior ministerial level: the appointment of David Davis as the Minister for Europe in the Foreign Office in 1994 was generally viewed as a guarantee that the department's pro-European sympathies would be kept in check. Outside government, the Eurosceptic camp could lay claim to other senior figures, the most notable (apart from Thatcher) being Jonathan Aitken, Norman Lamont and John Redwood. After his resignation as Chief Secretary to the Treasury in 1995, Aitken became an increasingly outspoken opponent of any further moves towards political integration in the EU, insisting that the government must keep open the option of withdrawal if it failed to secure satisfactory results at the IGC. Lamont similarly raised the possibility of British withdrawal from the EU at a fringe meeting of the 1994 Conservative Party conference.[8] The former Chancellor had by this stage become something of a loose cannon – embittered by his dismissal in 1993, convinced that he had been made a scapegoat for the ERM shambles of the previous year and, at the same time, retaining a strong dose of political ambition. Occupying a place on the backbenches, he was a troublesome critic of Major's policy on Europe. He now claimed that he had never been an enthusiast for sterling's membership of the ERM and that it would be a national disaster if it re-entered and if the government agreed to British participation in monetary union. Beyond that, he broadened

7. Major used the expression while being interviewed by Michael Brunson during the ITN news on 23 July 1993.
8. *The Times*, 12 October 1994.

the scope of his attack to embrace the Maastricht Treaty in its entirety. The force of Lamont's onslaught was somewhat diluted by the suspicion that he was largely motivated by malice and pique. The same could not be said about Redwood, with whom Lamont increasingly collaborated over tactics in the run-up to the IGC. Within the Conservative Party, Redwood was regarded as a heavy-weight thinker. Moreover, his decision – in sharp contrast to Portillo – to resign from the government (in which he had been Welsh Secretary) and challenge Major in the summer of 1995 boosted his standing as a leadership contender and intellectual standard-bearer of the Eurosceptic right. It was Redwood, working closely with the think-tank Conservative 2000, who provided much of the intellectual ammunition against EMU and Maastricht, including an 'alternative White Paper' for the IGC.[9]

Although the Eurosceptics were often referred to as though they represented a homogeneous set of ideas, their views in fact covered a wide spectrum.[10] Some of them might have been more accurately described as Europhobes, so deep was their dislike of the EU. For them the idea of life outside the Union was by no means unthink-able or even unattractive. Thus Teddy Taylor spoke in April 1996 of his longing for the day 'when Britain can be free again and can be disengaged from the Brussels nightmare which will inevitably pro-duce mass unemployment and misery'.[11] Teresa Gorman similarly told a radio interviewer the following July that she would like to stay in the Commons long enough to see the British people 'give two fingers to Europe' and recover their right to determine their own policies. Such a view was not universal among Conservative Eurosceptics, some of whom maintained that Britain had a duty to remain in the EU in order to lead the fight against dangerous federalist tendencies. Nevertheless, the tone of the comments does serve to convey the underlying suspicion and resentment that the overwhelming majority of them felt towards Brussels and Britain's EU partners. Beneath the differences of detail, there was a common determination to halt, indeed reverse, what was seen as a remorse-less drive towards the creation of a European superstate – hence the widespread demand for a wholesale 'repatriation' of the legal and political powers that had been ceded to the EU as part of the continuous process of pooling sovereignty. Assurances were sought

9. *The Independent*, Colin Brown and John Rentoul, 7 February 1996.
10. For a perceptive study of the different strands in the Eurosceptic tendency see Young, *This Blessed Plot*, ch. 10.
11. Cited in *The Independent*, Nick Cohen, 5 May 1996.

from the government that at the forthcoming IGC it would uphold Britain's opt-out from the Social Chapter, defend the national veto, prevent any extension of majority voting, resist attempts to give bigger roles to the European Commission and the EP and curb the jurisdiction of the ECJ. Most important of all, Eurosceptics were determined that Britain should never take part in EMU.

As free-marketeers, Conservative Eurosceptics objected in principle to a system based on fixed exchange rates. They were also opposed to EMU because they considered it to be driven by political rather than economic and financial considerations. Some saw it as a scheme for reinforcing German dominance. To others it was the price Mitterand had extracted from Kohl for his consent to the unification of Germany – a thesis that received support from a somewhat unlikely quarter in 1995 when Bernard Connolly, formerly the head of the EMS, National and Community Policies Unit in the European Commission, attacked EMU as essentially a French ploy in his book *The Rotten Heart of Europe: The Dirty War for Europe's Money*. But the fundamental reason for the Eurosceptics' resistance to British involvement in EMU was their belief that it would entail a significant loss of national sovereignty. Abolition of sterling and the adoption of a single currency, it was argued, would mean surrendering control over vital elements of economic management to an unelected ECB situated in Frankfurt. According to Redwood, Thatcher, Lamont, Tebbit and many others, that would represent a massive step towards the creation of a single European state. It was because they regarded the question as being at heart a constitutional one that Eurosceptics were unwilling to accept Major's tactic of postponing a decision until nearer to 1999. Ideally, they would have liked a government pledge that Britain would never enter EMU. Failing that, they wanted a pledge covering the lifetime of the current and next Parliaments. In addition, the government came under intense pressure to agree to a referendum on British entry.

By comparison with its Eurosceptic counterpart, the Europhile wing of the Conservative Party – represented by organisations like the One Nation Group, the Macleod Group and the Conservative Mainstream Group, and by individual MPs like Clarke, Heseltine, Hurd, Hugh Dykes, Quentin Davies, Edwina Currie, Peter Temple-Morris and, inevitably, Heath – presented fewer problems for Major. It is true that there were occasional bouts of irritation when it was felt that Eurosceptic rebels were being treated with excessive leniency or that the government was being pushed towards a position of outright hostility to the EU. On the whole, though, the Europhiles adopted a lower profile than their Eurosceptic colleagues and showed themselves to be far less disposed to disobey the party whip. This did not mean that their views could be totally ignored by Major and government managers, who had to be careful at the very least to avoid a situation where key Europhile ministers like Clarke were left with no alternative but to resign rather than accept a policy on Europe which they believed to be completely misguided.

Major was therefore faced with a considerable problem of party management. This involved, among other things, steering a careful course between Europhiles and Eurosceptics and producing a policy around which both tendencies could rally. His own position, which he labelled 'Eurorealist', was intended to provide such a rallying point. On the one hand, Major was adamant that Britain's fate was inextricably bound up with the EU and dismissed talk of pulling out as being in the realm of 'cloud cuckoo land'.[12] This was a message that went down well – as it was intended to – with the Europhiles. On the other hand, he was vehemently opposed to any further dilution of national sovereignty and went out of his way to convince doubters that there would be no concessions on that score at the IGC. As the Eurosceptics strengthened their position within the Conservative Party, Major responded with placatory gestures. His campaign for the European elections of June 1994, in which he castigated Labour and the Liberal Democrats as the pawns of Brussels, was characterised by crude Eurosceptic rhetoric.[13] Moreover, when it was agreed some two months earlier that Austria, Finland, Norway and Sweden should join the EU in January 1995, he had provoked a quarrel over consequent changes in the rules for QMV which was intended at least in part to demonstrate his determination to fight for British interests whatever the odds against him. His veto shortly afterwards of the appointment of Jean-Luc Dehaene, the Belgian Prime Minister, to replace Delors as President of the European Commission had a similar purpose. The fact that he was obliged to accept another candidate, Jacques Santer, the Prime Minister of Luxembourg, whose views were indistinguishable from those of the original one, was beside the point: Eurosceptic critics had been temporarily appeased by his show of defiance.[14]

During the months leading up to the first IGC session of March 1996, the Eurosceptics focused their attention on the single currency

---

12. Speech to the Institute of Directors: *The Daily Express*, 25 April 1996.

13. Stephens, *Politics and the Pound*, pp. 314–16.

14. Seldon, *Major*, pp. 448–54, 470–73; Stephens, *Politics and the Pound*, p. 316; Young, *This Blessed Plot*, pp. 456–7.

issue and, more specifically, on the possibility of holding a referendum on it. This was ironic, since EMU was not an item on the IGC agenda. As far as the French, German and most other EU governments were concerned, the matter had been settled at Maastricht and there could be no question of reopening it. Major, by contrast, took the view that the matter was far from settled and that there was one important question in particular that required further consideration: the relationship between those states which joined the monetary union from the date of its projected launch in January 1999 and those which remained outside, either through choice or failure to comply with the criteria set out in the Maastricht Treaty.

The issue was an extremely complicated and sensitive one. Conservative Eurosceptics denied that staying outside the EMU would place Britain at any disadvantage. There were many others, however, who took the view that such an assessment owed more to facile optimism than to sound economic and political judgement. Clarke, the Chancellor, thought it likely that Britain would pay a heavy price for not taking part in a single currency, and this was also the prevailing wisdom in business circles and among financial journalists. Expert commentators, like Gavyn Davies, warned of the costs that might be incurred – both financial and political – if Britain was not a member of the 'core club' of states that joined the EMU from its inception and that would certainly include France, Germany and the Benelux countries.[15] British non-participation in the single currency would mean exclusion from the governing council of the new ECB and from the right to vote in the Council of Ministers whenever it discussed monetary matters. Britain, in other words, would be effectively disenfranchised from the determination of interest rate, exchange rate and budgetary policy for the EMU, even though it was bound to be profoundly affected by such policy. There was a strong likelihood that the 'ins' would develop strict new rules for policing budgetary deficits and that Britain and the other 'outs' might be obliged to follow them by the dictates of the financial markets. It was also possible that the 'outs' would be faced by capital controls and even trade barriers around the single currency area, especially if they sought to give themselves a competitive advantage through devaluation. Finally, if the British government was to decide at some later stage that life outside the euro zone was not a viable proposition, the conditions for belated entry might be onerous.[16]

15. *The Independent*, business section, 22 January 1996.   16. *Ibid.*

That such a scenario was not merely the product of alarmist speculation was underlined by the attitude of Britain's partners. The French and Germans especially were increasingly impatient of the Major government's attempt, as they saw it, to have the best of both worlds by continuing to participate in the discussions leading up to EMU whilst refusing to give an undertaking to join it. They had no intention of allowing a similar situation to develop whereby Britain would enjoy the privilege of unrestricted access to the markets of the single currency bloc without disavowing the option of devaluing sterling against the euro. Given the benefits British exporters had derived from a depreciating pound since the latter's exit from the ERM in September 1992, their hard line was understandable. Following complaints from French and German industry, the European Commission conducted a study into exchange rate movements since the early 1990s, and the report it produced in the autumn of 1995 demonstrated conclusively that a decline in the international value of the pound, the lira and the peseta since 1992 had brought real competitive advantages which had not been frittered away in higher inflation. This conclusion was in sharp and embarrassing contrast to that of the Commission's 1990 report, *One Market, One Money*, which had argued that changes in exchange rate did not bring a long-term improvement in competitiveness. What the more recent report showed was that sterling had fallen in real terms by an average of 7 per cent against other European currencies between the third quarters of 1992 and 1995, a period which had also seen a rise of 1 per cent in Britain's share of total European exports. Spain and Italy had made even larger gains in cost competitiveness. Conversely, hard currency countries like France and Germany had experienced substantial increases in both nominal and real exchange rates and a resultant fall in their share of intra-European trade – by as much as 3 per cent in the case of Germany.[17] In the light of such findings, it is hardly surprising that Hans Tietmeyer, the President of the Bundesbank, Theo Waigel, the German Finance Minister, and Jean Arthuis, his French opposite number, demanded that Britain and other prospective 'outs' must renounce competitive devaluation and tie their currencies to the euro in the ERM 2. It was intolerable, Arthuis said in February 1996, that 'erratic monetary variations can, in a few seconds, wipe out real productivity gains obtained at the price of substantial sacrifices'.[18]

The experience of 'Black Wednesday' made the idea of British membership of the ERM distinctly unappealing to Major. His

17. *The Independent*, Paul Wallace, business section, 29 February 1996.   18. *Ibid.*

own contribution to the debate was a proposal, which had been accepted at the Cannes European Council of June 1995, that a study should be carried out by the European Commission into relations between the single currency 'ins' and 'outs' (or, as the Commission began to call them, the 'pre-ins'). If this proposal was designed to improve the chances that EMU would be placed on the IGC agenda, it was also meant to serve as a delaying tactic. By early 1996, however, Major's policy of simply playing for time on the question of whether or not to join the single currency was becoming almost untenable under the strain of conflicting pressures from other EU governments, on the one hand, and Conservative Eurosceptics, on the other. In these circumstances, Major was reduced to hoping that his problems would be solved by the collapse of the whole EMU programme. From the standpoint of the British government, indeed, that would be the optimal solution, at one stroke dealing a blow at the prospects of further integration within the EU and defusing the threat from the Eurosceptics.

For a time, in the opening months of 1996, there were some indications that Major's hopes might be fulfilled and that the agreed schedule for proceeding to the third stage of monetary union by January 1999 might, indeed, be on the point of disintegration. As has been seen, the Maastricht Treaty had laid down a number of financial criteria for membership of the EMU, the two most critical of which were a budgetary deficit of no more than 3 per cent of GDP and a public debt ratio that did not exceed 60 per cent of GDP. The decision on which states met these qualifying conditions was to be taken in March 1998 on the basis of economic performance over the previous year, but at the beginning of 1996 all the signs were that most of the candidates would be judged to have failed. At that stage only Luxembourg and Ireland were definitely on track to satisfy the criteria.[19] Italy's public debt in January 1996 was 124 per cent of GDP, while Spain had a budget deficit of 6 per cent of GDP. France and Germany, the main driving forces behind the EMU project, were also finding it extremely difficult to reach the designated targets, with the French budget deficit for 1995 standing at over 5 per cent of GDP and the German at 3.6 per cent. The revelation in January 1996 that Germany was not within the 3 per cent limit occasioned a certain amount of *Schadenfreude* throughout the EU. Waigel had been delivering some very tough lectures the previous autumn about the need to get budget deficits to as low as 1 per cent of GDP and to impose heavy fines, under a

19. *The Independent*, Sarah Helm, 16 January 1996.

so-called 'stability pact', on those members of the EMU who failed to stay below 3 per cent. He had also precipitated a massive run on the lira by publicly dismissing Italy's prospects of being ready for monetary union by 1999. Not surprisingly, therefore, his admission of Germany's own backsliding was greeted with relish in many European capitals, particularly in Rome.[20]

All EU governments were now impaled on the horns of a dilemma. There was general agreement that the only way to meet the Maastricht criteria was to cut public spending and raise taxes. But was that an appropriate policy to pursue when Europe was already suffering from persistent economic stagnation and mass unemployment? In early 1996 more than 18 million workers were without jobs in the EU as a whole, an average of 11 per cent of the labour force. The figure for Spain was considerably worse – 23 per cent of the labour force. In France more than 3 million were unemployed (11.5 per cent), while in Germany the corresponding number was 4 million (10.8 per cent). According to official forecasts, moreover, these levels were set to rise.[21] Under these circumstances, there was growing opposition to economic strategies based on retrenchment, and the view was increasingly expressed in all EU countries that efforts to meet the Maastricht criteria – arbitrary targets set for an arbitrary deadline – were deepening the recession and hampering recovery. Governments were seen to be faced with two stark alternatives. One was to press on with the deflationary policies considered essential for satisfying the EMU criteria, regardless of the rise in unemployment and political and social tensions that such a course would inevitably entail. The other was to acknowledge that the existing plans for monetary union were either unrealistic or attainable only at an unacceptable cost, and to modify them in a way that would make possible the adoption of measures for promoting economic expansion and job creation. During January and February 1996 many voices were raised, sometimes from the most unlikely quarters, in favour of this latter option. Thus Giscard d'Estaing, the former French President, called for relaxation of the Maastricht criteria, while Delors himself caused something of a stir by publicly conceding that the 1999 deadline might have to be postponed. In addition, several heads of government and other senior ministers were reported as making statements along similar lines. Franck

20. *Ibid.*, business section, 12 January 1996; Diane Coyle and Imre Karacs, 12 January 1996; Tony Barber, 15, 26 and 30 January 1996.
21. *Ibid.*, Tony Barber, 15 and 26 January 1996; editorial, 22 January 1996; *The Independent on Sunday*, Tony Barber, 4 February 1996.

Borotra, the French Industry Minister, indiscreetly declared on 25 January that if he had to choose between Maastricht and jobs he would choose jobs. At around the same time his colleague Hervé de Charette, the French Foreign Minister, said on radio that it might be useful to interpret the Maastricht criteria more flexibly.[22] Carlos Westendorp, Foreign Minister of Spain, insisted that the launch of monetary union would have to be delayed unless a 'critical mass' of countries met their financial targets on time. Lamberto Dini, the Italian Prime Minister, averred that it would be foolish to proceed to a single currency while unemployment in the EU stood at 11 per cent of the workforce and made it clear that his own priority was creating jobs; and Goran Persson, the Swedish Finance Minister, announced an easing of current austerity measures – a move which was regarded as tantamount to saying that Sweden would not be joining the EMU in 1999.[23]

Such pointers to a general weakening of resolve or loss of nerve were seized upon eagerly in London, where they were seen as promising evidence that the Maastricht blueprint for monetary union might soon be abandoned. The British government derived particular encouragement from the manifold problems facing Kohl and Chirac, the key players who would largely determine whether the project went ahead on schedule. Its aim was to exploit the French and German leaders' difficulties and generally fuel the atmosphere of crisis that was building up. 'Senior British sources' were reported as thinking that recession in Germany and social unrest in France had made it impossible to go ahead with the original timetable for EMU.[24] In a similar vein, Rifkind, the Foreign Secretary, told a press conference in Brussels on 29 January that plans for monetary union by 1999 could well collapse within a matter of weeks.[25] Clarke characteristically took his own line, one which was wholly at variance with the government's strategy. Having declared at the Madrid European Council of the previous December that he put the chances of EMU going ahead at 60/40, he repeated this assessment during a meeting of finance ministers at Brussels in January 1996.[26]

British expectations that economic and political exigencies might compel the French and German governments to backtrack on monetary union appeared to have some foundation in early 1996, though

22. *The Independent*, Sarah Helm and Tony Barber, 25 January 1996; Michael Sheridan and Sarah Helm, 26 January 1996.
23. *Ibid.*, Tony Barber, 26 January 1996.
24. *Ibid.*, Michael Sheridan and Sarah Helm, 26 January 1996.
25. *The Times*, 30 January 1996.   26. *The Guardian*, 23 January 1996.

there was certainly a substantial element of wishful thinking. Within a short time of his election as President in May 1995, Chirac had suffered a slump in popularity without precedent in the Fifth Republic. This was partly a result of disappointment at his failure to fulfil ambitious election promises, but it was also related to the deteriorating state of the economy and to a backlash against the Maastricht Treaty. The treaty had only been approved by a narrow margin in the 1992 referendum and the period thereafter had seen a growing tendency to condemn it as the unrealistic scheme of a political elite that was completely out of touch with the wishes of ordinary citizens – a sentiment which found an echo in most other EU countries. Rising unemployment was increasingly viewed as the price being paid for having to satisfy the Maastricht financial criteria, and the resentment generated by this belief had come to a head in December 1995 with the unveiling of the *Plan Juppé* which aimed at a drastic pruning of France's extensive state welfare provisions. Confronted by a wave of strikes and demonstrations on a scale not witnessed since the tumultuous 'events' of 1968, the government had retreated. It remained an open question in the months that followed, moreover, whether it could muster sufficient political will to force through measures which were deeply unpopular but which were judged necessary for reducing the budget deficit to the level stipulated by the Treaty of Maastricht.

The predicament of the Kohl government was almost as unenviable. Presiding over an economic slowdown caused by the expense of unification, high labour costs and an overvalued currency, Kohl had witnessed a 10 per cent drop in his personal popularity rating in the three months up to January 1996. He faced difficulties with his 47 Free Democrat coalition partners, who themselves were deeply divided and in turmoil. He also had to contend with an upsurge of 'Deutschmark nationalism'. This was reflected in a survey conducted by the Forsa Institute and published on 31 January in the Hamburg weekly *Die Woche*, which showed that four out of five Germans were either opposed to the single currency or wanted its introduction postponed.[27] On the party-political front, a powerful coalition against EMU was beginning to emerge, ranging from the Christian Social Union on the right to the Greens and Social Democrats on the left. The threat from the SPD was particularly serious. Under its new leader, Oskar Lafontaine, the party was moving towards a more sceptical stance on monetary union, arguing that attempts to satisfy

27. *The Independent*, Tony Barber, 1 February 1996.

the Maastricht criteria were aggravating the recession and unemployment. It campaigned for the March regional elections in Baden-Württemberg, Rhineland-Palatinate and Schleswig-Holstein on a platform of opposition to EMU and gave every indication of intending to make it a major issue in the federal elections due in 1998.

Given the situation in France and Germany, therefore, as well as developments in other countries, the British government had grounds for hoping for an acknowledgement that the single currency would not come into being in 1999. In the event, however, its hopes were disappointed. A crucial factor here was the attitude of the French and German leadership. Whatever the temptation for Chirac to try to escape from domestic political difficulties by seeking changes in the Maastricht plans, he could not afford to do so. There was a real risk that any hint of wavering on the part of the French government would unleash a disastrous bout of speculation against the franc. Besides, considerations of national prestige dictated that France must not be seen to take the initiative in admitting that the agreed schedule was not feasible. As for Kohl, he was absolutely committed to the existing arrangements and not prepared even to contemplate their modification. To Kohl, as was evident from his highly emotional speech of 1 February 1996 at the Catholic University of Louvain, what was at stake was nothing less than the preservation of European peace.[28] The single currency was the linchpin of the next phase of integration and any setback to that integration, he believed, could boost nationalism and plunge Europe into new wars in the next century.[29] Kohl's conviction on this point made him determined to press on with monetary union, whatever the obstacles, and his forceful lead provided much-needed encouragement to others throughout the EU who supported it.

During February and March 1996 there was a sustained counter-attack on critics of the single currency. In a show of solidarity, on 25 January Juppé, his Foreign Minister, Hervé de Charette, and Klaus Kinkel, the German Foreign Minister, put out a joint statement in Paris insisting that monetary union would definitely go ahead as planned. A few days later the French and German governments simultaneously announced synchronised packages of economic measures which were said to be designed not only to stimulate economic activity and reduce unemployment, but also to keep the single currency project on schedule – objectives which many people thought to be irreconcilable. Dehaene, the Belgian Prime Minister,

28. *The Guardian*, 2 February 1996.   29. *Ibid.*

issued a dire warning that failure to meet the 1999 deadline would 'start an irreversible disintegration process', and senior figures from the European Commission – notably Santer, Brittan, the Vice-President, and Yves-Thibault de Silguy, Commissioner for Monetary Affairs – weighed in with further prophecies of doom, as well as vigorous rebuttals of the charge that attempts to meet the Maastricht criteria were making the recession worse.[30] The relentless barrage of propaganda had its effect in helping to restore confidence in the single currency project. By mid-February nerves were beginning to steady, and a severe defeat for the SPD in the *Länder* elections, following its anti-EMU campaign, provided a clear sign that the tide of opinion was beginning to turn.

As it became apparent that plans for monetary union were not going to founder in the immediate future, Conservative Eurosceptics became increasingly insistent that the Major government must include in the next election manifesto a definite rejection of British membership. This was a non-starter. However, their demand for a pledge to hold a referendum on the subject was one that the government was eventually obliged to concede. Major only consented reluctantly and after more than a year of equivocation. As early as the autumn of 1994, Hurd had pressed the case for a referendum. At that time, though, Major was unpersuaded, and he remained so until the spring of 1996. Even then he had doubts. The idea of a referendum was not without attractions for the government: it would mollify the Eurosceptics and perhaps help to avert an open breach between the warring factions in the Conservative Party. But there were also drawbacks and risks. Major was desperately anxious not to give an impression of weakness. He had already, in January, given way to Eurosceptic pressure for a White Paper for the forthcoming IGC – 'not so much a white paper as a white flag', according to Blair[31] – and was worried that agreeing to a referendum would be interpreted as another surrender. An additional concern was that Cabinet disunity over the single currency might actually be exacerbated. A number of senior ministers were strongly opposed to holding a referendum on the question. Paradoxically, these included not only Europhiles like Clarke, Heseltine and Rifkind, but also Portillo, the Eurosceptic Defence Secretary, who had no wish to have to resign his post in order to fight against British membership

30. *The Independent*, Tony Barber, 26 January, 30 January, 1 February, 6 February 1996; business section, 30 January 1996; Leon Brittan, 2 February 1996; *Le Figaro*, 29 January 1996.
31. Interview on BBC Radio 4's *World at One*, 19 January 1996.

of the EMU if the Cabinet should decide to recommend it to the electorate in a referendum campaign. It was Clarke who presented the most intractable problem. Nobody else in the Cabinet shared his positive enthusiasm for the single currency, and this made him an isolated figure. The Chancellor believed that monetary union was a logical extension of the single market and that remaining outside it would prove costly for Britain: it would probably mean, for example, maintaining higher interest rates than in countries which were members, in order to satisfy the markets.[32] Nor did he share the opinion of the Eurosceptics and most of his Cabinet colleagues that joining the single currency raised questions of profound constitutional importance, since deregulation and globalisation of the financial markets had already greatly reduced the role of national governments in economic management. In evidence to the House of Commons Treasury Select Committee, he dismissed as 'myth' the idea that EMU would inevitably lead to a European superstate.[33] Clarke stuck to these views with great tenacity. Major's attempts to get him to tone them down for public consumption were generally ineffectual. His efforts to persuade him of the merits of having a referendum on the single currency were no more successful. Clarke was fundamentally opposed to the idea, and there was considerable press speculation during March that it was an issue on which he was prepared to resign.[34] His resignation, with a general election not far off, would have been disastrous for the Conservatives. As one of the more popular ministers and the man who was expected to retrieve the government's fortunes with tax cuts, the Chancellor was seen as a valuable electoral asset. In the light of such considerations, Major was understandably loath to risk losing him and therefore proceeded cautiously on the referendum question.

At the same time, the pressure to promise a referendum was becoming irresistible, the more so since the government's overall parliamentary majority was now wafer-thin and Major's leadership was again rumoured to be under threat because of anticipated large-scale losses in the forthcoming local elections. Virtually the whole of the Cabinet was by now either favourably disposed or reconciled to holding a referendum. Influential former ministers like Lord

---

32. Interview in *The Daily Telegraph*, 4 March 1996.   33. *The Times*, 2 May 1996.
34. Clarke himself later confirmed on Channel 4's documentary *Bye Bye Blues*, shown on 5 October 1997, that he had been prepared to resign rather than agree to changes in the referendum formula agreed by the Cabinet on 23 January 1997.

Lawson and Sir Norman Fowler were calling for one.[35] The clamour from Eurosceptic backbenchers was greater than ever and received powerful backing from most sections of the Conservative press, including *The Times*, the *Daily Telegraph*, the *Daily Mail* and the *Daily Express*. There was also the danger of being outmanoeuvred by Labour. On 14 January 1996, speaking on the television programme *Breakfast with Frost*, Blair had expressed his personal belief that a step of such enormous importance as joining the single currency should not be taken 'unless the people have a chance to make their views clear'. His remarks were widely interpreted as a hint that he was about to come out in support of a referendum, and subsequent comments by him and Robin Cook, the Shadow Foreign Secretary, seemed to confirm that Labour was edging towards a manifesto commitment to it. The recently formed Referendum Party, founded by the Anglo-French billionaire businessman and MEP Sir James Goldsmith, represented an electoral threat to the Conservatives from a different direction. As its name suggested, the new party aimed to pressurise the government into promising to hold a referendum. Goldsmith let it be known that he was ready to devote £20 million of his own money to the cause, and by early March 1996 the party organisation was beginning to take shape, with 300 candidates having been approved. These included Thatcher's former economics guru, Sir Alan Walters, who planned to stand against Clarke. The disclosure that Goldsmith's intended tactic was to put up a candidate in every constituency where the sitting MP was not committed to a referendum caused alarm among Conservative MPs, especially those holding marginal seats. Conservative Central Office was also thrown into a state of panic. A secret memorandum which it prepared forecast that intervention by the Referendum Party could cost the government up to 30 seats, and an exasperated Brian Mawhinney, the Conservative Party Chairman, urged Major to come to a decision in order to reassure backbenchers and spike Goldsmith's guns.[36]

Clarke continued to be the main obstacle. After a series of meetings between him and Major, however, on 3 April 1996 the Cabinet endorsed a formula, based on a paper prepared by the Foreign

35. See Lawson's comments to the House of Commons Treasury Select Committee on 6 March 1996: *The Times*, 7 March 1996. For Sir Norman Fowler's views see *The Independent*, Donald Macintyre, 9 March 1996.

36. *The Independent*, Colin Brown, 7 March 1996; Stephen Goodwin, 7 March 1996; Colin Brown and Donald Macintyre, 8 March 1996; Donald Macintyre, 9 March 1996; Patricia Wynn Davies, 11 March 1996; full-page advertisement by the Referendum Party, 11 March 1996; Paul Vallely, 12 March 1996; Donald Macintyre, 15 March 1996; Andrew Marr, 13 March and 15 March 1996.

Office, that the Chancellor felt able to accept: there was to be a general election manifesto commitment to hold a referendum if and when a future Cabinet opted to take Britain into the EMU and after Parliament had also given its approval.[37] For the Eurosceptics this was a hollow victory. British adherence to the single currency had not been ruled out. Nor was the referendum a pre-emptive one, as they had wanted, but would only come into play when the government and Parliament had decided in favour. Furthermore, unlike in 1975, when ministers had been given a licence to campaign according to their personal opinion, this time there was to be collective responsibility. Eurosceptic members of the Cabinet would therefore have to resign if they wanted to campaign for a 'no' vote in the referendum. Finally, the referendum was to be restricted solely to the subject of joining the single currency.[38] Goldsmith, backed by Redwood, dismissed such a limited referendum as 'an empty gesture', arguing that voters should be given an opportunity to express their views on the much broader question of Britain's future in the EU.[39] In almost every respect, therefore, the Eurosceptics had failed to achieve their objectives. Their dissatisfaction continued to simmer below the surface and was soon to break out into the open.

37. *The Sunday Times*, David Smith, 7 April; *The Independent*, Donald Macintyre, 3 and 4 April 1996.

38. *The Guardian*, editorial, 4 April 1996.

39. See the Referendum Party's full-page advertisement in *The Independent* (and three other national newspapers) on 11 March 1996. Redwood called for three referenda: one on the single currency; a second on the results of the 1996 IGC; and a third to ascertain the public's wider views on the EU.

CHAPTER TWENTY-TWO

'War at Last': the Beef Crisis of 1996

The issue that was to stoke up Eurosceptic fury and dominate Britain's relations with its EU partners throughout the late spring and summer of 1996 was the crisis that developed over 'mad cow disease' and British beef exports. This was triggered off by an admission from Dorrell, the Health Secretary, on 20 March that there might after all be a connection between bovine spongiform encephalopathy (BSE) in cattle and Creutzfeldt-Jakob disease (CJD) in humans, something which the government and its scientific advisers had previously dismissed as impossible.[1] Dorrell's statement to the Commons was made without any prior consultation with other members of the EU.[2] A meeting of agriculture ministers had taken place only two days earlier, but the British minister, Douglas Hogg, had not even attended. Nor was it thought necessary to give any advance warning to Franz Fischler, the Agriculture Commissioner, who learnt of what had happened through the media. As one EU official commented at the time: 'It was not simply that they [the Major government] didn't care . . . Europe simply didn't enter their calculations.'[3] The reaction from Brussels was swift. On 25 March, following a meeting of senior veterinary experts, Fischler announced a worldwide ban on all exports of British beef and beef derivatives. The imposition of the ban was confirmed by the full Commission two days later.

Despite its failure to consult, the British government was initially confident that the ban would soon be lifted. This was partly

1. *H.C.Deb.*, vol. 274, cols. 375–6. For the background to Dorrell's Commons statement see A. Seldon, *Major: A Political Life* (1997), pp. 639–40.
2. Seldon, *Major*, p. 642; H. Young, *This Blessed Plot: Britain and Europe from Churchill to Blair* (1998), p. 461; *The Independent*, Katherine Butler, 26 March 1996.
3. *The Independent*, Sarah Helm, 29 March 1996.

because it believed that scientific evidence showed British beef to be safe, but also because it expected unqualified cooperation from other governments. Certainly the early omens were promising. On 29 March EU leaders gathered in Turin to launch the IGC. The meeting took place on Major's birthday, and his colleagues provided a welcome present in the form of an impressive display of sympathy and what was described by Chirac as 'one hundred per cent solidarity with Britain'.[4] The French President spoke of the problem being a European rather than a British one, a sentiment echoed by Santer, who said: 'We are all affected by this.' The hope was held out to Major that the ban could be ended as soon as the Commission had approved a British package of measures to eradicate BSE. He was also promised that financial assistance would be available. Major's satisfaction with the degree of backing that had been offered was reflected in his comment that he only wished British Eurosceptics had been present 'to see how the rest of the European Union had rallied round in solidarity and support'.[5]

Such harmony proved short-lived and London's hopes of an early end to the ban were quickly dashed. Difficulties arose almost at once over the package of anti-BSE measures that Whitehall hurriedly prepared to present at an emergency meeting of agriculture ministers in Luxembourg on 1 April. Under intense pressure from the farming lobby to restore confidence in British beef as soon as possible, Hogg publicly contemplated a policy of slaughtering as many as 4.5 million cattle. This was ruled out by the Cabinet, however, which balked at the expense of a programme that might cost upwards of £2.5 billion and that it considered in any case to be unnecessary. As a result, the plans that Hogg took to Luxembourg were given short shrift, one Spanish official reportedly describing them as 'shit'.[6] Hogg's idiosyncratic personal manner managed to alienate all fourteen of his EC ministerial colleagues. Their real objection, however, was to the substance of his proposals. All cows over 30 months old were to be culled, and it was also intended to carry out a selective slaughter of herds with a proven record of infection. The reaction was cool. Other ministers felt that the plans were inadequate and lacking in detail. They were also unconvinced about the rigour with which existing abattoir controls were being enforced in Britain. In addition, there was considerable irritation

---

4. *The Independent,* Sarah Helm and Jojo Moyes, 30 March 1996; *The Times,* 30 March 1996.
5. *The Independent,* Sarah Helm, 31 March 1996.
6. *The Independent on Sunday,* Stephen Castle and John Lichfield, 26 May 1996.

over Hogg's demand that the EU should meet 80 per cent of the total bill, with Jochen Borchert, the German Agriculture Minister, pointing out that when Germany had experienced an outbreak of swine fever in 1994 the British government had urged that EU compensation payments should be kept to a minimum. After a marathon negotiating session, Hogg returned to London practically empty-handed.[7] The ban was to remain in force – a decision he denounced as 'unjustified' – and he had obtained a pledge of only 70 per cent of costs, not the 80 per cent he had sought. It soon transpired, moreover, that the financial assistance would not represent 'new' money but was to come instead from Britain's existing EU rebate.

A further meeting of agriculture ministers was scheduled for 29 April, and the British government was given until then to produce improved and more detailed proposals. The embattled Hogg was now in an extraordinarily difficult position. His performance since the beginning of the crisis was generally considered to have been woeful, not least by members of his own party. There were strong rumours, indeed, that he had offered his resignation. The farming industry was in chaos as consumption of beef plummeted, and there were serious knock-on effects on livestock slaughtering, meat processing, food retailing and other associated activities. Hogg was therefore under enormous pressure from the NFU and other influential groups to bring a return to normal conditions and, more specifically, an end to the EU ban. At the same time, there were limits as to what he could achieve in that direction. The restoration of foreign confidence in British beef was hampered by a number of factors. It was known that mass culling would present serious logistical problems, including a severe shortage of incinerators, while the uncertain state of scientific knowledge made it impossible to give a categorical assurance that any particular measures would definitely eradicate BSE. An outbreak of further cases of CJD in Britain added to the general mood of panic, as did publication in early April of a government-commissioned study showing that a disturbingly high proportion of abattoirs in England and Wales were falling well below acceptable standards of hygiene. Under all these circumstances, it is hardly surprising that Britain's EU partners required considerable convincing that what the British government intended to do would prove effective.

7. *The Guardian*, 4 April 1996; *H.C.Deb.*, vol. 275, cols. 406–8, 3 April 1996. Gavin Strang, Labour's agriculture spokesman, attacked the deal Hogg brought back from Luxembourg as 'the worst of all worlds'; *Ibid.*, col. 408.

A more fundamental difficulty was the existence of a great gulf between the perception of the nature of the beef crisis in British official circles and that obtaining in other EU countries. When Chirac said in Turin that BSE was 'a European problem', he was in one sense speaking no more than the literal truth. British farmers were not alone in suffering heavy financial losses because of the scare: French and German farmers were, if anything, hit harder still by a collapse in meat prices which was both steeper and more prolonged than that in Britain. In another sense, however, it was felt that the problem was essentially a British one. Only in the UK was there a serious incidence of BSE. Furthermore, it was believed that the disease had been allowed to reach its present disastrous proportions because of the persistent negligence of British producers and the British government. The view from the continent, therefore, was that it was the responsibility of the British government to take whatever action was needed to resolve the crisis. As for other governments, their prime duty was to protect their own citizens from the medical and commercial consequences of BSE. The ban on British beef exports must therefore remain in place until it was certain there was no longer any danger. To lift it before then would serve no useful purpose, since people could not be forced to eat meat they considered suspect.

As might be expected, matters appeared in a very different light in London. In government circles there the current crisis was regarded as being largely the product of media hysteria, irresponsible opportunism on the part of the Labour Opposition and lack of cooperation from other EU countries. There was acute disappointment at the alleged failure of Britain's partners to translate early promises of solidarity and help into deeds – hence Major's leaked private outburst that they had behaved 'like a bloody bunch of shits'.[8] This was accompanied by a strong conviction that the dangers of eating British beef had been grossly exaggerated. The fact that it was put on the menu for Kohl and Chirac when they paid official visits to London in April and May respectively was a rather crude attempt to ram home the message. According to the British government, the available scientific evidence offered no justification for the export ban.[9] It was even suggested that there were ulterior motives for its imposition. Michael Forsyth, the Scottish Secretary, expressed a common view among senior Conservatives

8. *The Daily Express*, 22 April 1996.
9. *H.C.Deb.*, vol. 275, cols. 405–7, 3 April 1996; *ibid.*, vol. 276, col. 1147, 1 May 1996.

when he said: 'What we are witnessing is the cynical elimination of a formidable competitor from the markets of Europe.'[10] Finally, there were grave doubts about the legality of the ban, especially as it applied to exports to non-EU countries, and the British government gave early notice of its intention to seek an interim order to overturn it from the ECJ.[11] Since the government was simultaneously announcing that a reduction of the same court's powers was one of the main items on its agenda for the IGC, this was ironic to say the least.[12]

Given such conflicting outlooks, it was highly improbable that the anti-BSE package that Hogg was due to produce in late April would prove acceptable to the other EU agriculture ministers. A scheme which he outlined to the Commons on 16 April envisaged the slaughter of cattle over 30 months old.[13] In response to warnings from Fischler and Santer that this would not suffice, its scope was subsequently extended to include an additional cull of 42,000 from herds that had been infected by BSE. When the modified plan was formally submitted in Luxembourg on 29 April, however, it was not considered radical enough to warrant setting a timetable for lifting the ban, which was what Hogg had demanded as a quid pro quo.

The failure of Hogg's latest efforts produced an explosion of anger in the Conservative press and among Conservative Eurosceptic MPs.[14] Xenophobic, anti-EU feeling had been building up in these quarters since the start of the BSE crisis in late March. As early as 4 April, Tebbit had written in *The Sun* of 'our masters' being 'intent on grinding Mr Hogg and this country into the dirt', and this set the tone for much of the tabloid press coverage that followed, especially in the *Daily Mail* and the *Daily Express*.[15] A typical offering from the latter newspaper was a 'Stop the Euro-Rot' campaign in which readers were invited to phone in their support for resisting the encroachments of Brussels. At the same time, prominent anti-EU figures, including John Biffen, Lamont and Bernard Connolly

10. Speech to the Scottish Conservative Party conference in Aberdeen: *The Independent*, 10 May 1996.

11. *The Times*, 17 April 1996; *H.C.Deb.*, vol. 276, col. 1147, 1 May 1996.

12. The irony of the situation was pointed out by Paddy Ashdown: *H.C.Deb.*, vol. 278, col. 104, 21 May 1996.

13. *The Independent*, Sarah Helm, Colin Brown and Paul Field, 27 April 1996.

14. For the hostile reaction to Hogg's Commons statement of 1 May 1996 from Nicholas Budgen, Sir Teddy Taylor, Sir Ivan Lawrence and William Cash see *H.C.Deb.*, vol. 276, cols. 1155, 1159, 1161–2.

15. *Daily Mail*, Simon Heffer, 24 April 1996; *The Daily Express*, leading article, 22 April 1996; *The Sun*, 23 and 26 April 1996.

– billed as 'the economist sacked by the European Commission for telling the truth about the single currency' – contributed articles.[16] In his article, Connolly suggested that the acronym BSE should stand for 'Britain Screwed by Europe'. Similar sentiments were voiced by Eurosceptics in Parliament. There, as in the press, the Eurosceptic refrain had four basic elements. First, there were repeated demands for retaliatory measures, either in the form of trade sanctions against selected imports or a suspension of Britain's payments to the EU. Second, there was continuous pressure on Major himself to take a tougher line, much of it threatening rather than encouraging in tone. Third, there was intense hostility towards Britain's EU partners. Germany, which was playing the principal role in blocking a lifting of the beef ban, bore the brunt of this, with frequent references being made to the danger of a 'Fourth Reich' and a Europe 'dominated by a reunified Germany'. Finally, there was a strong tendency to use the crisis over the beef ban as a weapon in the broader battle against European integration and even against British membership of the EU. Eurosceptics seized upon what was a highly emotive issue in order to whip up feeling against Brussels and to popularise their campaigns against a single currency and the ECJ and for a broad referendum of the kind being canvassed by Goldsmith.

When Hogg reported to the Commons on his lack of success at the agriculture ministers' meeting of 29 April, he sought to calm Eurosceptic backbenchers by the prospect of an early easing of the ban as it applied to gelatine, tallow and bulls' semen.[17] The Commission favoured such a move and it was to be considered in Brussels on 7 May by the EU's standing veterinary committee. In the event, a decision was postponed until a further session of the committee on 20 May. In the meantime, the Cabinet undertook a review of what measures to adopt if the ban was not relaxed. Trade sanctions and withholding Britain's financial contributions to the EU had already been ruled out on the grounds that they would be illegal. It had also been decided not to pursue the so-called 'empty chair' strategy of simply boycotting EU meetings.[18] Another option under discussion was that of systematically blocking all EU business where a unanimous vote was required. Opinion within the Cabinet on the merits of such a tactic was divided. Clarke and Heseltine were concerned about the long-term damage that might be caused to Britain's relations with its partners. They were in a minority, however. In

16. *The Daily Express*, 25 April 1996.
17. *H.C.Deb.*, vol. 276, col. 1150, 1 May 1996.   18. Seldon, *Major*, p. 648.

addition to Eurosceptics of long-standing like Howard, Lilley and Portillo, ministers who were generally regarded as more moderate in their views on Europe also argued for a policy of disruption. Dorrell and Rifkind, for example, now emerged as 'hawks' on the question.[19] Major was in equally determined mood. He was angered by what he saw as a breach of faith by Britain's partners in failing to carry out the promises given at Turin. In any case, his room for manoeuvre was extremely limited. Heavy Conservative losses in the local government elections of 2 May had weakened his position. Moreover, the Eurosceptics were on the rampage and demanding action, and they were joined by other middle-of-the-road Conservatives, especially those representing farming constituencies, who were infuriated by the beef ban. Major was warned by Alastair Goodlad, the Government Chief Whip, that if Hogg were to go to the Commons empty-handed to announce the failure of yet another attempt to secure a relaxation of the ban, he would be subjected to a terrible mauling by Conservative backbenchers. This seems to have been an important factor in making up Major's mind to go ahead with a programme of disruption should it prove necessary.

In the event, it did. On 20 May, despite a strong plea from Fischler, the standing veterinary committee declined to approve a recommendation by the Commission that the ban on exports of beef derivatives should be lifted. Hogg had hoped that a series of extra measures that he had announced a few days earlier, including an increase in the number of at-risk cattle to be culled from 42,000 to 80,000, might just tip the balance. Some of the experts voiced scepticism about the new proposals, however, as well as concern about reports from Britain that measures already set in train were not being properly implemented. The representatives of seven countries supported a relaxation of the ban, but opposition from Germany, Austria, Holland, Greece, Portugal and Spain produced the QMV necessary to reject it.

This outcome provoked an immediate response from the British government, with Major announcing in the Commons on 21 May that it would be embarking on a campaign of blocking EU business until agreement was reached on an easing of the ban plus 'a clear framework leading to a lifting of the wider ban'.[20] Even Thatcher had not been prepared to resort to such extreme methods. Major's statement aroused massive enthusiasm on the Conservative backbenches:

19. *The Independent*, Stephen Castle, 5 May 1996.
20. *H.C.Deb.*, vol. 278, cols. 99–101, 21 May 1996.

'This afternoon', declared Nicholas Winterton, 'my right hon. Friend has spoken for Britain.'[21] The Conservative press, hitherto highly critical of Major's inaction, was also delighted. On 21 May, following the negative decision of the standing veterinary committee, the *Daily Mail* had carried the headline 'Humiliation of Britain'. Its headline of the following day trumpeted 'Major Goes to War at Last', and there were equally belligerent and fulsome comments in the *Daily Express* and other Conservative newspapers.[22] While not giving unconditional support, the Labour Opposition offered general backing. As at the time of the Falklands and Gulf Wars, it was determined to avoid appearing unpatriotic.

The new policy of systematic obstruction – described by British officials as 'cumulative irritation rather than general buggeration' – came into operation on 23 May.[23] It began with the blocking of a convention on insolvency and an agreement on Europol, the latter being something to which Kohl was known to attach a lot of importance. Non-cooperation was then extended into all other areas of EU activity where a unanimous vote was required, as British officials and ministers – referred to ironically by critics as the BEEF (the British Eurosceptic Expeditionary Force) – went into battle to frustrate a whole series of EU initiatives on such diverse matters as targeting overseas aid, liberalisation of trade with Mexico, making 1997 anti-racism year and the simplification of single market legislation. The programme of disruption was pursued with relentless determination. But there were few signs that it was having its desired effect. On 3 June Hogg presented a new anti-BSE programme at a meeting of agriculture ministers in Luxembourg, only for it to be rejected. A revised five-point plan met a similar fate on 17 June.[24]

What had happened was that British obstructionism had produced a backlash. Apart from not being prepared to yield to what Lamberto Dini, the Italian Foreign Minister, denounced as 'strong-arm tactics' and 'blackmail', most EU governments were determined not to make any concessions that might help Major to retain power. With Blair calling for a more cooperative and constructive British approach, notably in a speech to the German equivalent of the CBI on 18 June, the advent of a Labour government was coming to

21. *Ibid.*, col. 108.

22. The exultant headline in *The Sun* of 22 May 1996 was 'Major Shows Bulls At Last'.

23. *The Independent on Sunday*, Stephen Castle and John Lichfield, 26 May 1996; Young, *This Blessed Plot*, pp. 461–2.

24. *The Independent*, Sarah Helm, 18 June 1996.

seem an increasingly attractive proposition.[25] Kohl, in particular, was anxious to ensure that Major should derive no political benefits from his confrontation with Britain's EU partners. This was an indication of the depth to which Anglo-German relations had sunk by this stage. As has been seen, one of Major's top priorities on becoming Prime Minister had been to rescue relations with Germany from the dire state to which they had been reduced by Thatcher. After a honeymoon period, however, a chill had set in once again as the 1992 ERM crisis had led to acrimonious public exchanges between Lamont and Major, on the one hand, and the President of the Bundesbank, Helmut Schlesinger, on the other.[26] Thereafter relations between Bonn and London had been correct rather than friendly, characterised on the British side by a certain amount of mistrust and envy of German dominance within the EU. It was this that had prompted Ashdown to lament in March 1996 that it had become acceptable in Conservative circles to talk about the Germans 'in the same tone which English politicians reserved for the Jews eighty years ago and for the Irish a century ago'.[27] With the onset of the beef crisis, crude anti-Germanism was given free rein among Eurosceptics. Open expressions of hostility to Germany were not voiced in government circles. Nevertheless, there were undoubtedly strong undercurrents of resentment at Germany's determined resistance to any lifting of the beef ban. The Germans, for their part, were no less irritated at the way in which progress within the EU was being impeded by a policy dictated (in their view) by the internal politics of the Conservative Party.

Loss of German goodwill was one unfortunate consequence of the British campaign of disruption. No less serious was a discernible hardening of attitudes on the part of the European Commission. By a curious irony, the Commission, much demonised and vilified by Conservatives in general, had for some time represented the best hope of getting the beef ban ended, with Fischler and Santer using all their influence to secure acceptance of the various proposals that Hogg had put forward. Now, however, its support could no longer be counted on. Most members of the Commission were outraged by the British government's tactics.[28] Santer insisted

25. *The Times*, 19 June 1996.

26. P. Stephens, *Politics and the Pound: The Conservatives' Struggle with Sterling* (1996), pp. 223, 228–31.

27. Speech to the Royal Institute of International Affairs, 6 March 1996: *The Guardian*, 7 March 1997.

28. *The Independent*, Sarah Helm, 30 May 1996.

that such 'absurd' methods 'had no place in a community based on the rule of law'. There could be no agreement on a framework for lifting the ban as long as they continued. Fischler, too, ruled out the possibility of a settlement until the disruption had ceased, arguing that Britain's partners could not be seen to yield to duress.[29]

Britain's growing isolation was not the only problem facing Major. There were other factors which raised doubts about the advisability of continuing on the present course. The CBI and many leading industrialists, including Sir Colin Marshall, chairman of British Airways, Niall Fitzgerald, chairman designate of Unilever, and Sir Iain Vallance, chairman of BT, spoke out about the damage being caused to British business interests.[30] Some senior ministers, notably Clarke and Heseltine, were increasingly uneasy about the long-term political consequences of the tactics being pursued. Their concern was shared, moreover, by a substantial element of the Conservative Party as a whole. Alarmed by the xenophobic hysteria displayed by sections of the press and the more extreme Eurosceptics, the normally quiescent Conservative Europhiles decided that it was time to fight back. They formed a new group, The Conservative Mainstream, headed by a former minister, David Hunt, which was to serve as an umbrella organisation for existing pro-European groups both inside and outside Parliament. A great deal of personal abuse was directed at prominent Eurosceptics: Hugh Dykes derided 'the pantomime figures of Teresa Gorman and Norman Lamont', and Tristan Garrell-Jones dismissed Cash as a 'pygmy'.[31] The Eurosceptics replied in kind, and the Conservative Party was convulsed by a mass of personal feuds and bitter disagreements. The tacit truce over Europe had manifestly broken down and the party was in a state of virtual civil war. Speculation was rife, indeed, both in the press and at Westminster, that it might well split in two after its anticipated defeat in the next general election. It is small wonder that Major was driven to confess to a meeting of Welsh Conservatives at Porthcawl on 14 June that he had 'had a bellyful'.[32]

All this presented serious problems of party management for Major. As usual, though, it was the Eurosceptics who were proving particularly difficult to control, as was evidenced by a parliamentary rebellion on 11 June, when 78 of them defied the whip to vote for a Ten Minute Rule Bill introduced by Cash calling for a referendum on progress towards a federal Europe. Despite the fact that

29. *Ibid.*, Sarah Helm, 10 June 1996.   30. *Ibid.*, Michael Harrison, 6 June 1996. 31. *Ibid.*, Colin Brown, 3 and 17 June 1996.   32. *The Guardian*, 15 June 1996.

the Referendum Party posed an electoral threat to the Conservatives, Cash, Redwood and Lamont were making overtures to Goldsmith. To Major's fury, it emerged that Cash was even receiving funds from him via the European Foundation, which Cash chaired.[33] In early June the 'whipless eight', now also known as the 'Westminster eight', embarked on a countrywide speaking tour on the theme 'In or Out?' Eurosceptic indiscipline was rampant. Major had won the temporary support of Eurosceptic malcontents by 'declaring war' on Britain's EU partners over the beef ban. The danger was that he might not be allowed to make peace. Having been marched to the top of the hill, the Eurosceptics were determined not to be marched down again.

On 17 June the British government's demand for a framework for a lifting of the beef ban was rejected at a meeting of EU foreign ministers at Rome. It was made clear that there could be no deal until disruption of EU business had ceased. In addition, there would have to be an even bigger slaughter programme for at-risk cattle. Major was now left with two broad options. One was to carry out his stated intention of blocking all progress at the forthcoming Florence European Council, which was due to start on 21 June. Such a wrecking tactic would certainly win him the plaudits of the Eurosceptic wing of his party. It might also provide the right atmosphere of anti-EU jingoism for a 'union jack' election. The alternative was to negotiate the best possible terms and try to present them as a resounding victory. The former was an extremely high-risk strategy and, in the event, Major chose a policy of stealthy retreat.

Success hinged on cooperation from both other EU governments and Conservative Eurosceptics. The latter proved to be more readily available. Britain's partners were in no mood to make concessions in order to save Major's face for domestic political purposes. This was reflected in the settlement on a five-stage lifting of the beef export ban reached at Florence which offered Britain nothing that could not have been obtained at an earlier date by patient negotiation. No timetable was fixed for ending the ban and Britain was obliged to accept a cull of up to 140,000 at-risk cattle. The only hint of a concession, and that a purely nominal one, came from the presiding Italian government, which tagged onto the framework agreement a declaration stating that if a non-EU country wished to import British beef solely for use in its own domestic market, its request might be granted – providing it secured approval from the

33. Seldon, *Major*, p. 651; Young, *This Blessed Plot*, pp. 507–10.

Commission on the basis of QMV by the standing veterinary committee. Since none of the other governments was willing to subscribe to this declaration, it was of little practical value, except as a fig leaf for Major.[34]

Trivial though this gesture was, it was enough to satisfy the Eurosceptics. When Major made a statement on the Florence beef deal to the Commons on 24 June, they joined with the rest of Conservative backbenchers in voicing their approval.[35] This marked the beginning of another party truce over Europe. Like previous ones, however, it was to be short-lived. It came to an abrupt end on 22 July with the announcement that David Heathcoat-Amory was resigning from his ministerial post at the Treasury in order to be free to campaign against the single currency.[36] Whether this represented a minor violation of the ceasefire or the prelude to a full-scale resumption of civil war remained to be seen. In the light of the extraordinary public row over the single currency that erupted in late September between Kenneth Clarke and Sir Nicholas Bonsor, a junior Foreign Office minister,[37] the latter seemed a distinct possibility – despite the approach of a general election.

34. *The Independent*, Sarah Helm, 22 June 1996.

35. For the reaction from Redwood, Sir Teddy Taylor, Sir Michael Spicer and John Townend see *H.C.Deb.*, vol. 280, cols. 27, 29, 31, 35–6, 24 June 1996. For Major's Commons statement see *ibid.*, cols. 21–2.

36. *The Times*, 23 July 1996.   37. *The Independent*, 25 September 1996.

CHAPTER TWENTY-THREE

Under New Management: the General Election of 1997

Conservative infighting over Europe continued unabated into 1997: neither Major's increasingly desperate appeals for party unity nor the imminence of a general election had any moderating effect on the warring factions. At the beginning of the year, Stephen Dorrell, the Health Secretary, triggered off a fresh bout of internecine conflict when he called for a renegotiation of Britain's relationship with the EU.[1] Such feuding was a regular feature of the next few months and proved extremely damaging to the Conservatives' electoral fortunes. On 17 March it was announced that voting would take place on 1 May. The unusually long period allowed for campaigning was clearly intended to give the government an opportunity to claw back the substantial lead registered by opinion polls for Labour. One of its consequences, however, was to provide more time for the Conservatives' deep divisions over Europe to be exposed to relentless probing. The outcome of the election was a resounding triumph for New Labour – as the party now called itself – and the worst defeat for the Conservatives for more than a century.

The Conservatives lost 177 seats, including that of leading Eurosceptic Michael Portillo. It would be simplistic to attribute their dismal showing solely to differences over Europe or, indeed, to any other single factor. Labour conducted a much more effective campaign than in the four previous elections and in Tony Blair possessed a leader whose breadth of appeal and decisiveness threw into relief the shortcomings of his Conservative opposite number. The outgoing government suffered from the intervention of the Referendum Party. Nor was it helped by an unenviable reputation

1. *The Times*, 3 January 1997; *The Independent*, Colin Brown, 3 January 1997; Fran Abrams, 4 January 1997; *The Independent on Sunday*, editorial, 7 January 1997. Dorrell's reported remarks had actually been made some weeks before.

for 'sleaze' resulting from a whole series of financial and sexual scandals.[2] It was widely believed that an unbroken run of eighteen years in power had bred ministerial arrogance and complacency. There was also some feeling, even among Conservative supporters, that it would not serve the interests of democracy if Labour was once again deprived of the chance to govern. That said, the Conservatives undoubtedly paid a heavy price for their disunity over Britain's relations with the EU. It was the issue of whether or not to participate in the single currency that provoked the strongest disagreement within the party. In much the same way as Labour's compromise line on nuclear disarmament had failed to withstand the pressures of the 1983 election, so the Conservatives' official stance on the euro began to come apart during the 1997 campaign. The Major government entered the campaign committed to a policy of 'wait and see' – the formula agreed by the Cabinet the previous January.[3] This, however, was not acceptable to the Eurosceptics who were convinced that ruling out British adherence to the single currency would be a certain vote-winner. Major refused to adopt such a policy, not least because it would have meant the resignation of his Chancellor. As a result, a growing number of Conservative candidates broke ranks, and by the time polling took place some 200 of them, including several ministers, had set out their personal opposition to the single currency in their own constituency manifestos.[4] A smaller number issued manifestos proclaiming exactly the opposite viewpoint. Such disarray can scarcely have impressed the electorate. Equally unimpressive was the sight of Major begging Eurosceptic critics not to bind his hands over negotiations on EMU.[5]

Even the disastrous defeat of 1 May did not bring an end to Conservative squabbling over the EU. Major announced his resignation the day after the election, and the ensuing contest for the party leadership quickly developed into a ballot on Europe. Four of the five candidates – Hague, Howard, Lilley and Redwood – vied

2. For the sleaze factor see A. Seldon, *Major: A Political Life* (1997), pp. 713–17.

3. The formula agreed by the Cabinet on 23 January 1997 stated: 'On the basis of information currently available, it is very unlikely but not impossible that the single currency can proceed safely on 1 January 1999, but if it did proceed with unreliable convergence we would not of course be part of it.' See *H.C.Deb.*, Major, vol. 288, col. 1071, 23 January 1997; *The Daily Telegraph*, 24 January 1997; *The Times*, 24 January 1997.

4. Senior figures who flouted the official Conservative 'wait and see' line on EMU included former minister and party vice-chairman Angela Rumbold whose election address stated, 'No more power to Brussels. No to the single currency': *The Guardian*, 15 April 1997.

5. *The Guardian*, 17 April 1997.

with each other to stake out the most strongly Eurosceptic position. The one exception was Clarke. Recognising that his support for the single currency was likely to count against him, the former Chancellor tried to deflect criticism by arguing that the issue should not be allowed to continue to cause damaging splits in the party and might be defused by allowing a free vote on it.[6] However, his appeal for a cessation of hostilities went unheeded. Those on the Eurosceptic right believed, as Tebbit wrote in *The Sun*, that 'Labour would never have had a dog's chance if he [Major] had ruled out the single currency'. They blamed Clarke for having vetoed such a move, and their determination to inflict revenge on him was a prominent feature of the leadership contest.[7] Clarke only added to the bitterness felt against him when he declared in early June that he had believed for several months that a delay in the introduction of the euro was both 'desirable and inevitable'.[8] One leading Eurosceptic was reported as saying: 'To have that fat, reckless, ill-disciplined lump as the future leader is laughable. Forget it.'[9]

The choice of William Hague as Major's successor represented a victory for the Eurosceptic tendency and reflected a shift in the balance of power within the Conservative Party. The most important positions in the new leader's team were allotted to noted Eurosceptics, with Lilley as Shadow Chancellor, Howard as Shadow Foreign Secretary and Redwood as spokesman on Trade and Industry. David Heathcoat-Amory, who had resigned from the Major government a year earlier in order to be free to attack the single currency, became Shadow Chief Secretary to the Treasury. Europhiles were not excluded, though none of them was given a key portfolio. Clarke himself declined an invitation to serve in the Shadow Cabinet, but others who shared his views on Europe – including Sir George Young (Defence), David Currie (Agriculture) and Ian Taylor (Northern Ireland) – agreed to do so. This was only after serious differences over the single currency had been effectively shelved.[10] During the leadership contest, Hague had come out decisively against British membership for the duration of two Parliaments and had indicated that he would expect every member of the Shadow Cabinet to

6. *The Independent*, Colin Brown, 3 May 1997,

7. Speaking on GMTV's *Sunday Programme* on 25 May 1997, Lord Parkinson, the former Conservative party chairman said: 'And there is a feeling that he [Clarke] held the last government to ransom – a feeling that is widely held, and that may count against him. I don't think he should be leader.'

8. *Daily Mail*, 3 June 1997.   9. *The Independent*, Colin Brown, 3 May 1997.

10. *The Independent on Sunday*, Stephen Castle, 22 June 1997; *The Independent*, Colin Brown, 2 July 1997; Donald Macintyre, 18 July 1997.

support this policy.[11] In the event, a special dispensation was granted to those who felt unable to defend the new line in public. At the same time, they were required not to attack it either. It was not long before this arrangement came under severe strain. Over the next few months Hague pushed the party in an increasingly anti-European direction, demanding a referendum on the Amsterdam Treaty of June 1997 and taking an ever firmer stance against participation in EMU. This development prompted warnings from Clarke, Heseltine and others about the danger of damaging traditional links between the Conservative Party and industry because of the latter's predominantly favourable attitude to the single currency.[12] There was considerable press speculation that some of the more Europhile Conservative MPs were contemplating what was termed a 'staged separation' from the party, as well as hints of resignation from the Shadow Cabinet.[13] The latter materialised when Taylor and Currie resigned at the end of October and the beginning of November respectively. One effect of this was to reinforce Eurosceptic influence on the front benches, a tendency which was accentuated by the reshuffle carried out by Hague in the early summer of 1998 when Francis Maude became Shadow Chancellor. By that stage, the Conservative leader's pronouncements on the single currency were assuming apocalyptic proportions. This was exemplified by his dire warnings that it could lead to a full-blown banking and financial crisis like that currently afflicting South-East Asia or to the kind of strife associated with Bosnia, and by his comparison (in a speech at Fontainebleau on 19 May 1998) of the risks of membership to those of being trapped 'in a burning building with no exits'.[14]

In the meantime, Labour had taken office at the beginning of May 1997 to the accompaniment of warm approval from Brussels and most EU governments. Throughout his brief period as leader of the Opposition, Blair had castigated Conservative policy on Europe as negative and uncooperative. Under his stewardship, he

11. Hague stipulated this condition in a letter to MEP Caroline Jackson: *The Independent*, Anthony Bevins, 14 June 1997.

12. Heseltine told BBC's Radio 4 *Today* programme on 29 October 1997 that Hague had exposed the Conservative Party to the real danger of 'fighting Britain's major companies over Europe'.

13. See, for example, *The Independent*, Anthony Bevins, 14 June and 30 October 1997; Colin Brown and Fran Abrams, 30 October 1997; editorial and article by Donald Macintyre, 31 October 1997; Stephen Castle, 2 November 1997.

14. *Ibid.*, Anthony Bevins, 21 May 1998. Hague had already used the image of a burning building without exits in a speech to the CBI on 10 November 1997.

had maintained, Britain would never be 'isolated' and bereft of its proper influence within the EU as it had been under both Thatcher and Major. During the election campaign, the Conservatives had sought to present his avowed determination to avoid isolation as an indication that he would be subservient to other EU leaders: a notorious example of this was the use of a poster depicting him as a ventriloquist's dummy on Kohl's knee. Blair's public response to this particular tactic was the adoption of a more Eurosceptic tone, notably in his jingoistic contributions to *The Sun*.[15] Even so, the message that he and other senior Labour figures continued to send out was that a change of administration would bring a much-needed improvement in Britain's relations with its European partners. It is hardly surprising, therefore, that the new government's advent to power was greeted with enthusiasm and optimism by EU officials and statesmen. Santer was quick to applaud Labour's 'outstanding victory'. Hervé de Charette, the French Foreign Minister, welcomed it as 'a blow against British scepticism', and Kohl went further to hold it up as a salutary lesson for Eurosceptics everywhere.[16] There was, in fact, a general sense of relief at the discomfiture of the Conservatives, whose resistance to any further integrationist measures was seen as the principal cause of faltering progress by the IGC since its launch at Turin in March 1996.

On the British side, too, there were hopes of a fresh start. On his first official visit to Brussels on 5 May, Douglas Henderson, the new Minister of State for Europe, emphasised that the Blair government viewed the EU as 'an opportunity not a threat' and wished to draw a line under past difficulties.[17] In a similar vein, Robin Cook, the Foreign Secretary, shortly afterwards told his German counterpart, Klaus Kinkel, that the confrontational approach of the Major government would be replaced by one of 'constructive engagement', adding: 'We want to make sure that from now on there are three players in Europe, not just two.' As might be imagined, this last assertion caused grave offence in Rome where it was pointed out that Italy, too, was a key player.[18]

The new approach to EU affairs displayed from the outset by the Blair government was not only a matter of rhetoric. Policy changes were also in evidence. As early as 4 May, Cook announced that

15. *The Sun*, Tony Blair, 17 March 1997.
16. *The Independent*, Sarah Helm, 3 May 1997.
17. *Ibid.*, Sarah Helm, 6 May 1997.
18. *Ibid.*, Donald Macintyre and Imre Karacs, 8 May 1997; Imre Karacs, 10 May 1997.

Britain would soon be signing up to the Social Chapter of the Maastricht Treaty.[19] In addition, there were several pointers to a more positive stance on the euro. Sir David Simon, the chairman of Unilever, was given a post within the Department of Trade and Industry and charged with the task of giving impetus to the drive for completion of the single market. Simon was known as one of the most high-profile supporters of the single currency in the business community, and his appointment was seen in many quarters as a strong signal that the government was favourably disposed towards EMU.[20] The same inference was drawn from the decision of Gordon Brown, the Chancellor of the Exchequer, to surrender control over interest rate policy to the Bank of England. Although Brown stressed that this move was for reasons of domestic economic management and denied that it was related to the question of the single currency, most expert observers took his disclaimer with a pinch of salt. Certainly Alexandre Lamfalussy, the President of the European Monetary Institute, was in no doubt that it represented an important step towards meeting the Maastricht convergence criteria, describing it as 'music to my ears'.[21]

Despite the establishment of better relations between London and other EU capitals, however, the Blair government quickly found itself at odds with the Commission and the majority of Britain's partners on a number of issues. Some minor skirmishing took place, for instance, over its decision to reduce from 8 per cent to 5 per cent the rate of VAT imposed on domestic fuel by its Conservative predecessor. Although this proposed change encountered strong objections from Brussels on the grounds that it ran counter to the spirit if not the law of directives aimed at harmonising taxation, it was nevertheless implemented.[22] A more serious disagreement arose concerning the Social Chapter. Here there were two main problems. First, the legal procedure involved in reversing the opt-out negotiated at Maastricht was a complicated one which would not be completed until the new EU treaty due to be finalised at Amsterdam in mid-June 1997 had been ratified by all member states. Since this might take anything up to two years, the British government wanted to have the right to participate in all relevant decision-making during

19. *The Times*, 4 May 1997.

20. *Financial Times*, Simon Kuper, 7 May 1997; *The Independent*, Diane Coyle, 5 May 1997; Sarah Helm, 8 May 1997; Chris Goldmark, 8 May 1997.

21. Speech to the European Parliament: cited in *The Independent*, Sarah Helm, 8 May 1997.

22. *The Independent*, Sarah Helm, 6 and 7 May 1997.

the interim. What it refused to accept was an alternative suggestion from the Commission, namely provision for a separate and speedier ratification of the Social Chapter on its own.[23] Secondly, there was considerable anxiety on the part of the Blair government, and the Prime Minister personally, about plans being prepared by Padraig Flynn, the Social Affairs Commissioner, for a substantial extension in the scope of the Social Chapter.[24] At the time Labour came to power, only two measures were in force, one relating to unpaid parental leave and the other to works councils. Proposals were in the pipeline, however, for further directives on sexual discrimination in the workplace and the rights of part-time employees,[25] and Blair immediately made it clear that he regarded such a development as highly undesirable. Speaking at a mini summit held at Noordwijk on 23 May and again at a meeting of European Socialists at Malmö on 6 June, he warned that his government would not tolerate a flood of new regulations under the Social Chapter which might serve to impair the competitiveness of British industry.[26]

The Blair government also found itself bogged down in the long-running disputes which it had inherited over the ban on British beef exports and quota hopping by foreign trawlermen. Initial confidence that the general spirit of goodwill generated by Labour's more cooperative attitude on EU matters would make it possible to resolve these difficulties without too much delay was soon dispelled. Although the Commissioners concerned, Franz Fischler and Emma Bonino, were eager to help, discussions between them and Jack Cunningham, the Agriculture Minister, and Elliot Morley, the Fisheries Minister, revealed that there remained serious obstacles to an agreement in both cases. As far as the beef question was concerned, the most promising approach appeared to be a progressive easing of the ban, starting with that on exports from Northern Ireland where all cattle were certified and traceable through computerised records.[27] It was clear, however, that this would be a lengthy business. The British were reluctant to see Northern Ireland treated as a special case because of the resentment that might cause among Scottish farmers in particular. Moreover, there was still no real confidence among Britain's partners in the adequacy of the measures

23. *Ibid.*, Anthony Bevins, 13 June 1997.   24. *Ibid.*, Sarah Helm, 19 May 1997.
25. *Ibid.*, Sarah Helm and Katherine Butler, 4 June 1997; Colin Brown and Katherine Butler, 5 June 1997.
26. *Ibid.*, Anthony Bevins, 23 May 1997; Sarah Helm, 6 June 1997.
27. *Ibid.*, Colin Brown, 10 May 1997; Sarah Helm and Anthony Bevins, 20 May 1997.

taken to eradicate BSE. On 11 June the EU veterinary committee flatly rejected proposals previously submitted by Douglas Hogg for a resumption of exports from healthy, grass-fed herds, and the likelihood was that the ban as a whole would remain in force for some considerable time.[28] The British government's exasperation at this disappointing prospect was reflected in threats to impose a unilateral embargo – in breach of EU rules – on beef imports from member states which refused to adopt the controls instituted by the UK to protect consumers against BSE.[29]

A satisfactory settlement over quota hopping proved similarly elusive. Unlike its predecessor, the Blair government refrained from threatening to wreck the IGC unless the entire practice was made illegal under EU law. Bonino suggested a deal under which all boats licensed to share in the UK quota should be required to land part of their catches in British ports and perhaps also to be manned by crews of which some members at least spoke fluent English. In return for this concession, Britain was to agree to cuts of up to 30 per cent of its existing quota, as proposed in the latest EU conservation plan. From the standpoint of the British government, this did not go far enough. What was needed, London argued, was the inclusion of a special protocol in the prospective Amsterdam Treaty providing a cast-iron guarantee that restrictions on foreign fishermen could not be overturned by the European Court as a violation of EU rules on free movement of capital and people.[30] As will be seen, this demand was not met.

One of the most significant issues on which the Blair government found itself out of step with most of its EU counterparts and with Brussels was EMU. By a supreme irony, at the time Labour took office the only large member state that was qualified to sign up for the single European currency on the appointed launch date of 1 January 1999 – Britain – was also the one that had no strong inclination to do so. While the political leaders of France, Germany and Italy were all eager to see their countries participating in the first wave, they were also experiencing great difficulty in ensuring that the key criteria established at Maastricht were satisfied. The British situation was exactly the opposite. Meeting the necessary economic and financial preconditions presented few real problems.

28. *The Times*, 12 June 1997.

29. *The Independent*, Charles Arthur and Katherine Butler, 6 June 1997; Katherine Butler, 16 December 1997.

30. *Ibid.*, Sarah Helm and Anthony Bevins, 20 May 1997; Sarah Helm, 21 May 1997; Stephen Castle and Sarah Helm, 15 June 1997.

What was lacking was political commitment. When in Opposition, Blair had repeatedly attacked the Major government for failing to make its position on the euro absolutely clear. Yet that was precisely the charge that critics tended to level at him when he, in turn, took up the task of formulating a policy on the matter. The prevailing opinion among political commentators, indeed, was that the new government appeared to be simply imitating its predecessor's 'wait and see' approach.

At the same time, there was undoubtedly a wide gap between the stance of the Labour government and that of the Conservative Opposition as it had evolved under Hague, with its concentration on the possible pitfalls rather than benefits of the single currency and its commitment to fighting the next election on the basis of opposition to British membership. In contrast to Conservative front-benchers like Howard, Lilley, Redwood and Hague himself, senior members of the Blair government did not regard the whole EMU project as inherently unworkable. On the contrary, they believed it to have considerable merits, especially in its potential for eliminating exchange rate risks and for bringing lower international transaction costs, a long-term reduction in interest rates and a greater element of financial stability.[31] There were, of course, varying degrees of enthusiasm within the Cabinet. Brown was by common consent the staunchest supporter of the single currency and Cook the leading sceptic. As for Blair, he was essentially a pragmatist on the matter. Whilst fully appreciating the possible benefits of membership to Britain, he nonetheless needed to be convinced that these were not outweighed by the economic and political risks involved in seeking to take the country in.

The question that preoccupied Blair and his colleagues was not whether Britain should sign up for the euro but when. For various reasons there was never any serious possibility that it would do so in January 1999. In the first place, all expert financial advice available to the government suggested that this would probably have severe adverse consequences, arising from lack of synchronisation or convergence between the UK's economic cycle and those of other EU members.[32] Eddie George, the Governor of the Bank of England,

31. See, for example, Brown's favourable comments in a major speech on EMU on 17 July 1997: *Financial Times*, 18 July 1997; *The Independent*, Anthony Bevins, 18 July 1997.
32. For the genuine difficulties created by cyclical divergence between the UK and its EU partners see Gavyn Davies, *The Independent*, business section, 15 September 1997.

who described himself as a 'Europragmatist' or a 'Eurorealist', made no secret of his anxiety on this score.[33] The Treasury shared his concern, warning that entry on the launch date would mean either cuts of £20 billion in public spending or an increase of taxation equivalent to 10p in the pound on the standard rate of income tax.[34] Secondly, business opinion, while overwhelmingly in favour of adopting the single currency at some stage, was nevertheless cautious about taking the plunge in the near future. This was partly because many companies had so far done very little to prepare themselves,[35] but also because of worries about the likely effect of such a move on domestic interest rates and the international value of sterling. It must be said that the attitude displayed by representatives of industry and commerce was deeply ambivalent. On the one hand, they were extremely critical of the upward trend of interest rates which the newly independent Bank of England quickly raised to a level of more than 3 per cent above the EU average during the summer and autumn of 1997. Their complaint was that this, combined with the prevailing high rate of the pound (peaking at DM3.07 in July and staying above DM2.80 for the remainder of the year), was hitting exports hard. It was for this reason that a deputation of seventeen prominent industrialists, including the chairmen of ICI and Guinness, pressed Blair in September for a firm government commitment to the euro as a means of bringing sterling down to a more manageable level of DM2.30–2.40.[36] On the other hand, there were also widespread fears in the business community that a fall in sterling, as well as in interest rates, because of a decision to adopt the single currency would add to resurgent inflationary pressures and perhaps produce an unsustainable boom of the 1988 variety. This sentiment was reflected in the findings of a survey of its members conducted by the CBI and published in July 1997. Although only 6 per cent of respondents expressed opposition in principle to membership of the euro zone, a substantial majority

33. See, for example, his end-of-year interview in which he spoke of the problems of sustaining long-term economic convergence. 'I think it would have been risky', he said, 'for the UK to join in the first wave': *Financial Times*, Richard Adams, 31 December 1997. See also his evidence to the Treasury Select Committee on 29 January and 2 April 1998: *The Independent*, business section, 30 January 1998 and 3 April 1998.

34. *The Independent*, Colin Brown; Colin Brown and Nigel Cope, both 20 October 1997.

35. For ignorance about the implications of the euro among small and medium-sized British companies see HM Treasury, *Getting Ready for the Euro*, First Report, July 1998.

36. *The Independent*, business section, 24 September 1997.

were against being part of the first wave on the grounds that it would fuel inflation.[37]

These factors apart, logistical considerations alone effectively ruled out British participation from 1 January 1999. When Labour took office, preparation of the necessary legal and practical groundwork was not sufficiently advanced to make that a feasible option. In addition, under the Maastricht Treaty all countries wishing to join the single currency at its launch date were to notify their partners of the fact before the end of 1997. This stipulation presented the new government with insuperable problems in pushing through the requisite legislation and holding a referendum – as it was pledged to do by its election manifesto – in a period of less than seven months.

If time was short for decisions relating to the euro, the government faced an even tighter schedule in preparing policy on the new EU treaty, the negotiations for which were due to be completed by 17 June, less than seven weeks after its election victory. During May, various drafts of the treaty continued to emerge from the deliberations of the IGC, and from London's reactions to these it was immediately apparent that in a number of important areas the Blair government was scarcely more willing to accept what was being proposed than its predecessor had been. It is arguable, indeed, that in his general approach to reform of the EU Blair himself was a great deal closer to Major than the rhetoric of both men suggested. Certainly the two shared an instinctive mistrust of the more ambitious plans for further integration issuing from the Commission and other quarters, as well as a belief that the EU would benefit greatly from a dose of British pragmatism. As a man in his early forties, Blair, unlike the older generation of European leaders, was not influenced in his attitude to European integration by personal experience of the Second World War.[38] His ideas were shaped less by a determination to prevent such a catastrophe from being repeated than by a mission to modernise and promote greater efficiency. Thus deregulation of the economy and a radical overhaul of the state welfare system at home were to be paralleled by an equally sweeping reform of outmoded practices within the EU. This reform, however, was to be directed towards improving the lives of ordinary

37. *The Independent*, Michael Harrison, 26 July 1997. Adair Turner, the Director-General of the CBI, described the result of a survey of members on joining the single currency as a 'contingent yes'.
38. H. Young, *This Blessed Plot: Britain and Europe from Churchill to Blair* (1998), p. 481.

citizens rather than devising increasingly elaborate institutional structures that were incomprehensible to all but a few. One of the main themes that Blair spelt out at Noordwijk and Malmö early in his premiership, and subsequently repeated in lectures to Kohl and other EU colleagues, was the need to create 'a people's Europe' instead of one run by and for a remote political elite.[39] As he told his Socialist audience at Malmö: 'We must stop talking about European theology and start doing things from which real people see real benefits.'[40]

At the top of the Blair government's agenda for Europe was tackling unemployment.[41] Other priorities included completion of the single market, progress on greater competitiveness, enlargement of the EU and far-reaching changes to the CAP.[42] Some of these objectives were shared by Britain's partners. Where fundamental differences arose was over the desire of the French, German and most other EU governments to improve the effectiveness of decision-making by increased use of QMV and by pooling sovereignty in spheres of activity which were currently based on intergovernmental cooperation: defence, foreign policy and justice and home affairs. The Major government had set its face against this sustained drive to integration and had pursued a strategy of systematic obstruction. Its successor was slightly more willing to make concessions, agreeing at an early stage to accept modest additional powers for the EP, as well as a reduction in the power of veto of individual states over joint foreign policy decisions and a limited extension of QMV to areas like anti-fraud measures, regional aid and environmental policy. There were a number of key points, however, on which the Blair government, too, refused to compromise. As the Conservatives had been, it was totally opposed to the idea floated by Bonn and Paris that the WEU should be absorbed into the legal and constitutional framework of the EU, fearing that this might pave the way for the development of a fully fledged common defence policy and undermine the Atlantic Alliance. The most that it was prepared to countenance was that the projected Amsterdam Treaty might lay down broad principles for EU involvement in humanitarian, peace-keeping and peace-making tasks of

39. *The Independent*, Anthony Bevins, 23 May 1997; Sarah Helm, 6 June 1997. For Blair's 'lecture' to Kohl see *ibid.*, Imre Karacs, 7 June 1997.
40. *The Independent*, Sarah Helm, 6 June 1997.
41. This was reflected in Brown's three-point action plan for unemployment presented to EU finance ministers on 9 June 1997: *The Times*, Philip Webster, 5 June 1997.
42. See, for example, Douglas Henderson's IGC speech in Brussels on 5 May 1997: *The Independent*, Sarah Helm, 6 May 1997.

the kind allotted to the WEU by the 1992 Petersberg Agreement.[43] Equally, it was no less determined than the Major government had been in its opposition to proposals for incorporating the Schengen agreements into the EU so as to eliminate completely internal border restrictions between all fifteen member states. What it demanded was that Britain must be given a legally binding guarantee, written into the Amsterdam Treaty, of its right to retain permanent control over its own frontier checks.[44] Other states were not unsympathetic to this claim and readily acknowledged that Britain (in common with Ireland) ought to be treated as a special case because of its island status.[45]

Ironically, a final point of disagreement between the Blair government and the majority of its EU counterparts stemmed from attempts to prevent such disagreements from leading to deadlock by introducing greater flexibility into the decision-making process. As was noted in Chapter 20, during the early months of 1997 considerable attention was devoted to the idea of a 'multi-speed' or 'variable geometry' EU whereby a group of members might agree to share sovereignty in particular areas without the participation of the rest. Such an idea had broad appeal. To the Major government it seemed to offer a measure of protection against being sucked unwillingly into the general drive for integration. As against that, after some initial misgivings, Kohl and Chirac came to view it as a useful tool for overcoming British obstructionism. There was, in any case, a growing recognition on all sides that the prospective accession of up to ten new members in the next few years made a reform of this nature essential if the EU was not to become completely unmanageable. While not disputing the logic of this argument, the Blair government shared the concern felt by its predecessor that Britain might be marginalised if an inner core of states, led by France and Germany, forged ahead with integration. It therefore insisted that such selective pooling of sovereignty should not be allowed in spheres like the single market or defence and that, even where it was allowed, the interests of those who chose not to take part must be protected. Thus a decision to proceed must be approved

43. See, for example, Cook's speech to the WEU on 13 May 1997: *The Independent*, John Lichfield, 14 May 1997.

44. See, for example, Blair's speech at Noordwijk on 22 May and Cook's talks with Hervé de Charette and Kinkel on 7 May 1997: *The Times*, 23 May 1997; *The Independent*, Donald Macintyre and Imre Karacs, 8 May 1997.

45. A concession to the British and Irish viewpoint was contained in the draft text of 6 May 1997 on the pooling of justice and immigration policy: *The Independent*, Sarah Helm, 6 May 1997.

by a unanimous vote of all fifteen EU members and would only be valid if more than half of these – perhaps as many as ten – wished to be involved.[46] Neither the French nor the Germans were prepared to accept such restrictions.

It would be wrong to think that the problems experienced in the course of the IGC were a product solely of differences between Britain and the rest of the EU. On the question of a common defence, the Danes and the four 'neutrals', Austria, Ireland, Finland and Sweden, took a similar position to the British. Moreover, the most serious clash by far in the run-up to the Amsterdam European Council was that which occurred between France and Germany over EMU. This originated in the electoral success of the French Socialists and their allies at the beginning of June 1997 and the subsequent formation of a left-wing government, headed by Lionel Jospin, the Socialist leader. Jospin campaigned on a pledge to cut unemployment by creating 700,000 jobs for the young and the introduction of a 35-hour working week without loss of pay. He promised an end to financial sacrifices to meet the Maastricht convergence criteria. He also indicated that France would not join the single currency zone if the so-called 'Club Med' countries – Italy, Spain and Portugal – were excluded, since that might place French farmers and manufacturers at a competitive disadvantage.[47] Such a programme was anathema to Bonn. It opened up the disagreeable possibility of a 'soft' euro or a delay in its launch and with that heightened opposition within Germany to giving up the Deutschmark. What made the situation all the more unwelcome was that the Kohl government itself had still not managed to meet the necessary budget deficit target of 3 per cent of GDP and was coming under heavy fire for resorting to 'creative accounting' – the most criticised aspect of this being an abortive attempt by Waigel to reduce the yawning DM10 billion gap between revenue and expenditure for 1997–8 by bringing forward a planned revaluation of the Bundesbank's gold and foreign exchange reserves.[48]

Worse was to come. Within days of taking office, Jospin and his Finance Minister, Dominique Strauss-Kahn, called for reconsideration of the single currency 'stability pact', the device which was intended

46. See, for example, Cook's comments to Hervé de Charette and Kinkel on 7 May 1997: *The Independent*, Donald Macintyre and Imre Karacs, 8 May 1997.

47. *The Daily Telegraph*, editorial and article by Toby Helm, 3 June 1997; *The Independent*, John Lichfield, 2 and 3 June 1997; Sarah Helm, 10 June 1997.

48. *Financial Times*, 'Lex' column and leader, 16 May 1997; Peter Norman, 16 and 17 May 1997. See also *The Independent*, business section, 16 May 1997; Imre Karacs, 16 May, 17 May and 2 June 1997; Diane Coyle, 29 May 1997; editorial and article by Sarah Helm, 30 May 1997.

to ensure a regime of strict fiscal discipline within the euro zone by a system of stiff fines – up to a maximum of 0.5 per cent of GDP – on participating states which failed to keep to the Maastricht guidelines. The pact had been proposed initially in November 1995 by Waigel as a form of reassurance for the Bundesbank and German opinion generally that the new currency would be as strong as the Deutschmark. From the outset, though, the French had argued that it should be concerned with fostering economic growth and employment as well as fiscal rectitude and, following pressure from Chirac at the Dublin European Council of December 1996, it had been renamed the 'stability and growth pact'.[49] The Jospin government wanted more than a change of name and pressed for the establishment of an economic 'government' or 'council' to act as a political counterweight to the ECB which, like the Bundesbank on which it was modelled, would have a narrowly monetarist remit. This provoked a row with the Germans during a meeting of EU finance ministers in Luxembourg on 9 June.[50] A Franco-German summit held at Poitiers four days later failed to produce a compromise, an outcome which lengthened the list of issues that had still not been resolved on the eve of the Amsterdam European Council.

The Amsterdam European Council met on 16 and 17 June 1997. Its central purpose was to finalise the work of the IGC and to fashion a treaty which would prepare the way for successful enlargement of the EU to up to 27 members by the early years of the new millennium. In this latter task it failed conspicuously. Indeed, the Amsterdam Treaty itself contained a tacit admission that this was the case in its provision for the convening of another IGC to complete unfinished business at least one year before the number of EU members had risen to twenty.[51]

Overall there was only modest progress at Amsterdam in carrying out the ambitious plans for reform that were originally envisaged when the IGC began. In some areas there was none at all. Small steps were taken to strengthen the EP. Its membership was capped at 700 regardless of how many new states entered the EU. It

49. A. Duff, *Reforming the European Union* (1997), p. 26.

50. *The Independent*, Sarah Helm and Imre Karacs, 3 June 1997; Sarah Helm, 7, 10 and 11 June 1997; Katherine Butler, 9 June 1997; John Lichfield, 11 June 1997.

51. For a detailed study of the Treaty of Amsterdam and the negotiations leading up to it see B. McDonach, *Original Sin in a Brave New World: An Account of the Negotiation of the Treaty of Amsterdam* (1998). For the text of the treaty and an analysis of its provisions see A. Duff (ed.), *The Treaty of Amsterdam: Text and Commentary* (1997). For a convenient summary of the terms of the treaty see *The Independent*, 16 June 1997.

was given the power to approve or reject the nominee for the post of President of the Commission. The number of functions that the EP was expected to perform was reduced to three: assent, consultation and co-decision with the Council. As well as being simplified and speeded up, the co-decision procedure was extended to new policy areas. The use of QMV in the Council was similarly broadened in scope to embrace twelve new fields, including employment guidelines and incentive measures, social exclusion, countering fraud, customs cooperation and equal opportunities. A clash of national interests made it impossible to reach agreement over changes to the composition of the Commission or the weighting of votes in the Council: these questions were simply shelved. Britain's reversal of its opt-out opened the way for incorporation of the Social Chapter into the Amsterdam Treaty. The Schengen agreements were also incorporated into it, and signatory states were required to remove all internal border controls within five years. Britain and Ireland were allowed to retain their own checks, whilst enjoying the right to collaborate with the others at any time and to the extent that they wished. Common procedures and standards were to be introduced for dealing with immigration, asylum, visas and other matters relating to the EU's external frontiers. Policy decisions concerning these questions would be taken by QMV after a period of five years from the coming into force of the treaty. In addition, the jurisdiction of the ECJ was extended to this sphere.

As regards foreign and defence policy, there was some advance towards closer cooperation, though not as much as the French and Germans had sought. The British and their supporters were successful in blocking the incorporation of the WEU into the EU. On the other hand, the treaty did call for the progressive creation of a common defence policy and established the principle of EU involvement in humanitarian, aid and peace-keeping tasks. Despite British resistance, the power of veto in foreign policy decision-making was somewhat weakened. In future it would be possible for the European Council to work out common strategies, as well as general foreign policy guidelines and joint actions. Once these had been agreed, they could be put into effect by QMV in the Council of Ministers. A 'constructive abstention clause' in the treaty permitted one or more member states to refrain from taking part in implementation of decisions, though without being able to prevent the rest from going ahead. A veto could only be exercised – by means of a fairly elaborate procedure – where a decision was opposed for 'very important reasons of stated national policy'.

A major innovation in the Amsterdam Treaty was the inclusion of a special section dealing with the issue of flexible decision-making. In this, a mechanism was established by which some EU states might move towards closer integration in certain fields without having to wait for others. As the British government had insisted, this procedure was subject to strict conditions and safeguards to protect the interests of non-participants. Thus it could only be utilised as a last resort, must involve more than half the member states and must be open to all.

Finally, there was the question of employment, the importance of which was underlined by a mass demonstration in Amsterdam shortly before the European Council got under way. The new treaty contained a chapter devoted to the subject in which, for the first time, promoting a high level of employment was set down as one of the EU's main objectives. However, most of the measures recommended were permissive, and it was emphasised that employment policy remained first and foremost the responsibility of individual governments. The Council of Ministers was charged with monitoring closely the efforts of each government to improve the unemployment situation in its own country. It was also authorised to adopt incentive measures to finance job-creating pilot schemes.

The Amsterdam Treaty's employment chapter was supplemented by a resolution on economic growth and employment. This originated in a package deal agreed by the French and Germans on 16 June by which the former were induced to abandon their objections to approval of the single currency stability pact. Like the treaty itself, the resolution was strong on promises to share experiences and examine good practices, but weak on financial and institutional back-up. Arrangements were made for it to be followed up by a 'summit for jobs' – to be held in the autumn in Luxembourg, which was scheduled to take over the EU presidency from The Netherlands at the end of June. At the summit, information would be exchanged on different experiences in fighting unemployment, and the British government was eager to seize this opportunity to give details of its 'welfare to work' programme.[52]

In addition to this side agreement on employment, which was separate from the treaty, there was another on the problem of quota hopping. Blair acclaimed this as a great achievement and a fulfilment of his pledge to protect the interests of the British fishing

---

52. *The Independent*, Sarah Helm, 17 June 1997; Anthony Bevins and Sarah Helm, 17 June 1997.

industry.[53] The reality, however, was less impressive. The British government failed in its original objective of securing a protocol which outlawed all quota hopping. Furthermore, the 'agreement' reached in Amsterdam consisted of nothing more than an exchange of letters between Blair and Santer on 18 June. In his letter, Blair suggested that any fishing vessel with access to the UK quota should be obliged to begin its voyage from a British port and land at least 50 per cent of its catch in one. Alternatively, most of its crew must live in Britain. These options were a variant on those discussed earlier by Bonino and Cunningham, and it was hoped that a combination of any or all of them would act as a powerful disincentive to foreign fishermen using UK-registered boats. Santer's non-committal reply merely stated that it might be legal to use such restrictions to ensure that the UK fish quota brought benefits to British communities. It was thought advisable not to disclose the existence of these letters during the Amsterdam European Council for fear of upsetting the Spaniards. Moreover, when Abel Matutes, the Spanish Foreign Minister, later sought assurances from Brussels that no deal had been done at Amsterdam, Santer confirmed that this was indeed the case. All he had done was to inform Blair of a long-standing legal remedy for the problem of quota hopping which was available to all EU members and well known to the British government.[54]

Despite its obvious deficiencies, Blair presented the Amsterdam Treaty as a whole as a triumph for his government and for Britain. The treaty, he told the Commons on 18 June, protected essential national interests over immigration, defence and foreign policy. It would also encourage flexible labour markets and job skills, and was based squarely on the prescription offered by the British government for tackling unemployment in the EU.[55] Not surprisingly, the Conservative Opposition was less enthusiastic. Major attacked what he called 'both a botched and an incomplete negotiation', claiming that the only good parts of the treaty were those that had been negotiated while he was still in power. His chief criticism, however, was that the Blair government had given in to moves towards a more integrated Europe on defence, on the role of the ECJ over immigration and asylum and on employment.[56] This was the main thrust of the Conservatives' onslaught on the Amsterdam

53. *H.C.Deb.*, vol. 296, col. 315, 18 June 1997.

54. *The Independent on Sunday*, Stephen Castle and Sarah Helm, 15 June 1997; *The Independent*, Sarah Helm, 18 June 1997; Nicholas Schoon and Sarah Helm, 19 June 1997; Katherine Butler, 26 July 1997.

55. *H.C.Deb.*, vol. 296, cols. 313–16.   56. *Ibid.*, cols. 316–18.

Treaty. According to Howard, the Shadow Foreign Secretary, it marked 'an unacceptable step towards an integrated federal superstate'. Deviating from the official party line as usual, Clarke spoke of a 'fair old mouse of a treaty'. In less provocative mode, he argued that on the whole it was 'a balanced document' that did 'not involve some fundamental transfer of power to Brussels'.[57]

It is hard to disagree with this last verdict. The institutional changes wrought by the Amsterdam Treaty fell well short of initial expectations and were certainly less substantial than those agreed at Maastricht. Indeed, the evident lack of appetite for more fundamental reform on the part of the negotiators in Amsterdam reflected a European-wide reaction against the Maastricht Treaty and its ambitious plans for further integration.

57. *The Independent*, Anthony Bevins, 1 November 1997.

CHAPTER TWENTY-FOUR

After Amsterdam: Enlargement, Employment and the Euro

The Amsterdam negotiations left a lot of loose ends to be tied up. A series of major reforms still needed to be carried out before enlargement of the EU could take place. It remained to be seen whether and how the well-meaning intentions expressed about reducing unemployment would be translated into action. In addition, many crucial decisions had to be taken about the launch of the single currency. The period following the Amsterdam European Council saw a great deal of hard bargaining on all these matters, with Britain seeking to play a pivotal role, especially after its assumption of the EU presidency at the beginning of 1998.

On 16 July 1997 the European Commission announced the names of those countries regarded as meeting the democratic and economic qualifications for entry to the EU laid down by the Copenhagen European Council of June 1993:[1] Poland, Hungary, the Czech Republic, Estonia, Slovenia and Cyprus. Negotiations with these would start in early 1998 and were expected to result in full membership by 2002. Another five of the total number of twelve applicants – Bulgaria, Romania, Slovakia, Latvia, and Lithuania – received a clear signal that they were next in line. Admission of the final applicant, Turkey, raised some delicate political issues, and there was little likelihood of its happening in the foreseeable future.[2]

Nobody doubted that the accession of so many widely differing states would place enormous strains on the EU. As one minor example of the difficulties ahead, it would mean catering for translation of another eleven languages. Far more serious was the basic

1. For the criteria set by the Copenhagen Council see A. Duff, *Reforming the European Union* (1997), p. 100.
2. *The Independent*, Sarah Helm, 17 July 1997. For information on the various candidates see Duff, *Reforming the European Union*, pp. 103–7.

problem of how to accommodate the interests of new members without imposing unacceptable sacrifices on some or all of the existing ones. The complete failure at Amsterdam to reform the composition of the Commission and the weighting of voting in the Council of Ministers provided a salutary warning of how hard this was going to be.

By the summer of 1997, earlier enthusiasm for admitting the newly democratised countries of central and eastern Europe was beginning to wane as some of the practical consequences came to be more fully appreciated. Britain remained strongly committed to enlargement of the EU, which was still seen as a useful way of slowing the pace of integration. Among many of the other member states, however, there was an evident wariness about the various economic and political costs involved. The French, for their part, had never been more than lukewarm about the project, worried that it might lead to institutional paralysis and preferring to focus attention instead on deepening integration within the existing EU. Some of the smaller members feared a diminution of their voting power, while those which derived substantial financial benefit from EU funding, like Greece, Ireland, Italy and Spain, looked askance at the prospect of subsidies being diverted from them to poorer newcomers. Perhaps the biggest change of attitude was on the part of the Germans, who had always been in the forefront of the movement for enlargement. There was no overt about-turn in the Kohl government's policy. Official opinion in Bonn was nevertheless more cautious than it had been, partly because of growing concern at the possibility of cheap eastern European imports flooding the German market, but mainly because of the realisation that it might well fall to Germany to bear most of the cost of expansion. The bill was bound to be huge – Santer called for a 'veritable Marshall Plan' involving expenditure of 75 billion ecus (£52.5 billion) – and the question inevitably arose of who was to pay.[3]

The prospect of having to provide massive subsidies to economically backward new members triggered an increasingly acrimonious debate about reform of the EU's financial arrangements. More specifically, it brought to a head the long-standing sense of grievance felt by the Germans about the level of their own payments to the EU budget. Germany's net contribution to EU expenditure for 1996 was £7.56 billion. Britain (£2.34 billion), Sweden and The Netherlands

---

3. *The Independent*, Sarah Helm, 15 and 17 July 1997. See also Duff, *Reforming the European Union*, pp. 107–8.

were also net contributors, albeit on a much smaller scale. Most of the other member states were net gainers. The Germans complained that they were paying a disproportionate amount relative to their wealth. During the summer of 1997 Kohl, Waigel and other senior ministers called for a fairer system based on GDP. This marked the start of a sustained campaign for change, which was to culminate in demands at the Cardiff European Council of June 1998 for an upper limit of 0.3 per cent of Germany's GDP on its budget contribution and a rebate similar to that which Thatcher had negotiated for Britain in 1984. Austria, The Netherlands and Sweden likewise pressed for a better deal for themselves. Any such alterations required a unanimous vote. They would also entail concessions by other states, and there was not the slightest evidence of a willingness to make them. Certainly the uncompromising response from the Blair government was that, whatever else happened, the British rebate was not negotiable.[4]

It was against this background of bitter financial wrangling that plans were laid for the radical reforms considered to be an essential precondition of EU enlargement. On 16 July 1997 the Commission issued a document called *Agenda 2000: For a Stronger and Wider Union* setting out proposals for a fundamental restructuring of the CAP and of regional funding which, between them, accounted for nearly four-fifths of the EU budget. The CAP alone absorbed some 50 per cent of a total expenditure of more than £60 billion and was a prime candidate for change. It was widely believed to be inefficient and expensive: studies by the OECD estimated that it added at least £20 a week to the food bill of a family of four. It was also thought to encourage overproduction. Reforms introduced in 1992 had failed to achieve the intended cutbacks, and the Commission warned in *Agenda 2000* of the need for further action to avert a return to the days of vast surpluses. What made an overhaul of the system imperative, however, was the planned accession of Poland and the other central and eastern European states. The inhabitants of these countries had disposable incomes which were far below the EU average, and any attempt to apply to them the CAP regime of artificially high prices would have produced serious economic and political tensions. Besides, an extension of the CAP in its existing form to regions in which a quarter of the population worked

---

4. *Handelsblatt*, 26 July 1997; *The Independent*, Imre Karacs, 26 July 1997; Katherine Butler, 16 June 1998; *The Courier and Advertiser*, 15 June 1998; *H.C.Deb.*, vol. 314, col. 368, 17 June 1998.

on the land would have been a sure recipe for bankrupting the
EU.[5]

The central feature of the Commission's proposals on agriculture was a phased replacement of price support, the cornerstone of
the CAP since its inception, by direct subsidies to producers. As a
first step, guaranteed prices for grain, beef, milk and dairy produce
were to be cut by up to 30 per cent between 2000 and 2002, the
hope being that this would lead – at least in the longer term – to
lower costs and cheaper food in the shops.[6] Since Blair and Cunningham had repeatedly criticised the CAP as indefensibly wasteful
and expensive, it came as no surprise when the British government
cordially welcomed the Commission's plans. Cunningham claimed
that they would save consumers £1 billion p.a. and indicated that
he would be pressing for even bigger cuts in guaranteed prices
than those prescribed in *Agenda 2000*.[7] However, the reaction from
the powerful farming lobbies in those countries which benefited
most from the existing system – including Germany – was overwhelmingly hostile, and it was from the outset highly improbable
that the programme would be implemented in anything like its
original form. The attitude of British farmers was mixed. On the
one hand, the NFU expressed broad support for moves towards
a more market-orientated approach and for the introduction of
direct income subsidies. In many respects, indeed, what was being
suggested represented a return to the system operating in Britain
before entry to the EC and adoption of the CAP. On the other
hand, there were misgivings. One of the new proposals was that EU
assistance might be supplemented by national top-up grants, and
the farming community was not entirely convinced that it would
receive sympathetic consideration in this respect from a Labour
government. Furthermore, some of the new proposals were inherently unfavourable to Britain. In particular, the idea of capping direct
subsidies so as to ensure that funds were channelled mainly to small
producers would necessarily work against the interests of British
farmers, whose holdings tended to be bigger than the EU average.[8]

The Commission's proposed changes in regional funding
threatened to be even more unsuited to British interests. Details of

5. Duff, *Reforming the European Union*, p. 178; *The Independent on Sunday*, editorial,
13 July 1997; *The Independent*, Katherine Butler, 9 and 17 July 1997.

6. *The Independent*, Katherine Butler, 17 July 1997.

7. *Ibid.*, Nicholas Schoon, 10 July 1997: *The Times*, Charles Bremner and Michael
Hornsby, 19 March 1998.

8. *The Independent*, Nicholas Schoon, 10 July 1997.

how the revised system would operate were released by Monika Wulf-Mathies, the Commissioner for Regional Policy, in mid-March 1998. From these it was obvious that Britain stood to lose a hefty slice of its current entitlement. Merseyside was expected to retain its existing share of aid and South Yorkshire to get more. But these were exceptions. Nine of the thirteen regions in industrial decline would see their funding slashed. Northern Ireland and the Highlands and Islands, which benefited to the extent of some £300 million a year between them, would cease to qualify as 'Objective 1' regions. The reason why Britain would be so adversely affected was simple. The yardstick of poverty would henceforward be unemployment, and the British rate – 5.3 per cent – was less than half of that in France and Germany, and barely a quarter of that in Spain.[9] Margaret Beckett, the President of the Board of Trade, and Peter Mandelson, the Minister without Portfolio, had lobbied hard in Brussels for other criteria, such as per capita GDP, to be taken into account as well, but they were given short shrift. Their task was not made any easier by the Blair government's repeated boasts about its success in reducing unemployment. There was also some feeling on the part of the Commission that the UK was more interested in financing grandiose Millennium projects than in providing 'matching' funds for long-term regional development schemes part-financed by the EU.[10]

If the disputes that developed about farming and regional aid reform were essentially a matter of conflicting national interests, those relating to unemployment contained a strong ideological element too. Soon after the Amsterdam European Council ended, preparations began for the Luxembourg jobs summit, which was scheduled to meet in mid-November. What these revealed was that beneath a common commitment to the goal of reducing unemployment there were deep differences over methods. Broadly speaking, there were two main schools of thought on the subject, each of which had support in the Commission and from individual member governments. First, there was the belief that the best way to create jobs was by giving Brussels more power to co-ordinate unemployment policy, setting definite targets for the EU as a whole and providing sufficient funds to make it possible to meet them. This was the approach associated with Padraig Flynn, the Social Affairs

9. See *The Times*, editorial, 19 March 1998; Alexandra Frean, 19 March 1998; Charles Bremner, 19 March 1998; *The Independent*, 16 March 1998; Katherine Butler, 19 March 1998; Katherine Butler and Kim Sengupta, 19 March 1998.

10. *The Independent*, Katherine Butler and Kim Sengupta, 19 March 1998.

Commissioner, and above all with the French government. The alternative model was the one vigorously championed by the UK and reflected in the proposals submitted by Brown to EU finance ministers in Brussels in mid-October 1997 and to the jobs summit a month later. Here the emphasis was on deregulation, increased competitiveness, a flexible and adaptable labour force, reform of state welfare systems and encouragement of small and medium-sized enterprises. Brown and his Cabinet colleagues denied that they were seeking to apply US-style practices wholesale to the EU. Rather, they claimed to be offering what was variously described as a 'new European model', a 'middle way' or a 'third way', in which dedication to improved economic efficiency was balanced by a concern for social harmony.[11]

Many of Britain's EU partners suspected that following the British lead might result in a low-wage, casual labour economy. At the same time, it could not be denied that the UK had enjoyed considerable success in reducing the level of its unemployment. Moreover, the persistence of sluggish economic activity in France, Germany and other member countries had prompted some debate there about the need for a change of direction. As a result, the lectures from London received a rather less sceptical response than they would otherwise have done – though Blair was doubtless guilty of exaggeration when claiming after the jobs summit that he had won backing from Denmark, The Netherlands, Italy, Luxembourg and Spain for the line advocated by Britain. What is certainly true is that there existed no great enthusiasm for dealing with unemployment through increased EU spending. To the Germans, in particular, such an approach seemed absolutely unthinkable at a time when they were already paying too much towards EU expenditure and were engaged in a desperate battle to balance their own budget and meet the Maastricht criteria.

On 1 October the Commission unveiled a new employment strategy which aimed at creating twelve million additional jobs over the next five years. This borrowed from each of the two main currents of thought about unemployment. The plan acknowledged the need for greater flexibility. It also called for member states to judge each other's performances in dealing with joblessness. As against that, it stressed the importance of job security and set ambitious targets for increasing the number of those on job training schemes from

11. Blair talked of a 'third way' in his Malmö speech of June 1997 and of 'a middle way' at the Luxembourg 'jobs summit' on 21 November 1997. Brown referred to a 'new European model' in an article for *The Independent* of 21 November 1997.

10 per cent to 25 per cent of the total EU workless. The latter measure, along with a reduction of taxation on employers, was designed to cut unemployment from its EU average of 11 per cent to 7 per cent. It was precisely this kind of centralised fixing of targets that the British government disliked, and it was largely as a result of its objections that many of the numbers contained in the Commission's blueprint were either omitted or scaled down in the package that emerged from the Luxembourg jobs summit on 21 November. Here again the outcome represented a combination of the two contrasting approaches referred to above. The European Investment Bank was to fund a £7 billion 'action plan' to assist small and medium-sized businesses. In addition, guidelines were laid down for boosting work training and job creation schemes. The responsibility for implementing these, however, rested with national governments whose success or failure in dealing with unemployment was to be vetted on an annual basis, starting at the Cardiff European Council in June 1998.[12]

From the standpoint of the British government, the most troublesome of the three main issues to be addressed following the Amsterdam European Council was the launch of the single European currency. More than anything else, it was this that provided the acid test of Blair's claim that the UK was now one of the leading players in the EU, setting its agenda, operating at the very heart of its decision-making process and generally exercising a decisive influence on its future development.

For reasons that have already been examined, British participation in the euro zone from its inception was a non-starter as far as the Blair government was concerned. The government was unwilling to say so publicly, however, principally because it wished to retain as much leverage as possible during the critical preparatory discussions. Initially, therefore, the official line from ministers and other authorised spokespersons was that nothing had been ruled out but that British entry in January 1999 was 'very unlikely'.[13] This formula was virtually identical to that used by the Conservatives during the general election campaign and, as in their case, reflected deep uncertainty over policy.

During the second half of 1997, as the deadline for a decision drew ever closer, the government came under growing pressure

12. *The Independent,* Katherine Butler, 2 October and 22 November 1997; Rupert Cornwell, 23 November 1997.
13. The words 'very unlikely' were used by Brown and Cook, for example: *The Independent,* business section, 9 May 1997; BBC1's *Breakfast with Frost,* 8 June 1997.

from its EU partners, business interests and domestic opinion in general to clarify its position. From July, the official mantra was modified somewhat to indicate that there were thought to be 'formidable obstacles' to British participation in the first wave.[14] It was also made clear by Brown in particular that when, at an appropriate (but unspecified) time, the government did come to make a 'hardheaded assessment' of whether adoption of the euro was in the national interest, it would do so on the basis of various economic tests.[15] There remained considerable doubt as to government intentions, however, and this gave rise to periodic bouts of market speculation. It was one of these that was instrumental in forcing the Chancellor of the Exchequer's hand.

On 26 September the *Financial Times* carried a report quoting an unnamed minister as saying that an announcement might soon be made on British conditions for joining the single currency shortly after the first wave. This was widely interpreted as a strong hint by the government that it was about to adopt a more positive stance on EMU. The result was a dramatic rise in shares and gilts and a fall in sterling of four Pfennigs against the Deutschmark – to DM2.83.[16] Brown and Cook appeared in two separate television programmes on 28 September to dismiss as nonsense talk of a change in government policy or a snap referendum on the euro. Their statements failed to put an end to fevered press speculation, however, and briefings by the Chancellor of the Exchequer's 'spin doctors', Ed Balls and Charlie Whelan, only added to the general atmosphere of confusion. It was rumoured that Brown was trying to bounce Blair into making an early decision in favour of British membership of the single currency area. An alternative theory had the two of them working together to 'talk up' the prospects of membership soon after the launch, their motives being to prepare the City and the public, to strengthen the government's hand in negotiations with Britain's EU partners and to help exporters by encouraging a fall in the value of the pound. An article in the *Daily Mail* of 13 October caused a fresh crop of rumours by suggesting that Blair was going to announce at the Luxembourg European Council of 21 November a decision to adopt the euro at the earliest opportunity. Not surprisingly, there were demands from the CBI and from the Conservative Opposition for a definitive statement of government policy.

14. 'A Treasury source': cited in *The Independent*, Anthony Bevins, 17 July 1997.
15. *Ibid.*, Anthony Bevins, 18 July 1997.
16. *The Independent*, Tom Stevenson and Magnus Grimond, 27 September 1997.

Brown had been intending to give such a statement to the Commons 'before the turn of the year'. He now brought it forward to 27 October.[17]

In his Commons statement, Brown ruled out British participation in EMU not only in January 1999, but also for the rest of the current Parliament – 'barring some fundamental and unforeseen change in economic circumstances'. At the same time, he left no room for doubt about the government's basically favourable attitude. As Brown himself put it: 'We are the first British Government to declare for the principle of monetary union.' It was announced that an intensive campaign was to begin to prepare business for membership should a decision be made in that sense during the lifetime of the next Parliament. In addition, Brown set out five key economic tests on which the government would base its judgement on the advisability of British adoption of the single currency: Would it help to create jobs? Would it promote investment in the UK? Would it be of assistance to the City and the financial services sector? Was the EU economy strong and flexible enough to withstand any shocks that might arise if there was a single currency? Was the British business cycle in harmony with those of other member states? A 40-page Treasury document which accompanied Brown's statement, and which had been five months in the preparation, provided an assessment of how far the British economy measured up to these tests. The verdict was strongly negative.[18]

After 27 October it was absolutely clear that Britain would not be part of the first wave. By that time it was equally clear that the launch of the euro would go ahead on schedule and that a substantial majority of EU states would be involved in it. For much of the summer there had appeared reason for doubt on both scores, not least because of French and German difficulties in meeting the Maastricht criteria. This had led the Blair government, like its predecessor, to indulge in wishful thinking about a postponement of the whole project. In the space of a few months, however, the situation had been completely transformed through a combination of creative accounting, political 'fudge', genuine austerity measures

17. BBC1's *Breakfast with Frost* and BBC Radio 4's *World This Weekend*, 28 September 1997; *Daily Mail*, 13 October 1997; *The Independent*, Anthony Bevins, 14 October 1997; Andrew Marr, 15 October 1997; Stephen Castle, 19 October 1997; editorial, 20 October 1997; Diane Coyle and Anthony Bevins, 21 October 1997.

18. *H.C.Deb.*, vol. 299, cols. 583–8, 27 October 1997; HM Treasury, *UK Membership of the Single Currency; Financial Times*, Philip Stephens, 28 October 1997. See also C. Johnson, 'British Membership', in A. Duff (ed.), *Understanding the Euro* (1998), pp. 94–103.

and a cyclical upturn in some of the continental European economies. Of critical importance was a sharp turn-around in the economic
and fiscal fortunes of France and Germany. In the case of both
countries, official figures released in September conveniently showed
that earlier estimates had overstated the size of their budget deficits
for 1996 and the first half of 1997. In the case of both countries,
too, the late summer and autumn of 1997 saw unmistakable signs
of economic recovery.[19] The improvement in France's position was
particularly impressive. After growing at an annual average of only
1.5 per cent for the previous seven years, the French economy
entered a new phase of rapid expansion, assisted by an emergency
package of spending cuts and tax increases, a boost to exports and
tourism from a fall in the value of the franc and an increase in
domestic demand. The fiscal situation also became a great deal
healthier. On 19 June Jospin had told parliament that public finances
were in a mess and predicted a budget deficit of 4 per cent for 1998
– yet in late September he was able to present a relatively painless
budget which was nevertheless consistent with the Maastricht criteria.
The French government's confidence in its ability to meet those
criteria was reflected in calls for the third stage of EMU to begin
before the planned date.[20]

On 14 October 1997 the European Commission produced a
report indicating that not only France, but all other EU countries
– with the sole exception of Greece – were on course to qualify
for membership of the euro zone from the beginning of 1999.[21]
Although a final decision on the starting line-up would not be
made until May 1998, the Commission's preliminary nod of approval
effectively banished any lingering fears that a number of major
states whose participation was seen as essential to the success of
the new venture might be refused entry. It also increased the risk
of British marginalisation in important areas of policy. The UK was
not completely isolated on the question of EMU since Greece, Denmark and Sweden would be 'outs' as well – the last two by choice.
Nevertheless, the Blair government faced a tough battle to prevent
its almost total exclusion from policymaking not only on management of the single currency, but also on a much wider range of economic and financial matters. As one illustration of the disadvantage

19. For the incipient turn-around in Germany see *The Independent*, business section,
Imre Karacs and Katherine Butler, 11 September 1997.

20. *Ibid.*, John Lichfield, 2 March 1998; Magnus Grimond, 26 July 1997; John
Lichfield, 12 and 25 September 1997.

21. *Ibid.*, Diane Coyle, 15 October 1997.

under which it would be obliged to operate, Britain was to have no representative either on the six-member executive board of the ECB or on the proposed 'euro council'.

The role of the latter quickly became a bone of contention between Britain and the eleven states that intended to take part in the single currency from the beginning of 1999. The French-inspired 'euro council' was a watered-down successor to the Jospin government's original proposal for the establishment of an 'economic government' which would serve as a political counterpoise to the ECB. The initial British assumption was that its influence and powers would be relatively small. This represented a serious misjudgement of French intentions, however, as became evident on 5 November 1997 when a Franco-German plan was unveiled giving details of how Paris and Bonn wanted the council to work. The new body was to be known as Euro-X – the X representing the number of countries in the single currency area. Its membership was to be restricted to the finance ministers of those countries, and it would meet each month immediately before the regular sessions of the EU Council of Finance Ministers (ECOFIN). Furthermore, the remit of Euro-X was to be wide-ranging, taking in such matters as EU budgetary policy, fiscal harmonisation and employment. Britain, along with Denmark, Sweden and Greece, immediately protested. All feared exclusion from a forum whose decisions could vitally affect their economic interests, the more so since there seemed a real danger that ECOFIN might gradually be reduced to a rubber stamp for policies agreed beforehand on Euro-X.[22]

The Blair government had no coherent strategy for countering this threat. At one and the same time it attempted to smother the proposed council at birth, to limit its terms of reference and to obtain agreement – by means of behind-the-scenes manoeuvring – that Britain should have a place on it with observer status. A fundamental problem was that there was no legal way of preventing the council from being set up: since the body was to be informal and outside the EU institutional structure, it could not be vetoed. Blair voiced his reservations about Euro-X at his 'Docklands summit' with Chirac and Jospin on 6 November. The issue was then discussed more fully by EU finance ministers in Brussels on the 17th of the month, with Brown – supported by his Danish and Swedish colleagues – insisting that ECOFIN must not be superseded by the

---

22. *Ibid.*, Anthony Bevins, Katherine Butler and John Lichfield, 6 November 1997; Katherine Butler, 17 November 1997.

new inner council as the main decision-making body on economic and monetary policy. At another meeting of finance ministers on 1 December, Brown raised the stakes by demanding full British representation on Euro-X. There was also a veiled threat that life could be made uncomfortable for members of the council by the withholding of EU-funded rooms and catering facilities.[23] The response from the French and German ministers was an uncompromising assertion of the right of single currency countries to exclude non-members from their 'club'. Waigel was reported to have said, with unimpeachable logic, that the UK could not 'both be in and out', while Strauss-Kahn allegedly compared the British attitude to that of a voyeur trying to gain access to a married couple's bedroom. In an attempt to salvage the talks, Luxembourg's Finance Minister suggested a compromise whereby the four 'outs' would be guaranteed full information on the proceedings of Euro-X through a representative of the Commission who would sit in on them. The British were unimpressed: 'We want a voice at the table not an ear at the door', commented one senior official. It proved impossible to resolve differences, and the matter was accordingly referred to the next European Council.[24]

Blair was desperate to avert a showdown at this meeting, knowing that defeat was certain and would not only expose the extent to which Britain was being sidelined, but also cast a shadow over the forthcoming launch of the British presidency. He therefore embarked on a hectic bout of personal diplomacy aimed at preparing the ground for a compromise agreement at the Luxembourg European Council of 12 December. He was concerned to secure acceptance of two key points: first, that Euro-X must be subordinate to ECOFIN; and second, that the former's terms of reference should be narrowly restricted to subjects, like the exchange rate of the euro against other currencies, which were unquestionably the business only of members of the single currency area. The stiffest resistance came from the French. It was they who took the lead in insisting that Euro-X should have a broad area of competence and in seeking to bar from its deliberations the four non-participants in the euro.[25] Their attitude had hardened as a result of Brown's demand on 1 December for full British membership, and this was reflected

23. *Ibid.*, Rupert Cornwell, 7 November 1997; Katherine Butler, 17 and 18 November, 2 December 1997.

24. *Ibid.*, Katherine Butler, 2 December 1997.

25. *Ibid.*, Colin Brown, 10 December 1997; Katherine Butler, 11 December 1997.

in Jospin's observation (reported in the *Financial Times*) that 'the UK, which invented clubs, should not say it is unfair to be excluded'.[26]

In the event, Blair managed to negotiate a deal on 12 December, though not before he had been involved in a series of angry exchanges, particularly with Kohl and Jacques Poos, the Foreign Minister of Luxembourg. Blair declared himself completely satisfied with the outcome, stating: 'I am absolutely delighted this has been resolved ... ECOFIN is the only decision-making body.' Yet the formula that had been agreed left plenty of room for differences of interpretation. The eleven 'ins' would be permitted to meet on their own to discuss issues related to management of the single currency. The four 'outs' would receive an agenda before each session of Euro-X, however, and could raise objections if they felt that any item was of 'common interest'. In the event of a difference of opinion over what constituted a topic of 'common interest', the dispute was to be referred to the next meeting of ECOFIN. As far as the British were concerned, this arrangement meant that the ultimate decision on whether a particular subject was one of 'common interest' rested with them and the other non-members of Euro-X. Since the French took exactly the opposite view, the scene was set for further clashes during Britain's EU presidency.[27]

26. *Financial Times*, interview with Jospin, 9 December 1997.
27. *The Independent*, Katherine Butler, 13 December 1997; *The Courier and Advertiser*, 13 December 1997.

CHAPTER TWENTY-FIVE

New Labour, Old Problems: the British Presidency of 1998

The period of Britain's EU presidency from January to June 1998 was dominated by final preparations for the launch of the third stage of EMU in January of the following year. On 27 February 1998 all of the eleven states that were likely to be in the euro zone from its starting date published self-assessments showing that they had managed to meet the Maastricht criteria or were on the way to doing so. On 25 March the Commission and the European Monetary Institute issued separate reports which broadly endorsed these findings, though not without reservations about Belgian and Italian public debt levels. At the beginning of May EU leaders met in Luxembourg to designate the founding members and to decide the exchange rates at which their currencies would be locked together. They also chose the first head of the ECB, thereby bringing to an end a bitter five-month-long wrangle. On 4 June the euro council – by now called Euro-XI – held its inaugural meeting. Finally, on 30 June, the last day of the British presidency, the ECB officially came into being.

The position of the British government while these momentous developments were taking place was a curious and at times invidious one. As representatives of the country exercising the EU presidency, Blair and Brown between them chaired nearly all of the meetings at which the key decisions were taken. Yet because of Britain's self-exclusion from the single currency, they were prevented from playing anything like a full role in the way that the political leaders of France, Germany and the rest of the eleven did. This reality of limited influence formed a sharp contrast with the expectations held out by Blair and other ministers at the start of the British presidency.

In a series of keynote speeches in the lead-up to the presidency, Blair and Cook promised strong leadership from the British government and set out its agenda for the next six months. One of the main themes they expounded was the need to make the EU more understandable and accountable to its citizens – to 'reconnect Europe to the people', as Cook put it. This meant, among other things, taking stronger action on issues that were seen to be relevant to the ordinary man in the street, like employment, crime, drug trafficking, pollution and global warming. Great stress was placed on promoting more flexibility in the labour market. In addition, Blair and Cook pledged to carry on the work of EU enlargement and to cooperate constructively in the launch of the single currency – despite the fact that the UK would not be a participant.[1]

So far as EU enlargement was concerned, matters proceeded smoothly enough during the British presidency. At the Luxembourg European Council of 12 December 1997 it had been confirmed that negotiations with Poland, Hungary, the Czech Republic, Estonia, Slovenia and Cyprus would begin on 31 March 1998. Another five applicants, Latvia, Lithuania, Slovakia, Bulgaria and Romania, had been officially declared candidates and were to be admitted in March to a 'screening process'.[2] Negotiations duly began on the appointed date, but were only at a preliminary stage when the British presidency ended. There was, however, an ominous cloud on the horizon. As has been seen, there was considerable dismay over the Commission's plans for reform of the CAP and regional subsidies in preparation for enlargement. Detailed proposals were released in mid-March, and these opened up the prospect of serious disagreements when the business of hard bargaining eventually got under way.

The problems caused by the projected launch of the euro were more immediate, especially for the UK. After Brown's statement to the Commons on 27 October 1997, it was known for certain that Britain would not be joining the single currency area during the lifetime of the current Parliament, i.e. for three to four years at least. It remained a matter of conjecture, however, when it would do so. One obvious possibility was 2002, the year when national currencies were due to be withdrawn from circulation and replaced by euro coins and notes. But the British government refused to commit itself to this or, indeed, to any other target date, in spite of

1. Speeches by Cook to the Institute of European Affairs in Dublin, 3 November 1997, and to the European Parliament, 14 January 1998; speech by Blair at Waterloo Station, launching the British EU presidency, 5 December 1997, and at a joint press conference with Santer in Brussels, 8 January 1998.
2. G. Avery and F. Cameron, *The Enlargement of the European Union* (1998), pp. 135–9; *The Independent*, Katherine Butler, 12 December 1997.

strong pressure from the UK's partners and the Commission to give a precise timetable. Its unwillingness to do so was a consequence of several factors. First, it was simply not possible to say in advance at what point there would be sufficient convergence between the British economic cycle and that of other EU countries. Second, it was also far from clear how much time would be needed to make the requisite economic and political preparations. Although the Chancellor of the Exchequer saw no reason why the question could not be put to a referendum soon after the next general election, others regarded this as unrealistic. Government policy was that a decision on entry would only be made when there had been adequate opportunity to judge 'clearly and unambiguously' whether the euro was a success and whether the five economic tests set by Brown had been met. According to a report published at the end of April 1997 by the House of Commons Treasury Select Committee, *The UK and Preparations for Stage Three of Economic and Monetary Union*, it would be at least 2004 before the government was in a position to make such a judgement. Third, and most important, senior ministers were acutely conscious of the political risks involved in giving an unequivocal public commitment to membership of the single currency area.

All available evidence indicated that a clear majority of the British public was opposed to adopting the euro. A poll conducted by British Social Attitudes and published in October 1997 found that 61 per cent of UK residents favoured keeping the pound as the country's sole currency, while only 17 per cent wanted to see it replaced by the euro. In the same month, similar results emerged from a MORI survey of how people would vote in a referendum on the question. It is true that a poll which MORI carried out for the European Movement in January 1998 recorded a greater degree of support for participation in the euro zone. This, however, was out of line with the general trend of polls since the general election, in which the figure for those who registered opposition tended to hover around the 60 per cent mark.[3]

An equally important consideration for the government was the attitude of the press, large sections of which, including pro-Conservative newspapers like the *Daily Mail*, the *Daily Express* and the *Daily Telegraph*, were sceptical about EMU and hostile to British membership. This was also the stance adopted by *The Sun*, whose

---

3. *The Independent*, Rupert Cornwell, 7 October 1997; 16 February 1998. For a useful analysis of public attitudes on the single currency see P. Kellner, 'EMU and Public Opinion', in A. Duff (ed.), *Understanding the Euro* (1998), pp. 117–37.

proprietor, Rupert Murdoch, was a fierce critic of the single currency. *The Sun*, which had recently switched its support from the Conservatives to Labour, had an awesome reputation – whether justified or not – for being able to influence the outcome of elections. Understandably, therefore, the prospect of holding a referendum in which it was to be found campaigning against the line recommended by the government was not one that Blair relished.[4] He was given a warning of what to expect in June 1998 when some favourable comments which he made about the euro at the Cardiff European Council prompted a series of vitriolic articles in *The Sun*. In typically knock-about fashion, one of these posed the question whether the Prime Minister was 'the most dangerous man in Britain'.[5]

Given the critical attitude of much of the popular press, as well as the unenthusiastic mood of the public, staging an early referendum on entry to the euro zone would have been a high-risk strategy. The government's preferred, and safer, option was to allow time for the climate of opinion to change, while taking steps to assist the process. There were two main interlocking strands in the government's approach. At the economic level, it offered encouragement and practical help to industry in its preparations for adjusting to the euro. With few exceptions, such as a small pressure group called Business for Sterling,[6] sentiment in business and commercial circles was strongly in favour of participation in EMU. Indeed, the general view among top industrialists was that after 1999 UK companies would be using the euro regardless of the fact that Britain would not be part of the first wave. Adair Turner, the Director-General of the CBI, spoke of a '*de facto* element of adoption', and at a joint CBI/Institute of British Management conference in January 1998, Peter Everett of ICI said: 'We must prepare and train as if we are in. Politics are irrelevant.'[7] A number of leading retailers, including

4. For an analysis of the hostility of *The Sun* and other newspapers to the euro and the Blair government's tactics for dealing with it see P. Riddell, 'EMU and the Press', in Duff (ed.), *Understanding the Euro*, pp. 105–16.

5. *The Sun*, 24 June 1998. See also *ibid.*, 25 June 1998; *The Independent*, Paul McCann, 25 June 1998; Colin Brown, 25 June 1998; *The Independent on Sunday*, Stephen Castle, 28 June 1998.

6. Business for Sterling was launched on 11 June 1998 and its principal supporters included Tim Melville-Ross, the Director-General of the Institute of Directors, Brian Prime, the Executive Director of the Federation of Small Businesses, Sir Stanley Kalms of Dixons, Sir Rocco Forte, the hotelier, Sir John Banham, a former Director-General of the CBI, and Lord Marsh, a former member of the Wilson government.

7. *The Independent*, Michael Harrison, 6 November 1997; *The Courier and Advertiser*, 22 January 1998.

Marks & Spencer and Sainsbury's, had already indicated that they would be accepting euro coins and notes at their tills from January 1999. Other companies, like BP, were considering switching their accounts to the euro.[8] The government welcomed such developments and worked closely with industry in ensuring that it was as ready as possible when the single currency was launched. Addressing the CBI annual conference at Birmingham on 10 November 1997, Brown declared: 'The euro will radically transform the whole single market. So my message is: "Let's get down together to the serious business of preparation."'[9] He also revealed that the government was planning a number of changes, including amendments to the Companies Act, to make it possible for businesses to pay their taxes and denominate their shares in the euro.

At the political level, the government was engaged in a parallel exercise of building up an irresistible groundswell of support for eventual adoption of the single currency. More specifically, it sought to construct in advance of the promised euro referendum a cross-party, pro-European grand coalition of the kind that had been so effective in the 1975 referendum campaign.[10] Little effort needed to be expended on gaining cooperation from the Liberal Democrats: they were wholehearted supporters of British participation in EMU and their leader, Ashdown, had already shown the extent to which he was willing to collaborate with the government by agreeing to sit on a Cabinet sub-committee on constitutional reform. The main targets for the government's charm offensive were members of the so-called Positive European Group and any other Conservatives who shared their disenchantment with Hague's Eurosceptic stance. As an added bonus, deepening the rift between these dissidents and the Conservative leadership could only work to the advantage of the Labour Party. On 5 January 1998, *The Independent* published a letter from a number of prominent Conservative politicians – popularly referred to as 'Tory grandees' – which was highly critical of their party's current approach to Europe. The signatories, who included Howe, Carrington, Clarke, Heath, Gummer, Tugendhat and Chris Patten, expressed strong support for the government's general approach on EU matters and, in particular, for its policy of

8. *H.C.Deb.*, vol. 299, col. 587, 27 October 1997.

9. *The Independent*, Michael Harrison and business section, 11 November 1997. See also Brown's speech to a City symposium at the Bank of England on 20 January 1998.

10. Speaking in The Hague in late January 1998, Blair called for a 'patriotic alliance'.

actively preparing for EMU. Blair immediately seized the opportunity thus presented by making overtures to senior figures like Clarke, Heseltine and Hurd about forming an all-party alliance to campaign in favour of the single currency.[11]

However necessary for domestic political reasons, the government's gradualist tactics entailed costs. Not for the first time, British policymakers discovered that a course of action dictated by the demands of national politics could have damaging consequences for relations between the UK and its European partners. In this particular case, growing irritation with the Blair government's equivocation about the single currency contributed to the adoption of a tougher approach by France, Germany and other states on a number of related issues. The two most important of these concerned the status of the euro council and the question of whether Britain, along with the other three 'outs', needed to spend two years in the ERM as a precondition of membership of EMU. Both matters were the subject of ill-tempered debate during the British presidency.

For his part, Blair was under the impression that the formula agreed at the Luxembourg European Council of 12 December 1997 on the respective powers of ECOFIN and Euro-X provided a guarantee that the influence of the latter would be minimal. He was confident that a British representative would be present whenever anything of importance was being considered. It later transpired, however, that this was not the case. The eleven 'in' states were adamant that they alone should have the power to determine when the four 'outs' should be invited to join them in discussing an item of 'common interest'. To compound British discomfiture, it was decided at a meeting of EU finance ministers held at York on 21–22 March that the first session of the euro council should take place during the British presidency. Most observers interpreted this decision as a deliberate attempt by the French in particular to humiliate the UK.[12] This may have been a factor in the Jospin government's calculations. At the same time, it must be borne in mind that the French had been concerned for some time that the Maastricht Treaty's timetable for launching the single currency left a seven-month hiatus between the date on which exchange rates were determined (May 1998) and that on which the launch actually took place. Their fear was that speculators would have a field day, and to counter this danger they wanted the euro council to be in

11. *The Independent on Sunday*, Stephen Castle, 18 January 1998; *The Independent*, Colin Brown, 22 January 1998; Fran Abrams, 14 February 1998.
12. *The Independent*, Diane Coyle, 23 March 1998.

place as soon as possible after the beginning of May to afford an
element of stability.[13] Whatever the truth about French motives,
however, the circumstances in which the inaugural meeting of Euro-
XI took place – in Luxembourg, on 4 June 1998 – were deeply
humiliating for the British government and for the Chancellor of
the Exchequer personally. Brown insisted on his right to chair the
opening formalities, but after a brief interval he was obliged to leave
– being replaced as chairman by Rudolph Edlinger, the Finance
Minister of Austria, the country that was due to take over the EU
presidency at the beginning of the next month. The outraged reaction from other EU finance ministers was that Brown had behaved
like a 'gatecrasher', and the whole incident provided a telling illustration of the extent to which Britain had become marginalised on
the key issue of EMU.[14]

A row over British membership of the ERM offered additional
evidence of this. Under the Maastricht Treaty, a two-year period
within the ERM was a necessary precondition of membership of the
euro zone. The Blair government was not prepared to accept this
stipulation – partly because the psychological scars left by Britain's
traumatic exit from the ERM in September 1992 made re-entry
difficult to contemplate, but also because it was felt that such a
qualifying test had been rendered meaningless by the substantial
widening in the fluctuation bands that had been effected in 1993.
All that should be necessary, argued Blair and Brown, was two years
of currency stability. Only the Swedes, who also refused to agree to
a two-year probationary period in the ERM, backed the British position. The overwhelming weight of opinion within the EU – both
banking and governmental – was that the provision set out in the
Maastricht Treaty must be scrupulously observed.

The disputes that occurred in connection with the ERM and the
euro council were overshadowed by a crisis over who should head
the new ECB. Here again, the British government was given a sharp
lesson in the limitations imposed on its influence by its prevarica-
tion over the euro. Blair was allowed no part whatever in the choice
of the ECB's first president. Instead, his role was restricted to that
of honest broker between the French, the Germans and the Dutch.

The first hint of trouble appeared in November 1997, when Jospin
and Chirac proposed Jean-Claude Trichet, the Governor of the Bank
of France, for the position of President of the ECB.[15] Until then, it

13. *Ibid.*, John Lichfield, 3 October 1997.
14. *Ibid.*, Katherine Butler, 5 June 1998.
15. *Financial Times*, Robert Graham, Gordon Cramb and Andrew Fisher, 5 November 1997.

had been generally assumed that the post would be filled by Wim Duisenberg, the former governor of the Dutch central bank and the current head of the European Monetary Institute. Duisenberg was strongly supported not only by the Dutch government, but also by the Germans, who were impressed by his ultra-orthodox views on monetary policy. As far as Bonn was concerned, the matter was already settled. A 'gentleman's agreement' had been reached with the French, by which the selection of Duisenberg was the quid pro quo for Germany's acceptance of Euro-X, as well as its reluctant acquiescence in admission to the euro zone of Italy and other states whose success in meeting the Maastricht criteria did not bear close scrutiny. From the German standpoint, therefore, the French appeared to be reneging on their part of the bargain.[16]

The ensuing squabble, which reflected basic differences of opinion between Paris and Bonn about how EMU should be managed, quickly escalated into a triangular power struggle involving the Dutch as well as the French and the Germans. It was initially hoped that an accommodation might be reached before the Luxembourg European Council of 2 May 1998. In the event, however, this proved impossible. When the matter was discussed by EU finance ministers at York in March, the French were isolated but determined not to give way. By the time of the next meeting of ECOFIN in Luxembourg on 20 April, feelings had hardened on all sides. The Dutch felt that national pride was at stake: Gerrit Zalm, their Finance Minister, said that to capitulate to French pressure would be 'worse than losing to Germany in the World Cup'.[17] In any case, their room for manoeuvre was severely restricted by electoral considerations. Wim Kok, the Dutch Prime Minister and head of a Socialist-led coalition government, faced a difficult general election in a few weeks' time, and for that reason alone could not afford to be seen making concessions to France. This was also a factor that affected the Germans, with federal elections looming in September for the politically embattled Kohl. As for the French, they were pressing their case as hard as ever and now threatening to veto Duisenberg's appointment unless it was agreed that his eight-year term would be shared with Trichet. They were made even more disinclined to compromise by a German proposal – to which they objected strongly – that each of the intending euro zone governments should submit drafts of their tax and spending plans for the next three years to Brussels.[18]

16. *Handelsblatt*, 29 January 1998.
17. *The Independent*, Katherine Butler, 22 April 1998.
18. *Ibid.*, Katherine Butler, 21 and 22 April 1998.

Not surprisingly under these circumstances, no agreement was reached on 20 April. It was not until the Luxembourg European Council of 2 May that the deadlock was at last broken. The decisive factor in ending the stalemate was acceptance of the French demand that Trichet should take over from Duisenberg after the latter had served half of his eight-year term. There were serious obstacles in the way of this arrangement. Not only did it contravene the Maastricht Treaty, which clearly stipulated that the term must be for eight years. It was also completely unacceptable to both the Dutch government and Duisenberg personally. These obstacles were swept aside in the course of eleven hours of arduous negotiations which saw Blair making desperate efforts to broker a deal between the Dutch, the French and the Germans. After putting up stubborn resistance, Duisenberg finally caved in to pressure from Chirac and gave an undertaking that, although his appointment would technically be for eight years, he would make way for Trichet after only four. The ostensible reason for his stepping down in 2002 was that by that stage he would be too old to continue. The harsh reality, however, was that he had been compelled to give a verbal assurance of his early resignation by a French veto.[19]

The general reaction throughout the EU to the job-share deal that emerged from the Luxembourg European Council was extremely unfavourable. Its many critics attacked it as a shabby 'fix' which undermined the credibility of the euro and set a dangerous precedent of political interference in the affairs of the ECB.[20] French tactics came in for widespread condemnation. There was also a great deal of critical comment about the way that Blair had handled matters in his capacity as chairman. One complaint – voiced by Romano Prodi, the Italian Prime Minister, among others – was that he had not prepared himself adequately for the task. Another was that he had spent too much time in private discussions with Chirac, Kohl and Kok, while completely ignoring other EU leaders. Jean-Claude Juncker, Luc Dehaene and Viktor Klima, the premiers of Luxembourg, Belgium and Austria respectively, all complained of being left in the dark. According to Klima, indeed, they had 'never seen anything like it'.[21]

19. *Ibid.*, Katherine Butler, 2, 3 and 4 May 1998.
20. The President of the European Parliament, Jose Maria Gil Robles, said that the job-share deal was a 'clear' violation of the Maastricht Treaty and there were threats that the EP would block Duisenberg's appointment.
21. See *The Independent*, leader; Katherine Butler; Jeremy Warner; Colin Brown and Jeremy Warner – all 4 May 1998.

In comparison with the Luxembourg European Council, that held at Cardiff on 15 June passed off relatively uneventfully, apart from insistent German demands for a rebate on their EU budget contribution. This enabled Blair to make good some of the damage done to his reputation by the Duisenberg affair. Nevertheless, the verdict on his performance, and that of his government, during the British EU presidency as a whole was at best a mixed one.[22] The Conservative Opposition had little good to say on the subject. Hague referred disparagingly to a presidency of 'disappointments, missed opportunities and poor diplomacy', while Howard called it 'a flop . . . one of the most timid and poor of recent times'.[23] This was entirely predictable. Even in quarters where a more sympathetic attitude might have been expected, however, there was little enthusiasm. Thus the EP took the unusual step of voting down the customary resolution congratulating the outgoing presidency.

All this was far removed from the Blair government's own assessment of its record.[24] A glossy mid-term report, unveiled by Blair and Cook at the end of March, listed 45 'achievements'. By the time the presidency ended, the number had shot up, with a paper prepared in the Cabinet Office noting well over 100 'items agreed and other successes'.[25] Among other things, the government claimed credit for successfully launching the single currency and the process of enlargement, as well as for setting a lead in the formulation of job creation policies. The lifting of the ban on beef exports from Northern Ireland – recommended by EU vets in March 1998 and given formal approval in June – was presented as another triumph.[26] But government claims went beyond such specifics. Speaking at the official opening of the ECB, Blair argued that the British presidency had produced a sea-change in the UK's approach to Europe, a move away 'from self-imposed isolation to full-hearted cooperation'.[27] According to Blair, moreover, a broad consensus had been created

22. The verdict of *The Observer* was that the British presidency had been 'undistinguished': leader, 14 June 1998. *The Independent* reached a similar conclusion: leader, 15 June 1998. See also *The Independent*, Fran Abrams, 15 June 1998.
23. *H.C.Deb.*, vol. 314, col. 370, 17 June 1998; *ibid.*, vol. 313, col. 1236, 11 June 1998. Howard was quoting from an article by the French journalist Pierre Beglau in the magazine *Le Pont*.
24. For a robust defence of the British presidency by Cook and Blair see *H.C.Deb.*, vol. 313, cols. 1230–34, 11 June 1998; *ibid.*, vol. 314, cols. 367–70, 372–84 *passim*, 17 June 1998.
25. *The Independent*, Katherine Butler, 1 April and 14 June 1998.
26. *H.C.Deb.*, vol. 313, col. 1233, 11 June 1998; *ibid.*, vol. 314, col. 380, 17 June 1998.
27. *The Courier and Advertiser*, 1 July 1998.

throughout the EU behind British ideas on flexible labour markets and the importance of decentralised decision-making. A joint letter from Kohl and Chirac, sent to Blair on 9 June, was offered as a vital piece of evidence on the latter point. The letter was intended to set the agenda for the impending Cardiff European Council, and in it the two leaders ruled out any attempt to establish a European super-state and called for the rich diversity of the EU to be respected. A Downing Street spokesman hailed the letter as an endorsement of Blair's call for a 'third way' in Europe. Blair himself took up its main themes at the Cardiff European Council, speaking of the importance of subsidiarity and securing agreement for an informal summit to be held in Innsbruck in October 1998 to explore ways of devolving power from Brussels.[28]

As observers of a more sceptical disposition pointed out at the time, ministerial claims contained an element of hyperbole. There was an undoubted tendency on the part of the government both to gloss over failures and setbacks and to exaggerate what had been accomplished. Many of the so-called achievements amounted to little more than routine continuation of processes already set in motion before the British presidency began. In addition, the assertion that there had been a fundamental transformation in relations between the UK and its European partners does not really stand up to close examination. Certainly the Blair government enjoyed a lengthy honeymoon period, a consequence partly of the Labour leader's personal charm and partly of the feeling in most EU capitals that virtually anything was an improvement on the previous Conservative administration. Long before the end of the British presidency, however, a familiar pattern had begun to emerge of a Britain relegated to the sidelines, being dragged along willy-nilly by forces it was powerless to control.

28. *H.C.Deb.*, vol. 313, col. 1231, 11 June 1998; *The Independent*, Colin Brown, 10 June 1998; Katherine Butler, 10 June 1998; Fran Abrams, 16 June 1998; Katherine Butler and Rupert Cornwell, 16 June 1998.

Suggestions for Further Reading

There is a growing body of literature on the subject of Britain and European integration since 1945. This very selective list identifies some of the introductory textbooks and also a few of the more detailed works covering particular aspects. Most of the books cited below contain extensive bibliographies.

A useful general study of British policy and attitudes towards the European Community is to be found in J.W. Young, *Britain and European Unity, 1945–1992* (1993). A more recent treatment of this subject is offered by H. Young, *This Blessed Plot: Britain and Europe from Churchill to Blair* (1998). For a detailed account of British membership of the European Community in the period 1973–89, see S. George, *An Awkward Partner: Britain in the European Community* (1990). An interesting collection of essays including eyewitness accounts of policymakers is provided by B. Brivati and H. Jones (eds), *From Reconstruction to Integration: Britain and Europe since 1945* (1993). A selection of primary source material is available in S. Greenwood (ed.), *Britain and European integration since the Second World War* (1996).

There is a large collection of books offering an overview of British political history, economic developments and foreign policy since 1945, including D. Childs, *Britain since 1945: A Political History* (1992), A. Cairncross, *The British Economy since 1945* (1992) and D. Sanders, *Losing an Empire, Finding a Role: British Foreign Policy since 1945* (1990). Wide-ranging studies of Britain's changing role and power in the international system of the twentieth century also provide much relevant comment, especially C.J. Bartlett, *British Foreign Policy in the Twentieth Century* (1989), B. Porter, *Britain, Europe and the World, 1850–1986: Delusions of Grandeur* (1987), R. Holland, *The Pursuit of Greatness: Britain and the World Role, 1900–1970* (1991), and D. Reynolds, *Britannia Overruled: British Policy and World Power in the Twentieth Century* (1991).

The evolution of the EC/EU is covered in a large number of publications. An introductory study of the history of European integration is offered by S. Henig, *The Uniting of Europe: From Discord to Concord* (1997). More detailed treatment is available in D.W. Urwin, *The Community of Europe: A History of European Integration since 1945* (1995), D. Dinan, *Ever Closer Union? An Introduction to the European Community* (1994), K. Middlemas, *Orchestrating Europe: The Informal Politics of European Union, 1973–1995* (1995) and C. Archer and F. Butler, *The European Community: Structure and Process* (1992). A selection of extracts from EC documents is contained in D. Weigall and P. Stirk (eds), *The Origins and Development of the European Community* (1992). The EC and the wider European context are also considered in a number of pan-European studies, including J. Story (ed.), *The New Europe: Politics, Government and Economy since 1945* (1993) and D.A. Gowland, B.C. O'Neill and A.L. Reid (eds), *The European Mosaic: Contemporary Politics, Economics and Culture* (1995).

Chapter 1: Britain, Europe and the audit of war

C. Barnett, *The Lost Victory: British Dreams, British realities, 1945–1950* (1995)

J. Becker and F. Knipping (eds), *Power in Europe? Great Britain, France, Italy and Germany in the Postwar World, 1945–1950* (1986)

M. Blackwell, *Clinging to Grandeur: British Attitudes and Foreign Policy in the Aftermath of the Second World War* (1993)

B. Brivati and H. Jones (eds), *What Difference Did the War Make?* (1993)

A. Deighton, *The Impossible Peace: Britain and the Division of Germany and the Origins of the Cold War* (1990)

K.O. Morgan, *Labour in Power, 1945–1951* (1984)

Chapter 2: Western Union and the reconstruction of Western Europe

J. Baylis, *The Diplomacy of Pragmatism: Britain and the Formation of NATO, 1942–49* (1993)

A. Bullock, *Ernest Bevin: Foreign Secretary, 1945–1951* (1983)

S. Croft, *The End of Superpower: The British Foreign Office Conceptions of a Changing World, 1945–51* (1994)

M.J. Hogan, *The Marshall Plan: America, Britain and the Reconstruction of Western Europe, 1945–1952* (1987)

A.S. Milward, *The Reconstruction of Western Europe, 1945–1951* (1984)

R. Ovendale (ed.), *The Foreign Policy of the British Labour Governments, 1945–1951* (1984)

Chapter 3: 'We are not ready': Britain and the Schuman Plan

E. Dell, *The Schuman Plan and the British Abdication of Leadership in Europe* (1995)

J. Gillingham, *Coal, Steel and the Rebirth of Europe, 1945–1955* (1991)

J. Monnet, *Memoirs* (1978)

K. Schwabe (ed.), *The Beginnings of the Schuman Plan* (1987)

P.M.R. Stirk and D. Willis (eds), *Shaping Postwar Europe: European Unity and Disunity, 1945–1957* (1991)

R. Woodhouse, *British Policy towards France, 1945–51* (1995)

J.W. Young, *Britain, France and the Unity of Europe, 1945–1951* (1985)

Chapter 4: The case for association

E. Di Nolfo (ed.), *Power in Europe? II: Great Britain, France, Germany and Italy and the Origins of the EEC, 1952–1957* (1992)

S. Dockrill, *Britain's Policy for West German Rearmament, 1950–1955* (1991)

E. Fursdon, *The European Defence Community: A History* (1980)

V. Rothwell, *A Political Biography of Anthony Eden* (1992)

A. Seldon, *Churchill's Indian Summer: the Conservative Government, 1951–1955* (1981)

F.R. Willis, *France, Germany and the New Europe, 1945–1967* (1968)

J.W. Young (ed.), *The Foreign Policy of Churchill's Peacetime Administration, 1951–1955* (1988)

Chapter 5: The 'special relationship' and European unity

C.J. Bartlett, *'The Special Relationship': A Political History of Anglo-American Relations since 1945* (1992)

J. Baylis, *Anglo-American Defence Relations, 1939–1984* (1984)

A.P. Dobson, *The Politics of the Anglo-American Economic Special Relationship, 1940–1987* (1988)

R. Edmonds, *Setting the Mould: United States and Britain, 1945–1950* (1986)

M.J. Hogan, *The Marshall Plan: America, Britain and the Reconstruction of Western Europe, 1947–1952* (1987)

W.M.R. Louis and H. Bull (eds), *The 'Special Relationship': Anglo-American Relations since 1945* (1986)

R.B. Manderson-Jones, *The Special Relationship: Anglo-American Relations and Western European Unity, 1947–56* (1972)

R. Ovendale, *The English-Speaking Alliance: Britain, the United States, the Dominions and the Cold War, 1945–1951* (1985)

Chapter 6: The Commonwealth dimension

J. Darwin, *Britain and Decolonisation: The Retreat from Empire in the Postwar World* (1988)

J. Kent, *British Imperial Strategy and the Origins of the Cold War, 1944–49* (1993)

J.E. Meade, *United Kingdom, Commonwealth and Common Market* (1962)

S. Newton, 'Britain, the sterling area and European integration 1945–50', *Journal of Imperial and Commonwealth History*, 13 (1985)

D. Sanders, *Losing an Empire, Finding a Role: British Foreign Policy since 1945* (1990)

C.R. Schenk, *Britain and the Sterling Area: From Devaluation to Convertibility* (1994)

Chapter 7: From Messina to Rome

S. Burgess and G. Edwards, 'The Six plus one: British policy-making and the question of European integration, 1955', *International Affairs*, 64 (1988)

M. Camps, *Britain and the European Community, 1955–1963* (1964)

M. Charlton, *The Price of Victory* (1983)

E. Di Nolfo (ed.), *Power in Europe? II: Great Britain, France, Germany and Italy and the Origins of the EEC, 1952–1957* (1992)

A.S. Milward, *The European Rescue of the Nation-State* (1992)

J.W. Young, ' "The parting of the ways"? Britain, the Messina conference and the Spaak Committee, June–December 1955', in

M. Dockrill and J.W. Young (eds), *British Foreign Policy, 1945–56* (1989)

Chapter 8: On the defensive

R. Aldous and S. Lee (eds), *Harold Macmillan and Britain's World Role* (1996)

E. Barker, *Britain in a Divided Europe* (1971)

A. Horne, *Macmillan, Volume II (1957–86)* (1989)

W. Kaiser, *Using Europe, Abusing the Europeans: Britain and European Integration, 1945–1963* (1996)

R. Lamb, *The Macmillan Years 1957–1963: The Emerging Truth* (1995)

H. Macmillan, *Pointing the Way, 1959–1961* (1972)

J. Tratt, *The Macmillan Government and Europe: A Study in the Process of Policy Development* (1996)

J. Turner, *Macmillan* (1994)

Chapter 9: From application to veto

O. Bange, *Europe at a Crossroads: Adenauer, de Gaulle, Macmillan and Kennedy* (1997)

N. Beloff, *The General Says No: Britain's Exclusion from Europe* (1963)

M. Camps, *Britain and the European Community, 1955–1963* (1964)

A. Deighton (ed.), *Building Postwar Europe: National Decision-Makers and European Institutions, 1948–1963* (1995)

Lord Gladwyn, *De Gaulle's Europe, or Why the General Says No* (1969)

R.T. Griffiths and S. Ward, *Courting the Common Market: The First Attempt to Enlarge the European Community, 1961–1963* (1996)

H. Macmillan, *At the End of the Day, 1961–1963* (1973)

Chapter 10: Ancient rivalries

P.M.H. Bell, *France and Britain, 1940–1994: The Long Separation* (1997)

I. Clark, *Nuclear Diplomacy and the Special Relationship: Britain's Deterrent and America, 1957–1962* (1994)

E.A. Kolodziej, *French International Policy under De Gaulle and Pompidou* (1974)

J. Lacouture, *De Gaulle: The Ruler, 1945–1970* (1991)
J. Newhouse, *De Gaulle and the Anglo-Saxons* (1970)

Chapter 11: Labour's retreat into Europe

G. Brown, *In My Way* (1972)
R. Coopey, S. Fielding and N. Tiratsoo (eds), *The Wilson Governments, 1964–70* (1993)
U. Kitzinger, *The Second Try* (1968)
R.J. Lieber, *British Politics and European Unity: Parties, Elites and Pressure Groups* (1970)
M. Newman, *Socialism and European Unity* (1983)
B. Pimlott, *Harold Wilson* (1992)
L.J. Robins, *The Reluctant Party: Labour and the EEC, 1961–1975* (1979)
H. Wilson, *The Labour Government, 1964–1970* (1971)

Chapter 12: Mission accomplished

J. Campbell, *Edward Heath: A Biography* (1993)
E. Heath, *The Course of My Life: My Autobiography* (1998)
U. Kitzinger, *Diplomacy and Persuasion: How Britain Joined the Common Market* (1972)
C. Lord, *British Entry to the European Community under the Heath Government of 1970–4* (1993)
H. Simonian, *The Privileged Partnership: Franco-German Relations in the European Community, 1969–1984* (1985)
D. Spanier, *Europe Our Europe: The Inside Story of the Common Market Negotiations* (1972)
S. Young, *Terms of Entry: Britain's Negotiations with the European Community, 1970–72* (1973)

Chapter 13: Renegotiating 'Tory terms'

J. Callaghan, *Time and Chance* (1987)
B. Castle, *The Castle Diaries, 1964–1976* (1990)
M. Holmes, *The Labour Government of 1974–79: Political Aims and Economic Reality* (1985)

B. Pimlott, *Harold Wilson* (1992)

H. Wilson, *Final Term: The Labour Government, 1974–1976* (1979)

Chapter 14: 'Full-hearted consent': the 1975 Referendum

T. Benn, *Against the Tide: Diaries, 1973–77* (1989)

D. Butler and U. Kitzinger, *The 1975 Referendum* (1976)

P. Goodhart, *Full-hearted Consent: The Story of the Referendum Campaign* (1976)

A. King, *Britain says Yes: The 1975 Referendum on the Common Market* (1977)

R. Jenkins, *A Life at the Centre* (1992)

R. Jowell and G. Hoinville, *Britain into Europe: Public Opinion and the EEC, 1961–1975* (1976)

B. Pimlott, *Harold Wilson* (1992)

Chapter 15: Semi-detached: the Callaghan government and Europe

S. Bulmer, S. George and A. Scott (eds), *The United Kingdom and EC Membership Evaluated* (1992)

C.D. Cohen (ed.), *The Common Market: Ten Years After* (1983)

R. Coopey and N. Woodward (eds), *Britain in the 1970s: The Troubled Economy* (1996)

A.M. El-Agraa, *Britain within the European Community* (1983)

F.E.C. Gregory, *Britain and the EEC* (1983)

K.O. Morgan, *Callaghan, A Life* (1997)

W. Wallace (ed.), *Britain in Europe* (1980)

Chapter 16: More U-turns: Labour and the EC in the 1980s

T. Benn, *The End of an Era: Diaries, 1980–90* (1992)

I. Bradley, *Breaking the Mould?* (1981)

B. Gould, *Goodbye to All That* (1995)

R. Harris, *The Making of Neil Kinnock* (1984)

R. Jenkins, *A Life at the Centre* (1992)

Chapter 17: 'Megaphone diplomacy': Thatcher and the EC, 1979–1984

P. Byrd (ed.), *British Foreign Policy under Thatcher* (1988)

F. de la Serre, J. Leruez and H. Wallace, *French and British Foreign Policies in Transition* (1990)

E.J. Evans, *Thatcher and Thatcherism* (1997)

I. Gilmour, *Dancing with Dogma: Britain under Thatcherism* (1992)

G. Howe, *Conflict of Loyalty* (1994)

R. Jenkins, *European Diary, 1977–81* (1989)

M. Thatcher, *The Downing Street Years* (1993)

H. Young, *One of Us: A Biography of Margaret Thatcher* (1991)

Chapter 18: Fatal attraction: Thatcher and the Single European Act

C. Grant, *Delors: Inside the House that Jacques Built* (1994)

G. Howe, *Conflict of Loyalty* (1994)

N. Lawson, *The View from No. 11: Memoirs of a Tory Radical* (1992)

P. Riddell, *The Thatcher Era and Its Legacy* (1991)

P. Stephens, *Politics and the Pound: The Conservatives' Struggle with Sterling* (1996)

D. Swann (ed.), *The Single European Market and Beyond: A Study of the Wider Implications of the Single European Act* (1992)

A. Watkins, *A Conservative Coup: The Fall of Margaret Thatcher* (1991)

Chapters 19–25

B. Anderson, *John Major: The Making of a Prime Minister* (1991)

T. Bainbridge and A. Teasdale, *The Penguin Companion to the European Union* (1995)

C.H. Church and D. Phinnemore (eds), *European Union and European Community: A Handbook and Commentary on the post-Maastricht Treaties* (1994)

B. Connolly, *The Rotten Heart of Europe: The Dirty War for Europe's Money* (1995)

P. de Grauwe, *The Economics of Monetary Integration* (1994)

D. Draper, *Blair's 100 Days* (1997)

A. Duff, J. Pinder and R. Pryce (eds), *Maastricht and Beyond: Building the European Union* (1994)

A.M. El-Agraa (ed.), *The European Union: History, Institutions, Economics and Policies* (5th edn, 1998)

P. Giddings and G. Drewry (eds), *Westminster and Europe: The Impact of the European Union on the Westminster Parliament* (1996)

D. Kavanagh and A. Seldon (eds), *The Major Effect* (1994)

M. Perryman (ed.), *The Blair Agenda* (1996)

C. Pilkington, *Britain in the European Union Today* (1995)

A. Seldon, *Major: A Political Life* (1997)

P. Stephens, *Politics and the Pound: The Conservatives' Struggle with Sterling* (1996)

Chronological Table

1945 May	End of the Second World War in Europe (8 May).
July	Labour Party under Clement Attlee wins the general election.
July/August	Potsdam conference of American, Soviet and British leaders.
1947 January	Merging of British and American occupation zones in Germany (Bizonia).
March	UK/France Treaty of Dunkirk signed.
	Announcement of the Truman doctrine.
June	Announcement of the Marshall Plan.
October	General Agreement on Tariffs and Trade (GATT) signed.
1948 March	Brussels Treaty signed by UK, France and the Benelux states.
April	Organisation for European Economic Cooperation (OEEC) established to administer the European Recovery Programme (Marshall Plan).
May	Congress of Europe at The Hague.
June	Berlin blockade begins.
1949 April	North Atlantic Treaty signed.
May	Statute of the Council of Europe signed by ten states.
1950 May	Announcement of the Schuman Plan.
June	Outbreak of the Korean War.
October	Announcement of the Pleven Plan for a European army.
1951 April	European Coal and Steel Community (ECSC) Treaty of Paris signed by France, Italy, West Germany and the Benelux states.
July	ECSC begins to function.

October	Conservative Party under Winston Churchill wins the general election.
1952 May	European Defence Community (EDC) Treaty signed by the six ECSC states.
1954 August	French National Assembly rejects the EDC Treaty.
October	Signature of the Paris Agreements and the formation of the Western European Union.
December	Treaty of Association between UK and ECSC.
1955 April	Anthony Eden succeeds Churchill as Prime Minister.
June	Messina conference of the six ECSC states.
July	Spaak Committee convened to consider plans for further European integration.
1956 March	Spaak Report on the creation of a common market.
October/ November	Suez crisis.
November	Announcement of British plan for a free trade area (FTA).
1957 January	Harold Macmillan succeeds Eden as Prime Minister.
March	Treaties of Rome signed establishing the European Economic Community (EEC) and the European Atomic Energy Community (EURATOM).
October	Formation of the Maudling Committee under the aegis of the OEEC to consider the plan for an FTA.
1958 January	Treaties of Rome come into operation.
December	France blocks further discussion of the FTA plan.
1959 January	First EEC tariff reductions and increases in import quotas.
1960 January	European Free Trade Association (EFTA) Convention signed in Stockholm by Austria, Denmark, Norway, Portugal, Sweden, Switzerland and the UK.
May	Failure of four-power summit in Paris.
December	OEEC reorganised into the Organisation for Economic Cooperation and Development (OECD).

1961 August	First UK application to join the EEC.
1962 January	Agreement on the main features of the EEC's Common Agricultural Policy (CAP).
December	Kennedy/Macmillan meeting at Nassau and the Polaris agreement.
1963 January	De Gaulle vetoes UK membership of the EEC.
October	Alec Douglas-Home succeeds Macmillan as Prime Minister.
1964 October	Labour Party under Harold Wilson wins the general election.
1965 April	Merger Treaty of the European Communities (EC) signed.
July	France begins a boycott of EC institutions.
1966 January	Luxembourg Agreement ends French boycott of EC institutions.
March	Labour Party wins the general election.
May/July	EEC negotiates an agreement on the CAP.
1967 May	Second UK application for EC membership.
November	De Gaulle vetoes UK membership of EC.
1968 July	Completion of the EEC customs union.
1969 April	De Gaulle resigns as President of the Fifth French Republic.
December	The Hague summit of EC leaders agrees in principle to enlarge the EC and to devise a plan for economic and monetary union (EMU).
1970 April	EC agreement on new arrangements for financing the budget through automatic revenue ('own resources').
June	Conservative Party wins the general election under Edward Heath. EC opens membership negotiations with Denmark, Ireland, Norway and the UK.
October	Publication of the Werner Report on Economic and Monetary Union and the Davignon Report on European Political Co-operation.
1971 March	EC Council of Ministers agrees to embark on the first of three stages towards EMU by 1980.

1972 January	Conclusion of EC membership negotiations and signature of Treaties of Accession by Denmark, Ireland, Norway and the UK.
October	UK Parliament votes in favour of the principle of UK membership of the EC.
	Paris summit of EC leaders reaffirms the goal of achieving EMU by 1980.
1973 January	Accession of Denmark, Ireland and the UK to the EC.
1974 March	Labour government under Wilson returned to power after general election with a commitment to renegotiate the terms of entry to the EC.
December	Paris summit of EC leaders agrees to establish the European Council.
1975 March	Conclusion of the UK's renegotiation of the terms of entry to the EC.
June	UK referendum results in a majority for the renegotiated terms of entry and continued membership of the EC.
December	Rome European Council meeting agrees to hold direct elections to the European Parliament (EP).
1976 April	James Callaghan succeeds Wilson as Prime Minister.
1977 November	Direct elections to the European Parliament postponed until 1979 due to UK failure to meet the original deadline.
1978 July	Franco-German proposal for a European Monetary System (EMS) announced at the Bremen European Council meeting.
December	Formal announcement of UK decision not to participate in the Exchange Rate Mechanism (ERM) of the EMS.
1979 March	EMS begins to function.
May	Conservative Party under Margaret Thatcher wins the general election.
June	First direct elections to the EP.
1980 May	EC Council of Ministers agrees to reduce UK contribution to EC budget for two years.

1981 January	Accession of Greece to the EC.
November	Genscher–Colombo Plan.

1982 January   Common Fisheries Policy (CFP) agreement.

1983 June   Conservative Party under Thatcher wins the general election.
                 Stuttgart European Council meeting adopts the Solemn Declaration on European Union.

1984 January   Free trade area established between the EC and EFTA.

June   Fontainebleau European Council meeting agrees a formula for reducing the UK contribution to the EC budget.
                 British paper entitled *Europe – The Future.*

1985 June   Milan European Council meeting agrees in principle to establish a single market by the end of December 1992 and to convene an intergovernmental conference (IGC) on EC reform.

December   Luxembourg European Council meeting agrees on the principles of the Single European Act (SEA).

1986 January   Accession of Spain and Portugal to the EC.
                 Single European Act signed in Luxembourg.

1987 June   Conservative Party under Thatcher wins the general election.

July   Single European Act comes into force.

1988 June   Hanover European Council meeting instructs a committee chaired by Jacques Delors to consider plans for the achievement of EMU.

September   Thatcher's speech at the College of Europe in Bruges.

1989 April   Delors Report on a three-stage progression towards the achievement of EMU.

June   Madrid European Council meeting agrees to begin first stage of EMU on 1 July 1990.

December   At the Strasbourg European Council meeting all EC states except UK approve the Charter of Basic Social Rights for Workers (Social Chapter) and also agree to establish an intergovernmental conference (IGC) on EMU at the end of 1990.

1990 June	Dublin European Council meeting agrees to convene an IGC on political union.
July	First stage of EMU comes into effect.
October	UK enters the ERM of the EMS.
	Rome European Council meeting agrees to implement the second stage of the Delors Plan for EMU by 1994.
November	John Major succeeds Thatcher as Conservative Party leader and Prime Minister.
December	The two IGCs on EMU and political union open in Rome.
1991 December	Maastricht European Council meeting agrees the Treaty on European Union (Maastricht Treaty). UK government secures opt-outs covering the Social Chapter and the third and final stage of EMU.
1992 February	Treaty on European Union signed in Maastricht.
May	Conservative Party under Major wins the general election.
	EC and EFTA sign a treaty establishing the European Economic Area (EEA).
June	Danish voters reject the Treaty on European Union in a referendum.
September	UK withdraws from the ERM.
1993 January	Single market comes into effect.
February	EC opens negotiations with Austria, Finland and Sweden (and Norway – April 1993) on their applications for membership.
May	Danish voters approve the Treaty on European Union (EU) after Denmark obtains opt-outs from the Treaty.
July	UK ratifies the Treaty on European Union.
November	Treaty on European Union formally comes into effect.
1994 January	Second stage of EMU comes into effect with the establishment of the European Monetary Institute (EMI) in Frankfurt.
July	Tony Blair elected leader of the Labour Party.

1995 June	Cannes European Council meeting recognises that the introduction of a single currency by 1997 is unrealistic.
1996 March	IGC convened to review the Treaty on European Union.
December	Dublin European Council meeting agrees a single currency stability pact.
1997 May	Labour Party under Blair wins the general election and announces its intention of accepting the European Social Chapter.
June	Amsterdam European Council meeting agrees the Treaty of Amsterdam following the IGC review of the Treaty on European Union.
	William Hague elected leader of the Conservative Party.
October	Gordon Brown, Chancellor of the Exchequer, specifies five economic tests for UK entry into the euro zone and indicates that the UK will not be ready for entry before the end of the current Parliament.
December	Luxembourg European Council meeting invites the Czech Republic, Estonia, Hungary, Poland, Slovenia and Cyprus to start membership talks in March 1998 with a view to entry to the EU early in the next century.
1998 January	UK's six-month presidency of the EU begins.
May	Eleven of the fifteen EU states agree to proceed to the third and final stage of EMU (scheduled for 1 January 1999) with provision for the establishment of a European Central Bank (ECB), the fixing of exchange rates and the introduction of a single currency – the euro. Denmark, Sweden and the UK have previously obtained opt-outs from this timetable, while Greece is deemed to have failed to qualify.
June	End of UK's presidency of the EU.

Map: The enlargement of the European Community

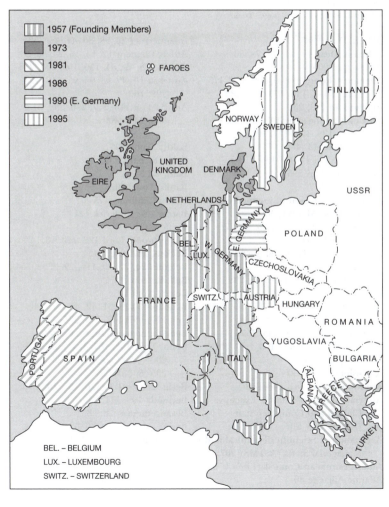

1957 (Founding Members)
1973
1981
1986
1990 (E. Germany)
1995

FAROES

FINLAND

NORWAY
SWEDEN

UNITED
KINGDOM
DENMARK

EIRE

USSR

NETHERLANDS

E. GERMANY

POLAND

BEL.
LUX.
W. GERMANY
CZECHOSLOVAKIA

FRANCE
SWITZ.
AUSTRIA
HUNGARY

ROMANIA

PORTUGAL
SPAIN
ITALY
YUGOSLAVIA
BULGARIA

ALBANIA
GREECE
TURKEY

BEL. – BELGIUM
LUX. – LUXEMBOURG
SWITZ. – SWITZERLAND

Index

Notes: names of people, places, organisations and institutions are included, with some passing references omitted. Some publications are also included. **Bold** indicates a major reference.

NB: For acronyms see pages ix–x.

Abbott, Diane 287

Acheson, Dean 41, 43, 77, 78, 80

Adams, Jad 200

Adenauer, Konrad 98–9, 106, 112, 113, 123, 136–7, 146, 170, 246, 284

Afghanistan 249, 251

African, Caribbean and Pacific (ACP) States 128, 173, 177, 191

Agenda 2000 343–4

Agriculture Act (1947) 129

Aitken, Jonathan 295

Algeria 143, 147

Amalgamated Union of Engineering Workers (AUEW) 199

Amsterdam Treaty (1997) 325, 327, 329, 333, 334, 336–40

Anglo-American Financial Agreement (1945) 17

Anti-Common Market League 208

ANZUS defence pact (1951) 95

Arab–Israeli war (1973) 179

Argentina 34, 250

Armstrong, Sir Robert 245, 255

Armstrong, Sir William 163

Arthuis, Jean 300

Ascension Island 250

Ashdown, Paddy 281, 318, 358

Association of Professional, Executive, Clerical and Computer Staff (APEX) 205, 206

Association of Scientific, Technical and Managerial Staffs (ASTMS) 207

Athens European Council (1983) 256

Atlantic Alliance 80

Atlantic Pact 26, 28, 30, 41, 48, 333

Attlee, Clement 11, 14, 16, 23, 52, 53, 71, 78, 79, 84, 156, 159, 160, 216

Australia 10, 85, 93, 94, 95, 117, 127, 128, 160

Austria 114, 115, 277, 290, 298, 316, 335, 343, 362

Baldry, Tony 286

Balfe, Richard 239

Balls, Ed 348

Banks, Tony 236

Barber, Anthony 175

Barclay, Sir Roderick 121

Bartlett, C.J. 153

Beaverbrook, Lord 122, 129, 131, 206

Beckett, Margaret 345

Belgium 24, 27, 40, 113, 290, 352, 354

Bell, Ronald 207

Beloff, Nora 121

Benelux 27, 29, 31, 42, 49, 66, 100, 117, 137, 142, 145, 265, 299

Benelux memorandum (1955) 96

Benn, Tony 158, 181, 187, 192–3, 195, 200–3, 209, 211, 217, 228, 232–3, 235–6, 281, 287

Berlin 28, 79, 120, 136, 137, 146

Bermuda 109, 111, 143

Bevan, Aneurin 78, 233

Bevin, Ernest 1, 10, 26–32, 34–9, 41, 43, 46, 48, 51–3, 55–8, 62, 63, 71–4, 77, 78, 81, 84, 89

Beyen, Jan 98

Biffen, John 271, 314

Blair, Tony 2, 287, 288, 306, 308, 317, 322
  as PM 325–34, 338–9, 343, 344–7, 350–3, 354–64
Blue Streak missile 119
Board of Trade 32, 34, 35, 90, 100, 106, 107, 112, 121
Body, Sir Richard 207, 294
Bonino, Emma 328, 329, 339
Bonn Contractual Agreements 66
Bonsor, Sir Nicholas 321
Boothby, Robert 18, 60
Borchert, Jochen 312
Borotra, Franck 302–3
Bosnia 286, 325
Bovine Spongiform Encephalopathy (BSE) 310–21, 329
Brandt, Willy 161, 164, 170, 171
Bretherton, Russell 100–1, 104, 225
Bretton Woods agreements 15, 185, 217, 223
Briand Memorandum 19
Bridges, Edward 102, 103
Britain
  beef crisis 310–21, 303
  economy 32–4, 52, 100, 211, 219–20, 227, 342, 355–9
  employment 345–6, 347
  entrance to EC 124–40, 168–84
  and European integration 1–5, 25–39
  Macmillan era 110–40
  postwar 9–24
  Presidency of EU 354–64
  referendum 187, 193, 197, 198–213, 280, 309, 356
  regions 344–5
  relationships with other countries *see* Commonwealth; France; US; USSR
  and Schuman Plan 40–54
  and the Six 55–68, 96–109
  sovereignty issue 175, 21
  and US 69–81 *see also* US: 'special relationship'
Britain in Europe 204, 205–6, 208, 212
British Budgetary Question 253
British Business in World Markets 208
British Empire 10, 13, 14, 19, 24, 33, 59 *see also* Commonwealth
British League of Rights 208
British Social Attitudes 356

Brittan, Leon 268, 275, 306
Brown, George 131, 132, 152, 153, 156, 158, 159, **161–3**, 164, 165, 166
Brown, Gordon 327, 346, 348–9, 351–2, 354–6, 359, 360
Bruges 269
Bruges Group 282, 294
Brussels Council of Ministers (1980) 255
Brussels European Council (1978) 223; (1984) 257; (1988) 262
Brussels Treaty Organisation (BTO) 29, 30, 36, 37, 41, 66
Budgen, Nicholas 294
Bulgaria 341, 355
Bundesbank 179, 216, 224, 274, 277, 281, 318, 335, 336
Burke, Edmund 202
Burma 13, 14, 83
Business for Sterling 357
Butler, David 213
Butler, Sir Michael 246, 267
Butler, R.A. 103, 104, 108, 115, 123, 124, 130, 131
Byrnes, James 71

Cadogan, Sir Alexander 11
Callaghan, James 153, 159, 184, 186–90, 192, 193, 196, 201, 205, 246, 248, 253, 271
  as PM 214–29, 230–1
Campaign for Labour Party Democracy (CLPD) 231, 233, 236, 239
Camps, Miriam 144
Canada 10, 14, 30, 66, 77, 80, 93–4, 95, 127, 128
Canadian Mutual Aid 17
Cannes European Council (1995) 301
Cardiff European Council 363, 364
Carrington, Lord 244–7, 255, 256, 358
Carter, Jimmy 217, 249, 251, 252
Cartiss, Michael 294
Cash, William 266–7, 281, 282, 294, 319, 320
Castle, Barbara 162, 163, 165, 166, 199, 203, 207, 212, 238, 240
Catholic University of Louvain 305
Ceylon 13, 83
Chaban-Delmas, Jacques 169
Chamberlain, Neville 136

Charette, Hervé de 303, 305, 326
Cherwell, Lord 79
China 21, 71
Chirac, Jacques 2, 286, 303–5, 311, 313, 334, 336, 351, 360, 362, 364
Christian Democrats 23, 38
Church of Scotland 184
Churchill, Winston 11, 15, 16, 19–21, 24, 37, 47, 52, 55, 58–60, 63, 65, 66, 78–81, 84, 90, 110, 147, 148
City of London 206, 226
Clappier, B. 225
Clarke, Kenneth 281, 289, 290, 297, 298, 299, 303, 306–8, 315, 319, 321, 324, 325, 340, 358, 359
Clayton, William 72
Clemenceau, Georges 49, 141
Cockfield, Lord 268
College of Europe 269
Colombo, Emilio 264
Combined Chiefs of Staff 15
Commission (EEC) 7, 142, 177, 221, 234, 240, 242, 259, 262, 264, 266, 268, 277, 278, 284–5, 292, 297, 300, 315, 318, 321, 341, 343–4, 346–7, 350, 354
Common Agricultural Policy (CAP) 4, 126, 129–30, 133, 134, 141, 169, 172, 173, 177–8, 185, 191, 196, 206, 212, 240, 253, 261–2, 333, 343–4, 355
Common Fisheries Policy (CFP) 286
Common Foreign and Security Policy (CFSP) 5
Common Market 5, 105, 106, 110, 114, 132
Common Market Safeguards Committee 207
Commonwealth 27, 41, 59, 62, 63, 97, 131, 132
  and Britain 10, 13, 14, 19, 24, 26, 81, 82, 83–95, 100–2, 107, 110, 116–19, 121, 126–8, 145, 160
  and EC membership 32–4, 124, 125, 133, 210
  and Heath 169, 177
  interests 21, 52, 108, 157, 160, 164, 173, 191–2, 226
  and Labour 160, 187
  and Rhodesia 160–1

Commonwealth Relations Office 102
Communist Party 209
Confederation of British Industry (CBI) 206, 319, 331, 348, 357, 359
Congress of Europe *see* Hague Congress of Europe
Connolly, Bernard 297, 314–15
The Conservative Mainstream 319
Conservative Mainstream Group 297
Conservative Party 55, 58, 60, 84, 90, 124, 180
  beef crisis 319
  Europhiles 297–9, 319, 325
  Eurosceptics 293–7, 299, 301, 306–9, 319–20, 323–4, 339–40
  General Election 1997 322–40
  Major's era 275–83, 284–92, 293–309
  membership of EU, attitudes to 37, 52, 110, 130–3, 174–5, 198–9, 230, 243
  referendum 203–13
  Thatcher era 184, 241–2, 244–58, 259–74
Conservatives Against the Treaty of Rome 208
Cook, Robin 308, 326, 330, 348, 354–5, 363
Cooperation on Justice and Home Affairs 5
Copenhagen European Council (1978) 223, 225, 341
Council of Europe 1, 36, 67, 41, 48, 58, 60, 62–4, 286
Council of Foreign Ministers 12–13 *see also* European Union Council of Foreign Ministers (ECOFIN)
Council of Ministers (EEC) 7, 8, 150, 172, 174, 175, 211, 221, 259, 260, 264, 266, 279, 338, 342
Court of Justice (EEC) *see* European Court of Justice (ECJ)
Couve de Murville, Maurice 133, 134, 137, 162
Couzens, K. 225
Craxi, Bettino 266
Creutzfeldt-Jakob disease (CJD) 310, 312
Cripps, Stafford 33, 35, 39, 47, 52, 53, 77, 89

Crosland, Anthony 161, 162, 163, 187, 215

Crossman, Richard 131, 153, 163, 164, 165, 166

Cunningham, Jack 328, 339, 344

Currie, David 324, 325

Currie, Edwina 297

Cyprus 109, 341, 355

Czech Republic 28, 290, 341, 355

Czechoslovakia 28

Daily Express 122, 206, 308, 314, 317, 356

Daily Mail 308, 314, 317, 348, 356

Daily Telegraph 308, 356

Daily Worker 122

Dalton, Hugh 18, 22–3, 37, 84, 90

Davies, Denzil 287

Davies, Gavyn 299

Davies, Quentin 297

Davis, David 295

Debré, Michel 150

de Freitas, Geoffrey 204

Dehaene, Jean-Luc 298, 305, 362

Dell, Edmund 228

Delors, Jacques 142, 242, 256, 263, 265, 269, 274, 298, 302

Delors Report (1989) 268, 288

Denmark 4, 114, 115, 172, 202, 223, 226, 254, 260, 265, 266, 280, 281, 283, 288, 290, 335, 346, 350, 351

Department of Economic Affairs (DEA) 153–4, 159, 163

Die Woche 304

Diefenbaker, John 127, 128

Dillon, Douglas 119

Dini, Lamberto 303, 317

Dixon, Sir Pierson 126, 135

Dohnanyi, Karl von 255

Donoughue, Bernard 189, 191, 193, 197

Dooge, James 259

Dooge Committee 259, 265

Dorrell, Stephen 293, 310, 316, 322

Douglas, Lewis 75

Douglas-Home, Sir Alec (*later* Lord Home) 102, 156, 175

Dublin European Council (1975) 177, 192, 194, 203; (1979) 246, 254; (1984) 262; (1996) 336

Duisenberg, Wim 361, 362

Dulles, John Foster 65, 66, 81, 111

Dumbarton Oaks conference (1944) 21

Duncan-Smith, Iain 280

Dundee Courier and Advertiser 208

Dunkirk Treaty (1947) 30

Dykes, Hugh 297, 319

East Germany 171

Eccles, David 114

Economic and Monetary Union (EMU) 5, 172, 176, 177, 179, 190, 241, 268, 272, 277, 279, 282, 288–90, 297, 299–309, 325, 329, 330, 335, 347–50, 354–61

Economic Cooperation Administration (ECA) 75, 77, 78, 89

Economist, The 18

Eden, Anthony 13, 20, 21, 55–6, 60–3, 64–8, 80, 84, 91, 97, 103–5, 109–12, 119, 143, 144

Eden Plan 62–3, 64, 80

Edinburgh European Council (1992) 288, 294

Edlinger, Rudolph 360

Egypt 14, 16, 109, 143

Eisenhower, Dwight 60, 81, 109, 111, 134, 143, 144

Enwright, Derek 239

Erhard, Ludwig 98–9, 112, 145

Estonia 341, 355

Eureka programme 263

Euro-X 351–2, 353, 359, 361

Euro-XI 354, 360

Europe – The Future (1984) 265

European Assembly 36, 41–2 *see also* European Parliament (EP)

European Atomic Energy Community 5, 96

European Central Bank (ECB) 8, 288, 351, 354, 360, 362, 363

European Coal and Steel Community (ECSC) 5, 7, 40, 43, 55, 63–4, 96, 97

European Communities 5

European Communities (Amendment) Bill 279, 280

European Communities Bill 181, 182, 201, 235

European Community (EC) 3–7, 20,
45, 61, 110, 119, 146, 148, 150–1
and beef crisis 310–21
Britain's entry negotiated 125–6,
128, 132–5, 137–9, 144, 168–84
Britain's entry terms renegotiated
184–97
Britain's referendum 198–213
Britain's relationship with 120–4
British Presidency 354–64
budget 172–3, 177, 178–9, 183, 184,
185, 191, 193–4, 219, 225, 228,
253–8, 261–2
Callaghan era 214–29
economy 24 *see also* budget (above)
employment 345–7
enlargement 172, 175, 179, 260, 261,
277, 290–1, 336, 341–3, 355
and Labour Party 152–67, 180–2,
184–97, 230–43
Major era 275–83, 284–92, 293–309
post-Amsterdam 341–53
reform and SEA 259–74
and Schuman Plan 40
the Six 15, 81, 108, 113, 115–18
Thatcher era 244–58, 259–74
European Council 218, 221, 225, 266,
320, 336–7, 338, 343, 347, 357
European Court of Human Rights 286
European Court of Justice (ECJ) 7,
286–7, 297, 314, 315, 337
European Currency Unit (ECU) 223,
229
European Defence Community (EDC)
56, 57, 60–8, 81, 97–9, 112, 144,
150, 171
European Economic Community
(EEC) 5–8, 31, 94–6, 99, 112
European Foundation 294, 320
European Free Trade Association
(EFTA) 114–15, 120, 125, 126,
132, 154, 156, 277
European Investment Bank 347
European League for Economic
Cooperation 204, 205
European Monetary Institute 288, 327,
354, 361
European Monetary System (EMS) 220,
223–4, 227–9, 254, 266
European Movement 204, 356

European Parliament (EP) 1–2, 7, 172,
174, 195, 218, 220, 221–3, 239,
259, 260, 266, 268, 278, 279,
284–5, 297, 333, 336–7, 363
European Payments Union (EPU) 78,
89
European Political Community Treaty
64
European Political Cooperation (EPC)
264, 266
European Recovery Programme (ERP)
26, 72, 74–7, 79, 100
European Regional Development
Fund (ERDF) 179, 180, 192,
195–6, 210
European Research Group 294
European Trade Union Confederation
(ETUC) 239
European Union (EU) 1–8, 277, 278
European Union Council of Foreign
Ministers (ECOFIN) 351, 352, 353,
359, 361
Europol 317
Evening Standard 122
Everett, Peter 357
Exchange Rate Mechanism (ERM) 223,
225–7, 229, 240–2, 270–4, 280–2,
288–9, 295, 300, 318, 359, 360

Falklands War 250, 256, 260, 317
Faure Plan 143
Feather, Victor 205
Federation of British Industries (*later*
Confederation of British Industry)
122
Fell, Anthony 123
Figgures, Frank 146
Financial Times 348, 353
Finland 290, 298, 335
Fischler, Fritz 310, 314, 316, 318, 319,
328
Fitzgerald, Niall 319
Florence European Council (1996)
320–1
Flynn, Padraig 328, 345
Fontainebleau European Council
(1984) 184, 245, 252, 257, 259,
261, 264–5
Foot, Michael 181, 199, 202, 203, 207,
211, 221, 232, 234, 236–8

Foreign Office 2, 11–13, 19–21, 24, 26, 27, 31, 32, 35, 41, 42, 44, 55, 61–3, 66, 69, 75, 77, 84, 97, 102–7, 121, 153, 227, 308–9
  Thatcher era 244–5, 267, 269
Forsa Institute 304
Forsyth, Michael 313
Fouchet committee 150
Fowler, Sir Norman 308
France 4, 19, 21, 23, 34–6, 38, 71, 74, 76, 80, 109, 175, 225, 242
  attitude to Britain 26, 29–31, 98, 141–51, 163, 164, 168, 169, 176, 185, 352–3
  and EC 123, 129, 277, 284, 285, 291, 292, 299, 300, 301, 303–4, 305, 334–6, 342, 352, 361–2
  economy 24, 108, 159, 170, 177, 226, 227, 263, 302, 349–50
  and EDC 60–2, 64–7
  and EMU 329, 359
  de Gaulle era 7, 112–13, 134, 135, 137, 139–40
  and Germany 99, 104
  oil 180
  and Pleven Plan 56–8
  politically 171
  referendum 202, 280
  and Schuman Plan 40–53
  single market 265
  and Six 172, 174
  and US 251
  veto 152, 166–7, 170, 174
Franco-British Union plan (1940) 19
Franks, Lord 9
Free Trade Area proposal (FTA) 62, 97, 100, 106–9, 112, 123, 125, 142–6 *see also* Plan G
Freeman, John 78
Fresh Start Group 281, 294
Fritalux proposal 42

Gaddafi, Colonel 250
Gaitskell, Dora 132
Gaitskell, Hugh 78, 129, 131, 132, 152, 153, 157
'Gang of Four' 234
Garrell-Jones, Tristan 319
Gaulle, Charles de 7, 21, 65, 80, 112, 113, 117, 120, 123, 124, 125, 126, 133, 134–8, 139, 140, 142, 144, **146–51**, 152, 164–5, 166–7, 172, 173–4, 185, 187, 195, 246, 248, 250
  resignation 168, 170, 171
General Agreement on Tariffs and Trade (GATT) 15, 17, 35, 88, 106
Geneva Summit (1955) 103
Genscher, Hans-Dietrich 264
George, Eddie 330
George, Stephen 153, 247, 269
Germany 10, 71, 72, 104, 107, 113
  attitudes towards 47–51
  postwar 18–21, 25, 27, 29, 30
  see also East Germany; West Germany
Get Britain Out 207
Ghana 118, 128
Gibraltar 286
Gill, Christopher 294
Gilmour, Sir Ian 244, 245, 246–7, 255–6, 273
Giraud, Henri 147
Giscard d'Estaing, Valéry 176, 194–5, 217, 218, 222, 225, 245–6, 254–5, 260, 302
Goldsmith, Sir James 308, 309, 315
Goodlad, Alastair 316
Gorbachev, Mikhail 252
Gordon Walker, Patrick 131, 154
Gore-Booth, Sir Paul 153
Gorman, Teresa 294, 296, 319
Grantham, Roy 205
Greece 4, 18, 71, 109, 260, 261, 265, 266, 286, 290, 316, 342, 350, 351
Grenada 249, 250
Grimond, Jo 198
Güggenheim, Charles 208
Gulf War 317
Gummer, John 358

Hague, William 323, 324–5, 330, 358, 363
Hague Congress of Europe (1948) 1, 36, 37, 58, 59
Hague summit (1969) 172, 175, 179, 185, 221
Hailsham, Lord 123
Hall-Patch, Sir Edmund 38
Harvey, Sir Oliver 46
Hattersley, Roy 181, 182, 234, 237

Hatton, Derek 238
Healey, Denis 155–6, 157, 163, 165, 166, 187, 201, 215, 227, 228, 230, 232, 234–6
Heath, Edward 122–4, 125, 127, 128, 130, 133, 156–7, 158, 181, 186, 187, 198, 199, 202, 205, 207, 297, 358
  as PM 168–9, 173–6, 177, 178–9, 180, 183, 191, 192, 194, 216, 226, 248–9, 253, 255
Heathcoat-Amory, David 321, 324
Heffer, Eric 209
Henderson, Douglas 326
Heseltine, Michael 275, 276, 281, 290, 297, 306, 315, 319, 325, 329, 359
Hoffmann, Paul 75, 77
Hogg, Douglas 310, 311–12, 314–18
Holyoake, Keith 127
Home, Lord 102, 156, 175
Horne, Alistair 118, 136, 146
Howard, Michael 281, 295, 316, 323, 324, 330, 340, 363
Howarth, Alan 293
Howe, Geoffrey 241, 244, 255, 256, 269, 271–4, 275, 358
Hoyer-Millar, Sir Frederick 121
Hungary 290, 341, 355
Hunt, David 319
Hurd, Douglas 272, 273, 276, 285, 289, 290, 291, 297, 306, 359

Iceland 14
Imperial Preference 33, 86, 87, 94, 101–2, 110, 117, 177
Independent 358
India 13, 16, 83, 84, 93, 119, 128, 161
Industrial Relations Act (1971) 199
Intergovernmental Conference (IGC) 266, 277, 283–6, 291, 295–9, 311, 314, 326, 329, 332, 335, 336
International Authority for the Ruhr 49
International Monetary Fund (IMF) 15, 215, 216, 217, 230
Iran 227
Iraq 14
Ireland 172, 202, 229, 254, 301, 334, 335, 337, 342
Irish Liberation Army (IRA) 286

Ismay, Lord 48, 74
Israel 143
Italy 23, 31, 38, 40, 59, 66, 226, 227, 229, 242, 265, 290, 300–2, 320, 326, 329, 335, 342, 346, 354, 361

Jamaica 210
Japan 13, 71, 93, 263, 265
Jay, Douglas 156, 157, 162, 163, 165–6, 187, 199, 207
Jebb, Gladwyn 97, 103, 113
Jenkins, Clive 207, 232
Jenkins, Roy 131, 132, 152, 158, 161–3, 181, 182, 187, 188, 197, 201, 202, 205, 206, 210, 211, 213, 221, 234–5, 246, 253, 254
Jobert, Michel 169, 176, 177
Johnson, Lyndon B. 155, 161
Jones, Jack 199, 207
Jordan 14
Jospin, Lionel 335–6, 350, 351, 353, 359, 360
Jowitt, Lord 52
Juncker, Jean-Claude 362
Juppé, Alain 285, 305

Kaufman, Gerald 237
Kaunda, Kenneth 160
Keep Britain Out (*later* Get Britain Out) 207
Kennedy, John F. 111, 120, 135, 139, 140, 148, 149, 150
Keynes, John Maynard 11, 16, 17, 18, 215
Keys, Brian 239
Khruschev, Nikita 120, 136
Kiesinger, Kurt 164
Kinkell, Klaus 305, 326
Kinnock, Neil 236, 237–8, 242
Kirkpatrick, Ivone 103
Kissinger, Henry 169, 171, 248
Kitzinger, Uwe 213
Klima, Viktor 362
Kohl, Helmut 2, 256, 257, 260, 276, 277, 284, 286, 290, 292, 297, 303, 304, 305, 313, 317, 318, 326, 333–5, 342, 343, 353, 361, 362, 364
Kok, Wim 361, 362
Korean War 56, 64, 78

Labour Campaign for Britain in
  Europe 205
Labour Coordinating Committee 231
Labour Party 1, 10, 22–3, 25, 90, 118,
  124
  beef crisis 313, 316, 317
  Callaghan era 214–29
  and EC 180–2, 184–97, 230–43,
    282–3, 287–8
  economic policies 33, 35, 53, 88
  into Europe 27, 37–8, 52, 55–7, 76,
    84–5, 86, 131–3, 152–67, 169
  General Election (1997) 322–40
  internal troubles 230–43
  membership, attitudes to 198, 199
  New Labour 322, 354–64
  referendum 198–213
  and Schuman Plan 41, 44
  and US 16, 17, 71, 78, 80
Labour Safeguards Committee 208
Lafontaine, Oskar 304
Lamfalussy, Alexandre 327
Lamont, Norman 275, 282, 289, 295–6,
  297, 314, 318, 319, 320
Latin America 71
Latvia 341, 355
Lawson, Nigel 241, 242, 270–3, 275,
  307–8
Lee, Sir Frank 114, 121, 122, 126
Leiden University 291
Leigh-Pemberton, Robin 271
Lend-Lease 14, 16, 17, 18
Lever, Harold 181, 201, 205, 228
Lib–Lab pact 186, 218, 222
Liberal Democrats 276, 281, 282, 358
Liberal 'No' to the Common Market
  Campaign 208
Liberal Party 180, 198, 205, 218, 222
Liberal–SDP Alliance 237, 240
Libya 14, 250, 251
Lilley, Peter 281, 295, 316, 323, 324,
  330
Limehouse Declaration (1981) 234
Lithuania 341, 355
Livingstone, Ken 287
Lloyd, Selwyn 119, 131, 144
Lloyd George, David 141
Lomas, Alf 239
Lomé Convention (1975) 191–2
Louis XIV 141

Lubbers, Ruud 277
Luxembourg 27, 40, 73, 174, 175, 301,
  338, 346, 352, 362
Luxembourg Compromise 174, 211
Luxembourg European Council (1985)
  252, 255, 266, 361, 362, 363
Luxembourg summit 345–7, 352, 355,
  359

Maastricht European Council (1991)
  277, 279
Maastricht Treaty on European Union
  (1992) 3, 5, 6, 7, 8, 264, 278–83,
  284–92, 295–6, 299, 301–2, 304,
  305, 327, 329, 332, 336, 340, 359,
  360, 362
Mabon, Dickson 205
MacDonald, Ramsay 189, 203
Maclean, Donald 30
Maclennan, Robert 234
Macleod, Iain 125, 175
Macleod Group 297
Macmillan, Harold 5, 60, 63, 65, 79,
  85, 91, 94, 97, 100, 102, 104–9,
  110–11, 112, 115–18, 119–20,
  122–4, 125, 127, 128, 130–1, 132,
  134–7, 138–40, 142–6, 148–53,
  169, 193
Madrid European Council (1989) 272;
  (1995) 288, 303
Major, John 142, 229, 272–3, **275–309**,
  311, 313, 315, 316–21, 322–4, 326,
  333, 334, 339
Makins, Sir Roger 121
Malaya, Malaysia 87–8, 155
Manchester Guardian (*later The
  Guardian*) 18, 123, 213, 233
Mandelson, Peter 345
Manifesto Group 232
Marlow, Tony 294
Marquand, David 205, 234
Marshall, Sir Colin 319
Marshall, George 25, 75
Marshall, John 128
Marshall Plan 26, 28, 30, 31, 34, 37, 41,
  69, 71–5, 87, 342 *see also* European
  Recovery Programme
Marten, Neil 201, 207
Matutes, Abel 339
Maude, Francis 325

Maudling, Reginald 112–13, 115, 123, 139, 142, 145
Mawhinney, Brian 308
Maxwell-Fyfe, David 60
McCarthy, Joseph 77
McMahon Act (1946) 111, 149
McNamara, Robert 149
Mellish, Robert 182
Mendès-France, Pierre 66, 144
Menzies, Robert 127, 128
Messina conference 96–100, 103–6, 108, 126
Mexico 317
Mikardo, Ian 199, 233
Milan European Council (1985) 259, 265, 267
Militant 231, 237
Milward, Alan 50
Mitterand, François 241, 256–7, 260, 263, 265, 277, 286, 291, 297
Mollet, Guy 143
Monnet, Jean 19, 22, 40, 41, 43–5, 50, 56, 64, 133, 150
MORI 356
Morley, Elliot 328
Morning Star 208
Morrison, Herbert 53, 58, 84
Mouvement Républicain Populaire (MRP) 38, 64
Murdoch, Rupert 357
Mutual Aid Agreement (1942) 14

Napoleon 141
Nassau agreement (1962) 138–9, 149, 150, 190
Nasser, Gamal 109, 143
National Coal Board 210
National Council of Anti-Common Market Associations 207
National Enterprise Board 193
National Executive Committee (NEC) of the Labour Party 37–8, 52, 199, 200, 201, 218, 221, 233, 235–9
National Farmers Union (NFU) 130, 206, 312, 344
National Front 207, 209
National Liberal Club 204
National Plan (1965) 155, 159
National Referendum Campaign 204, 206, 207, 208

National Union of Railwaymen (NUR) 206
Nehru, Jawaharlal 128
Netherlands 24, 27, 40, 46, 59, 112, 113, 145, 254, 316, 338, 342, 343, 346, 361, 362
New Zealand 10, 85, 93–5, 127, 128, 173, 177, 191, 192, 210
Nicholson, Emma 276, 293
Nigeria 128
'92 Group 294
Nixon, Richard 169, 179, 211, 248
No Turning Back Group 294
North Atlantic Treaty (Atlantic Pact) *see* Atlantic Pact
North Atlantic Treaty Organisation (NATO) 25, 26, 48, 56, 57, 66, 68, 69, 77, 79–81, 144, 149, 150, 252
Northern Ireland 294, 328
Norway 114, 172, 202, 212, 298
Nott, John 226

Observer, The 121
One Market, One Money (1990) 300
One Nation Group 276, 297
O'Neill, Sir Con 153, 163, 175, 176
Organisation for Economic Cooperation and Development (OECD) 217, 343
Organisation for European Economic Cooperation (OEEC) 25, 30, 36, 38, 41, 43, 48, 74–8, 80, 88, 89, 92, 99, 100, 103, 106–8, 112, 113, 142
Organisation of Petroleum Exporting Countries (OPEC) 179, 248
Ostpolitik 171
Ottawa Agreements (1932) 86
Owen, David 233, 254

Pakistan 13, 16, 83, 128, 161
Palliser, Sir Michael 255
Pannell, Charles 132
Paris Agreements (1954) 66
Paris conference (1975) 196
Paris summit (1960) 119; (1972) 179
Partnership of Nations, A 284, 285
Patten, Chris 358
Peart, Fred 156, 157, 163
Peel, Sir Robert 130
Pella Plan 100

Persian Gulf Territories 14
Persson, Goran 303
Petersburg Agreement 334
Petsch Plan 100
Pimlott, Ben 158, 165, 188
Pineau, Christian 144
Pisani, Edgar 140
Plaid Cymru 207
Plan G 106, 107, 112
Plan Juppé 304
Pleven Plan 56–7, 58
Pohl, Karl Otto 216
Poland 171, 290, 291, 341, 343, 355
Polaris missile 139, 149, 250
Pompidou, Georges 162, 168, 169,
    170–2, 176–8, 185
Ponting, Clive 161
Poos, Jacques 353
Portillo, Michael 281, 285, 295, 296,
    306, 316, 322
Portugal 114, 260, 261, 290, 316, 335
Positive European Group 358
Post Hostilities Planning Committee 14
Potsdam conference 10, 103
Powell, Charles 267, 269, 276
Powell, Enoch 174, 181, 207, 209, 211
Private Eye 133
Prodi, Romano 362
Public Sector Borrowing Requirement
    (PSBR) 214–15
Pym, Francis 181, 256

Reagan, Ronald 249–52, 263
Redwood, John 293, 295–7, 309, 320,
    323, 324, 330
Referendum (1975) on EEC
    membership 187, 193, 197,
    198–213
Referendum Party 308, 320, 322
Reilly, Sir Patrick 121
*Reinforcing Political Union and Preparing
    for Enlargement* 284, 292
Rhodesia 155, 160–1
Riddell, Peter 262
Ridley, Nicholas 270, 273, 276, 281
Rifkind, Malcolm 285, 303, 306, 316
Rippon, Geoffrey 175, 176, 178, 203,
    204
Robinson, John 175
Rodgers, William 181, 233

Roll, Sir Eric 126, 154
Romania 341, 355
Rome European Council (1990) 274
Roosevelt, Franklin D. 12, 15, 71, 147,
    148
Roper, John 182
Ross, William 163, 201, 203
Rothschild, Robert 101
Russia 286 *see also* Union of Soviet
    Socialist Republics (USSR)

Sanders, David 253
Sandys, Duncan 60, 123, 127, 143
Santer, Jacques 298, 306, 311, 314, 318,
    326, 339, 342
Sargent, Orme 13, 22
Scandinavia 74
Scanlon, Hugh 199
Schengen agreements 334, 337
Schlesinger, Helmut 318
Schmidt, Helmut 191, 194–5, 196,
    216–18, 223–6, 245–6, 254–5, 260
Schulmann, H. 225
Schuman, Robert 40, 41, 43, 45, 48,
    64
Schuman Plan 25, 40–7, 49–53, 55–8,
    61, 62, 96, 98, 99, 125, 156
Schumann, Maurice 169–70
Scottish Daily News 208
Scottish National Party (SNP) 207
Servan-Schreiber, Jean-Jacques 148
Shepherd, Richard 294
Shinwell, Emmanuel 84
Shore, Peter 187, 203, 207, 211, 287
Shuckburgh, Sir Evelyn 121
Silguy, Yves-Thibault de 306
Silkin, John 164, 203, 236
Simon, Sir David 327
Singapore 13
Single European Act (SEA) 3, 8, 241,
    253, 259–73, 279
Single Market 5
Skinner, Dennis 287
Skybolt missile 139
Slovakia 290, 341, 355
Slovenia 341, 355
Smith, Ian 155, 160
Smith, John 242, 282, 287
Soames, Christopher 123, 130, 169,
    176, 177, 210, 248

Social Chapter 279, 283, 285, 287, 288, 297, 327, 328, 337

Social Charter (1989) 241, 242, 268

Social Democratic Party (SDP) 213, 234, 235

Solemn Declaration on European Union (1983) 264

Soustelle, Jacques 113

South Africa 10, 93, 119, 251

Spaak, Paul-Henri (and Committee) 61, 74, 96–8, 100–6, 150

Spain 260, 261, 286, 290, 300–2, 316, 335, 339, 342, 346

Spectator 208, 270

Spicer, Sir Michael 293

Spinelli, Altiero 264

Stalin, Joseph 64

Star Wars 250, 252

Steel, Sir Christopher 146

Steel, David 205

Stephens, Phillip 273, 280

Sterling Area 14, 16, 17, 33, 78, 86–9, 93–5, 121

Sterling balances 16, 176

Stevens, Roger 44

Stewart, Michael 154, 155, 163

Stikker Plan 100

Stockholm Convention (1959) 114

Straits 14

Strasbourg European Council (1979) 254

Strategic Arms Limitation Talks (SALT) 171

Strategic Defence Initiative (Star Wars) 250, 252

Strauss-Kahn, Dominique 335, 352

Stuttgart European Council (1983) 256, 264

Suez 109, 111, 119, 143

Sun 314, 324, 326, 356–7

Sunday Express 122, 206

Sunday Times 122

Sweden 114, 277, 290, 298, 335, 342, 343, 350, 351, 360

Switzerland 114, 115

Tanganyika 90

Tapsell, Sir Peter 267, 280

Taylor, Ian 324, 325

Taylor, Teddy 181, 280, 294, 296

Tebbit, Norman 271, 280, 281, 297, 314, 324

Tehran conference 10, 11

Temple-Morris, Peter 297

Thatcher, Margaret 184, 203, 205, 230, 240–2, 275, 277, 279, 280–1, 297, 316, 318, 326, 343

as PM 244–58

Third World 160

Thomas, Michael 234

Thomson, George 157, 181, 201, 205

Thorn, Gaston 263

Thorneycroft, Peter 90, 104–5

Thorpe, Jeremy 198, 202

Tietmeyer, Hans 300

Times, The 206, 308

Townend, John 280

Trade Union Alliance for Europe 205

Trades Union Congress (TUC) 32, 205, 242

Transport and General Workers Union (TGWU) 199, 208

Treasury 32–4, 73, 89, 102, 106, 107, 112, 121, 146, 154, 159, 163, 177, 179, 226, 227, 273, 331

Treaty of Dunkirk (1947) 30

Treaty of Friendship and Cooperation (1963) 137, 146, 218

Treaty of Paris (1951) 5, 7, 40

Treaty of Rome (1957) 5, 7, 31, 67, 91, 96, 108–11, 113, 125, 126, 134, 138, 174, 221, 266

Treaty on European Union (1992) *see* Maastricht Treaty on European Union (1992)

Trend, Burke 101

Trend Report 102, 103, 106, 121

Tribune 208, 236

Tribune group 206, 235–6

Trichet, Jean-Claude 360, 361, 362

Trident missile 250

Tripolitania 14

Truman, Harry S. 25, 71, 73, 76

Tugendhat, Christopher 246, 358

Turin 284

Turkey 14, 18, 71, 286, 341

Turner, Adam 357

Union of Post Office Workers (UPW) 206

Union of Shop, Distributive and Allied Workers (USDAW) 206
Union of Soviet Socialist Republics (USSR) 27, 28, 29, 30, 48, 56, 69, 81, 146, 161, 164
  and Britain 11
  economy 91, 159, 251–2
  foreign relations 9, 20–1, 71–3, 136, 137, 171, 251–2
  technology 263
  and US 12, 14, 22, 26, 37
United Kingdom 14 *see also* Britain
United Nations 13, 21, 71
United States (US) 66, 68, 88, 91, 100
  and Britain 48, 49, 51, 56, 59, 89, 110–11, 119, 122, 143, 248–52
  and Europe 30–2, 34, 57–8, 65, 105–6
  foreign relations 22, 25, 26, 28, 37, 62, 95, 97, 109, 144, 171
  and de Gaulle 147–50
  and Labour government 155, 215, 216, 225
  postwar 9–12, 14–19, 21
  and Schuman Plan 41–5
  'special relationship' 69–82, 138, 160, 161, 167, 168
  technology 135, 263, 265
  and USSR 249
United Ulster Unionists 198, 208, 294

Vallance, Sir Iain 319
Value Added Tax (VAT) 172, 190, 257, 258, 268, 327
Vandenberg, Arthur H. 75, 80
Vandenberg resolution 28
Varley, Eric 203
Vietnam 155, 161, 162, 166
'Visegrad' states 290

Waigel, Theo 300, 301, 335, 336, 343, 352
Walker, Peter 256

Walters, Alan 271–2, 308
Warsaw Pact 252, 286
West Germany
  attitudes towards 56–60
  beef crisis 315, 318
  EC 4, 23, 106, 179, 277, 284, 291, 299, 300, 301, 302, 303, 304–5, 334–6, 342–3, 352, 361–2
  economy 24, 227, 349–50
  and EMU 329, 359
  and de Gaulle 137
  oil 180
  rearmament 56–60, 62, 64, 67, 81, 144
  reunification 281
  and Schuman Plan 40–5
  single market 265
Westendorp, Carlos 303
Western European Union (WEU) 66, 67, 68, 74, 97, 167, 285, 333, 334, 337
Westminster Eight 320
Whelan, Charlie 348
Whitelaw, William 205, 271
Wilkinson, John 294
Williams, Shirley 181, 202, 205, 233
Wilson, Harold 78, 85, 173, 181, 182–4, 186, 199, 200–2, 212–14, 221, 231, 248, 253, 254
  as PM, and entry to EC 152–67, 169, 172, 177, 187–97, 209–10
  and referendum 200, 205, 212, 213
Winterton, Nicholas 317
Woche, Die 304
Woolley, Harold 130
World Bank 15
Wulf-Mathies, Monika 345

Yalta conference 10, 21
Young, Sir George 324
Young, Hugo 247
Young, John 278

Zalm, Gerrit 361